OZARK MAGIC
AND FOLKLORE

formerly titled *Ozark Superstitions*

OZARK MAGIC AND FOLKLORE

formerly titled *Ozark Superstitions*

by

VANCE RANDOLPH

Dover Publications, Inc.
New York

This Dover edition, first published in 1964, is an
unabridged and unaltered republication of the work
originally published in 1947 by Columbia University
Press under the title *Ozark Superstitions*. This edition is published by special arrangement with
Columbia University Press.

Library of Congress Catalog Card Number: 64-18649

International Standard Book Number

ISBN-13: 978-0-486-21181-7
ISBN-10: 0-486-21181-9

Manufactured in the United States by Courier Corporation
21181920
www.doverpublications.com

TO THE MEMORY OF G. STANLEY HALL

Preface

For obvious reasons it is not practicable to credit every item in this collection to the individual from whom it was obtained, as I have done in *Ozark Folksongs* and some of my other books. But for the sake of the record, I set down here the names of certain persons who have directly furthered my investigations. Among these must be listed Mrs. Anna Bacon, Galena, Mo.; Dr. Charles Hillman Brough, Little Rock, Ark.; Miss Nancy Clemens, Springfield, Mo.; Dr. George E. Hastings, Fayetteville, Ark.; Mr. Charles S. Hiatt, Cassville, Mo.; Mrs. Dorn Higgins, Sulphur Springs, Ark.; Mr. Earl Keithley, Day, Mo.; Mr. Lewis Kelley, Cyclone, Mo.; Mr. Maurice Lamberson, Bentonville, Ark.; Mr. Cass Little, Anderson, Mo.; Mr. Ernest Long, Joplin, Mo.; Mrs. May Kennedy McCord, Springfield, Mo.; Mrs. Mary Elizabeth Mahnkey, Mincy, Mo.; Mrs. Mabel E. Mueller, Rolla, Mo.; Mrs. Geraldine Parker, St. Louis, Mo.; Miss Rubey Poyner, Southwest City, Mo.; Mr. Otto Ernest Rayburn, Eureka Springs, Ark.; Dr. Oakley St. John, Pineville, Mo.; Mr. Clyde Sharp, Pack, Mo.; Mr. Elbert Short, Crane, Mo.; Mrs. Isabel Spradley, Van Buren, Ark.; Mr. Fred Starr, Greenland, Ark.; Mrs. Olga Trail, Farmington, Ark.; Mrs. Ruth H. Tyler, Neosho, Mo.; Mr. John Turner White, Jefferson City, Mo.; Mrs. Marie Wilbur, Pineville, Mo.; and Dr. J. H. Young, Galena, Mo. I wish to acknowledge my indebtedness to these people, but they are in no way responsible for my interpretation of the material, nor for the general character of the book.

Some of the preliminary studies upon which this volume is based were printed as early as 1927, in the *Journal of American*

Folklore. My books *The Ozarks* and *Ozark Mountain Folks,* published by the Vanguard Press in 1931 and 1932, contained accounts of backwoods folk belief. Many supernatural narratives, and some notes on water witching, first appeared in *Ozark Ghost Stories* and *Tall Tales from the Ozarks,* published and copyrighted by E. Haldeman-Julius, of Girard, Kansas. Several yarns about witchcraft were printed in *Folk-Say,* a regional annual edited by B. A. Botkin and brought out by the University of Oklahoma Press; other related items first saw the light in the quarterly *University Review,* published at the University of Kansas City. I am grateful to the owners of these copyrights for permission to reprint the material here.

V. R.

Galena, Missouri
June 10, 1946

Contents

OZARK MAGIC
AND FOLKLORE

formerly titled *Ozark Superstitions*

1. Introduction

The people who live in the Ozark country of Missouri and Arkansas were, until very recently, the most deliberately unprogressive people in the United States. Descended from pioneers who came West from the Southern Appalachians at the beginning of the nineteenth century, they made little contact with the outer world for more than a hundred years. They seem like foreigners to the average urban American, but nearly all of them come of British stock, and many families have lived in America since colonial days. Their material heirlooms are few, but like all isolated illiterates they have clung to the old songs and obsolete sayings and outworn customs of their ancestors.

Sophisticated visitors sometimes regard the "hillbilly" as a simple child of nature, whose inmost thoughts and motivations may be read at a glance. Nothing could be farther from the truth. The hillman is secretive and sensitive beyond anything that the average city dweller can imagine, but he isn't simple. His mind moves in a tremendously involved system of signs and omens and esoteric auguries. He has little interest in the mental. procedure that the moderns call science, and his ways of arranging data and evaluating evidence are very different from those currently favored in the world beyond the hilltops. The Ozark hillfolk have often been described as the most superstitious people in America. It is true that some of them have retained certain ancient notions which have been discarded and forgotten in more progressive sections of the United States.

It has been said that the Ozarker got his folklore from the Negro, but the fact is that Negroes were never numerous in the hill country, and there are many adults in the Ozarks to-day who have never even seen a Negro. Another view is that the hillman's superstitions are largely of Indian origin, and there may be a measure of truth in this; the pioneers did mingle freely with the Indians, and some of our best Ozark families still boast of their Cherokee blood. My own feeling is that most of the hillman's folk beliefs came with his ancestors from England or Scotland. I believe that a comparison of my material with that recorded by British antiquarians will substantiate this opinion.

The collection of some types of folklore—riddles, party games, or folksongs, for example—is a comparatively easy matter, even in the Ozark country. If a hillman knows an old ballad or game song any reasonably diplomatic collector can induce him to sing it, or at least to recite the words. But the mention of superstition raises the question of one's personal belief—a matter which the Ozarker does not care to discuss with "furriners." The stranger who inquires about love charms or witchcraft will meet only blank looks and derisive laughter.

Authentic data in this field cannot be gathered by running "Old-Timer" columns in newspapers, because the people who contribute to such columns are not typical backwoods folk at all; the real old-timers seldom read newspapers, much less write letters for publication. The questionnaire method, too, has been tried at our whistle-stop colleges and among rural schoolmarms without any conspicuous success. The man who wants to study the Ozark superstitions must live with the Ozark people year after year and gradually absorb folklore through the rind, as it were. The information obtained in this manner is more trustworthy, in my opinion, than that elicited by any sort of direct questioning.

I first visited the Ozark country in 1899, and since 1920 I have spent practically all of my time here, living in many parts of the region, sometimes in the villages and sometimes in the wildest and most isolated "hollers." I fished and fought and hunted and danced and gambled with my backwoods neighbors; I traveled the ridge roads in a covered wagon, consorting with peddlers and horse traders and yarb doctors and moonshiners; I learned to chew tobacco, and dabbled in village politics, and became a deputy sheriff, and solicited local items for the newspapers. By marriage and otherwise I associated myself with several old backwoods families, in both Missouri and Arkansas. I spared no effort to become intimately acquainted with Ozarkers of the hillbilly type, and succeeded insofar as such intimacy is possible to one who was born a lowlander.

The Ozarker's wealth of folk material fascinated me from the very beginning. I carried scraps of newsprint in my pocket, and along with locals for the paper I recorded other things that interested me—folksongs, tall tales, backwoods jokes, riddles, party games, dialect, old customs, and superstitions. This stuff was later typed on cards and placed in a trunk which I had converted into a filing cabinet, indexed and classified so that I could put my finger on any given item at a moment's notice. I made no secret of the fact that I was gathering old songs and intended to publish a book of them some day, but the other material was collected more or less surreptitiously.

The cards in the file marked SUPERSTITIONS accumulated very slowly for the first three or four years, but my neighbors gradually became accustomed to seeing me around, and began to talk a bit more freely in my presence. In 1924 some witchcraft material which came to my attention seemed so extraordinary that I suspected my friends were greening me—*greening* is a dialect word which means spoofing. It was only after checking and double-checking these tales, and getting almost identical items from different people in widely separated sections of the hill country, that I began to realize the extent to which superstition still flourished in this region.

In all the years of my collecting I have never known a hillman to admit a belief in anything which he regarded as superstition. "I aint superstitious myself," one old man told me,
"but some things that folks *call* superstitious is just as true
as God's own gospel!" Most of the real old-timers adhere to
traditions wild and strange, and the fact that many of them
contradict each other matters not at all. Nobody could possibly believe, or even remember, all of the items listed in this
book, but nearly every one of them is credited by hillfolk
within my own circle of friends and neighbors. The man who
laughs at witchcraft and supernatural warning is found to be
a firm believer in the moon's influence upon crops, while the
woman who doesn't believe in dummy suppers takes the question of prenatal "marking" very seriously indeed.

One might expect to find a definite negative correlation between superstition and intelligence, or at least between superstition and education, but this does not seem to be the case.
Perhaps the most famous water witch who ever lived in southwest Missouri was a physician, a graduate of Washington
University, and a man of really extraordinary attainments.
One of the most credulous and superstitious hillmen I ever knew
was intelligent enough to learn surveying and had sufficient
book learning to enable him to teach the district school with
unprecedented success.

It must be admitted that some of the items in this collection
are folktales rather than superstitions proper. That is, they
are not really believed by intelligent adults, but are repeated
to children just as parents elsewhere tell the story of Santa
Claus or assure their offspring that rabbits lay parti-colored
eggs on Easter Sunday. The old sayin' that killing a toad
will make the cows give bloody milk, for example, is probably
just a way of teaching children to let toads alone; the farmer
knows that toads destroy insects, and he likes to see them
around his doorstep on summer evenings. Every backwoods
child has heard a little rhyme to the effect that one who

defecates in a path will get a "sty" on his posterior—a notion doubtless promulgated by barefoot housewives who wish to keep the catwalks clean. Perhaps the children don't really believe all this either, but it sometimes amuses them to pretend that they do, and thus the stories are preserved and transmitted from one generation to the next. But even here I do not presume to define the exact limits of credulity. Sometimes it appears that backwoods parents begin by telling outrageous whoppers to their children and end by half believing the wildest of these tales themselves.

Many of the civic boosters in the Ozark towns are sensitive about their hillbilly background and regard anybody who mentions the old customs or folk beliefs in the light of a public enemy. This sentiment is reflected in the Ozark newspapers, particularly in the smaller cities. An address of mine, delivered before the State Historical Society at Columbia, Missouri, in 1938, offended people all over the Ozarks because it dealt in part with backwoods superstition. Once in Springfield, Missouri, during a dinner at which I had been invited to speak by the Chamber of Commerce, a casual reference to superstition so moved the president of that body that he suddenly sprang up and denounced me and all my works. Another time, in the dining room of a hotel at Joplin, Missouri, an old gentleman cursed me at the top of his voice and even made as if to strike me with his stick, because I had published something about Ozark superstition in *Esquire*. Others who have spoken or written on the subject have had similar experiences. The general feeling is that the persistence of the old folklore is somehow discreditable to the whole region, and the less said about it the better.

A Little Rock attorney who read this book in manuscript says that "it applies only to a few ignorant old folks who live in the most backward and isolated sections of the Ozark country." Well, it is true that much of my information was obtained from elderly people in the back hills. The educated young folk are certainly less concerned with witchcraft and the like than were their parents and grandparents. And yet I have known college boys, proud possessors of dinner jackets and fraternity pins, to say and do things which would be quite inexplicable to anyone not familiar with the superstitions of their childhood. And there was a pretty girl once, a senior at one of our best Ozark colleges, who obtained her heart's desire by a semipublic "conjuration" which would not seem out of place in a medieval book on demonology.

The wildest kind of superstition was accepted as a matter of course by the grandparents of these backwoods collegians, and resistance to change has always been the chief regional characteristic of the Ozark people. The principle of organic evolution has been pretty well accepted everywhere for a long time, but as I write these lines it is still against the law to teach evolution at the University of Arkansas.

A Missouri politician writes me that "the old superstitions you describe may have existed in my district fifty years ago. In fact, I know personally that some of the most fantastic did exist as late as 1900. But you may rest assured that the folks down there do not believe any such nonsense today." To this I can only reply that nearly all of my material was gathered since 1920, and that many of the most striking items in the collection came from the locality indicated in this man's letter.

It is difficult to see why our civic leaders and politicians should be so concerned about these matters. Surely they must know that people in other sections of the country, even in the great cities, have superstitions of their own. Some very eminent gentlemen in Washington are known to consult mediums and fortunetellers on occasion, and there are many women in New York who still believe in astrology and numerology.

I think that the hillfolk are somewhat less superstitious today than when I began this study, twenty-five years ago. Much

of my best material came from men and women who were old
in the 1920's, and nearly all of them are dead now. One has
only to compare the young people with their grandparents, or
the isolated settlements with the villages along our new motor
highways, to appreciate the present status of folklore in the
Ozark country.

Wherever railroads and highways penetrate, wherever newspapers and movies and radios are introduced, the people
gradually lose their distinctive local traits and assume the drab
color which characterizes conventional Americans elsewhere.
The Ozarkers are changing rather rapidly just now, and it
may be that a few more years of progress will find them thinking and acting very much like country folk in other parts of
the United States. This standardizing transformation is still
far from complete, however. A great body of folk belief dies
very slowly, and I suspect that some vestiges of backwoods
superstition will be with us for a long time to come.

2. Weather Signs

Signs and superstitions about the weather naturally seem important to a people who live by tilling the soil, and are taken very seriously in the Ozark country. There is no denying that some old hillmen are extraordinarily acute in their short-range predictions of rain and frost. The old-timer generally speaks dogmatically of bad luck, death bells, ghosts, witches and the like. But he becomes a bit more cautious in discussing the weather. "Nobody ever claimed that them old signs was *always* right," a gentleman in Jasper county, Missouri, said reasonably. "But I've been a-watchin' the weather for sixty years, an' I believe these here goosebone prophets are just about as good as the government men we've got nowadays."

The spotty nature of the Ozark weather, with conditions varying widely between one hollow and another a few miles distant, may also give the local weather predictor a slight edge. "Them government weathermen do pretty well on a flat prairie, like Kansas or western Oklahoma," an old man told me, "but they aint worth a damn in a hilly country."

The most colorful official of the United States Weather Bureau in the Ozarks is C. C. Williford, who has been giving a daily broadcast over a local station at Springfield, Missouri, since 1933. Williford differs from most of his colleagues in his readiness to argue with the "groundhog watchers" and other defenders of superstition. He takes a lot of ribbing about this, particularly when the goosebone meteorologists predict the weather more accurately than the government weather prophets, as sometimes happens. The backwoods Christians known as "Holy Rollers," in Taney county, Missouri, have more than once held public prayers for "that feller in Springfield that lies so much about the weather." Williford gets many astonishing items by mail; as an example of Ozark innocence in these matters, here is a letter dated Oct. 21, 1939:

We thought maybe you would say something about the moon falling Sunday night. There might not have been many saw it but we sure did. There was six of us witnessed it. It looked to be about 1 or 2 hours high when it just suddenly turned over and fell like a star would fall, making a ball of fire which could be seen down low for 5 or 10 minutes. No one around here ever heard of the moon falling, even people 50 years old. Some wouldn't believe it. It was between 7:30 and 8 o'clock. If you or anyone else ever heard of this before I wish you would please mention it.

Paul Murrell
Strafford, Mo. Route 3

To this communication Mr. Williford replied soberly that what Paul Murrell and his friends saw was probably a pilot balloon from the Weather Bureau, since one was lost that night. The records show, he added, that at the hour mentioned the new moon was almost invisible—a faint sickle riding low on the horizon. An account of this episode was printed in the Springfield *News & Leader*, Oct. 22, 1939, under a two-column head: "Extra! The Moon Falls on Strafford Route Three!"

There are so many rain signs, and they vary so widely in different sections of the Ozarks, that one frequently encounters contradictions and differences of opinion as to their proper interpretation. One old fellow told me that when the tall grass is bone-dry in the morning he "allus figgered on rain afore night" but he also insisted that a heavy dew is one of the most reliable rain signs known. Some time later, during a prolonged drouth, I showed him that neither statement had any great merit, but he was not at all disturbed. "All signs fail in dry weather," quoth he and seemed perfectly satisfied to let it go at that. And even Will Talbott, who used to be the government weatherman of Greene county, Missouri, in 1930, was quoted as saying "the only *sure* thing about the weather is that a dry spell always ends with a rain."

Many common indications of rain are found in the activities of animals. If rabbits are seen playing in the dusty road, if dogs suddenly begin to eat grass, if cats sneeze or wash behind their ears or lick their fur against the grain, if large numbers of field-mice are seen running in the open, if sheep turn their backs to the wind, if wolves howl before sunset, the hillman expects a shower. Any backwoods farmer will tell you that when a hog carries a piece of wood in its mouth there is bad weather a-comin', and I am almost persuaded that hogs do sometimes pile up leaves and brush for nests several hours before a storm.

When horses' tails suddenly appear very large, by reason of the hairs standing erect, it means that a drouth will soon be broken. If cattle and horses refuse to drink in very dry weather, the farmer expects a cloudburst. When horses suddenly stop feeding and begin scratching themselves on trees or fences, it is a sign of heavy rains. Farmers who live in the river bottoms are alarmed when they see dogs or cats carrying their young to higher ground, believing that these migrations indicate floods or cloudbursts.

Mrs. Mabel E. Mueller, of Rolla, Missouri, says that "if the cat lies in a coil, with head and stomach up, bad weather is coming, but if it yawns and stretches, the weather will be good."

Some country women believe that chickens are somehow able to tell what the weather is to be for several days in advance. When chickens or turkeys stand with their backs to the wind, so that their feathers are ruffled, a storm is on the way. If hens spread their tail feathers and oil them conspicuously, it is sure to rain very soon.

A rooster's persistent crowing at nightfall is regarded as a sign that there will be rain before morning:

> If a cock crows when he goes to bed,
> He'll get up with a wet head.

This jingle is evidently very old and is one of the few instances in which the male fowl is called a *cock* in the Ozark speech. In ordinary conversation the hillman says crower or rooster instead.

In front of my cabin near Sulphur Springs, Arkansas, a rooster crowed repeatedly at high noon. "What's that a sign of?" I asked an Ozark girl who sat beside me. "Oh, that aint no sign at all," she answered. "I reckon he's just a-crowin' up company."

In this same connection Mrs. Mueller says that her neighbors are much impressed when chickens suddenly go to roost outside the henhouse. One might suppose that, if the fowls really know what they are about, this would be an indication of fair weather, but the people near Rolla regard it as a sure sign of rain. A storm is expected, too, if the chickens are seen going to roost earlier than usual. Mrs. Mueller says also that "if chickens stand on the woodpile and pick their feathers, rain is on the way."

When chickens and other fowls are seen feeding in the fields during a shower, it means that the rainy weather will continue for at least twenty-four hours longer. When ducks or geese or guineas suddenly become very noisy, without any visible reason, it is a sure sign of rain. When crows, or woodpeckers, or hawks make more racket than usual, the hillman expects rain in twenty-four hours or less. If robins suddenly begin to sing near the cabin, when they are not accustomed to sing there, the housewife prepares for a shower. The call of the yellow-billed cuckoo, which the Ozarker knows as the rain crow, is widely recognized as a sign of wet weather. If a big owl hoots in the daytime, or calls loudly and persistently near the house at night, there will be a heavy rain within three days.

When kingfishers and bank swallows nest in holes near the water, the hillman expects a dry season; if these birds nest high above the stream, the hillfolk prepare for much rain and flooded rivers. If wild ducks nest close to the water's edge a fairly dry summer is expected; if they make their nests farther back, the Ozarker looks for a wet season.

If quail are found sunning themselves in coveys, or if brush rabbits are lying in shallow, unprotected forms, the Ozarker feels safe in expecting two or three days of pleasant weather. The latter sign in particular inspires great confidence, and I am almost persuaded that there may be something in it. I have often seen farmers go out and flush two or three rabbits, and examine their nests carefully before deciding to go on a journey.

It is generally believed that snakes—particularly rattlesnakes and copperheads—become very active just before a rain. Thus an abundance of snake trails in the dusty road is regarded as a sign that a drouth will soon be broken.

The voices of tree toads always forecast a shower, according to the old-timers. Men who hunt bullfrogs say that the skin of these creatures turns dark about twelve hours before a rain. Old rivermen claim that when they see a great many fish coming to the surface and "stickin' out their noses," there is sure to be a rainstorm in three or four hours.

When flies and mosquitoes suddenly swarm into a cabin, or snails become very abundant, or spiders leave their shelters and crawl aimlessly about, or glowworms shine brighter than usual, or crickets chirp louder, or bees cluster closely about the entrance to their hives, or a centipede appears where centipedes are not usually seen—all these are signs of an approaching storm. When the burrows of ants and crawfish are "banked up" about the entrance, the mountain man looks for a cloudburst, or a sudden rise in the water of the streams.

If the sun "rises red" it is a sign of rain, according to the old rhyme:

> When the morning sun is red
> The ewe and the lamb go wet to bed.

When the sun rises into an unusually clear sky, even if it isn't red, many farmers expect showers before night. Others contend that the meaning of this depends upon the season of the year —in summer a misty dawn means a dry spell, but in winter it is a sign of rain.

A red sunset is supposed to promise at least twenty-four hours of dry weather. If a dull blue line shows around the horizon at sunset, one may expect rain the following day. When a "sundog" circle is seen about the sun, there will be some radical change in the weather. Some say that a sundog means a prolonged drouth. When a fringe of cloud hides the sun, just before sunset, it is a sign of rain.

A rainbow in the evening means clear weather, but a rainbow in the morning indicates a storm within twenty-four hours. If the weather clears between sundown and dawn there will be more rain within forty-eight hours. When fog rises rapidly it is always a sign of rain:

> Fog goes up with a hop,
> Rain comes down with a drop.

If a fog descends and seems to disappear into the ground, the hillman expects several warm, bright days.

Lightning in the south is a dry-weather sign, while lightning in any other direction usually indicates rain.

When the crescent moon rides on its back, with the horns turned up, there will be no rain for some time. This is the moon that will "hold water," the moon a feller can "hang a powder horn on." When one of the horns seems much higher than the other, the concavity will no longer hold water, and one may expect rain shortly. If the moon remains low in the southern sky, the old folks say that it is well to prepare for a severe drouth.

A ring around the moon is said to be a sure sign of bad weather—usually rain or snow. You can tell how many days will elapse before the storm by counting the number of stars inside the circle; if there are no stars in the ring, the rain is less than twenty-four hours away. There is a very general notion that if it doesn't rain at the change of the moon, there will be little rain until the moon changes again. In the midst of a drouth, one of my neighbors remarked that it *couldn't* rain until the new moon appeared. When the stars appear faded and dim, some people say that a big rain is on the way, no matter what the moon signs may be.

A great many hillfolk believe that an abrupt drop in the water line of a spring or well is a sure indication that wet weather is coming soon. When the surface of plowed ground appears damp, or moisture seems to gather on the gravel in dry gullies, a rain is expected within a few hours. Nearly all of the old-timers seem to believe this. One of the most successful and progressive farmers in my neighborhood told me that he does not believe in many weather signs, but that he is prepared to wager even money up to a thousand dollars that whenever the flint-rocks in his field suddenly begin to sweat, there will be some precipitation within twenty-four hours.

A man in Greene county, Missouri, has a cave on his place. He says that when the roof of this cave begins to drip, after a spell of dry weather, it always rains within two or three days. He used to crawl into the cave, particularly at harvest time, to see what sort of weather was coming.

When a housewife is boiling food in a kettle, and it seems necessary to add more water than usual, she expects a rain shortly. Mrs. Mabel E. Mueller, of Rolla, Missouri, says that her neighbors watch the coffeepot—if the coffee boils over too often, they regard it as a sign of an approaching rain. The lumping of table salt, the unusual creaking of chairs, the loud sputtering of a kerosene lamp, an extraordinary amount of crackling in a wood fire, the "warping up" of a rag carpet, the sudden flabbiness of hitherto dry and crisp tobacco leaves —all these phenomena are supposed to indicate rain.

If the leaves of a tree turn up, so as to show the undersides which are usually lighter in color, the hillfolk expect a rain within a few hours. When the upper blades of corn begin to twist, as they do in very hot dry weather, many farmers predict rain. If dead limbs fall in the woods, with no perceptible wind blowing, it is regarded as a sure sign of rain; but when an entire tree topples over, under the same conditions, it is not so considered.

If oaks bud earlier than ash trees in the spring, a wet summer is expected; if the ash buds first, look out for a drouth in July and August.

It is said that certain flowers, which ordinarily close at dusk, sometimes remain open all night—this is a positive indication that it will rain very shortly. A sudden appearance of toadstools or mushrooms is regarded as a sure sign of rain within twelve hours. If a hillman sees thistledown or milkweed or other hair-winged seeds flying in the air, when no breeze is otherwise apparent, he predicts rain.

When rain falls while the sun is shining, it will be of short duration—"a sunny shower won't last an hour." A sunny shower means that "the Devil is a-whuppin' his wife," according to the old-timers, and is a sign that there will be more rain on the following day. If drops of water hang on twigs or leaves for a long time after a rain, you may be sure that more rain is coming. It is said also that if one sees many large bubbles in roadside pools after a rain, it means another shower within a few hours. The belief that showers which begin early in the morning do not last long is recorded in the old sayin':

> Rain before seven
> Shine before eleven.

Many hillfolk believe that large raindrops mean a brief shower, while small drops indicate a long siege of rainy weather.

A series of hot days and cool nights, some old-timers say, is a sign of a long dry spell to come. If it seems very warm in the evening, and unusually cool next morning, the hillman concludes that a rain has "blowed over" or "went around," and he expects three or four days of dry weather.

There are farmers in Arkansas who insist that the blood of a murdered man—bloodstains on a floor or garments—will liquefy even on dry sunshiny days, as a sign that a big rain is coming. Burton Rascoe, who once lived in Seminole county, Oklahoma, told me that this notion is common in many parts of the South, and that the field hands on his father's farm used to go to a cabin where a Negro had been shot and examine the bloodstains on the planks to see whether a rain was about due.

Many persons believe that twinges of rheumatism, unusual soreness of corns and bunions, or attacks of sinus trouble inform them when it is going to rain.

Country women say that when milk or cream sours sooner than usual, a rain may be expected—and they insist that this works in fairly cold weather as well as in the heat of summer. Also that the little globules of fat in a cup of coffee to which cream has been added collect at the edges of the cup when a rain is coming, and in the center when there is dry weather ahead.

Little whirlwinds in the dusty road are regarded by many as sure signs of rain. If the wind blows suddenly and strongly from the east, many old-timers expect a heavy rain soon.

People in some parts of Taney county, Missouri, live so far from a settlement that they do not ordinarily hear trains or motor cars or church bells. Once in a while, however, they *do* hear these sounds, very faintly. When this happens, the people expect a good rain before many days. It is generally believed, in many sections of the Ozarks, that gunshots, church bells, whistles and the like may be heard at a greater distance when rain is approaching than when continued dry weather is in store.

A rain on Monday, according to some backwoods folk, means that it will rain more or less every day that week. Others say that if it rains on Monday there will be two more rainy days in the week, and maybe three, but that Friday will be bright and

fair. There is a common notion that Friday is always either the
fairest or the foulest day of the week. If the sun "sets clear" on
Tuesday, it is sure to rain before Friday. If the sun sets behind a
cloud on Tuesday, there will be showers before the *next* Tuesday.
If the sun "sets cloudy" on Thursday one looks for heavy rains
before Saturday night.

Many people insist that "the sun shines every Wednesday"
even if only for a moment, but if a Wednesday *should* pass
without a sunbeam, there will be some sudden, violent change—
perhaps a cloudburst or a tornado.

When rain falls on the first Sunday in the month, most old-
timers expect showers on the three following Sundays. If it rains
on the first day of the month, at least twenty days of that month
will be wet. This is really taken seriously by farmers in some
localities, and they consider it in planting and cultivating their
crops.

A number of farmers in Greene county, Missouri, have told
me that, during the month of July, it *never* rains at night. One
old gentleman said he had watched the weather for nearly sixty
years and had never yet, during the month of July, known rain
to fall after dark or before dawn.

There is a common notion, in rural Arkansas, that it never
rains during dog days—that is, the period in July and August
when Sirius the dog star is supposed to rise at dawn.

Many old-timers are obsessed with the notion that there is
always a big storm at Easter time. Mrs. May Kennedy McCord,
of Springfield, Missouri, writes: "I have lived to be 'over twenty-
one' in the Ozarks and I have never failed to see an Easter squall
yet. I believe if Easter came as late as the Fourth of July we
would still have that squall. When I was a girl we used to always
depend on it for our Easter picnics, and dread it." There is
also the common belief that if it rains on Easter Sunday, the
seven Sundays following Easter will be rainy too.

It is said that the last Friday and Saturday of each month
rule the weather for the next month—that is, if the last Friday

and Saturday in May are wet or cloudy days, the month of June
will be wet or cloudy.

I have known hillfolk who more or less seriously forecast the
weather for many months in advance by splitting open a persimmon seed in autumn. If the little growth at one end, between the
two halves of the seed, looks like a spoon, it means that the next
summer will be moist and warm, and that everybody will raise
bumper crops. But if the seed carries a tiny knife and fork,
instead of the spoon, the growing season will be unsatisfactory
and many crops will fail.

Some hillfolk claim to predict the rainfall, in a general fashion, for a whole year in this wise: take twelve curved pieces of
raw onion, set them in a row, and place an equal amount of salt
in the hollow of each piece. The first piece represents January,
the second piece February, the third March, and so on. Let all
the pieces stand undisturbed over night. The one which contains
the largest amount of water in the morning shows which month
will have the greatest rainfall.

In any case, a dry March is supposed to mean plenty of rain
and good growin' weather later on. There is an old sayin' that
"a bushel of dust in March is worth a bushel of silver in September." Many farmers say that if dandelions bloom in April,
there will be both rain and hot weather in July.

Will Rice quotes a patriarch at St. Joe, Arkansas, as saying
that "for every 100-degree day in July there will be a 20-below
day in the following January." [1] Rice assures his readers that
this idea has come down from grandpappy's day, and that many
hillfolk believe it absolutely.

July 2 is a mysterious and important day to some backwoods
weather prophets. The idea is that if rain falls on that day the
season will be moist and prosperous, but if it does not rain on
July 2 there will be no rain for six weeks.

July 15 is also an important date in connection with weather

1 *Rayburn's Ozark Guide,* Lonsdale, Arkansas (September–October, 1943),
p. 17.

prediction, but I have been unable to get any definite information about this. There are many hillfolk who insist that if November 1 is clear and cool, it means that big rains or snowstorms
are coming soon. Others say that if November 11 is cold, we
may expect a short, mild winter.

Some people think that the weather on December 25 is somehow correlated with the rainfall and temperature of the following summer. A mild Christmas, according to many Ozark
farmers, always means a heavy harvest. A good season for the
crops is supposed to be bad for human life, however, hence the
old saying that "a green Christmas makes a fat graveyard."

If there is no wind on New Year's Day, the Ozarker expects a
very dry summer; a fair breeze mans sufficient rainfall to make
a crop; a real windstorm on New Year's is a sign of floods the
following autumn.

Many hillfolk believe that the first twelve days of January
rule the weather of the entire year. That is, if January 1 is
cloudy, the whole month of January will be cloudy; if January 2 is clear, the whole month of February will be clear; if
January 3 is stormy, the whole month of March will be stormy,
and so on. One finds Alice Curtice Moyer-Wing [2] rejoicing with
her neighbors that January 6 was dry, therefore June would
be dry enough to permit work in the cornfields; it was fortunate
also that January 7 and 8 were wet, since that assured rain
enough in July and August to make a crop. Clink O'Neill, of
Day, Missouri, remarked to me that there may be something
in this theory "if it aint carried too far," adding that he doubted
whether snow on January 8 means that there will also be snowstorms in August.

Mr. Ora McGrath, a farmer of Taney county, Missouri,
tells me that in his family it has always been believed that the
twelve "old days"—the last twelve days in December—rule the
coming year. Some old-timers near Farmington, Arkansas, think
that the "ruling days" are the last six days in December *plus*

[2] St. Louis *Post-Dispatch,* Jan. 28, 1917.

the first six days in January. Still other hillfolk believe that it is Old Christmas (January 6) and the eleven days which follow Old Christmas which really determine the weather for the year.

The dates of the first and last frosts are matters of considerable import to the Ozark farmer, and he has many curious ideas about the prediction of these frosts. There is a very general notion that katydids sing to bring on cold weather in the fall. A writer in the St. Louis *Post-Dispatch* (Aug. 25, 1936) says that the katydids "can sing for frost, and get it in about two weeks," but the old-timers say that it can't possibly be done in less than six weeks. In some parts of Arkansas and Missouri the farmers expect the first frost exactly six weeks after the katydids' singing begins; others say that nine weeks is the correct figure, and many Missourians hold out for three months. Mr. Elbert Short, of Crane, Missouri, says that it was always three months to the old folks in his neighborhood. Whatever the period, nearly all Ozarkers feel that there must be something in the katydid-frost theory. I know many hillfolk who listen for the katydids and arrange their agricultural schedules accordingly, and I have interviewed very few old-timers who did not believe in this sign to a certain extent.

An old man in Washington county, Arkansas, told me that he always marked on the calendar the date when he saw the first Devil's-darning-needle—the walking-stick insect, that is. His prediction was that the first real frost comes just six weeks later, and he swore he had missed it only twice in twenty-seven years.

In Taney county, Missouri, they say that the first killing frost comes ten weeks after the "locusts begin to holler"—the locust or jarfly is really a cicada. The locusts usually began to holler about the Fourth of July, when I lived in Taney county, but the first killing frost, in the average year, doesn't come to the Ozarks before the middle of October.

There seems to be some correlation between the date at which deer change their coats and the time of the first frost. In southwest Missouri, in 1943, it was said that fawns "lost their spots" about the middle of July; old-timers who observed this all agreed that it indicated an early fall.

Butterflies seen late in the autumn are signs that cold weather will be here very soon. The same is true of big woolly caterpillars. The intricate designs made by the tiny larvae that work inside leaves are said to be significant in weather prediction, but I have been unable to learn just how to read their signs.

Many Ozarkers tell me that it never frosts until the cockleburs are ripe—nobody ever saw a frostbitten cocklebur. As long as green cockleburs are in evidence, one may be sure that there will be no frost for several weeks. It is said that persons who suffer from hay fever are reliable weather prophets—the first attack of the season always comes just ninety days before the first frost. When angleworms and grubs are found close to the surface there is no danger of frost. When crab grass lies flat on the ground, many country folk say that there'll be a frost within twenty-four hours.

I have known old-timers in Carroll county, Arkansas and in Taney county, Missouri, who believe that thunder in February always means frost on the corresponding date in May; that is, if it thunders on February 12, there'll be a frost on May 12, and so on. Others contend that there are always as many frosts in May as there are thunderclaps in February but do not insist that the dates must correspond exactly.

Several old hillfolk tell me that the number of fogs in August is always equal to the number of snows in the following winter. Some say that the number of days the first snow remains on the ground indicates the number of snows to be expected during the winter. Another view is that the whole thing depends upon the date of the first snowfall. One man told me that if the first snow falls on December 1 it means that there will be twenty-four snows altogether. "What if the first snow came on November sixteenth?" I asked. "Then thar'll be a hunderd an' seventy-six," he answered after a moment's thought but refused to tell me how he arrived at these conclusions. Another old-timer whom I consulted gave me the same figures for these two dates, adding that every man should obtain the method of "figgerin' it out" from the elders of his own family, and that it would be very bad luck for him to tell me about it. I "figgered it out" for myself later on, however; one simply multiplies the number of the month by the number of the day, and in case the latter is less than fifteen doubles the result.

Mrs. Mabel E. Mueller, of Rolla, Missouri, tells me that people in her neighborhood count the number of sunny days between July 1 and September 1 and multiply by two—this gives you the number of freezing cold days to be expected the following winter.

Some old folks take careful note of the age of the moon, at the time the first snow falls. It is said that the number of days the moon is old, at that time, is always equal to the number of snows which will come that winter.

The deepest snow of the winter, according to some Ozarkers, is forecast by the height to which the brush rabbits gnaw the sassafras sprouts in the fall. I have heard this mentioned in all seriousness at least fifty times, from Mena, Arkansas, to the suburbs of St. Louis. But I do not think that the genuine old-timers take much stock in it. Personally, I am not even sure that brush rabbits are accustomed to gnaw sassafras sprouts in the autumn.

There is an old saying that "clouds on frost means bad weather," and many believe that when a heavy frost is accompanied or immediately followed by a cloudy sky, it is well to prepare for severe storms and lower temperatures.

Nearly all of the old-timers believe that when a frost comes in cloudy weather it is less harmful to crops than a frost in clear weather. Many insist that a frost in the light or increase of the moon is much less harmful than a frost in the dark or waning of the moon. Some go so far as to say that fruit is *never* killed by frost in the light of the moon, though anybody who has lived in this country a few years can see that it isn't so.

I know deer hunters in Arkansas who think that if an autumn campfire spits and sputters more than usual, it means that a snowstorm is not far off. The firewood, they say, is "stompin' snow." Mr. Elbert Short, of Crane, Missouri, agrees with the deer hunters. "If your wood fries an' sings an' pops an' cracks," says he, "it's a sure sign that snow is a-comin'."

Children in the backwoods sometimes make a great show of counting the nodules on cane, the knots on lilac bushes, the spots on bass in September, the freckles on their left hands and so on, to determine the number of cold spells to be expected in the coming winter, but I do not believe that any of these signs are taken very seriously by adult hillfolk.

Many of them do believe, however, that they can make some general forecasts about winter weather by examining the breast-bone of a wild goose killed in the fall. If the bone is thin and more or less transparent, the winter will be mild; if the bone is thick and opaque, the winter will be severe. If the bone is white, there will be a great deal of snow; if the bone is red, or has many red spots, the winter may be very cold, but the snowfall will be unusually light.

These goosebone weather prophets are still common in some sections, and their predictions are often recorded and discussed solemnly in the country newspapers. J. O. Wadell, veteran newspaperman of Springfield, Missouri, used to comment editorially upon the weaknesses of the goosebone school of weather forecasting. In the Springfield *Press*, he wrote: "The fact that one goose-bone may be thin and another from the same flock be thick, as has often been demonstrated, has no effect upon the old superstition. Folks believe it just the same." [3]

The severity of the approaching winter is indicated by the thickness of furs and feathers and cornshucks and so on. If hair

3 Oct. 31, 1930, p. 3.

on muskrats, skunks, coons, and possums is unusually thick, the hillman expects a hard winter. If goose feathers are "veined close" it means severe weather ahead. Every backwoods child has heard the little rhyme:

> Onion skin mighty thin,
> Easy winter comin' in.

Some old men tell me that a summer in which the foliage on trees is unusually dense, or exceptionally bright in color, is followed by a very cold winter. When great numbers of squirrels are seen moving toward the south, it is regarded as a sign of an early fall and hard winter.

Many old people say that if the hornets build their nests low in the trees, it means that a severe winter is coming; if the hornets' nests hang high, the following winter will be mild.

A big crop of walnuts indicates cold weather to come. A great abundance of *mast*—which means acorns—is a sure sign of a severe winter. If cherries or lilacs bloom in the fall, the winter will be unusually long and severe. If woodpeckers begin at the foot of a tree and work clear to the top, it means that cold weather is coming very soon. When a cat sits down with its tail toward the fire, the hillman looks for a cold spell. If the moon appears farther north than usual in the fall, the Ozarker predicts an unusually cold winter. Most old-timers feel that a very hot summer is likely to be followed by a winter of extraordinary severity.

When snowflakes are very large, it means that the storm won't last long; if the flakes are small, it may be only the beginning of a heavy fall of snow. If snow *lays* on the ground, without melting appreciably, it is a sign that another snowfall may be expected soon.

Pick up a handful of snow, and try to melt it with a lighted match. If it melts quickly, the snow on the ground will soon disappear. But if the snow in your hand does not melt easily, it means that there will be snow on the ground for a considerable time.

Old hunters say that when a deer lies down casually in the snow, there will be another snowstorm within a few days. But when deer paw out places in the snow, as if to make beds for themselves, it means that there will be no more snow for a week or two at least.

The old belief regarding Groundhog Day is very widely accepted in the Ozarks. The groundhog is supposed to emerge from his burrow on Groundhog Day, and if the sun is shining he goes back to sleep, knowing that there will be six more weeks of winter weather.

February 2 is recognized as Groundhog Day in most sections of the United States, and is so marked on our calendars and almanacs. Otto Ernest Rayburn says that the Missouri Legislature has established February 2 as the legal and official Groundhog Day of Missouri.[4] But there are thousands of people in Missouri and Arkansas who regard February 14 as Groundhog Day, and it is February 14, not February 2, that they consider in deciding the proper dates for plowing and planting.

The publisher of the Crane (Missouri) *Chronicle* comments editorially: "In Pike county, Ill., where I was born, groundhogs saw or failed to see their shadows on February 2nd. That date prevails to this day as far west as the Mississippi. Down here, the official date is February 14th." [5]

Uncle Jack Short, Galena, Missouri, told me in 1944 that he never heard of February 2 being called Groundhog Day until after 1900. "February fourteenth is the real old-time Groundhog Day," he said. Mr. Short was born up on Crane Creek, not far from Galena, in 1864. His father came from Tennessee in the 1840's.

4 *Arcadian Magazine* (February, 1932), p. 18.
5 Feb. 18, 1943.

In 1933 I was in Greene County, Missouri, where February 2 was clear, while February 14 was dark and cloudy. The "fur-riners" prepared for six weeks of cold weather, but the old-timers shucked their sheepskin coats and began to spade up their garden patches. The following is clipped from the Spring-field (Missouri) *Press*, Feb. 16, 1933.

"What's all this talk about February 2 being groundhog day?" asked a man at the courthouse Wednesday who is old enough to know what he is talking about. "It was always February 14 until late years. Suppose the darned hog has caught the spirit of the times and is stepping on the gas—working under high pressure and starting his year 12 days earlier than in the good old days when men and ground-hogs both took time to live in a rational manner.

"My father and my grandfather, and all the generations from Adam down to 20 years ago pinned their faith to February 14—St. Valentine's day. That is the correct date, and it matters not what the younger generation may say about it. There was no shadows Tues-day and Winter is about over."

Three years later the people in Greene County were still wrangling. Here is an editorial comment from the Springfield (Missouri) *Leader*, Feb. 4, 1936:

Groundhog saw no shadow here and a large faction says it makes no difference whether the hog saw a shadow or not on February 2, as the correct date for such an observation is February 14. The second-of-February faction claim that those who stand by the four-teenth have mixed the date up with Valentine Day. A great many people are neutral on the subject, or pretend to be in order to avoid making enemies.

The last sentence of the above quotation shows how seriously the controversy is taken by some persons. Springfield is a town with a population of perhaps 60,000 souls, and many of these, including some newspapermen, are not native Ozarkers at all. Most of the weekly papers in the back-country villages do not even mention this controversy about the date. Their readers all know that Groundhog Day falls on February 14, and there is no need for any argument about it.

It is said that Deacon Dobyns of the Oregon (Missouri) *Sentinel* kept careful records of Groundhog Day for more than forty years and discredited the see-your-shadow prophecy in his section of the country, for either February 2 or February 14. But that doesn't matter in the least to the old-time hillman, who still believes in Groundhog Day. I have encountered, in some isolated localities, traces of an ancient notion that birds and rabbits begin their mating on February 14, and some old folks say that it is unlucky to eat rabbit meat after this date.

There are other ways of determining whether winter is really over, regardless of Groundhog Day. Even though many warm days come early in the spring, if the moon appears just a hair farther north than it should be, many an Ozark farmer fears another killing frost. Some people say that the moment a sign of green shows on the bodark tree (*bois d'arc*, or Osage orange) the cold weather is definitely over, but many hillfolk are skeptical even of this sign.

One often hears frogs piping very early. Mr. Rufe Scott, attorney at Galena, Missouri, has noticed for many years that during court week (the second week in March) the frogs holler for the first time. In this locality it is commonly believed that the frogs always come out too soon, and are "froze back" three times before spring really arrives. The birds known as killdeers are much more reliable than frogs, but even killdeers are sometimes mistaken about the weather. One certain sign of spring, however, is the return of the turkey buzzards; the old-timers all agree that there is never any freezing weather after the first buzzard is seen.

There are occasional violent tornadoes or cyclones in the Ozark country. I have seen long lines of big trees uprooted in the timber, and sometimes one of these storms destroys a settlement with considerable loss of life. But somehow the hillfolk as a rule are not much concerned about windstorms, and there is little of the tornado-phobia that used to be so common in the cyclone-cellar belt of Kansas and Oklahoma.

I have heard farmers declare that the wind always slacks up at milkin'-time, both morning and night. Some of them really believe this, while others tell it to their children along with the old story that a boy who rubs a sow's milk in his eyes can *see the wind*.

Some people say that the angle at which a star falls somehow indicates the direction of the wind which will arise next morning. Charles J. Finger, of Fayetteville, Arkansas, tells me that his neighbors believe that the "set" of the Milky Way shows the direction of the prevailing wind for a month in advance.

Many hillfolk think that cats are able to tell when a windstorm is on the way; some even say that just before a storm a cat always scratches itself and points with its tail in the direction from which the wind will come. When crows fly erratically, or pitch about high in the air, the hillman expects a strong wind within the next hour or so.

If a hog is seen looking up, when nothing is visible which would ordinarily attract his attention, some folk conclude that a terrific storm or tornado is imminent. Several farmers near Green Forest, Arkansas, and Berryville, Arkansas, where windstorms have destroyed houses and killed many people, claim to have seen hogs looking up at the sky not long before the big winds came.

There are still a few diehards in the Ozarks who believe that men can control the weather to some extent by charms and incantations, but the average farmer has little confidence in such methods. The wild rain dances of the Cheyennes, not uncommon across the Oklahoma border, excite only laughter among the mountain folk. One hears occasionally of certain preachers, particularly those of the Pentecostal or "Holy Roller" cults, who have big meetings at which the whole congregation prays for rain—but apparently without much effect.

Other hillmen try to produce rain by burning brush along the creeks, or hanging dead snakes belly-up on fences, or killing frogs and leaving them in the dry road, or putting salt on gravel bars, or suspending live turtles above the water. Singing late at night is said to "fetch on a shower," as explained in the little rhyme:

> Sing afore you go to bed,
> You'll git up with a wet head,

but I have never known any grown-up hillfolk to take it seriously.

In very dry periods a farmer may try to "charm up" a rain by pouring a gourdful of water on the ground in the middle of a dusty field. Children are sometimes told to do this by their elders, but I don't think that many adults have any real confidence in it.

In some localities people imagine that they can cause a rain by submerging a cat in sulphur water—they don't drown the animal, but make sure that it is completely under water for a moment at least. I once saw this tried at Noel, Missouri, but without any success.

There is an old saying to the effect that "rain follers the plow," and this is sometimes interpreted to mean that a farmer can actually bring on a rainstorm by plowing in the dust. I have met farmers who repeated this saying and said that they believed it. But the only man I ever knew who actually put the idea into practice was a religious fanatic, not a typical Ozark hillman at all.

Mr. G. H. Pipes tells me that in 1929 an old man appeared at Reeds Spring, Missouri, and announced that he was a professional rain maker. The country was mighty dry just then, and the tomato crop seemed certain to fail. Mr. Pipes says that Jim Kerr, who owned the tomato cannery in those days, offered fifty dollars for a good soaking rain. The old man begged a lot of used motor oil from a filling station and carried it to the top of a high hill near the village. That night he set the stuff afire, and the blaze could be seen for miles around. Next day came a good rain, and Jim Kerr paid him the fifty dollars without any quibbling. The rain maker stayed around Reeds Spring for several months, and the old-timers claim that he produced several other showers when they were sorely needed.

Mrs. May Kennedy McCord says [6] when she was a child the rain maker knelt down facing the sunrise, bowed three times, and repeated the 6th verse of Psalm 72: "He shall come down like rain upon the mown grass, as showers that water the earth."

Some say that if one kills a spider it won't rain for seven days, and in certain families the children are very careful not to kill spiders in dry weather. It's only a sort of childish game, though. And I doubt if many of the children really believe that there is anything to it.

Mr. Elbert Short, of Crane, Missouri, quoted for me an old sayin' that if a farmer doesn't provide sufficient cook wood for his womenfolk, his crops will suffer from lack of rain. I have heard this in several remote sections of Arkansas and Oklahoma, but very few backwoods farmers pay any attention to it, and the women still split most of the cook wood.

Some Ozark farmers are very careful, at corn-planting time, to save the cobs from the seedcorn and soak them in water— this is said to insure plenty of rain to make the crop. Once the crop is safe, these cobs are buried in the ground or thrown into a running stream. On the other hand, I am told that the people who live in the White River bottoms burn every seedcorn cob, contending that this prevents floods which would otherwise damage the corn. Will Rice of St. Joe, Arkansas, remarks that his neighbors believe that "if after you shell the seedcorn from the cobs, you throw the cobs in the creek, your corn will have all the moisture it needs. But if you burn the cobs in the stove, your corn crop will burn up in a drought." [7]

Many hillfolk feel that it is best not to call a tornado or cyclone by name. I remember a man near Pineville, Missouri, who viewed a sudden black cloud with considerable alarm. But

[6] *KWTO Dial*, Springfield, Mo., October, 1946, p. 3.
[7] Kansas City *Star*, May 5, 1943, p. 2.

he was careful to avoid the word cyclone. "I'm afeared *somethin'* *bad* is a-comin'," he quavered.

There is an old story to the effect that when a farmer sees a cyclone coming he should run into a field and stick his knife into the ground, with the edge of the blade toward the approaching cloud. The knife is supposed to "split the wind," so that his dwelling and barn will be spared. This notion is widely known in the Ozarks, and it is said that it is still practiced in Carroll county, Arkansas. I know a lot of backwoods people in Carroll county but have never found a man who would admit having done such a thing himself. Several of them have told me, however, that such "foolishment" is common among their neighbors.

I was once present in a backwoods settlement when the place was struck by a high wind—trees uprooted, some buildings turned over, and so on. The natives ran wildly about, cursing and screaming, exactly as people do elsewhere in similar situations. One bewhiskered citizen prayed a little and then sprang into a pigpen where he somehow broke one of his legs. But if anybody stuck knives into the ground, or worked any sort of magic spells against the approaching storm, I found no evidence of it.

3. Crops and Livestock

The changes of the moon and the signs of the zodiac are very important in determining the best dates for planting certain crops. What the hillman calls the "dark" of the moon is the period from the full moon to the new, the decrease or waning of the moon; the other half of the lunar season, from the new moon to the full, when the moon is waxing or increasing in size, is known as the "light" of the moon. In general, it is said that vegetables which are desired to grow chiefly underground such as potatoes, onions, beets, turnips, radishes, and peanuts are best planted in the dark of the moon. Garden crops which bear the edible part above ground, such as beans, peas, tomatoes, and so on, are usually planted in the light of the moon.

Besides the moon's phases, there are also the signs of the zodiac to be considered, and almost any hill farmer can make out these signs in the almanac, even though he cannot read a line of ordinary print. Merchants in the backwoods settlements distribute large calendars in which the phases of the moon and the signs of the zodiac are graphically and plainly represented. If a man can "read figgers" and knows the date he can see at a glance just what the situation is for any day in the year. Instead of using the names of the twelve constellations as the astrologers do, the hillman usually designates the portion of the human body with which each is associated. Some very successful farmers believe that underground crops, such as potatoes, should be planted "when the sign's in the feet"—that is, when the moon is in Pisces. If a hillman wishes to indicate Aquarius he says "when the sign's in the legs." In the same way

Capricornus is connected with the knees, Sagittarius with the thighs, Scorpio with the sex organs or "privates," Libra with the kidneys, Virgo with the bowels, Leo with the heart, Cancer with the breast, Gemini with the arms, Taurus with the neck, and Aries with the head. It is interesting to note that some Ozarkers say "the sign of the crawpappy" when they mean Scorpio, simply because the picture of the scorpion in the almanac looks rather like a crawfish.

Mr. C. C. Keller, farm agent in Greene County, Missouri,[1] stirred up a great controversy once by advising farmers to plant their potatoes on March 17 every year, with no regard to the signs of the zodiac or the changes of the moon. One of my neighbors in McDonald county, Missouri, was so horrified at this heresy that he decided not to send his son to the village high school. "If education don't learn a man no better than that," said he, "I don't want none of it in my family!"

Uncle Jack Short of Galena, Missouri, told me that some farmers back in the 1880's used to plant potatoes on February 14. Mr. Short himself thinks that this is much too early; he plants his own spuds on March 17, or even later—sometimes as late as March 30. I have met a few old-timers who say that the one-hundredth day of the year is the proper day to plant potatoes, regardless of the weather or any other considerations.

However farmers may differ about the proper date for planting, they are generally agreed that potatoes should be dug in the light of the moon, as they will rot otherwise.

There are men in Arkansas who are always careful to plant onions and potatoes on opposite sides of the garden, believing that potatoes will not do well if onions are growing too close. A little boy who asked about this was told that the odor of onions "makes a 'tater cry its eyes out." This was only a joke, of course, but the fact remains that these people *do not* plant potatoes and onions together.

It is very generally agreed that beans should be planted when

1 Springfield (Missouri) *Press*, Mar. 15, 1933.

the sign is in the arms. Plant them in Virgo, the old-timers say, and you'll get large plants and plenty of bloom, but mighty few beans and poor quality at that. An old woman fingering some very inferior beans at a crossroads store remarked: "They must have been planted when the maid held the posies"—in Virgo, that is. Bunch beans should be started on Good Friday regardless, according to some very successful bean growers. All beans should be planted in the morning rather than in the afternoon, and there is a widely accepted theory that beans planted in May never amount to much. Some old hillmen contend that one should never plant beans until after the first whippoorwill's cry is heard, no matter what the weather conditions are, or what the signs indicate. The farmer who burns the hulls of his seed beans or peas will get no crop anyhow, no matter what happens.

Cucumbers are best planted in Gemini, other things being equal, but some old-timers insist that cucumber seeds must be planted on May 1 before sunup—this protects the vines against insects. Many hillmen believe that the size of a cucumber depends upon the virility of the man who plants the seed—cucumbers planted by a woman or an old man never amount to much. A feeble-minded person is particularly successful in growing certain crops, and there is an old saying that "it takes a damn fool to raise gourds." Peppers thrive best if the individual who plants them is angry at the time, and if a lunatic can be induced to do the planting, so much the better. It is considered very bad luck to plant sage in one's own garden—the backwoods housewife always calls in a stranger to do this job if possible.

The old-timers around Marionville, Missouri, tell me that watermelon seeds should be planted on May 10, regardless. Many farmers in Arkansas, however, plant watermelons on May 1, before sunrise, just like cucumbers. Some hillmen soak watermelon seeds in sweet milk overnight before planting them, and one fellow near Clinton, Arkansas, told me that this trick is supposed to make the melons sweeter.

Cabbage, head lettuce, or any vegetable that heads, is supposed to be planted in Aries. There is a widespread notion, however, that all lettuce is best planted on Saint Valentine's day—February 14, which the old-timers still call Groundhog Day. Otto Ernest Rayburn tells me that once, when Valentine's Day fell on Sunday, the people at Kingston, Arkansas, got up before daylight to plant their lettuce, so as not to be seen violating the Sabbath. Peas are always planted on February 14— many gardeners cling to this idea after they have discarded most of the other superstitions.

People who used to raise hemp for cordage—the same weed that is called marijuana by the moderns—say that this stuff is best planted on Good Friday. Flax *must* be planted on Good Friday no matter what the weather conditions, according to the old settlers, but not much flax is grown in the Ozarks nowadays.

Farmers who differ widely about the proper signs and dates for other crops are pretty well agreed that turnips should be planted on July 25, regardless of signs, weather, or the phases of the moon. Uncle Jack Short, of Galena, Missouri, quoted a little rhyme:

> Sow your turnips the 25th of July,
> You'll make a crop, wet or dry,

and he tells me that this has been known and followed in his family for more than a hundred years.

Oats which are to be thrashed must be sowed in the light of the moon, to insure good full heads. But many hillmen believe that oats intended for fodder should be planted in the "olden moon"—the dark of the moon, that is. Some people near Forsyth, Missouri, contend that all wheat and oats are best sowed in the dark of the moon—if planted in the light of the moon the stalks will be too tall and spindlin', and likely to fall down.

One of the men who told me about this remarked also that a man who is raising oats should not have his hair cut during the growing season, but the younger members of the family smiled at this "old fogy notion."

The best time to plant corn is when the oak leaves—or the hickory buds, according to some hillmen—are as big as squirrels' ears. Some think that it is better to plant corn immediately after the first dove coos in the spring, or when the first martins appear, usually in late March or early April. There is an old saying that one should never plant corn the first two days of May, no matter what the circumstances or the weather. Corn never amounts to much if it is planted on one of the "blind days" —the day before the new moon, the day of the new moon, or the day following the new moon. If a man laughs loudly while planting corn, it is said that the grains on the cob will be irregular and too far apart. Many farmers plant corn in the dark of the moon. Roy Cole, of Taney county, Missouri, says that the light of the moon grows tall stalks and lots of top fodder, but mighty few ears of corn. Many hillfolk believe that corn is best planted in Scorpio, other things being equal.

Some hillmen always plant sugar cane on a certain day in July, and it is said that this is figured from the number of snows in the preceding February, but I have never been able to learn just how it works. Mrs. Pearl DeHaven, of Springfield, Missouri, says that "when the katydids first begin to sing it is time to plant cane, if you want your stock to eat it." There are substantial farmers in Arkansas who believe that a man with a child less than one year old should never plant cane or "soggrums" at all, though what the penalty is for violating this rule I do not know.

Fruit trees are set out in one of the "fruitful" signs, such as Scorpio, and in the dark of the moon, although any country boy will tell you that trees must be *pruned* in the light of the moon. Transplanted trees should be set in their old positions relative to the points of the compass—the north side of the tree must still face the north. Some farmers contend that any sort of tree may be transplanted at any time of the year (in the dark of the moon, of course) if one is careful to water it every day exactly at noon, and keep this up until the first rain falls.

In planting peach trees, it is always well to bury old shoes or boots near the roots. Not far from Little Rock, Arkansas, I have known farmers to drive into town and search the refuse piles for old shoes to be buried in peach orchards. The older and more decayed the leather, the better it works as fertilizer.

Many hill people drive nails into peach trees, but just what effect this is supposed to produce I do not know. Some say that nails are driven into barren trees in order to make them bear fruit, or to keep the peaches from falling off before they are ripe, but others are noncommittal or evasive. "Them's *family* matters," one old man growled when I asked why a certain peach tree was so thickly studded with big old-fashioned nails.

I have met intelligent and educated farmers in Arkansas who believe that if the wind is in the south on February 14, the peach crop will fail. Some farmers prefer to express this notion in another way, saying that "if the wind *aint* in the south on Groundhog Day, we'll get peaches no matter how cold it is."

There is an old saying in southern Missouri that a big yield of peaches means that certain other crops—especially corn, wheat, and oats—will be poor and scanty; this notion is stoutly defended by farmers who pay little attention to other superstitions. Akin to this is the theory that a season which is good for tomatoes is somehow bad for walnuts; a man who has run a "tomater factory" (a cannery, that is) for many years tells me that when the tomato crop is exceptionally good there aren't any walnuts at all.

Up around Marshfield, Missouri, many farmers say that if it rains on May 23, there'll be no blackberries that summer. Near Rogers, Arkansas, I met a family of berrypickers who believe that even a few drops of rain on June 2 will ruin the prospect for berries, while other hillfolk claim that June 13 is "blackberry day"—if it rains or even thunders on June 13, the blackberries will not be worth picking. Many people feel that rain on June 1 is bad for the grape crop, both wild and cultivated. Otto Ernest Rayburn, of Eureka Springs, Arkansas, told me of the belief that if it rains on June 20, the grapes will fall right off the vines.

Some people insist that mushrooms must be gathered when the moon is full—gather 'em at any other time and they will be unpalatable, or perhaps even poisonous. It is said that any mushroom which grows in an orchard where apple trees are blooming is edible.

The clearing of underbrush and the killing of sprouts is a serious matter to the Ozark farmer. There is a widespread belief that on *some certain day* one can kill large trees merely by touching the trunk with the blade of an ax, but there is so much difference of opinion about the proper date that little practical use is made of this theory. Nevertheless, nearly all of the old-timers are convinced that there is something in the idea.

Some hillfolk believe that if sprouts are cut on the ninth or tenth of May, they will never grow again. One of my neighbors near Pineville, Missouri, insisted on clearing his garden patch on these two days, although his wife and child lay dying only a few yards away.

Roy Cole, of Taney county, Missouri, says that "if you stick an ax in a saplin' in the spring, *when the sign's in the heart*, the leaves will wither in a few hours, and the tree will be dead in three or four months." Uncle Jack Short, of Galena, Missouri, would not commit himself about the *sign*, but told me that he had killed big oaks in May, when the oak leaves had not quite reached their full size, by making two or three deep cuts. The trees were positively not "ringed" or "girdled," he said, as in an ordinary deadening, but the leaves shriveled up in about six hours.

A woodsman near Walnut Shade, Missouri, told me that June 2 was "tree-killin' day" in his neighborhood, and that one man cutting brush on this day can accomplish more than ten men working at any other season.

In general, I think that most Ozarkers believe it is best to cut weeds and grub sprouts and deaden timber in August—some say between August 1 and August 20. There is a pretty general opinion that the dark of the moon is better than the light of the moon for this work. I have met men who prefer to grub sprouts in Virgo, or Gemini, but the great majority speak for Leo— "when the sign's in the heart."

By the same token, experts in these matters say that one should never cut hay when the sign is in the heart: if you do, it'll kill the roots, and you'll have no hay next year. "Lots of these here book farmers, when their clover or alfalfa dies, think it was froze out," one old man told me. "But the facts o' the matter is, the damn' fools cut it when the sign's in the heart, and that's what killed it."

A man who owns land near Carl Junction, Missouri, tells me that some farmers in his neighborhood cut sprouts only on the dates marked "Ember Days" in the almanac; they hire all the men they can get on these days and "sprout" large areas, claiming that this is more economical than the ordinary way of sprouting fields.

Ask almost any Ozark farmer, and he will tell you that if you fell a tree in the dark of the moon the log will show a definite tendency to sink into the ground, while a log cut in the light of the moon will not sink. Shingles or "shakes" rived out in the dark of the moon lie flat, but if made or put on during the moon's increase they warp and turn up. In recent years I have met several men who say this is all wrong, that shingles must be made and roofs laid in the *light* of the moon. All agree, however, that "board trees" from which shingles are made *must* be cut in the dark of the moon, otherwise they will rot. Rail fences are subject to the same principle; if the rails are split and laid in the light of the moon they are sure to curl and twist, and decay much more rapidly than if they are cut when the moon is dark. Even seasoned planks, if laid on the ground in the light of the moon, invariably warp or cup, while in the dark of the moon there is no such difficulty. Hog raisers sometimes build their fences during the moon's last quarter; they believe that this causes the bottom rail to sink into the ground, so that hogs cannot root under the fence.

Many Ozark farmers say that it is very bad luck to drive fence posts in the light of the moon, but just why this is so I have not been able to learn. Mrs. C. P. Mahnkey, Mincy, Missouri, tells me that a posthole dug in the dark of the moon can be filled up level full with the dirt that was taken out of it; when a posthole is dug in the light of the moon, however, there is always more dirt than can possibly be replaced. In Baxter county, Arkansas, I was told that in making posts one should sharpen the end that was nearest the ground in the living tree; it's bad luck to set a post upside down.

The old-timers long ago discovered, or at least believed, that chickens which roost in cedar trees are healthy and free from mites and other parasites, so that many farmers periodically cut cedar boughs and put them in their hencoops. A few years ago, when bananas became common in the village stores, people somehow got the notion that a banana stalk hung up in a chicken house would rid the whole place of mites and chicken lice, and these stalks are still seen in outbuildings occasionally.

Some chicken raisers tell me that it is a mistake to keep chickens near a potato patch, or near a place where potatoes are stored. The smell of potatoes, it is said, makes hens quit laying and want to brood. I have often seen hens with corn shucks fastened to their tails—this is supposed to discourage a settin' hen in a few days.

It is generally thought best to set eggs in the light of the moon. Never set a hen or an incubator when the wind is blowing from the south, or mighty few of the eggs will hatch. Eggs carried in a woman's bonnet, it is said, invariably make pullets. Mrs. Pearl DeHaven, of Springfield, Missouri, repeats the story that if eggs are carried in a man's hat, they all hatch roosters. Unusually long eggs, or eggs with shells noticeably rough at one end, are also regarded as "rooster eggs." It is said that eggs set on Sunday produce roosters, but one hears also that eggs placed under a hen in the forenoon, no matter what the day, always hatch a majority of pullets. Some hillfolk believe that chicks hatched in May, regardless of how favorable the other conditions may be, will never mature properly.

There are several magic tricks to protect domestic fowl from birds of prey. Mrs. Lillian Short, of Galena, Missouri, tells me that one of her neighbors used to take a smooth stone from a runnin' branch, just about big enough to fit the palm of the hand, and keep it in the oven of the cookstove—this was supposed to prevent hawks from killing the chickens. Most hillfolk of my acquaintance use a horseshoe instead of the stone, and some think that a muleshoe is even better. It is frequently fastened in the firebox of the stove rather than in the oven. In the old days the muleshoe was hung up in the fireplace, or even set into the mortar at the back of the chimney.

Some chicken grannies pull one feather out of each chicken in their flock and bury these feathers deep in the dirt under the henhouse or henroost. As long as the feathers remain there, it is believed that those particular chickens cannot be carried off by hawks or varmints, or stolen by human chicken thieves.

I once saw a large flock of chickens in the Arkansas backwoods, and about half of them had dirty rags fastened round their necks, like collars. "There's coal oil on them rags," an old woman remarked, "an' it cures the roup."

Mrs. C. P. Mahnkey, Mincy, Missouri, says that a handful of "polecat brush," put into the chickens' drinking water, will stop an epidemic of roup or chicken cholera quicker than any other treatment. Polecat brush is a shrub with tiny yellow flowers —I have not been able to identify this plant. Some people call it aromatic sumac.

It is very commonly believed that people who raise chickens

should never give away a chick—always take some sort of payment, even if it is only a matter of form. A neighbor told me that when she wanted to give some chicks to her mother-in-law, the old lady insisted on "paying" her with a handful of wild strawberries, carefully counting out one berry for each chick. The old saying is that if you give away a chick, your luck goes with it. I remember a woman who had two black chicks that the hen wouldn't own, so she gave them to a little girl from the city. The old-timers predicted ruin for the whole family, and the prediction came true with a vengeance. Before the year was out, my neighbor's husband was sent to the penitentiary, and her only daughter "went wrong."

Down around Rogers and Bentonville, Arkansas, there are many people who believe that healthy geese lay the first eggs of the season on March 17—if the eggs appear very much later, it means that the geese will have a bad year. Most backwoods women are taught that live geese must be picked in the new moon, and never at any other time; some say that this makes the birds produce a fine new crop of feathers, others think that it somehow affects the quality of the feathers already plucked.

There are several peculiar taboos against mentioning aloud the exact number of chickens in a flock, or cattle in a herd, particularly if it happens to be an *even* number—one divisible by two. A real old-timer never counts aloud the flowers or fruit on a tree, or the number of peas in a pod, or even the number of ears on a stalk of corn, because of an ancient notion that this counting may injure the crop.

A hill farmer, when asked how many bee-gums he has, never mentions the exact number—if he did so, he would get no honey that season. Some beekeepers believe that every hive must be moved an inch or so on February 22, in order to prevent an infectious disease called foul brood. Moths which destroy the honeycomb are driven away by scattering splinters from a "lightnin'-struck" tree over the hives, and I am told that the same treatment will rid a cabin of fleas and bedbugs—which latter pest the Ozarker calls "cheenches." When a death occurs in the family, the hillfolk attach a bit of black cloth to each hive; if this is not done, the bees are likely to leave the place and carry their stored honey away to bee trees in the woods. Honey is best removed from the hive in accordance with the state of the moon and the signs of the zodiac, but a man who can hold his breath is never stung by honeybees, anyhow. In the case of yellow jackets one protects himself by chanting:

Jasper whisper jacket!
You caint no more sting me
Than the Devil can count sixpence!

There are many cattlemen in the Ozarks who will not feed an even number of cattle. I knew one man who bought forty-one steers, expecting to feed them through the winter and sell them in the spring. When he discovered that one was missing he was much disturbed and immediately tried to buy another animal to replace it. Failing in this, he *sold* one at a very low price, preferring to winter thirty-nine steers rather than forty. When I asked what would be the penalty for violating this rule against even numbers, he said that the cattle would not be "thrifty," by which he meant that they would not fatten properly. The same man told me that it was bad luck to pull a pig's tail, as this may cause the animal to become "unthrifty."

Mr. Blaine Short, of Carl Junction, Missouri, tells me that his neighbors always dehorn cattle in Aquarius, believing that this prevents hemorrhage and infection. My friends in all sections of the Ozarks know better than to castrate pigs without considering the signs of the zodiac, for animals cut when the sign is in the heart are almost sure to become infected and die. The best time for this operation is "when the sign's in the legs."

Many hillfolk, in both Missouri and Arkansas, repeat the saying that "a man with lots of hair on his legs is always a good hog raiser," but whether this is meant literally I do not know. Perhaps akin to the above is a hillbilly crack reported by Nancy Clemens, of Springfield, Missouri, to the effect that "pigs born in January always have black teeth." Miss Clemens isn't sure just what this means, and neither am I.

Some of the old folks are very careful to see that hogs, at least hogs which they intend for their own use, do not have access to garlic. Several country women have told me that if a hog eats one little sprig of garlic and is butchered within a week, all the meat is so impregnated with garlic that "it aint fitten to be et." To feed hogs on soft, frostbitten corn is another sure way to ruin the pork; some farmers believe that this spoiled corn spreads the cholery, but the best hogmen say there's nothing to it.

The hillfolk believe that sweet milk is not very good for grown-up human beings to drink, and that it is frequently fatal to hogs. Very few of the real old-timers can be induced to give sweet milk to pigs—they prefer to wait until the stuff has "clabbered up." Many backwoods fox hunters think that sweet milk is poisonous to dogs, too, and are horrified to see tourists feed valuable hunting dogs with messes containing sweet milk.

In many parts of the Ozark country I have heard stories of "mule-footed" hogs—a breed of swine with solid hooves. It was my impression at first that the mule-footed hog must be a mythical creature, comparable to the willipus-wallipus or the jimplicute, but Uncle Jack Short of Galena, Missouri, tells me that he once saw several mule-footed hogs exhibited at a carnival or street fair in Stone county, Missouri. The *Christian County Republican*, a weekly published at Ozark, Missouri, carried the following advertisement:

INFORMATION WANTED: Concerning what used to be known in this locality as "mule-footed" hogs. Anyone still having this strain or any information pertaining is asked to communicate with me. Floyd C. Goddard, Box 234, Olds, Alberta, Canada.[2]

I have always intended to write Mr. Goddard and try to find out just what he learned about this subject, but never got around to it, somehow.

2 Dec. 30 1943, p. 8.

Some people believe that to steal a very young pig will bring them luck. I knew a man who caught a boy in the act of stealing one of his little pigs. He let the boy get away with it and made no complaint—which was not in character at all. I kept pestering the old man about it, and finally he said that the boy "didn't steal it just for the *pig*."

The best time for butchering hogs is a very important matter in the Ozarks, because apart from wild game pork is the hillman's only meat. Few Ozarkers will eat mutton, and they don't care much for beef even when they can get it. The real old-timers butcher in the light of the moon, believing that pork killed in the dark of the moon is tough, has an inferior flavor, and does not keep well. Besides, most women claim that pork butchered in the decrease of the moon will "all go to grease" and curl up in the skillet when it is cooked.

Many farmers keep a few sheep for the wool, and goats are valued because they eat underbrush and thus help to clear the land. The old-timers never shear sheep or wash wool in the decrease of the moon, believing that the wool will shrink if handled at this time. Some Ozarkers who have no interest in breeding goats nevertheless buy or borrow a male goat occasionally and turn it in with sheep, cattle, or even horses. The idea is that a goat in the same pasture keeps other animals healthy, and is especially good for horses and cattle with diseases of the respiratory tract.

Barn swallows are supposed to bring good luck to cattlemen, and it is said that a barn in which swallows are nesting will never be struck by lightning. To shoot a barn swallow is always unlucky, and sometimes it makes the cows give bloody milk. It is generally believed that eating persimmons makes cows go dry; there may be some truth in this, and all cows seem to eat persimmons whenever they can get at them. Eating large quantities of acorns or turnips is also supposed to make cows go dry. "If a cow loses her cud, give her a dishrag to chaw" is an old sayin' in the Ozarks, but I am not sure just what is meant by it.

There is a very widely known superstition that to kill a toad will make one's cows give bloody milk. Most people think that nothing can be done about this, once the toad is dead, but Otto Ernest Rayburn found hillfolk in Arkansas who claim to be able to repair the damage, particularly if the toad was killed accidentally.[3] "Get seven pebbles," says Rayburn, "and throw them over your left shoulder into an open well at sundown. The milk will be all right after that."

Many farmers say that it is a good idea to bury a bit of a cow's afterbirth under a pawpaw tree, as this will cause her to bring forth female calves thereafter. It is best to begin weaning calves on the third day before a full moon—this makes 'em grow into big healthy cattle. Most Ozarkers wean calves when the moon is in Aquarius, without considering any other factors. When a calf is sold, some hillfolk always drag it out of the pen tailfirst, so that the cow will not miss it so much; I saw a man doing this once, and he said that it was all foolishness, but he always pulled 'em out by the tail to please his children.

Even today, in some parts of the Ozark country, cattle are not fenced up in pastures but merely marked or branded and allowed to roam the hills at will, so that the matter of finding one's cows is often difficult. However, a boy has only to consult a harvestman, or daddy longlegs, and cry out:

> Longlegs, longlegs,
> Tell me where the cows are

whereupon the creature will immediately crawl in the direction of the strayed animals. If a daddy longlegs is not available, the farmer may spit in his hand and strike the spittle smartly with a finger; the fluid is supposed to fly toward the lost cattle.

If the white of a horse's eye shows all around the iris it means that the animal is a killer—many hillfolk believe that human beings whose eyes protrude are dangerous, too. Horses with certain white markings are looked upon with disfavor, according to an old rhyme:

[3] *Ozark Country,* p. 271.

Four white feet an' a white nose,
Take off his hide an' throw him to the crows.

A horse foaled in May, it is said, always has a tendency to lie down in a running stream and often does so with a rider on his back. No matter when a colt is born, the old folks insist that it should be weaned when the sign's in the legs. "Try to wean a colt when the sign's in the belly," an old woman told me, "an' see what happens! He'll raise hell sure, an' maybe git sick besides."

Roy Cole, who lives on Bear Creek in Taney county, Missouri, says that it is easy to tell whether a colt will make a big horse or a small one. When a colt is first able to stand, measure the distance from the ground to the point of its shoulder—this is exactly one-half of the height the horse will attain at maturity. Some horsemen measure from the hairline of the colt's front hoof to the center of the knee joint—this distance is one-fourth of the height the horse will be when full grown. In other words, if the colt's hoof-to-knee measurement is sixteen inches, the grown horse will be sixteen hands high—a hand is four inches.

A great many hill people claim that when a mare's first colt is a mule, her second, although sired by a stallion, is sure to have a stripe down its back. Professional horse breeders ridicule this notion, but a lot of old-time hillmen still believe that there is something in it.

Akin to the superstition regarding prenatal influence and the "marking" of babies is the idea that a horse breeder can color a colt to suit his taste simply by hanging a cloth of the desired color before the mare's eyes when she is bred.

The fact that a horse rolls on the ground has no particular significance, but near Harrison, Arkansas, they say that if a horse rolls over *and back*, it means that he's worth a lot of money.

It is very bad luck to change a horse's name; to sell a man a horse and tell him its name incorrectly is regarded as a dirty trick, since it means that he will never get any satisfactory service out of the animal. There is an old saying that one should "always name a good dog after a bad man," but a long list of dog names which I once collected in the Ozarks shows no evidence that the hillman really puts it into practice.

There are many outlandish remedies and treatments for the ailments of domestic animals. Ordinary soft soap made with wood ashes is regarded as a sort of universal tonic for hogs, so the hillman just mixes a little soap with the hog feed occasionally. "Soap will cure a hog no matter what ails him, if you git it to him in time," said one of my neighbors. Equal parts of soft soap and lard are administered to cattle as a cure for the murrain. Many old-timers mix soot from the chimney with the salt they give their cattle, but I have been unable to learn the reason for this.

To cure holler horn in cattle, some hillmen take a gimlet and bore a hole in the horn just above the hairline, leave the hole open for several days, and then plug it with a small cork. Others fill the cavity with salt, which seems to work as well as the stopper.

If a cow has the disease known as holler tail, you must split the tail open and apply a mixture of salt and vinegar, then bind it up with woolen yarn. Mrs. Pearl DeHaven, of Springfield, Missouri, thinks that salt and pepper is a better combination than salt and vinegar. "Of course," she writes, "modern veterinaries tell us there is no such thing as *holler tail*, but these young squirts have a lot to learn." Any disease which involves paralysis of the hindquarters seems to be called holler tail.

A neighbor of mine, when several of his horses were sick, spent an entire day rounding up every horse and mule on the place. With a sharp knife he split the end of each animal's tail just a little, and let it bleed a few drops. I tried to find out what was wrong with the horses, but the man had no idea. He said that splittin' their tails always cured them, no matter what the trouble was.

When a horse has colic, these amateur vets just blow a little salt into each of its nostrils. If an animal's legs are cut by barbed wire, the hillman burns a bit of wool and blows the smoke over the wounds by way of antisepsis; sometimes he twists a cord tightly about the creature's tail, believing that this stops the injured legs from bleeding.

Farmers sometimes mix gunpowder with a watchdog's food, believing that it renders the animal more vicious. I have never known a hillman to give gunpowder to a foxhound or a tree dog. I did see a boy in Galena, Missouri, dosing an Irish setter with gunpowder—somebody had told him it was a sure cure for distemper. Many hillfolk treat distemper by rubbing kerosene on the back of the animal's neck. Others claim to cure distemper by burning chicken feathers in a paper sack and holding the sack over the dog's head so he is forced to inhale the fumes. A dog's nose, the hillman thinks, should be black, and a red-nosed dog is always regarded with suspicion. Many old-timers imagine that a dog whose nose isn't black must be sick, and they keep their own dogs away from such an animal, fearing infection.

Here is a "recept" from an old manuscript book belonging to Miss Miriam Lynch, Notch, Missouri.

CURE FOR A DOG WITH A SORE MOUTH

apple sider vinegar .... ¼ pint
blue stone .... teaspoon ½ full
allom .... teaspoon ½ full
borax .... teaspoon ½ full
coppers .... teaspoon ½ full

then Take yellow rute and make
a strong Tea and Disolve
the rest in it.

The "blue stone" mentioned is copper sulphate; "allom" is alum; "coppers" is ferrous sulphate, which is often called copperas; "yellow rute" is probably golden-seal (*Hydrastis*), also known as yellow puccoon.

To cure a dog of fits, just cut up some of your own hair into pieces about one-eighth of an inch long, mix these pieces with lard, and make the dog swallow a spoonful once a week.

The best way to keep a dog at home, according to some of the old-timers, is to bury a little of its hair under the hearth or the doorstep. I once knew a hunter in southwest Missouri who had ten or twelve foxhounds. He was a man who moved frequently from one shack to another, as he owned no property and was unable to pay any rent. His wife told me that every time they moved he cut a little hair off each dog's tail and buried it carefully somewhere about the new cabin. This woman admitted that the hounds stayed at home better than most, but she attributed it to the vast quantities of "dog cornbread" which her husband required her to bake for them, rather than to the hair which he buried under each shanty. "Them dogs' hair is planted under ever' old shack for miles around," she said, "but I take notice they allus come home where the bread is at!"

Some hillfolk say that to keep a dog at home one has only to cut a green stick exactly the length of the animal's tail and bury it under the doorstep. Another method is to cut off the tip of his tail and nail it on a gate; I have twice seen this tried, but without any good result so far as I could perceive.

If a night dog will not bark "treed," some old hunters profess to cure him of this fault by smashing green gourds on the tree above his head. Otto Ernest Rayburn mentions this,[4] and I have heard of it in many different places. But experienced dogmen tell me that it is "just an old hillbilly joke" and was never meant to be taken seriously.

[4] *Ozark Country*, p. 157.

4. Household Superstitions

The signs and omens listed in this chapter are mostly concerned with matters of no great import, but they are seriously considered none the less, especially by women and children. The arrival of a visitor, for example, is an important event in a backwoods cabin, and there are numerous signs and portents of his coming.

When a woman drops a dishrag she knows at once that some dirty individual is coming toward the cabin; if the cloth falls in a compact wad the visitor will be a woman, if it spreads out upon the floor a man is to be expected. It is bad luck to drop a dishrag anyhow, and many women take the cuss off by throwing a pinch of salt over the left shoulder immediately. To drop the towel used in drying dishes means that a stranger will arrive very soon, and if the towel is dropped twice it means that the newcomer will be hungry, and a meal must be prepared. The accidental dropping of cutlery also signifies a guest—a fork means a man, a case knife a woman. If you help yourself to something at table, when you already have some of the same stuff on your plate, it means that somebody is coming who is hungry for that particular article of food.

If the coffeepot rattles back and forth on the stove, or a rocking chair moves along the floor as the woman rocks in it, she expects company before night and makes her household preparations accordingly. If she accidentally drops a bit of food on the floor, she knows that the visitor will be hungry. Children sometimes try to "fetch company" by running in one door and out another, or jumping out the window if the cabin has only one door, which is frequently the case. If coffee grounds cling to the sides of the cup, high up, it is a sign that company is coming with good news.

When two roosters fight in the yard, it is said that two young men will soon arrive; if two hens fight, female visitors are expected. If a dog rolls on the ground before the door, the children watch him closely, knowing that when he gets up his nose will point in the direction from which a stranger is approaching.

If the housewife's nose itches, it means that some unexpected company is on the way. An itching on the right side of the nose indicates a man, an itching on the left side means a woman. Some hillfolk say that such a visitor will be poor or needy, according to the old rhyme:

> If your nose itches, if your nose itches,
> Somebody coming with a hole in his britches.

If the woman's right hand itches, it means that she will soon shake hands with an unexpected guest. When the joint of either thumb itches, she expects an unwelcome visitor within an hour or two.

A pretty girl who lives appropriately enough in a town called Blue Eye, Missouri, told me that "if your right eye itches you'll be lucky, but if your left eye itches it means a disappointment." Most Ozarkers don't see it this way, however—they believe that an itching of the right eye signifies bad luck, but when the left eye itches it means that good news is a-comin'. "Never in all my life," an old lady told me, "did my right eye itch *real bad*, without I got into some kind of trouble before the day was out!" Some people think that if your right ear burns, a man is talking about you, while if your left ear burns, a woman is taking your name in vain. Others say that an itching of the right ear means that someone is speaking well of you, but a tickling of the left ear means that someone is talking unfavorably about you. If your left hand suddenly begins to itch, the old folks say, you will shortly receive an unexpected present.

When a woman sneezes before breakfast, it means that company will arrive before noon. If she sneezes during breakfast, it is a sign that two or more people will leave the house before sundown. If she sneezes with food in her mouth, it means that she will hear of a death before twenty-four hours have passed. If she sneezes while telling a story, it is a true story—even though she may believe that it is a lie. Some people say that the girl who sneezes on Monday is sure to kiss a stranger before the week is out.

Mrs. Coral Almy Wilson, of Zinc, Arkansas, quotes the following sneezing-rhyme:

> Sneeze on Monday, sneeze for danger,
> Sneeze on Tuesday, kiss a stranger,
> Sneeze on Wednesday, sneeze for a letter,
> Sneeze on Thursday, sneeze for better,
> Sneeze on Friday, sneeze for sorrow,
> Sneeze on Saturday, a friend you seek,
> Sneeze on Sunday, the Devil will be with you all week.

Here is a different version from Reynolds county, Missouri.

> Sneeze on Monday, sneeze for fun,
> Sneeze on Tuesday, see someone,
> Sneeze on Wednesday, get a letter,
> Sneeze on Thursday, something better,
> Sneeze on Friday, sneeze for sorrow,
> Sneeze on Saturday, see your beau tomorrow,
> Sneeze on Sunday, the Devil will control you all week.

Mrs. Mabel E. Mueller, of Rolla, Missouri, tells me that the old-timers were careful never to let the supply of salt get too low—they believed that to run completely out of salt meant a whole year's poverty and privation for the family. Above all one should make sure that the salt shaker is full on New Year's Day, since this insures prosperity for the coming year.

When I first came to the Ozarks I heard several vulgar wisecracks about candle salt as somehow connected with the sex life of elderly persons; when I asked what candle salt was, they told me that the old folks used to put salt on tallow candles in the belief that it made them last longer.

At table it is bad form to take a salt shaker from another person's hand, since this may bring evil fortune to both parties; the correct thing is to wait until your neighbor sets the salt shaker down on the table and withdraws his hand, then you are free to pick it up.

If one spills salt at the table it is said that there will be a violent family quarrel, ending only when someone pours water on the salt that has been spilled. Some folks try to "take the cuss off" by throwing a pinch of salt into the fire, or over the left shoulder, but most of the old-timers regard this as childish —the only thing that really helps is to pour water on the spilled salt.

It is bad luck to lend salt, often causing some sort of a "fraction" between the lender and the borrower. The mountain housewife seldom borrows salt if she can possibly avoid doing so, and if she does borrow the stuff, is careful never to pay it back. When a woman borrows a cupful of salt she replaces it with an equal amount of sugar, or molasses, or some other household staple—never salt.

Many people think it is a bad omen to spill pepper, and that the person who does so will have a serious quarrel with one of his best friends.

When a woman burns light bread, so that the crust is black, it is a sign that she will fly into a rage before the day is over. The person who eats this blackened bread will have good luck, however, and among other blessings will never be troubled by intestinal worms.

Some people say that when a woman burns pancakes or biscuits it means that her *old man* is angry. There are many jokes and wisecracks about this notion. I once boarded at the home of a widder woman, and when she burnt the biscuits one morning another lodger cackled: "Well, I don't know which one is the maddest, Randolph or old man Miller!" The widder woman scowled at this, which she regarded as a very coarse and vulgar remark, and an outrageous falsehood besides, since neither Mr. Miller nor myself had been overintimate with our hostess.

Among the real old-timers, when one gives a neighbor something to eat or drink, the housewife returns the vessel unwashed, since to send it home clean is a sign of an early quarrel with the donor. I have known women in the hill country deliberately to smear a pot or kettle before returning it, in case the vessel had been washed by mistake.

It is very bad luck to give away yeast. A careful housewife doesn't like to lend yeast, either. If one *must* get yeast from a neighbor, it is best to buy it. Women who would be insulted by an offer to pay for any other article of food are glad to accept a penny or a nickel for yeast.

If two persons use the same towel at the same time there is sure to be a quarrel, or some sort of difficulty:

> Wash an' dry together,
> Weep an' cry together.

In case two persons *should* unthinkingly start to dry their hands on the same towel, they hasten to twist the cloth between them —this is supposed to take the cuss off'n it, in a measure at least.

When two friends are talking together, and a third person suddenly comes between them, they instantly turn away from the intruder for a moment, so as to prevent a quarrel—not a quarrel with the third party, but between themselves. May Stafford Hilburn refers to something of this sort when she says cryptically that "girls turned their backs to each other *to ward off an untoward event* if a third party stepped between them during a conversation." [1]

If two friends are walking side by side, and "unthoughtedly" allow a tree to come between them, it means that they will have a serious quarrel soon. One way to break this spell is for both parties to cry instantly and in concert "Bread-and-Butter!"

[1] *Missouri Magazine* (October, 1933), p. 14.

In Galena, Missouri, some children insist that one of the persons involved should say "Salt-and-Pepper" instead. Another way is for them to touch hands and hook their little fingers together while they chant a certain verse—it is very bad luck to repeat the verse at any other time, so I am unable to obtain the words of it.

No hillman would think of giving a steel blade to a friend—such a gift is sure to sever their friendship. Whenever a knife changes hands, it must be paid for, even if the sum is merely nominal. I have seen a salesman, a graduate of the University of Missouri, present his son with a valuable hunting knife—but he never let it out of his hand till the boy had given him a penny.

The accidental crossing of two case knives at the table must be avoided, as it is likely to cause a desperate fight between members of the family; if knives *are* crossed inadvertently, they must be touched only by the same person who crossed them. If an Ozark woman finds a pair of scissors open, she closes them instantly—if she fails to do this she will quarrel with her dearest friend before the moon changes. If one finds an open clasp knife he snaps the blade shut immediately; if it is a sheath knife of the rigid kind, he thrusts the blade into the ground at once.

A thoughtful hillman is careful to leave a neighbor's house by the same door through which he entered, knowing that to violate this simple rule may cause a serious quarrel. The host, on his part, always politely turns away as a guest leaves his cabin —if he were to watch a departing friend out of sight he feels that they might never meet again.

If the fire spits and sputters without any apparent cause, it means that two members of the family will quarrel within twenty-four hours.

It is very bad luck to return to the house for anything which has been forgotten, or to come back to the house when you have started to go somewhere. If you *must* return, however, always make a cross in the dust of the road and spit on the cross, before setting out again. Some old-timers insist that the cross must be marked on the doorstep. Other people take the cuss off by sitting down in a chair and counting ten, or sitting down and making a wish, before leaving the cabin for the second time. Some say one has only to sit down for a moment and spit three times on the floor. Others think it is necessary to walk backward out of the house, while counting "ten, nine, eight, seven, six, five, four, three, two, one, AMEN!"

When a hillman starts out on a journey which he regards as important, he is careful never to look back as he leaves his own premises.

Some people won't drive down a road if they see a little whirlwind in it—a journey which takes one through a whirlwind is always unlucky.

It is bad luck to close a gate which one finds open, and the mountain man who inadvertently does so is often quite upset; some hillfolk, starting on a journey, regard this matter of the gate as such an evil omen that they postpone the trip until another day.

I once knew a man near Pine Bluff, Arkansas, who threw little pieces of tobacco into the river whenever he was about to start on a journey. He was a white man, of some education, but he had learned this propitiation of the river gods from Negroes, I think.

When you meet a cross-eyed woman at a place where the road forks, always spit in your hand, or on the ground, and mark a cross in the saliva. One fellow told me that he always spit in his hat on such occasions and "let the cross go by." Some say it is well to cross one's fingers and count ten backward, also.

When starting to visit someone, if you meet a flock of geese you'll be a welcome guest, but if you find hogs in the road you will not be so well received.

To encounter a red-haired girl on a white horse is always a good omen; to meet a red-haired girl on a white *mule* is superlative.

Some people of Polk county, Arkansas, believe that it is bad luck to ride in a vehicle painted green. When a local sportsman suffered a series of accidents on the new highway, Mrs. Emma Dusenbury, of Mena, Arkansas, was heard to ask: "Well, what could he expect, with that old green car?"

Never let anyone step directly into your tracks in mud or snow, for this may cause headaches or even blindness. It is wise not to step in anybody else's tracks, either.

When you find a pin in the road, never fail to pick it up:

> See a pin, pick it up,
> All day long, good luck;
> See a pin, leave it lay,
> Have bad luck all day.

Another view is that if the head of the pin is toward the finder he will have good luck, but if the point is toward him it means that he has a dangerous enemy to contend with.

To find a hairpin in the path means that you will soon meet a new friend. If the prongs of the hairpin are of equal length, the new friend will be a girl; if one prong is a bit longer than the other, it's a boy.

Never pick up a spoon lying in the road. Women who are unlucky in their household affairs sometimes throw away a spoon, believing that their bad luck will pass to the person who picks it up.

Many of the old settlers say that it is good luck to find a rock with a hole in it, but that such a stone found in running water is superlucky. At several homes in the Ozarks I have seen little boxes containing stones with holes in them, placed under the porch or the wooden doorstep. Near Marvel Cave, in Taney county, Missouri, the Lynch sisters who own the cavern used to have a lot of these stones strung on wire; when Nancy Clemens and I visited the place in 1936, Miss Miriam Lynch took down one of these wires and gravely presented each of us with a lucky stone. Some say that lucky stones keep off witches and evil spirits; others tie one of the stones to a bedpost in the belief that it somehow prevents nightmare. Near Harrison, Arkansas, children are told that it is good luck to find a round stone with a hole in it, but that such a stone must be thrown away at once and never carried in the pocket.

Do not pick up a black or dark-colored button in the road. There is some tale about such buttons being left by people who think they are sick because of witchcraft, and that the sickness will go to whoever picks up the button. I haven't been able to get any definite information on this. Everybody agrees, however, that it is *some* sort of bad luck to pick up a black button in the road. Children near Southwest City, Missouri, say that when you find a button in your path it means that you will soon receive a letter with as many pages as there are holes in the button. Asked if they picked up these "letter buttons" the children answered that they always picked up white buttons and carried them home, but that "Mommy don't want no *black* buttons."

A button received as a gift is always lucky, no matter what the color. Years ago, many an Ozark girl collected buttons from her friends and strung them together into a sort of necklace called a charm string. A charm string not only brought good fortune to the owner but also served as a sort of memory book for women who could not read—one button recalled a beloved aunt, another a friend's wedding, still another a dance or a quilting party or an apple-peelin' or some other pleasant occasion. Nancy Clemens, of Springfield, Missouri, says that the craze for charm strings once reached a point in Douglas county, Missouri, where girls had to borrow pins to fasten their dresses before they could go home from a party. May Stafford Hilburn remarks that "each donor of a choice button came under the charm, and nothing could break the friendship between that person and the owner of the charm string." [2]

Many hillfolk think that the man who finds a horseshoe with the closed end toward him will do well to "leave it lay." If the open end is toward the finder, he sometimes spits on it and throws it over his left shoulder, a procedure which is supposed to bring good fortune. Or he may place it in a tree or on a fence, saying: "Hang thar, all my bad luck!" In this case, whoever touches the hanging horseshoe falls heir to the misfortune of the man who placed it there. In some parts of the Ozarks one sees dozens of bad-luck horseshoes hanging in trees along the roads, but no real old-timer will touch one of them for love or money. Near the village of Day, Missouri, I have noticed that even my old friend "Doc" Keithley walks wide of these horseshoes, although he is scornful of most taboos and superstitions.

Members of the older generation feel strongly that cornbread must be broken—it is very bad luck to cut it with a knife. Some old-timers are much upset to see a stranger, even in a hotel, cutting cornbread. I have known several who refused to eat at the table where such a thing occurred but got up and left at once. A "furrin" schoolmarm in McDonald county, Missouri, having her first meal at the boardinghouse, offended everybody by cutting a piece of cornpone. "Dang it, she's sp'iled the bread!" muttered one young man, jumping up from the table.

I know several families near Big Flat, Arkansas, who have a strange notion that one should never allow a piece of bread to fall upon the ground—the idea is that to do so will somehow injure the next crop of corn.

There is an old saying that eating bread crusts brings good luck in fishing and hunting, and also makes one's hair curly. I think, however, that this is told to children in order to cajole them into eating the crusts and is not taken very seriously by adults.

When a small boy plays at stirring the fire, it is a sign that

2 *Missouri Magazine* (December, 1933), p. 11.

he will urinate in his bed that night. This old saying prevents many a little boy from messing with the fire, since whenever he goes near it the other children begin to giggle. People in Baxter county, Arkansas, tell a long story about a girl who was sitting up with her beau, while her little brother kept running in and stirring the fire; this was regarded as very embarrassing, and the poor girl's friends "plagued her plumb to death 'bout it."

To eat or drink at the same time one urinates or defecates is very bad luck, and I have known children to be severely whipped when the mother caught them eating candy in the privy. The child who eats anything under such conditions is said to be "feedin' the Devil an' starvin' God."

There is a persistent notion that Providence is somehow tempted by stepping on cracks in the floor. Some people think that a boy who fails to "miss the cracks" in the schoolhouse steps will fail in his lessons that day and probably be punished for it. Other hillfolk say that by stepping on cracks a boy does some injury to his parents, and I have heard children quote the rhyme:

> Put your foot onto a crack
> An' you will bust your mother's back.

It is bad luck to put the left shoe on before the right, or to put the left foot out of bed first in the morning. Nearly everybody in the Ozark backwoods is familiar with these notions, but no one has ever told me just what will happen to a man if he should violate such rules of conduct.

A woman mixing a cake always stirs the batter in one direction—if you stir it first one way and then another you'll spoil the cake sure. Another thing to remember is that the person who begins the stirring must stay with it and complete the job, because if two persons try to divide the labor they may as well throw the cake away. Mrs. W. D. Mathes of Galena, Missouri, one of the best pastry cooks in the Ozarks, tells me that cakes must be stirred by hand; she has tried several sorts of electric mixers but never had any luck with them. It is said that a good cook never allows anyone else to stir the dough that *she* is to bake, but what is supposed to result from the violation of this rule I have never been able to learn.

One often encounters an ancient notion that a woman rendering out lard will never have any luck unless she stirs it with a sassafras "bat," and I have known women to walk quite a distance in order to get a proper stick for this purpose; some say that the bark of the sassafras actually flavors the lard or keeps it from becoming rancid.

There are several interesting superstitions about soft soap, which is made by cooking lye with waste fats from the kitchen. Lye is obtained by pouring water through wood ashes, which are carefully saved in a wooden trough called an ash hopper. Some old-timers say that it is impossible to make lye from the ashes of cherry wood; it is said that the remains of a small twig from a cherry tree, or even a single chip that got into the fire by mistake, will ruin a whole hopperful of good ashes.

Nearly all of the old-timers think that soap will not "make" unless it is stirred by a member of the family—"a strange hand skeers the soap," as the old saying goes. Some believe that soap cooked in March thickens quicker and is somehow superior to that produced at any other season. In the dark of the moon, soap "biles high round the edges an' low in the middle," but in the light of the moon it "spatters up high in the middle of the kettle." Soap made in the increase of the moon is light in color; that made in the decrease of the moon is considerably darker. I believe that the majority of soapmakers prefer to work in the dark of the moon, but there is no unanimity about this. "You can make good soap when the moon's a-fullin', or you can make it right *on* the full," said an old woman in Stone county, Missouri, "but don't never try to cook soap when the moon's a-wanin', or it won't be no good at all."

In making vinegar from molasses and rain water, the Ozark housewife hastens fermentation by putting in nine grains of corn, which she *names* for the meanest, sourest persons of her acquaintance. This is usually regarded as a sort of joke, but I know many women who never fail to do it, even while they laugh at the idea that it really helps the vinegar. Mrs. C. P. Mahnkey, Mincy, Missouri, tells me that she never troubled to name the grains of corn, but was always careful to put in nine grains, no more and no less. It was mighty good vinegar too, she says.

Some hillfolk believe that there is no use in trying to make cider or wine when the moon is waning—it will turn sour every time. Others tell me that the best cider is made in clear weather, with the wind a-blowin' from the west, and the moon has nothing to do with it. There is an old proverb to the effect that the best way to keep cider sweet is to drown a water snake in it, but this is not to be taken literally. Who wants to keep cider sweet, anyhow?

Ordinary sauerkraut can be put up without any reference to the moon's phases, or the signs of the zodiac. What is called turnipkraut, however, must be made in one of the "fruitful signs," after the full of the moon; the brine comes to the top and runs over, if you try to make turnipkraut in the increase of the moon.

It is generally believed that a menstruating woman can perform all of her ordinary household tasks save one—she can't pickle cucumbers. I have known women who laughed at most of the backwoods superstitions yet were convinced that there was something in this idea. One girl told me that she and her sister had tried it out repeatedly, and that the pickles prepared by a girl who was menstruating were always soft or flabby, never properly crisp.

Akin to this is the notion that a "bad woman can't make good applesauce"—it will always be mushy, and not sufficiently tart. This is so generally accepted in some sections as to have passed into the language, and the mere statement that a certain woman's applesauce is no good is generally understood as a slighting reference to her morals.

Many apparently insignificant actions must be avoided

simply because they are regarded as unlucky, although no specific penalty is attached to them. For example, it is bad luck to sit on a trunk, or for two persons to sit in one chair at the same time, or to rock a rocking chair when there is nobody in it, or to enter a strange house by the back door, or to count the cars in a train, or to throw water out of a window, or to sleep too near a spring, or to set two lights on one shelf, or to put a stamp upside down on a letter, or to tell a dream at the table, or to begin any important task on a holiday which falls in the light of the moon. Nobody knows just what would happen if one should violate these "chimney-corner laws," but many hillfolk avoid doing so whenever possible, anyhow.

To turn a chair around with one leg as a pivot is always bad luck, and leads to family quarrels. Otto Ernest Rayburn quotes a backwoods girl: "If anybody twirled a chair on one of its legs, we knew father would come home mad as a wet hen about something." [3]

The typical hillman is upset by any trifling piece of ill luck which happens on his birthday, knowing that one who is unfortunate on this particular day is likely to have bad luck all year.

It is unlucky to cut your fingernails on Sunday—you'll have a pain in the neck for seven days, or the Devil will rule your house all week, or something of the sort. It's bad luck to trim fingernails on Friday, too. Monday is the best day for this, and it is said that people who cut their fingernails on Monday will always have plenty of money.

White spots on fingernails are supposed to represent lies, and little boys often hide their hands to avoid betraying falsehoods. However, there is a fortunetelling rhyme children use when counting these white spots:

> A gift, a ghost, a friend, a foe,
> A letter to come, a journey to go.

Some people say that a large white spot means a journey—

3 *Ozark Country*, p. 156.

when the spot grows to the end of the nail, you will start on a trip to some distant place.

It is unwise to laugh early in the morning, particularly before getting out of bed. There is an old saying that the woman who laughs before breakfast will cry before supper. Another version lingers in the jingle:

> Laugh before it's light,
> You'll cry before it's night.

Singing before breakfast is also discouraged in the familiar verse:

> Sing before you eat,
> You'll cry before you sleep.

The child who sings in bed, or at the table, is likely to bring misfortune upon the whole family and come to a bad end as indicated in the old rhyme:

> Sing at the table,
> Sing in bed,
> Bugger-man will get you
> When you are dead!

It is also very bad luck to whistle or sing while urinating or defecating, and the child who does so is certain to get a whipping before sundown, but there isn't any little verse about this so far as I know.

There is some sort of sign in the flame of a candle, which indicates that a letter is coming. While the "letter sign" lasts, a girl who spies it begins to count, rapping on the table with each numeral, and thus determines how many days will pass before the letter arrives. Otto Ernest Rayburn mentions this but doesn't make it clear just what happens in the candle flame.[4] There is an old song entitled "The Letter in the Candle," which apparently refers to this business.

The woman who suddenly finds a large hole in her stocking regards it as a sign that there is a letter waiting for her at

4 *Rayburn's Roadside Chats*, p. 23.

the post office. When a hillman sees a big spider exactly in the middle of the path, he knows that he'll get a letter within a few days. If coffee grounds cling to the sides of a cup, near the bottom, one may expect a letter with good news in it.

When a woman is opening a jar of fruit, and some of the juice spatters into her face, it means that she will hear some welcome news very soon. It is also a sign of good tidings to drop a glass vessel without breaking it. If a man gets charcoal into his hair, accidentally, his friends assure him that he is about to receive a letter containing money.

Mrs. Coral Almy Wilson, of Zinc, Arkansas, reports that her neighbors pay close attention to sweat flies, which they call news bees. A yellow news bee buzzing round one's head means that good news is coming, while a black news bee is a sign of bad tidings.

If a woman accidentally splits a wooden clothespin, so that it falls in two separate pieces, she may expect some bad news from her husband's people.

If there happens to be a snowfall in May, the housewife is supposed to melt some of the snow in the fireplace—a sure way to kill all the fleas and bedbugs in the house. The same happy result is said to be obtained by burning a dirty dishrag the first time you hear it thunder in March. Some Ozark women scatter fresh walnut or butternut leaves about their houses to repel insects, but I can't see that it does any good. Burning old shoes on the hearth is a well-known method of driving snakes out of a house; a schoolmaster who has been to college and made a particular study of reptiles tells me that there may be some truth in this, but I suspect it is merely another superstition.

When backwoods people are troubled by fleas, they just bring a sheep into the cabin for a few days; the fleas all flock to the animal's wool and are thus disposed of. I knew a man in Springfield, Missouri, who wanted to put a sheep into the basement of his daughter's fine new house, but she was too highfalutin; said she'd rather put up with fleas in the bedroom than have a damned stinking sheep in the cellar. A smart fellow from Lincoln, Arkansas, tells me that there are never any fleas in a sheepherder's house, but where a farmer has lots of hogs and no sheep, you'll find fleas all over the place.

A mountain girl who wants a new dress has only to catch a butterfly of the desired color and crush it between her teeth; she mutters some sort of a charm, too, while the insect is in her mouth, but I have never been able to obtain the magic formula. It is said also that the woman who shakes her apron at the new moon, under certain conditions, will get a new dress very shortly —but this latter observation is regarded as somehow improper, and I am not certain just what is meant by it. I have heard allusions to this saying many times, however, all the way from Hot Springs, Arkansas, to Poplar Bluff, Missouri, so I record it here for what it may be worth.

Mrs. May Kennedy McCord, of Springfield, Missouri, says that the old women she knew as a girl were very careful never to make what is called a "diamond fold" in ironing table linen or bed sheets—anything folded "diamond-shaped" is likely to bring bad luck on the entire household.

Handwoven coverlets and the like should always be washed in snow water, according to the old grannies; some say to ease the spirits of the dead women who made them years ago; others contend more practically that snow water does not cause the old homemade colors to run or fade. Many hillfolk believe that it is bad luck to mend an old quilt or comforter by patching, although there's no harm in darning small rips or tears.

The Ozark housewife seldom begins to make a garment on Friday—never unless she is sure that she can finish it the same day. Many a mountain man is reluctant to start any sort of job on Saturday, in the belief that he will "piddle around" for six additional Saturdays before he gets it done.

A woman who breaks a needle while making a garment for her own use is horrified, fearing that she will never live to wear it out. If the garment is intended for somebody else it doesn't matter at all, as in that case the broken needle has no sinister significance.

A mountain woman who sews after sunset, or who pours water on a window sill, will be poverty-stricken all her life. A basting inadvertently left in a garment is also a sign of poverty; some people think it means that the cloth is not paid for.

It is very unfortunate for a woman to button a new garment before it has been worn; a   y made shirt should be buttoned first on the person who is to wear it, but if this person is not available, button it around somebody else.

If you put on a garment wrong side out, it means good luck, but you must wear it that way until bedtime. There are many tales of men who refused to do this and were carried home dead before the day was over. It is not uncommon for girls in high school and even in college to attend classes with their petticoats wrong side out because of this superstition.

Many of the old folks figure that May 1 is the proper day to shed heavy winter underwear. Children begin to go barefoot on May 1 too, for the first time that summer. "If you start on May Day," an old woman told me, "you can go bar'foot plumb till snow flies, an' it won't hurt ye a bit!"

Winter clothing is packed away with fresh sassafras leaves, which are said to keep out insects much better than mothballs. The sassafras leaves don't work, however, unless a certain secret sayin' is repeated as the clothes are being packed.

Every old quiltmaker knows that when a quilt is once stretched on the frame it must never be turned around; if it is turned, at least one of the quilters will lose her skill, or her eyesight will fail, or her hands become paralyzed.

It is bad luck to burn floor sweepings or shavings that have been produced inside the house. An old-time Ozark housewife seldom sweeps her cabin after dark, and she never sweeps anything out at the front door. Otto Ernest Rayburn observes that "one of the most progressive merchants in Arkansas will not permit his janitor to sweep dirt out through the door after dark." [5] A woman in Madison county, Arkansas, told me that ghosts and spirits are accustomed to stand about near cabins at night, and it is dangerous to offend these supernatural beings by throwing dirt in their faces. Sweepings are best gathered up and carried out of the house or swept down through a wide crack in the floor so as to fall beneath the cabin, although there are hillfolk who see no harm in sweeping dirt out at the *back* door—always in the daytime, of course. Some people say that once you begin to sweep a room, it is bad luck to stop before the job is done. Many women are careful never to sweep the house on Monday, even in broad daylight, as this is likely to sweep away the family's "money luck" for the entire week.

Mrs. C. P. Mahnkey, Mincy, Missouri, tells me that no true hillbilly ever burns walnut shells. If a walnut shell is inadvertently cast into the fire, some member of the family hastens to snatch it out at any cost.

The hulls or skins of certain vegetables, on the other hand, are always burned, never disposed of in any other manner. I have known households where the women made a great show of saving onion peelings, which were carefully gathered up and burned in the fireplace or the cookstove. One woman told me that people who throw onion peel out on the ground are likely to suffer some financial reverses, and that she knew personally of a case in which carelessness in this matter caused a Civil War veteran to be deprived of his pension.

Never look directly into a fire that is being kindled; if you do it will not burn properly and may bring bad luck to the whole household besides. Some hill people become quite irritated if a guest persists in staring straight into a stove or fireplace, when it is not burning well. To do so is very bad manners and somehow appears to cast discredit upon the family.

It is said that lightning often strikes a cookstove but has never been known to strike one with a fire in it. In Baxter county, Arkansas, several persons warned me never to sit in the "dog

5 *Ozark Country*, p. 146.

run"—the covered passage between the two rooms of a log house—during an electrical storm; it seems that lightning often goes through such a passage, killing dogs which have taken refuge there, without damaging the house proper. I know many backwoods families who always try to drive the hounds away from their cabins during a thunderstorm, in the belief that "a dog's tail draws lightnin'."

In some sections of Arkansas there are people who bury the entrails of a black hen under the hearth on "Old Christmas." This is said to protect the house against destruction by lightning or fire. A gentleman at Hot Springs, Arkansas, told me that people used to do this when he was a boy, but added contemptuously that it was "just an old nigger superstition," and that he did not believe it was taken seriously by any white people nowadays. However, I know that some "peckerwood families" did bury chicken guts under their hearths as recently as 1935, not far from the enlightened metropolis of Hot Springs.

A lot of backwoods families are very careful not to use the wood of a lightnin'-struck tree for fuel, in the belief that this renders the cabin more likely to be struck by lightning.

Many hillmen believe that black walnut trees draw lightning and will not go near them in a storm. It is quite common for hillfolk to cut down all the walnuts, even little ones, that grow near their cabins.

When lightning strikes the ground, some woodsmen pretend to look around for the thunderbolt, which is supposed to be a piece of iron about three feet long, forked at one end. These thunderbolts are said to be used in making fish gigs, and a finger ring hammered out of thunderbolt iron is a sure cure for rheumatism. I have myself seen, in Washington county, Arkansas, an old iron ring which the owner told me was made of a thunderbolt recovered in Kentucky before 1815.

I have met hillmen who think that it is bad luck to use the word *thunder*, particularly during an electrical storm. They feel that people who keep talking about thunder are likely to get struck by lightning. Instead of saying thunder, they use some familiar circumlocution, such as "the 'tater wagon is a-rollin'," or "they're crossin' the old bridge now." Some Ozark farmers deliberately cross their "galluses" on stormy days to guard against lightning, but the man who gets his galluses crossed accidentally, when he puts on his trousers in the morning, will have bad luck all day.

It is very generally believed that thunder and lightning cause milk to sour in a few hours, even in the coldest weather. This can be prevented, however, by putting a rusty nail in the crock or pan. A man who was looked upon as exceptionally intelligent and "well posted," who served several terms in the Missouri state legislature, assured me that this was no superstition at all but a well-established scientific datum, adding that the rusty nail "works somethin' like a lightnin'-rod."

In November, 1943, a big flock of wild geese was struck by lightning at Galena, Missouri, and about three hundred of the birds fell near the village. People went out and picked them up. I got one myself, which we roasted next day, and found it very good indeed. Many people in the vicinity ate them, with no bad results so far as I could find out. But several families would not touch these geese, saying that it was dangerous to eat any creature killed by electricity.

It is very bad luck to bring cedar boughs or mistletoe into the house, except during the Christmas season. Mrs. Isabel Spradley, Van Buren, Arkansas, says that every bit of green stuff must be out of the house before midnight on January 5, or some unspeakable calamity will overtake the whole family. Many old people feel that it is better not to have mistletoe in the house at all. It is always bad luck to carry peacock feathers into a cabin, and several hillfolk actually refused to sleep in my cottage because an old-fashioned fan made of peacock feathers was nailed to the wall as a decoration.

Never carry a hoe or a mattock into the house, even to prevent the tool from being stolen. If a hillman does bring a hoe into his cabin by mistake, he must carry it out again at once, walking backward. Most people agree, however, that there is no harm in keeping hoes or mattocks under a porch, or even beneath the floor of the cabin itself.

It is always bad luck to place a hat or a shoe or a rifle on a bed. Mountain men sleep with pistols under their pillows, however, without any bad results. Never place a shoe or shoes on the table in a hillman's cabin; this applies even to brand-new shoes in a box, or in a sealed mailing carton just arrived from Montgomery Ward or Sears and Roebuck.

The mountain housewife is careful never to drop a broom so that it falls flat on the floor, and it is doubly unfortunate for a woman to step over a broom handle. Some people say that when a girl, even a very young girl baby, steps over a broom it is a sign that she will be a slovenly housekeeper all her life.

A person may go barefoot or shod anywhere, but it is tempting fate to go out of doors in one's stocking feet, or to walk even in the house with one shoe off and one shoe on.

Hillfolk seldom remodel their houses, except to add a lean-to or "shed room" when an increasing family demands more space. It is bad luck to cut a doorway between two rooms after the house is built, and the average backwoods family will not do this under any condition.

A hillman courts misfortune if he moves his family from one house to another in the dark of the moon, and I have known otherwise intelligent people to put up with a deal of inconvenience rather than make such a move. Even in a case where a house is destroyed by fire, some hillfolk prefer to camp under a ledge, or sleep in a wagon, until such time as the moon is "favorable"—that is, at the appearance of the new moon. The idea is that the family's prosperity will increase as the moon waxes.

In building a new dwelling, the old-time hillman was careful to use a few timbers from an older building. A house composed entirely of new lumber is sure to bring bad luck, usually sickness or death, upon the persons who live in it. If you find your initials in spider webs near the door of a new home, it is a sign that you will be lucky as long as you live there. No furniture or supplies should be carried into a new house until the salt and pepper are in their proper places on a shelf. An empty hornets' nest is hung up in the loft of nearly every old-time mountain cabin, and I have seen such a nest tied to the rafters of a new house that had not yet been occupied; some people say that this brings good fortune to the whole household, particularly in connection with childbirth and other sexual matters.

Most people think that it is good luck if a strange black cat visits the house, but very bad luck if the animal takes up its permanent abode there. To *carry* a stray cat into a house brings bad luck, and children are often warned against this folly. It is always bad luck to kill a cat, but the hillfolk do not hesitate to drive a cat away by all sorts of cruel treatment. One of my neighbors in McDonald county, Missouri, would not kill a cat which had annoyed him, but he chopped off one of its feet and threw the animal out into the snow. Whatever happens, *never* burn a dead cat; bury it deep in the ground, or throw it into a running stream.

A few hillfolk say that it is good luck to see a white cat on the road; there is some difference of opinion about this, but everybody agrees that it is a very bad sign when a black cat crosses ahead of a traveler. Many Ozark people turn back or detour to avoid crossing a black cat's trail. I have seen countrymen near Little Rock, Arkansas, take off their hats and turn 'em around on their heads, after seeing a black cat in the path. Black cats are worst, of course. But many people are a bit leery of all cats, particularly on the highways. "I'd just as soon there wouldn't be *no* cat runnin' acrost the road ahead of me," said an old man near Elsey, Missouri, in 1944.

It is very bad luck to be photographed with a cat. I was at Rose O'Neill's place in Taney county, Missouri, when a photographer came out from St. Louis to make some pictures of Miss O'Neill and her house. He took one photo which showed a group of us in the O'Neill library, with the family cat crouching on a table. This was later published in the St. Louis *Post-Dispatch*, and I showed the paper to one of the neighbors. "God Almighty," she shivered, "I wouldn't have set in that there picture for a hundred acres o' land!"

A girl who drops the comb while combing her hair is doomed to some sort of disappointment, but she may "take the cuss off" in a measure by counting backward from ten as she retrieves the comb. To open an umbrella inside a house is tempting Providence, but very few of the real backwoods women own umbrellas anyhow, so it doesn't matter much.

It is said that misfortunes always go in threes, and this is especially true of household mishaps. The housewife who smashes a dish, or burns the cornbread, or barks her shin on the oven door generally expects two more minor accidents before the spell is broken.

The woman who happens to get her first glimpse of the new moon unobstructed by foliage—"cl'ar o' brush," as the old folks put it—considers herself lucky. "Everyone knows," writes May Stafford Hilburn, "that to see the new moon through the leafy branches of a tree means bad luck throughout the month. It still gives me cold shivers to see the moon behind treetops, and I hastily close my eyes, remembering an old 'charm' of childhood, clasp my hands over my heart and say 'bad luck, vanish!' Then I feel better." [6] A housewife who sees the new moon through a windowpane fears that she will break a valued dish, or some other piece of household equipment, before the moon is new again.

Some of my present associates do not profess religion and never go to church but are nevertheless convinced that it is very

[6] *Missouri Magazine* (September, 1933), p. 20.

bad luck to do any work about the house on the Sabbath. An old man who is known all over the country as an outspoken free-thinker told me soberly: "I don't hold with this here church business, an' I don't never feed no preachers. But I believe that if a man works six days a week he'll have plenty, and if the same man works seven days a week he's liable to starve out!" Another neighbor assured me that a roof mended during the Christmas holidays will leak worse than ever, and that a spring or well cleaned out on Sunday is likely to go dry.

A great many of the old-timers call December 25 "New Christmas" in order to distinguish it from "Old Christmas," which falls on January 6. They tell me that in pioneer days nearly everybody celebrated Christmas twelve days later than they do now. Old folks say that elderberry always sprouts on the eve of Old Christmas—even if the ground is frozen hard, you'll find the little green shoots under the snow. A man at Pineville, Missouri, told me that bees in a hive always buzz very loudly exactly at midnight on the eve of Old Christmas; if several bee gums are set close together, the "Old Christmas hum" can be heard some distance away. This shows that January 6, not December 25, is the *real* Christmas.

Mrs. Isabel Spradley, Van Buren, Arkansas, tells me that the old folks in her neighborhood sometimes call January 6 "Green Christmas" or the "Twelfth Night." It is on January 5, the eve of Old Christmas, that the cattle are supposed to kneel down and bellow, exactly at midnight, in honor of the birth of Jesus. Some say that the critters have the gift of speech on this night, so that they may pray aloud in English. Mrs. Spradley quotes an old woman with reference to the family water supply: "Our well had a charm put on it *the night the cows talked,* and I wouldn't clean it out for silver!" I don't know what the *charm* is that this old woman referred to, but there are people in Arkansas today who say that the water in certain wells turns into wine at midnight on January 5.

It is said that on the morning of Old Christmas there are

two daybreaks instead of one—I have talked with men who claim to have seen this phenomenon. Boys born on Old Christmas are supposed to be very lucky in raising cattle; some say that these "Old Christmas children" can actually talk the cow brute's language.

There are old men in the Ozarks today who swear that they have actually seen cattle kneel down and bellow on Old Christmas eve. But skepticism sometimes prevails, even in the Ozarks. A neighbor tells me that when he was a boy he watched repeatedly to see his father's oxen kneel but was always disappointed. His parents told him, however, that the presence of a human observer broke the spell, and that cattle must always salute the Saviour in private. "But I just drawed a idy right thar," he added thoughtfully, "that they warn't nothin' to it, nohow."

In some settlements this notion about the cattle kneeling has shifted from Old Christmas to New Year's. Mr. Elbert Short, of Crane, Missouri, told me that his sister slipped out to the barn one New Year's Eve "to see the critters kneel down and talk." At exactly twelve o'clock one old cow fell on her knees and let out two or three low moans. A moment later another animal knelt—but with this the girl suddenly became frightened and ran back to the house. Another funny thing, says Mr. Short, is that if you go out before midnight on New Year's Eve and cut an elderbush off flush with the ground, by sunrise it will have "pooched up" at least two inches.

Every backwoods family, even if no member of the group is able to read, has a calendar and probably an almanac as well, in order to keep track of the signs and phases of the moon. But it is very bad luck to hang up a calendar or almanac before sunup on New Year's Day, and I have known children to be severely punished for doing so.

An unexpected visitor on January 1 signifies that many others will come to the house during the year; this prediction is often regarded with mixed emotions, since hillfolk do not care for too many uninvited callers. If the first visitor to cross the threshold on New Year's is a man the family may expect good luck, but if the first visitor is a woman the prospects are not so good. A large group of visitors on New Year's is regarded as a favorable omen, though nobody seems to know just what sort of good fortune may be expected to follow such an invasion.

Many Ozark natives believe that whatever a person does on January 1 is an indication of what he will be doing all the rest of the year. On this account many people are very cautious on New Year's Day, and drunkards often make a superhuman effort to keep sober. In Pineville, Missouri, I have seen men sit with watches in their hands and whiskey jugs before them, waiting until midnight before taking a drink. A woman who washes clothes on New Year's will have to work very hard all year; many hillfolk think that to do a washing on New Year's Day will cause the death of a relative before the year is out. On the other hand, some people feel that it is well to be occupied with some useful task on New Year's Day, in the belief that if a person does not get something accomplished on that day he will be more or less "idlesome" during the twelve months which are to follow.

I have been personally acquainted with several Ozark families who always opened their windows for a few minutes on New Year's Eve, just before midnight, no matter what the temperature or weather conditions. Asked about the purpose of this, the younger people grinned tolerantly, saying that it was supposed to let bad luck out and good luck in. But the old folks said nothing at all and looked very solemn indeed. It was plainly no laughing matter to them.

It is considered very important, in some districts, to have black-eyed peas for dinner on New Year's Day. I have known country folk who rode a long way to get these peas for a New Year's dinner, even though they did not care particularly for black-eyed peas, and seldom ate them at any other time. Fred Starr quotes a granny-woman near Fayetteville, Arkansas, as saying: "On New Year's you just eat black-eyed peas, with a dime under your plate, an' wear a pair of red garters, an' you'll have good luck the whole year."

A dish known as hoppinjohn, which consists of black-eyed peas cooked with hog jowl, is the traditional New Year's dinner in many well-to-do families who would not eat such coarse food on any other day. Mr. Walter Ridgeway, of West Plains, Missouri, always contended that this custom began in Civil War days; some planters who had nothing to eat but black-eyed peas at a New Year's dinner were lucky enough to regain their fortunes, and later on they somehow connected this good luck with the New Year's hoppinjohn. Other hillfolk, however, have told me that the custom of eating black-eyed peas on New Year's is much older than the War between the States. The Ridgeways say that the name hoppinjohn originated when a guest named John was invited to "hop in" and help himself to the food.

Perhaps the most striking feature of the Ozarkers' New Year's behavior is their reluctance to allow anything to be taken out of the house on January 1. I once knew a woman who absent-mindedly carried a bucket of ashes out on New Year's morning; she was shaken almost to the point of hysteria, and the whole family was horrified, although nobody seemed to know just what specific calamity was supposed to result.

Many broad-minded modernists pretend that there is no harm in carrying something out, provided you are careful to take something else in; thus it's permissible to throw out a pan of potato peelings if one immediately lugs in a bucket of water or an armload of wood. The real old-timers figure it is safer not to carry *anything* out of the cabin on January 1, but to pack in as much stuff as possible. Some old folks take this so seriously that they will not allow anyone to enter on that day without depositing something, even if it is only a few walnuts or a handful of chips. This precaution, according to the old tradition, insures a whole year of plenty for the people who live in that house. "It aint much trouble, just for one day," an old man said as he insisted that I get a stick from the woodpile before coming into his shanty, "an' me an' Maw don't aim to take no chances."

5. Water Witches

Nearly all of the old settlers in the Ozark country believe that certain persons can locate underground streams by "cunjurin' round" with forked sticks. These characters are called *water witches* or *witch wigglers*, and the forked switches they carry are known as *witch sticks*. Despite this sinister terminology, the waterfinder has no dealings with the Devil, is not regarded as dangerous by his neighbors, and has nothing to do with witchcraft proper.

I have known several water witches intimately and have seen more than a score of them at work, and there is no doubt that they themselves are sincere believers in their ability to find water. Nearly all of the really old wells in the Ozarks were located by witch wigglers. Even today there are many substantial farmers who would never think of drilling a well without getting one of these fellows to *witch* the land.

When I first came to Pineville, Missouri, in 1919, Dr. Oakley St. John was the only educated person in the village. He was an outspoken atheist and materialist, the last man whom one would expect to find involved in any superstitious practice. But the neighbors all told me that Doc was the best witch wiggler in the Ozarks, with the possible exception of old John Havard, who used to live over in Greene county. So I took to hanging around St. John's little drugstore, and tried to talk with him about these matters.

The doctor parried my questions for a long time, but finally admitted that he had located a large number of wells.

"I used to laugh at this water-witch business," he told me, "but I got to fooling with it one day, and discovered that I'm a pretty good witch wiggler myself. I can't defend the thing scientifically, but I can find water in these hills. I've never staked a dry hole yet."

"But how do you do it, Doctor?" I asked.

"Well, I just cut me a green fork off a peach tree—some fellows use witch hazel or redbud, but peach always works better for me—and take one prong in each hand. Then I walk slowly back and forth, holding the fork in front of me, parallel with the ground. When I cross an underground stream the witch stick turns in my hands, so that the main stem points down toward the water. Then I drive a stake in the ground to mark the place, and that's where I tell 'em to dig their well."

After a little more talk we went to an old peach orchard, where the doctor trimmed up a nice witch stick. The thing looked very much like a slingshot handle, except that it was nearly three feet long. Climbing through the fence, we strode out into a big pasture. Thrusting the stick forward, St. John walked across the rocky hillside, with me close at his heels. Suddenly, he hesitated, then moved forward very slowly, the green switch turning and twisting in his hands. There he stood, holding the thing as if it were a living, writhing reptile.

"Look at that!" he cackled triumphantly. "I couldn't hold it still if I tried! It would twist the bark right off the God damn' stick!"

I shivered a little and felt as if the hair were rising on the back of my neck. There was something uncanny and obscene about that witch stick.

"Let me have the thing a minute," I said shakily.

St. John handed it over, and I carried it back and forth exactly as he had done. But nothing happened. The stick in my hands was just a stick, and nothing more.

The moment I returned it to the doctor the thing began to twist about and point to the ground, just as it had before. Evidently the power, whatever it is, resides in the man and not in the witch stick itself.

"If you were to dig right here," St. John declared, "you'd get a good well, sure. And you wouldn't have to go more than thirty feet, either."

"How do you tell about the depth, Doctor?"

"Well, I judge by the strength of the pull on the stick," he answered. "If the water's too far down it doesn't register at all, and the nearer it is to the surface, the stronger it pulls. I just kind of guess at it," St. John added, "but you'd be surprised how close I come to the truth!"

Another water witch named Truman Powell, who lived near Reeds Spring, Missouri, and is still remembered as one of the explorers of Marvel Cave, used to defend a different method of estimating depth. Powell always marked the spot where he first felt a pull on the stick and then drove another stake at the place where the pull was most intense. The distance between these two points, he said, was equal to the depth of the well.

Otto Ernest Rayburn, of Eureka Springs, Arkansas, tells of a witch wiggler who determined the depth by walking away from the stake, counting his steps, until the stick regained its normal horizontal position; multiply the number of steps by three, and this gives the number of feet it is necessary to dig.

There was also the veteran waterfinder interviewed by Betrenia Watt in Hickory county, Missouri, who claimed that his witch stick moved downward by a series of separate jerks. Each of these "nods" or "beats," said he, represents a foot, and one has only to count them in order to determine how far the water lies beneath the surface of the ground.

Dr. St. John told me about a chap named Patterson, of Carter county, Missouri, who was rated as the best "witcher" in all that region for many years. Using a peach-tree switch, he once located "living water" at a depth of only five feet, in the middle of the dryest summer that ever hit the Ozarks. One of Patterson's aunts "follered the witchin' trade" for awhile but gave it up because some tourists laughed at her.

J. O. Jackson, an early settler in Springfield, Missouri, used to "project round" with a hazel or peach-tree stick. "Dig right there," he would say, "an' if ye don't git water at forty feet I'll pay for th' diggin'." There is no record of his ever having to pay. It was Jackson who located the big well behind the Lyon House on Commercial Street, the best hotel in Springfield in the seventies and early eighties. Jackson always refused to accept money for his witching, being convinced that to do so might weaken his mysterious power.

The late A. M. Haswell, of Joplin, Missouri, was a well-known water witch but never became superstitious about it. "The switch certainly does move in my hands," said he. "Whether that movement is caused by underground water, I do not know. All I know is that without the least aid from me—indeed in spite of the strongest grip I can apply to it—the switch does move." Haswell experimented with several varieties of wood, but always claimed that a hazel twig was much superior to any other. "Some fellows prefer the wahoo, which used to be called 'witch elm,' but a good hazel fork works better for me." The hazel bush preferred by Mr. Haswell is still known as witch hazel in some localities.

There is a very general notion that virility has something to do with this "power," and that certain physical qualifications are essential to a good witch wiggler. "A feller has got to be a *whole man*," one old gentleman said, "if he aims to take up witch wigglin'." He meant that a water witch must be normal sexually; a man who has anything wrong with his genitals can never locate wells with a witch stick. Some hillfolk say that women and children can't work the forked stick; I have never seen a child operate the thing successfully, though I have known many who tried it. I have met several women witch wigglers, however, and they seemed to do about as well as their male colleagues.

Mrs. Ethel Davis, of Huggins, Missouri, differs from most water witches in that she uses a wild-plum branch instead of peach or witch hazel. Mrs. Dinnie B. McBride, of Licking,

Missouri, has been very successful in locating wells and is quoted as saying that most any sort of green switch will do in a pinch; if one forked stick doesn't work to suit her, she throws it away and tries another. Mrs. Bettie Williams, of Bolivar, Missouri, is firmly convinced that water witching somehow runs in families. She cites several cases in which the "power" seems to have been inherited. "My mother-in-law witched all the country around Bolivar, and *always* found water," she declares, "and my oldest son, E. A. Williams, can do the same thing." Mrs. May Kennedy McCord, of Springfield, Missouri, agrees with Mrs. Williams and others that the necessary magnetism must be an hereditary trait. "I have seen the power of water-witching run in families," she writes, "*girls and all!*"

My old friend Otto Ernest Rayburn, of Eureka Springs, Arkansas, himself an amateur water witch, told me that it may be true that the ability runs in families, but he thinks that only one member of each generation has the "power" to witch water.

There used to be so many witch wigglers at Butler, Missouri, that in 1934 they organized a "Water Surveyors' Club," with George Hartrick as president. The following is taken from a signed article which Mr. Hartrick published in the local newspaper:

Last Summer we located many a good well during the drouth, by the use of the stick. Many of the members learned how to tell the depth of the water, and so forth. . . . We do not feel that this is a divine gift any more than the power of music or art. It is the duty of all to use their gifts for the progress of humanity. All persons cannot locate objects with the water-witching stick any more than all can be musicians. Everyone is welcome to our meetings, and we welcome any information on the subject. Water-witching is not a new activity, as Jacob in the Bible located his living well of water by this method.[1]

Dr. F. A. Middlebush, president of the University of Missouri, has experimented with witch wiggling. "I can vouch for the fact that a properly selected and trimmed branch will move in my hands," he writes, "but I failed to apply this mysterious

[1] Springfield (Missouri) *News*, April 28, 1938.

art when I had a well dug at my place in the Ozarks, near Camdenton, Missouri." Dr. Middlebush says that Professor J. W. Rankin, of the English department at the University of Missouri, also claims to be an expert water witch. Mayor Bryce B. Smith of Kansas City is another amateur witch wiggler, according to his friends. It appears that Middlebush, Rankin, and Smith all use the conventional peach-tree fork.

In the 1930's, when a well was to be drilled at a golf club near Springfield, Missouri, it appears that those in authority wanted to have the ground witched but were laughed out of it by the younger members. The well was said to be three hundred feet deep, but it never produced water enough for the clubhouse. So they decided to drill another well, and this time, rather surreptitiously, they called in the water witches. These fellows went over the golf course with their peach-tree switches and located a new place for the drillers. And this second well, according to local testimony, was quite satisfactory to all concerned.

Several witch wigglers have told me that in southeast Missouri, along the Mississippi River, there are men who claim to locate wells with willow switches. "But I don't put no confidence in willer myself," said an old fellow in Neosho, Missouri. "Them folks down at Cape Girardeau must be a turrible ignorant set, or else they'd know better'n that."

Near Everton, Missouri, lives a famous water witch named Fred Goudy, distinguished from other members of his profession by the fact that he uses no switch at all, but only a piece of heavy copper wire. When J. M. Jones, a wealthy cattleman of the neighborhood, needed a well he called in Fred Goudy to witch the land. "The water-witch used a copper rod," said the *Kansas City Times* (Oct. 13, 1936), "and locating a desirable spot, paused above it while the divining rod 'nodded' thirty-nine times." The idea is, I take it, that the underground stream lay thirty-nine feet below the surface.

There used to be a man in Christian county, Missouri, who enjoyed considerable success as a water witch and attributed his power to the fact that he always wore rubber boots and worked in dry weather besides. "You got to be insulated from the ground," said he. This gentleman was quoted as saying that anybody could witch water if he were properly insulated and had sense enough to hold the stick correctly. "There's no magic about it, and no superstition," he said. "There's something in running water that pulls the stick. It must be electricity, or maybe magnetism."

Some people say that the witch stick can also be used for locating coal, gas, and oil, but I have never heard of this being successfully practiced in the Ozark country. Old W. H. Johnson always claimed that the artesian well which supplies the village of Hollister, Missouri, was drilled by one Dr. Diemar, upon information furnished by an "oil witch" who professed to feel "a peculiar wiggling in the fingers" when he approached oil-bearing sand. The well has produced a lot of excellent water, but never a drop of oil.

Many hillfolk are interested in the search for lost mines and buried treasure, and some of these people have tried to use the witch stick in their quests. If a man is looking for buried gold, he fastens a gold ring to the end of his stick; if it is silver that he expects to find, he splits the end of the wand and inserts a silver coin. Rayburn says that to locate mixed ores one uses two different metals—usually a dime and a penny.[2] Witch sticks thus equipped for treasure hunting are sometimes called "doodlebugs," but I don't know if this is an old backwoods term or a recent importation. I have seen perhaps a dozen doodlebugs in operation but have yet to hear of any treasure being found by the doodlebuggers in the Ozarks. It is said that a switch loaded with metal will not react to water, or to any other substance save the particular metal which is attached to the stick.

I am told that there are a few witch wigglers in the Ozarks who have commercialized this sort of thing, and make their living by the manufacture and sale of doodlebugs. There are

2 *Ozark Country*, p. 128.

others who offer to locate treasure at so much per diem, or even to work on a percentage basis in some cases. There used to be a man near Steelville, Missouri, who professed to locate mineral deposits at a flat rate of five dollars per deposit. He even claimed that he could tell, by the behavior of his witch stick, whether the alleged deposit was a vein of the mineral, or a mere pocket.

When I lived in McDonald county, Missouri, I had occasion to drill a well near my cabin. A local water witch came out to witch the land for me, and he indicated a spot high up on the hillside, in a most inconvenient place. "Dig there," said he, "and you'll get a good strong flow at sixty-five feet." It was a very unhandy place for the well, and I asked the man to check on a little clearing just behind the cabin. He picked up his witch stick again and tested every foot of the ground about the house, without any result. "Dry as a bone," he decided. So I reluctantly drove the driller's stake in the designated spot on the hillside.

But when the well-drilling outfit came out from the nearby town of Anderson, I had a talk with the boss driller. His name was Lee Cantrell, and he was a man of very decided opinions on all matters pertaining to his craft. Cantrell said that he had been drilling wells for many years, and that water witching was all damned foolishness. "If I was in your place," said he, "I wouldn't pay no mind to this witch business. I'd just drill that there well wherever I wanted it."

This advice seemed so eminently sane and sensible that I agreed at once and blushed to think that I should have even for a moment considered any other course. And so we disregarded the location stake on the hillside and set up the drill rig in the little clearing behind the house. At a depth of fifty-two feet we struck a great underground river, "clear as crystal an' cold as ice," as Cantrell assured me. That well is still in use, and there is no better drinking water in southwest Missouri.

The witch wiggler could hardly believe that we had really found water in the place he said was dry as a bone. He came out with a plumb line and sounded the well long before we could get a pump in. He tasted the water, too, and shook his head as if greatly puzzled. That water witch and I were good friends. We got drunk together sometimes and discussed our common prejudices and detestations freely enough. But I do not recall that he ever mentioned water witching in my presence again.

Charles J. Finger, in a book entitled *Ozark Fantasia*, recounts his experience with a water witch near Fayetteville, Arkansas.[3] The chief difference between Finger's experience and my own is that the stick turned in his hands. I have met Mr. Finger, and he impressed me as a very practical sort of man, with no place in his mind for any kind of backwoods superstition. He could not believe in any such hocus-pocus, even though he *did* hold the witch stick himself. And so he ends his dissertation thus: "My notion, without any ingenious assumptions, is that there is water almost anywhere; that the waterfinders act in good faith; and that the dipping of the stick is the result of unconscious fatigue." But even Finger, evidently, is not quite satisfied with this explanation, for he qualifies his statement with the final sentence: "This, of course, fails to account for certain coincidences."

It is surprising how many intelligent people do believe in this sort of thing. In 1931 I published a book about the Ozarks, in which there was some mention of witch wigglers. Several months later, in the New York *Sun* I saw a review of my book by Burton Rascoe, eminent literary critic. Rascoe resented my referring to this method of finding water as a backwoods superstition.

I believe in water-witches [wrote Mr. Rascoe]. When my father bought a tract of land down in Seminole county, Okla., in 1911, there was no drinking water on the place except that to be had from the streams. My father engaged a water-witch, whose fee was $25—a lot of money in that part of the country in those days. The water-witch wandered about and took in the topography of the farm pretty

[3] Pages 125–130.

thoroughly. He cut himself a forked willow switch and carried it along in front of him until the end of it bent toward the earth. Then, having found the underground stream, he followed it along to where he knew it was widest and deepest. This happened to be in a most unlikely looking place, on top of a hill. The old gentleman told my father that if he dug forty-five feet into the ground at that spot he would find a plentiful and continuous supply of excellent water. The well that was sunk there went just forty-five feet into the ground. To this day that well supplies an abundance of fine water, even in periods of prolonged drought.[4]

Since that time I have received many letters on the subject, and nearly all of them took me to task for my skepticism regarding the claims of water witches. But it seems to me that there is no scientific basis for a belief in water witching. Systematic records show that where several witch wigglers are called to work on the same plot of ground, there is no consistency in the results—their drill stakes are scattered from one end of the field to the other. It appears that hundreds of dry wells have been drilled in places where the water witches were sure of finding water in abundance. Witch wigglers have been kidded into walking directly over great underground torrents in unlikely places, even water mains and reservoirs, and their witch sticks didn't move at all.

The scientific conclusion is summarized by Dr. O. E. Meinzer, of the United States Geological Survey, who expressed himself as follows: "It is difficult to see how, for practical purposes, the water-witch theory could be more thoroughly discredited. To all inquiries the United States Geological Survey therefore gives the advice not to expend any money for the services of any water-witch, or for the use or purchase of any machine or instrument devised for locating underground water or minerals."

[4] New York *Sun*, Oct. 30, 1931.

6. Mountain Medicine

Regular physicians are not very numerous in the Ozarks, and a great many "chills-an'-fever doctors" are practicing illegally. Most of these are men who had a year or two of training at some Southern medical college, but others have just "picked up doctorin' " by assisting some old physician whose practice they have inherited. The "chills-an'-fever doctors" save the overworked M.D. many a long night ride and are frequently protected and advised by the medical profession. The average hillman, of course, knows nothing of this distinction between qualified and unqualified physicians. He calls 'em all "Doc" and lets it go at that.

Besides the regular and irregular physicians, who live mostly in the villages, the backwoods country swarms with "yarb doctors" and "rubbin' doctors" and "nature doctors" who have never studied medicine at all. Some of these nature doctors are women, others are preachers who do a little doctorin' on the side, and many of them are unable to read or write. They rely mainly upon herbs, barks, roots, and the like. For internal medication these substances are steeped in hot water, and "horse doses" of the resulting teas are administered at frequent intervals. In some cases the tea is boiled down to a thick paste called ooze, or mixed with strained honey to make a syrup. The yarb doctors are great believers in poultices, which are applied both hot and cold for all sorts of ailments. Doubtless some of these homely remedies have real value and may be listed in the *Pharmacopoeia* for all I know. The hillfolk, however, seem to feel that the efficacy of a treatment varies directly with its unpleasantness; bitter tea is always best, and the more a poultice hurts the better they like it.

"God Almighty never put us here without a remedy for every ailment," said old Jimmy Van Zandt of Kirbyville, Missouri. "Out in the woods there's plants that will cure all kinds of sickness, and all we got to do is hunt for 'em."

Mullein-flower tea is supposed to be good for colds, sore throat, flu, and even pneumonia. A tea made of sumac berries is favored for coughs and sore throat. Strong cider vinegar, with salt and pepper added, is used as a gargle. Cranesbill (*Geranium maculatum*) is brewed into a fine astringent medicine for sore throats. Pine needles, steeped in water over night and boiled down with sorghum, make another popular cough remedy, but a tea made of linn or basswood flowers is better for a cold in the head. Mrs. C. P. Mahnkey, Mincy, Missouri, says that she has broken up many a bad cold with "red-pepper tea, simmered in butter and water, and made pretty sticky with sugar."

Horehound is one of the best cold remedies. Just take a panful of horehound leaves, add water, and keep warm on the back of the stove for several days. Then pour off the liquid and concentrate it further by boiling. This is the standard cough medicine of the Ozarks, but it's pretty bitter. Many people think that horehound tea should be mixed with wild honey— the blacker the honey the more effective the syrup. Some young folk like it better if the mother adds a lot of sugar to make horehound candy, which is poured out on a buttered platter and allowed to harden, then broken into pieces and distributed among the children.

Many Ozark youngsters are dosed with large quantities of skunk oil for throat ailments, particularly croup. This stuff is rendered from the fat of skunks trapped in the winter—a strong stinking mess which makes many children vomit. There are tales also of yarb doctors who use liniments made of rattlesnake oil, but I have never seen any of this myself. Croup is treated externally by a poultice of lard and fried onions, applied very hot.

Charley Cummins, veteran newspaperman of Springfield, Missouri, always called a severe cold a *tissic*—that's his own spelling. He said the only way to cure such a cold was to apply a poultice of lard, camphor, turpentine, and fried onions.

Dr. W. O. Cralle, of Springfield, Missouri, writes me that some backwoods friends of his have used a tea of onions and wild lobelia with great success, in cases of "pneumony fever." Some old settlers make poultices of chicken manure mixed with lard as a treatment for pneumonia; it is said that the dung of black chickens is best. A hot poultice of hopvine cones and leaves is a famous remedy for pneumonia; I have seen this used hour after hour, fresh poultices always in the making, and a new one applied every fifteen minutes.

A tea made from the roots of butterfly weed (*Asclepias*), also known as pleurisy root, is used for "lung trouble," which usually means the late stages of tuberculosis. Some hillfolk believe that drinking fresh warm blood is the best treatment for "lung trouble"; I knew an elderly couple who sold their farm and moved to a city so that their consumptive daughter could get fresh blood from a slaughterhouse every day. One old man said that he had kept his family free of disease by putting ground dandelion root into their coffee, but many hillfolk use dandelion root as a coffee substitute or adulterant with no thought of tuberculosis.

A pinch of gunpowder, washed down with a glass of warm water or sour milk, was regarded as a sure cure for diphtheria in the Ozark country, long before we ever heard of vaccines or antitoxin.

A family at Lamar, Missouri, claims to cure hay fever by feeding the patient honey made from Spanish needles. Sumac leaves are supposed to cure asthma and hay fever; some people make a sumac tea, others dry the leaves and smoke them in a pipe. Jimson-weed (*Datura*) is used in treating bronchial troubles and asthma. Wild plum bark, *scraped down*, is a specific for asthma; most yarb doctors just make a strong tea with a little sweetening, but some add a great deal of sugar or molasses and make a regular syrup of it. In scraping bark from a tree or shrub, the direction in which it is cut may make a vast difference in its effect as medicine. Peach-tree bark, for example, if the tree is shaved upward, is supposed to prevent vomiting, or to stop a diarrhea. But if the bark is scraped downward, the tea made from it is regarded as a violent purgative. In general, the old-timers say that if the pain is in the lower part of the body, it is best to scrape the bark downward, to drive the disease into the legs and out at the toes. If the bark in such a case were stripped upward, it might force the pizen up into the patient's heart, lungs, or head, and kill him instantly.

The root of the yellow puccoon or golden-seal is fine for all sorts of stomach and intestinal troubles. If a hillman "gets to pukin' an' caint keep nothin' on his stummick," he just drinks a little yellow puccoon tea, or eats a bit of the fresh root every day. Some people carry a piece of this root in their pockets and chew it like tobacco or chewing gum.

The inner lining of a chicken's gizzard, chopped fine and made into a tea, is used in cases of dyspepsia, stomach cramps, colitis, and so on. They tell me that this stuff "settles the stummick" quicker than anything found in the drugstore.

Rattlesnake weed (*Polygala senega*) is good for bellyache, flatulence, and intestinal pains; the natives make a strong tea from the dried root and drink it hot.

Many hillfolk chew angelica root, which is another famous stomach remedy, supposed to cure everything from gastric ulcers to appendicitis; six-year-old Dorothy Farris died near Hartville, Missouri, in 1938, because she mistook poisonous water hemlock (*Conium*) for the aromatic angelica, which her mother had told her to gather and eat every day.

Red-pepper tea, catnip tea, horsemint (*Monarda*) tea—all of these are mightily cried up as remedies for stomach cramps or bellyache. Strong onion tea without salt, taken in small doses every fifteen minutes, is said to be a sure cure for "wind-on-the-stummick." Dr. W. O. Cralle, Springfield, Missouri, tells me that a decoction of "milk pursley" is highly recommended in all sorts of stomach and bowel trouble. Wild ginger (*Asarum*) and Indian turnip (*Arisaema triphyllum*) are also good for digestive difficulties; the root of the latter can't be eaten in its natural state, but they say that it loses its bite when boiled. Snakeroot (*Aristochia serpentaria*) is often made into a tea and substituted for the more drastic Indian turnip.

Mrs. C. P. Mahnkey, Mincy, Missouri, tells of a neighbor who "burned a saucer of whiskey, the blue flame toasting a rancid bacon rind, the juice dripping down into the saucer." When the flame went out, this "witchified potion" was given to a man with severe stomach pains. He made a rapid recovery, too.

Slippery-elm bark, boiled down to a thick ooze, is a common remedy for all sorts of digestive troubles—particularly such as are caused by excessive use of alcoholic liquors. The gelatinous bark is widely used also as a capsule for quinine, or any other medicine that has an unpleasant taste. Some yarb doctors treat typhoid by administering large doses of slippery-elm ooze, forbidding the patient to eat any solid food, and finally building up a great smudge of corncobs under the bed.

Slippery-elm bark is sometimes given in cases of poisoning, to produce vomiting, and seems very effective. A thick ooze of peach-tree leaves is another valuable emetic, according to Mr. Lewis Kelley, of Cyclone, Missouri. So is a tea made of puke root (*Gillenia stipulata*), also known as wild ipecac. Some yarb doctors get the same result by taking a living fly, preferably a green stable fly, and washing it down the patient's throat in a cup of coffee or a glass of warm milk.

The yarb doctors are familiar with many purgatives or "loosenin' weeds." One of the most violent and griping is the root of the May apple or mandrake, made into a thick tea or ooze. The so-called black physic (*Veronica virginica*) is another root with a strong cathartic action. The inner bark of the white walnut or butternut is also a popular laxative; most people boil this down to a thick syrupy mess, then thicken it with flour and roll it into pills, which are allowed to dry with a little sugar on the outside. Flaxseed is also highly recommended for chronic constipation.

Near Walnut Shade, Missouri, a man told me that the early settlers didn't bother much with vegetable purgatives, as they all preferred to take Epsom salts. When I asked where the pioneers obtained Epsom salts, he said that there was a whole mountain of it down the road. At the time it did not occur to me that the man was in earnest, but I learned later that there is a high ridge nearby called Salts Bluff. I went to this place and saw for myself the white powdery substance on the rocks under some overhanging ledges. I tasted the stuff, and it is like Glauber's or horse salts rather than Epsom. But it is evidently cathartic in its action, and there is no doubt that the early settlers did gather this material and use it as medicine.

Ragweed tea, made by steeping the fresh leaves in cold water, is a famous cure for diarrhea—what the hillfolk call *flux*. An old woman at Pineville, Missouri, talked me into trying this once, and it worked like magic in my case. Smartweed (the kind with red stems) is used in the same way, except that in this case the tea is made with hot water instead of cold. The root of a plant called cranesbill (*Geranium maculatum*) is also a popular "flux stopper." A tea of white-oak bark is good for diarrhea too, and in small frequent doses is indicated in chronic indigestion or colitis.

Backwoods babies seem particularly subject to an intestinal disorder known as "summer complaint." Many children die of this ailment, and the only sure cure is a tea made from the roots of the wild artichoke. A young couple in Tulsa, Oklahoma, came near losing their baby, and the city doctors didn't seem to do the child any good. The father went out and searched the country around Tulsa but could not find any wild artichoke. Finally he got into his car and drove back to his old home in Taney county, Missouri, where he obtained a good supply of artichoke roots. When he got back to Tulsa the doctors thought the baby was dying, but the artichoke tea brought relief within a few hours, and a week later the child was as well as ever. This is the story, anyhow, and there are many old-timers around Forsyth, Missouri, who believe it.

Where no artichoke is obtainable, some folks treat summer complaint with a tea made by mashing up sow bugs and steeping them in hot water; some mountain healers give large doses of this mess to sick babies. I have seen this tried, and the child recovered in spite of the sow bugs.

A young girl near Forsyth, Missouri, used to take large quantities of tea made by boiling toasted egg shells in water, but I was unable to find out what was the matter with her, or what effect this "egg-shell tea" was expected to produce. Children are sometimes dosed with chamber lye—which means urine—mixed with sweet oil; it is said that this is a sure cure for stomach cramps.

When an Ozark child has colic, the mother squeezes a little of her own milk into a teacup. Then she takes a reed pipestem and blows clouds of tobacco smoke into the cup, so that it bubbles up through the milk. When the baby drinks this nicotinized milk it becomes quiet at once and soon falls asleep. Other people treat a "colicky" infant simply by blowing tobacco smoke up under its clothes; I have seen this done several times, and it really did seem to relieve the pain—or at least to distract the child's attention for the moment.

Tobacco is used in other ways by the yarb doctors and granny-women. I have seen severe abdominal pain, later diagnosed as appendicitis and cured by surgery, apparently relieved at once with a poultice of tobacco leaves soaked in hot water. The tobacco poultice is very generally used for cuts, stings, bites, bruises, and even bullet wounds. A poultice of tobacco leaves in cold water is often applied to "draw the pizen" out of a boil or a risin'. Some people think such a poultice is more effective if fresh mullein leaves are bound on outside the tobacco.

For rectal troubles the yarb doctor favors a salve made by boiling bittersweet berries in lard. Sometimes, however, the patient is merely directed to sew a piece of sheep's intestine to the tail of his shirt. Charley Cummins, old-time newspaper reporter of Springfield, Missouri, always claimed that he could make an "almost infallible pile cure" out of mullein leaves, but he would never give me any details of the treatment. Several herbalists have told me of the "balm-o'-gilly" tree, doubtless identical with the Balm of Gilead, said to be a kind of poplar; they cook the waxy buds of this tree with tallow, and the resulting salve is used in treating burns and abrasions as well as hemorrhoids.

There are several outlandish semimagical methods of curing piles, which involve some hocus-pocus with urine. The following story is vouched for by a sober and respectable business woman in Mountain Grove, Missouri, who would never have believed such a tale had she not known all the parties involved and seen the thing for herself:

An old woman on relief at Mountain Grove, Mo., kept asking for a suit of brand-new underwear. Finally a member of the Ladies' Aid bought it for her. The old woman did not wear the suit, but sent it, with a dollar bill attached, to one of her neighbors; she asked the neighbor to wear it ten days, then send it back to her unwashed, and she would wear it for three days—this would *cure her piles,* she said.

The neighbor wanted to humor the old woman, so she sent back the dollar and put on the union suit. A few days later the old woman wrote again, saying that she hated to tell the whole story at first, but that the cure demanded something more. After wearing the suit ten days, the neighbor was to take it off and urinate on it, wetting it all over, and then drying it in the sun without washing. Next, the old woman would wear it for three days, then wash it and return it to the neighbor, as the whole process had to be gone through with again.

The neighbor was kind of discouraged by this time, and sent the underwear back to the old woman, with a note saying that she did not believe in superstitions, and recommending a certain patent medicine for piles.

It is not stated what happened after that, but at last reports the old woman still had her hemorrhoids.

Some years ago a prominent Ozark farmer suffered from hiccoughs, which continued for many days, so that his life was endangered. One yarb doctor said that if the man would just grind up some white beans, mix the resulting powder with vinegar, and take a teaspoonful every thirty minutes, he would stop hiccoughing within twenty-four hours—this was tried without any results. Other local healers contended that a big dose of dill tea, or tea made of the inner lining of a chicken gizzard, would cure hiccoughs almost immediately. An old woman from Rocky Comfort, Missouri, wrote the man's doctor suggesting that he "drench" the patient with sweet milk and black-pepper tea. A poultice of raw potatoes, fastened tightly across the abdomen, was also highly recommended. An amateur herbalist at Pineville, Missouri, told me that a tonic mixture of whiskey, tansy, and ragweed leaves was indicated in all such cases; "I take it every day myself," said he, "an' it agrees with me fine. I aint had the hiccoughs but once in fourteen year!"

Many hillfolk treat sprains by tying on rags soaked in hot vinegar to which salt has been added. Others put mullein leaves in the vinegar instead of salt. A poultice of red clay moistened into a paste with vinegar is also common. Another application for sprains is a hot mixture of cornmeal and buttermilk, with a little bran stirred into it. A poultice made by boiling down the inner bark of black oak, stiffened with bran or sawdust, is said to reduce the swelling of sprains and bruises. Also recommended are the leaves of horse balm (*Collinsonia canadensis*), widely used to poultice bruises and even open wounds.

A poultice made of the root bark of polecat weed (a little aromatic bush with yellow flowers) chopped fine and boiled in salt water is very good for wounds and bruises. Some folk seem to think that a poultice of mullein leaves simmered in vinegar is helpful in almost any sort of painful condition. I have seen such a poultice applied to a wound made by a charge of bird shot; it not only eases pain, I was told, but "loosens up the shot" so that the doctor can easily extract the pellets.

A weed called square stalk, apparently a kind of figwort, is used in making poultices to reduce swelling. At the same time, it is supposed to "bring a risin' to a head." A mixture of soft soap and brown sugar seems to get the same results. Some people cure boils by soaking a piece of snake skin in vinegar and tying it on the affected part. Sour-dock leaves are also used to bind up boils or carbuncles. Fresh possum-grape leaves are tied on open sores, or on boils which have come to a head.

Dr. W. O. Cralle, Springfield, Missouri, tells me that Aunt Mary Johnson, of Theodosia, Missouri, treats "proud flesh" or "blood poison" with a poultice of prickly pear, beets, and sweet milk cooked together and applied as hot as the patient can bear it. Old leg sores, and the condition called milk-leg, are said to be relieved by binding "the pup bag of a bitch dog" on the affected part and wearing it for seven days. A wound made by a rusty nail is best treated by fastening a very old corroded penny over the puncture—it is believed that the "green moss" on the copper will draw out the poison and prevent tetanus. Another method is to burn woolen rags in a copper kettle and hold the injured member in the thick smoke for several minutes.

Chimney soot, thoroughly mixed with molasses, is good for cuts and open wounds. Spider webs are used for this purpose, too, and are said to stop bleeding at once. Best of all is the dry dust from the fungi called puffballs, especially the big yellow kind known as the Devil's snuffbox. Golden-seal root, ground into a fine dry powder and dusted on an open wound or sore, seems to cure it up about as well as anything. The pain of a bee sting is relieved by applying the crushed leaves of three plants—any three will do, just so they are of different species —to the painful area.

The hillfolk use kerosene or coal oil both externally and in-

ternally, for many minor ailments and injuries. Some of them
claim Biblical authority for this treatment in the passage:
"Nothing but the *oil of the earth* will cure ye in the latter days,"
but I have not been able to locate this in the Bible, so far. I
have seen snake bite treated by sticking the swollen leg into a
bucket of kerosene; if the snake was really poisonous, it is said
that the "pizen" forms a greenish scum on the top of the oil;
many of those present claimed to see the green venom very
distinctly, but I saw nothing but the iridescent surface color
of the kerosene. A poultice of soft soap mixed with salt is
sometimes used for snake bites and is believed to draw out the
poison if it is applied in time. Mrs. C. P. Mahnkey, of Taney
county, Missouri, recommends "a bit of real snake-weed, boiled
in sweet milk," but it is a rare plant, and I have not been able
to find a specimen. "The leaves are slender, almost like blades
of corn," she writes, "but four come out of the stalk, all exactly
opposite each other, and at the top is a little white blossom."

For kidney and bladder trouble, the yarb doctor usually
burns the dried blood of a rabbit and makes a tea by boiling the
ashes in water and decanting off the liquid. Gravelroot (*Eupa-
torium*) is good too—it is boiled down to a strong tea, and then
diluted with water as taken. A tea brewed from parsley is also
a popular kidney medicine. The root of sevenbark (*Hydrangea
arborescens*) is a remedy for scanty or difficult urination, as
is the shrub known as ninebark, which looks very much like the
common white spiraea seen in flower gardens.

Corn-silk tea, made by steeping corn silks in very hot water,
is said to cure bed wetting in children. Some people think that
sumac-berry tea is better, however. Similar claims are made for
a strong decoction of finely chopped watermelon seeds. Another
sure cure for bed wetting is to feed the child a pancake with
bedbugs cooked into it; I saw this tried once and noted that
the patient was not told about the bugs until several hours after
he had eaten the pancake. Miss Betrenia Watt, who taught the
village school at Preston, in Hickory county, Missouri, tells

me that the old-timers use *seven* bedbugs to each pancake, but the folks in my neighborhood didn't bother to count the "cheenches."

I remember a young woman near Pineville, Missouri, who was very ill indeed. The local m.d. said that she had Bright's disease and held little hope for her recovery. One of this woman's male relatives searched the hills for days and finally dug up a root which seemed to do her more good than any of the doctor's prescriptions. She was still alive several years later, apparently much improved in health. I interviewed the man who found the magic root. He boasted that he had cured the woman "after all the doctors done give her up" but refused to tell me the name of the root that did the business. A yarb doctor who saw the stuff, however, told me that it looked to him like yellow-root, by which he meant golden-seal (*Hydrastis*).

Plenty of sexual intercourse is regarded as a sure cure for bladder and kidney ailments in women. It is often said of a widow who remarries: "Well, I guess Lizzie has throwed away her gravel medicine." Perhaps this is somehow related to the hillman's habit of saying, as a sort of toast when he takes a drink of whiskey: "Well, this is for my wife's kidneys!" I have heard this remark many times, in different parts of the Ozark country, but am not certain just what is meant by it.

The yarb doctor is brother to the witch and close cousin to the preacher, and not infrequently mixes a little religious hokum with his teas and plasters. People who visited Hollister, Missouri, in the spring of 1934 will not soon forget the "prayin' corn doctor," a bewhiskered old herbalist who specialized in corns and bunions and prayed loudly over his remedies. As late as 1940 there was one of these fellows in Taney county, Missouri, a long-haired chap with beaded moccasins and a deerskin vest. He carried many little bags of dried herbs, each marked with a mysterious sign supposed to be Cherokee picture writing. This medicine man treated all ailments and agreed to cure anything for six dollars in cash. He asked every patient "You believe in God, don't you?" and they all answered that they did. Muttering strange words as he opened each little sack of medicine, he put several kinds of dried leaves into a pint of water for each patient. The leaves were so finely divided that they were not easily identified, but I tasted the tea made from them, and I think it was mostly senna and gentian.

A woman in McDonald county, Missouri, had some sort of kidney trouble—her body was enormously swollen. The m.d. said there was no hope for her, but the family called in an illiterate healer from the backwoods. This yarb doctor glanced at the patient and said that he *could* reduce the swelling in a few minutes, but this might endanger the patient's life, so he had best do the job gradually. He muttered some gibberish and applied a green poultice of his own making. He told me privately that this poultice was made of turnip tops, which he had "blessed with the power of Christ Jesus." The woman died two or three days later. "You orter have called me sooner," said the yarb doctor.

Perhaps the most famous yarb doctor ever known in the Ozarks was Omar Palmer, who lived in the village of Hurley, Missouri. I went to see Palmer once, and the cars in front of his office sported tags from five different states. He had a larger practice, and made more money, than any of the licensed m.d.'s in the neighborhood. The Missouri State Board of Health had him arrested once for practicing medicine without a license, but at the last moment his patients refused to testify. The yarb doctor walked out of court a free man and was greeted with loud cheers from the assembled yokelry. Somebody even shot off some firecrackers, ordinarily reserved for Christmas and the Fourth of July. Palmer kept five or six men and women busy, collecting roots and herbs in the woods near Hurley. He sold his various teas in pint bottles. Unwilling to use alcohol to preserve the stuff, Palmer could not prevent its spoiling in a few days, so that the customer had to return to Hurley for another bottle.

Sassafras tea, made from the bark of sassafras roots in the

spring, is supposed to thin or purify the blood. It has the color of tawny port, and a very fine flavor—though too much boiling makes it bitter. Some people put small quantities of May apple, wild cherry, and goldenseal into their sassafras tea, but most of the old folks take it neat. Sassafras is used not only in the backwoods but more or less all over the country. I have seen men selling little bundles of sassafras roots in the streets of Kansas City, St. Louis, Springfield, and Joplin, Missouri, and also in Fort Smith and Little Rock, Arkansas. The old-timers use only the fresh red roots—the smaller and redder the better. The fellows who sell the stuff split larger whitish roots up to look like young ones, but the big roots don't make the best tea.

The drugstores sell dried sassafras bark the year round, and some people buy this stuff in the winter, but the hillfolk claim that only the fresh roots have any value as medicine. Many of them say that sassafras is no good until Groundhog Day—February 14.

Many Ozark people make a tea from the bark of the spice-bush (*Benzoin aestivale*) in March and April. They drink this just as they do sassafras tea and regard it as a tonic and blood thinner. It tastes quite as good as sassafras, I think. Some old folks say that in pioneer days the spicebush was used to season game—it softened the wild taste of venison and bear meat. Spicebush twigs are still used as a mat beneath a possum, when the Ozark housewife bakes the animal in a covered pan or a Dutch oven.

Choctaw-root or dogbane (*Apocynum*) is also made into a tea, mildly laxative, which is said to "thin the blood an' tone up the system." I have never tasted this but have met men who say that it is better than either sassafras or spicebush. Some yarb doctors fortify their choctaw-root with wild-cherry bark and "anvil dust," whatever that may be.

A strong tea of red-clover blossoms is highly regarded in some quarters as a blood purifier and general tonic. It is used in the treatment of whooping cough, too, but if the whooping cough is really bad nothing will help it but mare's milk. Many a father has been routed out in the night to ride to some farm where a mare has lately foaled.

Bloodroot or red puccoon (*Sanguinaria*) is also supposed to be a great blood remedy, apparently because it has blood-red sap. By the same token a leaf shaped like a kidney, or a liver, or an ovary, or what not is supposed to designate a remedy for disorders of the organ which it resembles. The yarb doctors are all familiar with this principle, but they don't seem to take it very seriously or follow it consistently.

Some hillfolk in southern Missouri gather the roots of the big purple coneflower (*Brauneria*) and brew a tea which is given to sick persons apparently regardless of what ails them. I know a man who was confined to his bed with a broken leg, and the doctor was no sooner out of sight than the womenfolks began to dose the patient with this "niggerhead" tea. "It made him sweat wonderful," an old woman told me later, "an' sweatin's good for a big man layin' in bed that-a-way!"

Many of the old-time druggists make up *bitters* by putting wild cherries, together with the inner bark of the wild-cherry tree, into whiskey. This is a fine spring tonic, and some prefer it to sassafras tea. It is good for almost any ailment, in a pinch, and even families who are notoriously dry keep a quart of bitters in case of sudden sickness. A mixture of whiskey and rock candy is popular too but is not so highly recommended as the famous wild-cherry bitters.

Children in Arkansas are sometimes encouraged to chew the gummy resin melted out of pine wood before the fireplace; I have seen children chewing this stuff by the hour, just as city children chew gum. The parents think that the turpentine in this resin keeps the children free of worms. A tea made from peach leaves is also a common remedy for worms, while some favor a mess made by stewing vermifuge seeds in molasses. Horsemint tea is supposed to be a sure cure for rectal worms in children. A decoction of pumpkin seeds is used to expel tape-worms, and it seems to be effective, too.

Boneset tea is a favorite remedy for chills, fever, and ague. A tea made of elderberry roots is good, too. Some people have great confidence in blade-fodder tea, especially if the fodder has been kept in a dry place. Seneca-root or rattlesnake weed (*Senega*) is said to make a mighty fine chills-and-fever medicine. The unfermented juice of the little wild possum grapes is supposed to cure malaria. Uncle Jack Short of Galena, Missouri, says that he used to drink gallons of peach-bark tea every fall for his "ager"; also a tea made by boiling sheep manure, with a little spicewood added to kill the unpleasant ..e. Fanny D. Bergen observes that "in central Missouri one is recommended to take for ague a whole pepper-corn every morning for seven consecutive mornings." [1] The plant known as fever-root (*Corallorhiza odontorhiza*) is also used to reduce fevers and is a mild sedative as well. A gentleman in Cyclone, Missouri, tells me that his family made a "chill remedy" that was in great demand; the exact formula was kept secret, he says, but the main ingredient was crushed burdock seeds.

A good strong tea of saffron, taken often and in large doses, is said to be a sure cure for the "yaller janders." Another jaundice remedy is made by cooking fishworms in lard and rolling the result into big evil-smelling pills.

Nanny tea, consisting of sheep manure and hot water, with a little sugar, is a very powerful medicine for measles; it is believed to make the patient "break out" at once, which the yarb doctors say is desirable. Spicewood tea, made by boiling the tender green twigs of the spicewood or feverbush (*Benzoin aestivale*), is another famous remedy for measles.

Mrs. Coral Almy Wilson, of Zinc, Arkansas, tells me that her neighbors treat rheumatism with an infusion of wahoo (*Euonymus*) bark. In other parts of the Ozarks the yarb doc-

[1] *Journal of American Folklore,* V (1892), 21.

tors administer pokeroot (*Phytolacca*) tea for rheumatism,
while people in eastern Oklahoma seem to think that celery
leaves are about as good as anything. Mrs. May Kennedy
McCord, Springfield, Missouri, claims that a mixture of sulphur
and homemade sorghum molasses *does* cure rheumatism, no matter what the doctors say. The so-called rheumatiz root (*Dio-
scorea*) is much favored in some sections. A man near Marionville, Missouri, used to eat pokeberries, generally supposed to
be poisonous, in the belief that they might help his rheumatic
joints. A tea made by boiling cockleburs in water is another
remedy for rheumatism.

Water drunk from a gourd is somehow cleansed of all impurities, according to the old-timers, and is regarded by some
as a specific for rheumatism. I knew a lawyer in Pineville, Missouri, who always kept a gourd in his office, hidden behind the
water cooler; he said that a man who was inclined to be rheumatic should not drink from cups or glasses.

Stiff joints are treated with a grease made by hanging a
bottle of dead fishworms up in the sun—a horrible stinking mess
it is, too. The grease from skunks or civet cats, mixed with
peppermint leaves, is highly praised by some hillfolk as a
lubricant for rheumatic joints. It is said that the fat of a male
wildcat is best of all. Big black ants are dried and powdered
and mixed with lard; this is rubbed on the legs of babies who
are slow in learning to walk, or who seem weak in the legs.

Sometimes a severe pain in the ear is relieved with a vinegar
poultice—just soak a piece of light-bread in hot vinegar and
hold it against the ear until it cools. Some yarb doctors treat
earache simply by blowing tobacco smoke into the ear; if this
doesn't give relief, they blow the smoke into a cup of warm
water with a reed or pipestem and put a few drops of this
smoke water into the ear at intervals. Others prefer to pour
sweet oil, or skunk oil, or goose grease strained through silk
into their ears. Some use human urine in the same way, although
it is claimed that mule's urine is better. An infusion of sheep

manure, called nanny tea or sheep-dumplin' tea, is also much in favor as a remedy for earache. If the pain is caused by a bug getting into the ear, however, one has only to squirt water into the *other* ear, and the insect will be washed out immediately. Fresh urine is the best lotion for chapped hands, sore feet, and chilblains. I once knew a lady south of Joplin, Missouri, who thought that the practice of rubbing urine on one's feet was disgusting; she contended that a nice salve made of hog bristles cut very fine and mixed with skunk oil was more efficacious, anyhow.

A mess of peach roots, ground up and mixed with lard, is said to cure the seven-year itch. Some people prefer a salve made of hopvine leaves. Bloodroot or red puccoon, pounded up fine and steeped in vinegar, is another very popular itch medicine. Some claim to cure the itch by taking sulphur and molasses internally, but most yarb doctors scoff at this. Others treat itch with a paste made of gunpowder and wood ashes mixed with sweet cream, applied at frequent intervals. In Pineville, Missouri, my old neighbors asked the druggist for "a dime's worth of acker fortis an' a nickel's worth of quicksilver," by which they meant nitric acid and mercury, to make some kind of itch medicine. Otto Ernest Rayburn, of Eureka Springs, Arkansas, says that boiled pokeroot used to be a famous remedy for itch, but "it burned like fire, and the cure was probably worse than the ailment." A strong ooze of pokeberry root, a man from Madison county, Arkansas, assures me, "will make you think hell aint a mile away, but it sure does cure the eetch."

The skin disease called tetter is treated with spunk water or stump water—simply rain water which happens to be retained in a hollow stump. Bloodroot is good for tetter also, and there is another herb known as tetter weed, but this latter I have not been able to identify. The yarb doctors all insist that tetter weed is not identical with bloodroot (*Sanguinaria*) which is called tetterwort in some parts of the United States. The root of the bull nettle is used in the treatment of skin diseases, according to Otto Ernest Rayburn, of Eureka Springs, Arkansas. I have seen skin eruptions treated with mud supplied by crushing dirt-dobbers' nests and adding water—mud from these nests is credited with some astringent virtue not found in ordinary earth. A poultice of pokeberry leaves is said to cure ivy poisoning. Some people say that a big dose of sulphur and molasses, with a pinch of saltpeter, will render a person immune to poison ivy for several weeks.

Many hillfolk treat ringworm by daubing it with the juice of a green walnut; this smarts a bit but really does seem to arrest the ringworm in some cases. Another way of curing ringworm is to burn a bit of flannel on a flatiron, so as to leave a tiny drop of dark-colored oil; this oil is applied directly to the ringworm, care being taken not to get any of it on the surrounding tissue.

I have heard of Ozark yarb doctors who claim that they can cure epileptic fits, but I have never met one of these gentlemen. The old folks say, however, that a poultice of colts-tongue leaves, applied to the sufferer's forehead, often affords a measure of relief. "Mirandy" Bauersfeld tells of an Ozark granny who chewed up *fitweed* leaves and then thrust them into the patient's mouth, but I have not been able to find any plant called fitweed.[2] A tea made of fresh parsley is supposed to be beneficial in epilepsy, and some yarb doctors prescribe it for hysteria and other nervous diseases. It is often said that parsley will stop an epileptic fit, but only in the light of the moon. I talked with one epileptic boy about this, but he said that he seldom had a seizure in the light of the moon, whether he drank parsley water or not. A human bone, pulverized, is sometimes given internally for epilepsy—just a pinch of the powder stirred into a hot toddy, or a cup of coffee.

Old sores, syphilitic lesions, and skin cancers are sometimes treated with powder made from the bones of a person long dead. In order to obtain this material the hillfolk dig into Indian

2 *Breezes from Persimmon Holler*, p. 129.

graves and Bluff Dweller burials under the ledges. The hillman always tells strangers that he's digging for arrowheads and the like, which can be sold to tourists; but I have seen these old bones broken into small pieces with a hammer and ground up to be used as medicine.

Some people named Carney, living near Cape Fair, Missouri, have for several generations been treating skin diseases. They claim to have cured many cancers. The treatment is simply a poultice of crushed, boiled sheep sorrel. Some say it must be boiled in a copper kettle. This stuff is applied freely to the sores and cures a lot of them, but it is terribly painful. I asked Dr. J. H. Young of Galena, Missouri, about this, and he said that the oxalic acid in sheep sorrel was effective, if the patient could stand it. Of course, he added, the sores that the Carneys had cured were not really cancers.

Judge Gerrit Snip, Lamar, Missouri, in 1919, announced publicly that he had healed a cancer on his hand with an infusion of "sheep shower"—probably the same as sheep sorrel. He said it hurt like hell but cured the cancer.

To prevent hives, one has only to put several buckshot into a glass of water and drink a spoonful of the water every two hours; some people say that there must be exactly nine buckshot in the glass, no more and no less, but others think that this numerical idea savors of superstition. If one does get hives despite all attempts at prophylaxis, maple-leaf tea is the best remedy; the hard maple or sugar tree is better than the ordinary kind. Some hillfolk soak cloths in the tea and apply them to the skin, others get equally good results by taking large doses of the stuff internally.

Nearly every hillman has heard of the strange disease called *bold* hives or *boll* hives, supposed to be invariably fatal. Ozark M.D.'s tell me that there is no such thing, but they have all been called in great haste to treat the mythical disease. "When I get there," said Dr. J. H. Young, "I generally find a case of ordinary hives, and they always get well." Babies are supposed to be especially susceptible to *bold* hives, but adults sometimes have 'em too, according to the old settlers.

The fat found on rabbits' kidneys in the fall is said to be a specific for sexual debility; I have known several old men who obtained large quantities of this fat from rabbit trappers and claimed great things for it. A tea made from black snakeroot (*Cimicifuga*) is another powerful aphrodisiac, according to the wise men of the mountains, but it seems to upset the stomach if large doses are taken, and is best mixed with whiskey. There is a widespread belief that a man who "loses his manhood" is doomed to die before the year is out; a gentleman ninety-three years old told me that he used to believe this himself but had finally been forced to the conclusion that "there aint nothing to it."

Ginseng or sang root is supposed to prolong life and to strengthen the sexual powers in aging men. There are probably a few old fellows in the Ozarks who still use it, and there are reports of secret sang patches here and there. But wild ginseng is almost extinct now, and it sells for between ten dollars and fifteen dollars per pound. Not many hillfolk can be induced to eat anything that they can sell for that much money. There are some people down at Compton, Arkansas, who have been growing the stuff in sang arbors since old "Frost" Petree started the practice about 1900, but the domestic roots do not bring the high prices paid for wild sang. The plants don't bear seeds until they are three years old, and the seeds won't sprout until two years after they are picked. Roots less than five years old are hardly big enough to market—some of the four-pronged wild roots are said to be twenty or thirty years old. The whole project of sang raising is too slow for the hillman's taste.

Most yarb-doctors gather their own yarbs, but there are many root diggers and herbalists in the Ozarks who collect such stuff for the market. Much of this material is sold or bartered to country storekeepers, who ship it to a famous root-and-herb broker in St. Louis. This man operates a business founded by his father some ninety years ago and sends out a yearly price-list of nearly one hundred roots, herbs, and barks that he will buy.

People near Walnut Shade, Missouri, still tell the story of how an amateur root buyer named Cummins went broke through buying counterfeit sang. Lou Beardon, who lived on Bear Creek, discovered that two-year-old pokeroots, properly dried, look very much like ginseng, and it is said Cummins bought nearly a hundred dollars' worth of this so-called *bogue sang* before he learned to distinguish the two.

Roots for the market must be dug in the fall—dig 'em in the growin' season and they shrink away to nothing. Bark is best gathered in late winter and early spring. Leaves and herbs should be collected while the plants are blooming. Flowers are picked when they first open, seeds are gathered as soon as they are ripe. All of these things must be dried slowly in the shade and not shipped until they are perfectly dry, otherwise they will become moldy and lose their value as medicine. I have known several backwoods wanderers who lived by gathering roots and herbs; it seemed to me that they worked harder than most farmers, and I don't think many of them earned more than fifty cents a day. Some of the herbs gathered in the Ozarks are ultimately sold to legitimate drug houses, while others are no longer prescribed by regular physicians but are used in various patent medicines and also by the medicine-show quacks who still flourish in many parts of the United States.

The yarb doctors are not very well provided with sedatives or soporifics. They sometimes try to quiet the nerves of alco-holic patients by rubbing the head with a paste of sunflower seeds; I let a woman at Rogers, Arkansas, smear some of this stuff on my head once, but it didn't seem to do much good. A thick sassafras-bark shampoo is sometimes used in similar cases and has the added advantage that it kills headlice as well as soothing jangled nerves.

A tea made from the roots of the butterfly weed (*Asclepias*) is supposed to be good for nervousness and restlessness. A pillow stuffed with dried hopvines relieves pain and puts the patient to sleep. Mistletoe leaves are made into a remedy for dizziness and head noises. Catnip tea is a common sedative, taken warm just before going to bed. Lady's-slipper (*Cypripedium*) roots are boiled in milk to make some sort of "nerve medicine." An infusion of fresh alfalfa, taken in large doses, is said to quiet the nerves and produce sleep. Mr. Lewis Kelley, Cyclone, Missouri, tells me that his neighbors used a tea made of skullcap root (*Scutellaria*) for nervousness, and it was more effective than the "nervine" sold at the drugstore. For persistent insomnia, one has only to put a handful of Jimson-weed (*Datura*) leaves into each shoe and set the shoes under the bed with the toes pointing toward the nearest wall. A few Jimson-weed leaves, placed in the crown of a hat, are believed to protect the wearer from apoplexy or sunstroke. A tea made from Jimson weed is used in the treatment of nervousness, hysteria, and delirium, but without much success so far as I can see.

The shell of a black walnut is supposed to represent the human skull, and the meat is said to resemble the brain, therefore people who show signs of mental aberration are encouraged to eat walnuts. I know of one case in which an entire family devoted most of the winter to cracking walnuts for a feeble-minded boy. They kept it up for years, and I believe the poor fellow ate literally bushels of walnut goodies.

A few years ago I visited an aged couple in northwest Arkansas, and noticed a lump of brown resin-like stuff, about as big as a baseball, on the fireboard. "What is that?" I asked. The old man grinned. "That's gum opium," said he, "it's been settin' there since the fall of 1904. They tell me it's agin the law to sell opium now, but you could buy it at any drugstore in them days. Whenever I don't feel right peart, or Maw either, we just scrape off a little o' that stuff and it fixes us right up." From what I have heard elsewhere it seems that a great many pioneers took opium or laudanum freely, and always carried it with them, or kept it in their cabins. One might think that they would have all become dope fiends, but the old-time doctors say that there was very little drug addiction in those days.

I am told that the early settlers raised hemp, great fields of it, and used the fibers to make rope and coarse cloth. They never thought of smoking it, but it was genuine hemp all right (*Cannabis sativa*), the same plant that is called marijuana nowadays. Many people believe that fried fish and sweet milk, taken into the human stomach at the same meal, combine to form a deadly poison and several persons have told me that hemp tea is the only known antidote for this fish-and-milk poisoning.

Some otherwise intelligent and progressive mountain people patronize the yarb doctor rather than the regular M.D. because of their fear of surgery. This is understandable when one remembers that in the early days, with little attempt at aseptic conditions, often without any anesthetic, even minor operations were horrible indeed and very often fatal.

Another thing which prejudices the hillfolk against the M.D. is the fact that so many modern drugs are administered hypodermically. In the old days, the hypodermic needle was used chiefly for injecting opiates. Very often the doctor was not called until the patient was desperately ill. When he arrived to find some poor devil dying in great pain, the physician just sighed and gave the sufferer a big shot of morphine. Thus the pioneers came to regard the needle as a kind of death warrant, and to this day the backwoodsman is afraid of hypodermic medication. Even children in the schools, who make very little fuss over being vaccinated against smallpox, often raise a terrific disturbance when the doctor tries to give them a "shot" of antityphoid serum.

There is a widespread belief that physiological phenomena are somehow connected with the increase and decrease of the moon, but the various healers have such divergent ideas of this that no general principles are apparent to me. The matter is often mentioned by the yarb doctors in talking with their patients, and I have heard some of these conversations, but can make little of them. On the whole, it seems that yarb medicines for internal use are best taken in the "dark" of the moon, when the moon is waning, since most of them are supposed to *stop* some deleterious process, or to *arrest* some injurious growth.

There are also the signs of the zodiac to be taken into account. A great number of people believe that stomach trouble is most likely to be acquired or aggravated when the moon is in Cancer, diseases of the throat during the sign Taurus, venereal infections in Scorpio, and so on. The treatment of disease is tied up with these constellations also, and many people, if forced to undergo a surgical operation, are careful to postpone it until an appropriate sign is indicated on the calendar.

In discussing this matter of operations, May Stafford Hilburn says that all operations are best performed "when the sign is going into the feet or legs," unless the operation is to be performed upon the feet or legs. "We *know*," she writes, "that if an abdominal operation is to take place, and the sign is in the bowels, we can look for trouble." [3]

Dr. J. H. Young, of Galena, Missouri, told me that he had a patient all ready to go to the hospital once, when the man's relatives suddenly discovered that the sign wasn't right for his operation and said it must be postponed for about a week. Young warned them that the patient might be dead before the week was out, if they didn't let the surgeon operate. They still refused, so Dr. Young withdrew from the case and washed his hands of the whole business. The patient survived, and all his kin are still great believers in "operatin' by the sign."

Dr. Glenn Jones, dentist at Crane, Missouri, told me that many of his patients waited until the sign was right before having teeth extracted, even when they were in considerable pain. Hillfolk generally agree that a tooth should never be pulled when the sign is in the head—to do this is to risk a serious hemorrhage. Most people think that extractions go best in

3 *Missouri Magazine* (September, 1933), p. 20.

Aquarius or Pisces, but there is no certainty about this. The old-timers say that it is better to pull a tooth in the morning than in the afternoon, no matter what constellation the moon's in.

Some hillfolk imagine that if a pain or disturbance in any part of the body coincides with the sign as shown for that date in the almanac, there is no cause for alarm. I once found a neighbor writhing on the floor with a terrific cramp in his abdomen. It occurred to me that the fellow probably had a hot appendix, and I urged him to call a doctor at once. He asked me to fetch him a calendar from the kitchen, and when he saw the picture of Virgo he relaxed with a sigh of relief. "The sign's in the guts," he gasped, "I'll be all right in the mornin' "—and sure enough he was completely recovered five hours later. I have often known men to complain of sharp pains here and there, which they explained by saying "the sign's in the ———," naming the part of the body which seemed to be affected. Had the sign been elsewhere on that particular day, these pains would have been taken much more seriously.

An old friend showed me a bottle of medicine prescribed for him by a very competent M.D. named Wade, who used to practice in Christian county, Missouri. "Take a dose of that stuff every day," Dr. Wade had told him, "and keep it up *till snakes crawl.*" Wade prescribed this medicine in late February, and no snake was seen thereabouts that year until March 24. Instead of saying so many days or weeks, this physician used a real backwoods expression, which pleased the patient much more than an arbitrary date. He felt that his recovery was somehow tied up with the orderly processes of Nature, rather than governed by some man-made rule in a medical book. When a neighbor boy came running in, on March 24, shouting that some woodcutters had found a snake, my friend put away the medicine. He was a well man.

Most of the backwoods healers do little harm, and even the worst of yarb doctors seldom poison anybody. They kill their patients indirectly sometimes, simply by preventing them from getting proper medical or surgical treatment. One of my neighbors suffered a ruptured appendix, whereupon the local yarb doctor assured him that there was no need of an operation and applied a poultice of hot boiled potatoes. The man died, of course—not because of the poultice, but because the yarb doctor's bad counsel prevented him from calling in a surgeon. Most of the damage done by yarb doctors and granny-women is of this negative type.

Occasionally, however, one encounters a bit of medical practice that seems ill-advised, not to say hazardous. A physician in southwest Missouri tells me that a young woman in his neighborhood had some sort of colitis—painful and depressing, but not dangerous. Along came a granny-woman who induced this patient to swallow a half-tumblerful of turkey shot, and she died a few days later. It appears that people in this vicinity often take small doses of fine shot for "bowel trouble," without any apparent damage. "But it certainly doesn't do 'em any good," said the doctor grimly.

Another case is that of a hillman who had what was called "locked bowels." The doctor from a neighboring town said that he would probably die anyhow but recommended that he be taken to a hospital at once. Instead of doing this, the patient's brother, in the presence of the whole family, knocked the patient unconscious by striking the back of his head with a small sack of salt. The young physician, who had not been long in the Ozarks, thought that the patient was being murdered before his eyes and left the house immediately. But the man's people were trying desperately to save him, working on the theory that unconsciousness allows the internal organs to relax and might thus dispose of the obstruction. After knocking the patient cold, they "cupped" him with fruit jars of boiling water—poured the water out and clapped the empty jars against his abdomen. The poor fellow died, as the doctor had predicted. The father of the dead man said sadly: "Too bad we couldn't save Jim. I've saw several fellers with locked bowels cured that-a-way." It is said that the physician asked the county officers to place manslaughter charges against the bereaved family, but nothing was ever done about it.

Sometimes when an infant does not grow and function properly, the granny-women decide that the child is "liver-growed" —meaning that the liver has somehow become attached to the body wall. In such cases a stout old woman grasps the baby's left hand and right foot and twists them together behind its back, then does the same with the right hand and left foot. She has to pull pretty hard sometimes, and the child hollers somethin' turrible, but it's the only treatment for a liver-growed baby. The more difficult it is to bring the hands and feet together in this fashion, the more certain it appears that the child is really liver-growed. This is a rather alarming thing to witness, but physicians tell me that it does not seem to do any particular harm.

Another dubious item, to my mind, is the idea that if a small boy has a fit, the parents should strip him instantly and make him walk home stark naked. Such treatment may be harmless in warm weather, but it surely must be a bad thing to force a little naked screaming child to walk through the snow in the dead of winter. But there is no doubt that it is still practiced, in some sections, by parents who are firmly convinced that it is the proper scientific procedure.

Many yarb doctors insist, when a bullet wound goes clear through an arm or leg, on trying to pull a silk handkerchief through the wound. The connection between bullet wounds and silk handkerchiefs is common enough to have passed into the language, and there are several stories and backwoods wisecracks about it. A boy who once lived in my home was insulted and enraged when a girl sent him a fine silk handkerchief as a Christmas present. "She'd orter sent it to Bob Taylor, that's allus a-kickin' up dust round there," he said grimly, " 'cause Bob's the one that's goin' to need it !"

A farmer in McDonald county, Missouri, had a persistent headache which the yarb doctors failed to relieve. Finally one of them told him that his only hope was to have a thin silver plate set under the scalp at the back of his head. The yarb doctor remarked that he *could* do the job himself but advised the patient to have some "town doctor" attend to it. "It'll cost ye four or five dollars—maybe six," said the yarb doctor, "but it's worth the money." The patient was so charmed with the idea of having a silver plate in his head that he rushed into the office of Dr. Oakley St. John, at Pineville, Missouri, demanding that the operation be performed immediately. It was with some difficulty that St. John persuaded him that a silver plate was not indicated in his case.

Physicians in the Ozark towns have remarked upon the practice of giving turpentine as a worm medicine. Turpentine is still administered by many yarb doctors and granny-women, large doses being given to small children. The stuff may eliminate the worms, but it seems to be bad for the child's kidneys. A lot of little children in the Ozarks die of nephritis, and the M.D.'s say that nephritis is caused or aggravated by this indiscriminate dosing with turpentine.

7. The Power Doctors

Very different from the yarb doctors described above are healers of another type, who make no pretense to scientific knowledge but depend entirely upon charms, spells, prayers, amulets, exorcisms, and magic of one sort or another. These are the so-called "power doctors," backwoods specialists, each claiming to be endowed with supernatural power to cure certain specific ailments. They seldom attempt any general practice, and most of them take no money for their services, although they may accept and even demand valuable presents on occasion. Some of these people, usually old women, can cool fevers merely by the laying on of hands; others draw out the fire from burns by spitting or blowing upon the inflamed areas, while still others claim to heal more serious lesions by some similar hocus-pocus. One old lady who specializes in burns says that she always mutters a few words which she "l'arnt out'n the Book"—the Bible, that is—but refuses to tell me what particular text is used.

A gentleman near Crane, Missouri, has enjoyed a great success in relieving the pain from superficial burns. He just blows gently upon the burned place, touches it with his finger tips, and whispers a little prayer. The prayer may be told to persons of the other sex, but never imparted to one of the same sex. This man said he had learned the magic from Mrs. Molly Maxwell, an old woman who lived in Galena, Missouri. Since he could not tell me, I asked a young woman to get the secret words from him. This is what she heard:

One little Indian, two little Indians,
One named East, one named West,

The Son and the Father and the Holy Ghost,
In goes the frost, out comes the fire,
Ask it all in Jesus' name, Amen.

In teaching this prayer to a member of the opposite sex, the healer said, one should whisper it three times and no more. If a person cannot learn the prayer after hearing three repetitions, I was told, "he aint fit to draw out fire nohow!"

Mrs. May Kennedy McCord, of Springfield, Missouri, knows how to "draw out fire" from a burn. She learned it from Harry N. Force, an old-time druggist who spent many years in Cotter, Arkansas. You just mutter: "Two little angels come from Heaven, one brought fire and the other brought frost, go out fire and come in frost." As you say the last word you blow gently on the burn. This "sayin'" is supposed to be a great secret and must be learned from a member of the opposite sex.

I met an old-time healer near Gainesville, Missouri, who cured sores, sprains, and bruises in this way: he laid his right hand on the wounded place, and his left hand on a corresponding part of his own body. Then he shivered for a moment, threw back his head, and muttered some gibberish under his breath. Many people declared themselves benefited by this treatment. I asked the old man if the magic words were from the Bible. "No, they *shore* aint!" said he.

There used to be a woman at West Plains, Missouri, who had a great reputation as a "blood stopper." A wounded man was brought to her home in a wagon. The whole wagon bed seemed to be covered with blood, and the man's friends were unable to stop the bleeding from two deep knife cuts. The woman looked at the patient, then walked out to the barn alone, with a Bible under her arm. In about three minutes the bleeding stopped, and the healer returned to her house. She would take no money for "blood stopping," and she would not discuss the method. She was not a religious woman, and rarely looked at the Bible except when she was asked to stop the flow of blood. The old woman confided to a friend that she had already imparted the secret to three persons, and that if she ever told a fourth the "power" would be taken from her.

"About this blood-stopping charm, it really works," wrote Otto Ernest Rayburn, of Eureka Springs, Arkansas. "We had a neighbor at Caddo Gap, who could do it. Our eleven-year-old son had a severe case of bleeding, and we were unable to stop it by ordinary methods. We told our neighbor and he asked the boy's full name, then went out into the yard and repeated a few words—we couldn't hear them. And lo and behold, the bleeding stopped! I do not know how to explain such things, but they *do* happen." Later on Rayburn reports his encounter with another power doctor who stops bleeding; this man "repeats a certain verse from the sixteenth chapter of Ezekiel. He walks toward the East while repeating the lines. . . . A man who has the power may tell the secret to three women; a woman may tell three men. Some think they will lose the power if they tell the secret to the third person."

Mrs. Anna L. Coffman, of Marshfield, Missouri, says that to stop bleeding you repeat the sixth verse, sixteenth chapter, of Ezekiel: "And when I passed by thee, and saw thee polluted in thine own blood, I said unto thee when thou wast in thy blood, Live; yea, I said unto thee when thou wast in thy blood, Live."

Mrs. Callie Brake, Seymour, Missouri, used the same verse, adding: "You call the person by name and the wound by name and walk toward the sunrise repeating God's Word and the bleeding will stop. My daddy always kept that chapter at hand so he could find it right quick. He would read it if we cut ourselves dangerously and the great God of Israel would stop the bleeding. There is no 'charm' about this stopping blood, it is God's own words." [1]

Another old woman, perhaps the best blood stopper in McDonald county, Missouri, simply held up both hands and cried:

> Upon Christ's grave three roses bloom,
> Stop, blood, stop!

[1] Springfield (Missouri) *News*, July 29, 1940.

An old gentleman who told a girl reporter the secret of blood stopping cautioned her never to write it down or publish it, as in that case the charm would lose its efficacy. Several blood stoppers tell me that the secret can only be passed to a person of the opposite sex, and one said that he could tell it to three persons, and no more. He had already told two women, and was saving the third telling for his little granddaughter.

In a letter to Mrs. May Kennedy McCord, written by Mrs. M. R. Smith, Marionville, Missouri, dated March 7, 1941, Mrs. Smith says:

Speaking of stopping blood, I can do it. I have on several occasions. My mother had cancer of the face, and it would bleed till she would almost pass on. So my brother-in-law told us about an old man in the neighborhood who could stop blood, and all he needed was to be *told* —did not have to see the person. So we sent him word one day and the blood just stopped, all at once. Why or how you will have to decide for yourself, but it did stop. So my mother wanted that I should learn how, and this old man taught me, and I stopped my mother's face bleeding many times. Last time I tried it I stopped my son-in-law's throat bleeding when he had his tonsils taken out and they started bleeding after he had worked too hard and got too warm. So between me and my God, it *will work*. I can tell only one more person, and that takes the charm away. A woman tells a man, who is not a blood relative, and a man tells a woman, who is not a blood relative. Can only tell three, and the third one takes the charm.

An old man in Joplin, Missouri, told me that perhaps "all that Bible stuff" was necessary to stop serious hemorrhage, as when somebody had cut his throat, but an ordinary nosebleed could easily be "chipped off" without any religious monkey business. You just catch a number of drops of the blood on a chip —one drop for each year of the patient's life. Put the chip with the blood on it in a dry, safe place—on a high rafter, for example, or seal it up in a dry glass jar. As long as the chip is not disturbed, the nose will not bleed.

If a patient is suffering from a deep cut or knife thrust, some power doctors burn the sole of his shoe and apply the ashes to the wound. This is said to stop bleeding and make the cut heal without "blood poisoning." If the cut is on the right side of the body, the right shoe is burned; if the left side of the body is injured, the healer burns the left shoe. In case a man received a knife wound in the exact center of his chest, I don't know just what the power doctor would do; I asked one backwoods healer about this, but he smiled thinly and made no reply.

One hillman of my acquaintance treats boils, ulcers, and the like in this wise: he reaches behind him, picks up a stone without looking at it, and spits upon it. Stirring the saliva about with his finger, he repeats the words:

> What I see increase,
> What I rub decrease,

and with that he rubs a little on the growth, which is supposed to disappear in a week or so. All this must be done, however, when the moon is waning; if it should be attempted before the full moon the sore would grow larger and larger instead of wasting away.

One way to cure boils, according to an old neighbor, is to rub a greasy string on a rusty nail and then throw the nail away where it will not be found. Hang the string on the inside of the cabin door, and touch the boil with the string several times a day.

A woman in Stone county, Missouri, is known far and wide as a healer of goiters, boils, carbuncles, tumors, open sores, and even skin cancers—though she says modestly that she can't cure the latter unless she gets them in the early stages. She uses no drugs nor herbs, just makes a few magic passes and mutters some secret old sayin's, supposed to be adapted from the Bible. She says she is "not allowed" to tell how it's done; the secret is handed down in the family; her mother was a healer and "blessed her with it"; she intends to pass the knowledge on to one of her own daughters before she dies. This woman makes no charge for her services, but if somebody offers her a present, such as a new dress or a side of bacon, she seldom refuses the gift. It is said that those who do not reward her liberally always come to some misfortune shortly afterward. She must know the name of the disease before she can treat it; therefore many of her patients go to the local m.d. for diagnosis and ask him to write the medical name of their ailment down on a piece of paper. The whole business is very hush-hush for some reason. I lived next door to this woman for several months before I learned that she was a power doctor.

Warts are common enough in the Ozarks, but it is surprising that so many of these folk remedies should refer exclusively to warts. Mrs. May Kennedy McCord, Springfield, Missouri, has collected and written down 125 wart cures. There is a high degree of specialization in these matters, too. I once visited a renowned wart witch and showed her an infected tick bite on my ankle. "I'm the best wart taker in this country," she said, "but that thing on your leg aint no wart—it's a *risin'*. I don't never monkey with risin's. You better go to town an' git Doc Holton to lance it for ye."

John Proctor Gentry, in Springfield, Missouri, assured me that he could "conjure" warts. He refused to tell me how it was done, but Mrs. Gentry says he just touches the wart and mutters something which begins "hocus-pocus" and ends in "unintelligible gibberish."

Mr. Rube Cummins, of Day, Missouri, eighty-five years old, tells me that he has been curing warts in the neighborhood since he was a boy. "I just tetch 'em, an' then I say a little *ceremony* to myself. I don't never tell nobody what the *ceremony* is." Asked if the ceremony was something out of the Bible, he said emphatically that it was not.

There used to be a wart witch at Seneca, Missouri, who tied a string around the wart, muttered a few words under her breath, and pulled the string off with a great flourish. Then she presented the string to the patient and told him to bury it in the ground where nobody could find it. If the string lay undisturbed for nine days and nights, she said, the wart would soon shrivel and gradually disappear.

Another old-timer tells me that it is only necessary to tie a woolen string around the wart, then spit on the wart and rub it with the finger tip. This done, remove the string and burn it secretly.

Warts may be disposed of by hiring some boy to "take them off your hands"—two or three more warts don't matter to a chap who has a dozen or so already. Just give the boy a penny or a nickel for each wart, and they will pass from you to him as soon as he spends the money.

Some specialists go through a kind of wart-buying ceremony, but no money actually changes hands. You show the man your wart, and he says: "Want to sell it?" You answer "Yes, sir." Whereupon the wart taker produces a big safety pin with many buttons strung on it. He selects one of these and hands it to you saying: "Carry that there button in your pocket till the wart's gone. Hit's mine now, 'cause I done bought an' paid for it."

Another way to "pass" a wart is to spit on it, rub a bit of paper in the spittle, fold the paper, and drop it in the road; the wart is supposed to pass to the first person who picks up the paper and unfolds it. Children are always trying this, and one can find these little folded papers in the road near most any rural schoolhouse.

Some hillfolk prefer to lose their warts at a crossroad, or better still at a place where the road forks three ways. Take a grain of corn for each wart and place each grain in the road under a small thin stone. The warts will be taken over by the person or animal that moves the stones and uncovers the grains of corn.

Or you may put as many pebbles as you have warts in a paper bag, walk down the road alone and throw the whole thing backward over your right shoulder. Whoever picks up the bag and counts the stones will fall heir to the warts.

One old lady who has cured warts for a large family says

that she just lets 'em alone until she happens to dream of a man, then seeks this fellow out and induces him to spit some tobacco juice on a penny; after rubbing the warts with the penny she gives it to the man, and as soon as he spends the coin the warts drop off. I asked her if the warts "passed" to the men who spit on the coins. She looked a bit disturbed by this query but answered stoutly that she "never had no complaints."

The exact number of warts is important in some of these ceremonies. When a hillman tries to remove warts by applying stump water he repeats this formula:

> Stump water, stump water,
> Kill these ———— warts!

The dash represents the number of warts that the patient has, and it is essential to state this number correctly. If a man says *six* when he has only five warts, the warts will not be cured, and another one will appear in a few days.

An old man near Bentonville, Arkansas, had quite a local reputation as a wart specialist, though he made no secret of his method, and said that anybody could perform similar cures if they only "knowed how." He told me that he just fastened a bit of cloth to the wart, blindfolded the "warty feller," and turned him around seven times; then he buried the cloth in the ground, and very seldom did the wart last more than three or four days thereafter.

One school of wart catchers place their trust in dirty dishrags, and some healers say that they require *stolen* dishrags. After touching each wart with the rag, one either buries it secretly in the earth or hides it under a flat rock, being careful to replace the rock in exactly the position in which it was found. Sometimes the patient is told that the wart will disappear in three days, or seven days, or nine days, or twelve days. More conservative practitioners say rather that as the dishrag decomposes, the wart will grow smaller and finally disappear. A variation of this procedure is to steal a dishrag and burn it secretly, then rub the ashes on your warts, and rest assured that they will soon be gone. But it is essential to avoid telling anybody that you have done this, else the warts are likely to come back.

An old man in Pineville, Missouri, told me as a great secret that he could cure any wart by squeezing a drop of blood out of it on a grain of corn and feeding the corn to a red rooster. According to another version of this story, it is best to rub the wart with two grains of corn, feed one to the rooster, and carry the other in your pocket. When you lose the grain from your pocket, the wart will be gone. The losing must be accidental, but that is not difficult; most cabins are full of rodents, and a grain of corn in the pocket of one's overalls will soon "turn up missin'."

Another "sleight" for getting rid of a wart is merely to prick it with a thorn until it bleeds, then throw the thorn over the left shoulder and walk away without looking back.

If the weather conditions are favorable, one has only to hold a hailstone against his warts; as soon as the hailstone melts, the warts will crumble and fall away. If no hailstone is at hand, just wet your finger and mark a circle about the wart, and then make sure that your hand doesn't get wet again for twenty-four hours. A schoolteacher in Barry county, Missouri, believes that the best way to get rid of warts is to rub them with a green bean leaf until each wart looks green and then go to bed without washing your hands. Another common theory is that it is only necessary to touch a wart with nine beans and then throw the beans one at a time over the right shoulder. Or cut a small potato in two equal parts, and rub the wart with *the same half* for three mornings in succession. Or you may just rub the wart with a piece of onion, then throw the onion backward over your right shoulder and walk away without looking back. Another school contends that it is best to touch your wart with a whole red onion; then you cut the onion in two, eat half of it and bury the other half; when the buried part decays, the wart will disappear.

The stick-notching treatment used for many other ailments is also adapted to the removal of warts. A little boy near Hot Springs, Arkansas, showed me a green switch with four notches in it, tied to the end of an old wooden gutter; each notch represents a wart, he said, and as the water rushes over the notches, it gradually dissolves away the warts.

Other hillfolk say that it is best to use an elderberry stick, and to cut the notch carefully so that it just fits over the wart to be cured. Then bury the stick on the north side of the cabin and never mention it to a living soul.

A prominent Arkansas lawyer tells me that in his boyhood the essential thing was to cut big notches in a stranger's apple tree with a stolen knife, one notch for each wart to be removed. This was quite an undertaking, for knives were highly prized and hence difficult to steal. Even more serious was the fact that the people in the neighborhood were all acquainted, so that a boy had to travel a considerable distance before he could find a stranger's apple tree.

Some hillfolk say you can remove warts simply by spitting on a hot stovelid—one expectoration for each wart. Another method favored in some quarters is to get up exactly at midnight and make faces at yourself in a mirror; if you do this on three successive nights your warts will disappear within a fortnight. Dr. W. O. Cralle was told in Taney county, Missouri, that the best way to cure warts is to smother a mole and hold the dead animal above your head for a moment.

I know several healers in McDonald county, Missouri, who pretend to do the job by letting a big grasshopper or katydid bite the wart. They just hold the critter's head up to the wart, and he'll bite it all right. It is painful for the moment, but they tell me that the wart soon dries up and falls away.

A group of old-timers in Phelps county, Missouri, contend

that the best way to dispose of warts is to carry a black cat, freshly killed, into a graveyard at night. Some say that the dead cat must be placed on the grave of a person buried the same day, and if this person has led a wicked life, so much the better.

Or one may kill a toad, rub its intestines on the wart, then bury the entrails under a stone. All this must be kept secret, otherwise it won't work. The boy who acquainted me with this method still had several large warts; when I asked why the toad's guts hadn't cured them, he explained that he had told his mother what he was doing, in order to escape punishment for killing the toad. The mother was opposed to killing toads in the dooryard; she said it was an unlucky and senseless practice and might make the cows give bloody milk.

At the funeral of a close friend, a "warty feller" is supposed to touch his warts and repeat the following jingle:

> They are ringing the funeral bell,
> What I now grasp will soon be well,
> What ill I have do take away
> Like ——— in the grave does lay.

This is believed to benefit tumors, sores, boils, and even cancers as well as warts.

There is a widespread belief that warts can be "charmed off" by touching them with the hand of a corpse. I have seen this tried several times. The warts disappeared after a while, just as they generally do under any other treatment, or with no treatment at all. On the other side of the balance, I have met an undertaker who handles many bodies every year, and both his hands are covered with warts!

Ringworms are no trouble to an old-fashioned power doctor. He just draws a life-sized picture of the ringworm in the soot on the bottom of a mush pot and burns off the picture in the presence of the patient. I was once in a cabin where this was being done, and the "doctor" himself described it to me a few minutes later, but they would not let me witness the treatment because my unbelieving gaze might somehow spoil the charm. I came back two weeks later to see the ringworm and found that it had almost disappeared.

Otto Ernest Rayburn reports a variation of this method of curing a ringworm. "Go to a tea kettle of boiling water," he writes, "rub your thumb in a circle the size of the ringworm on the inside of the lid, and then around the ringworm. Do the same with the forefinger, then with the thumb again. Do this with all the fingers on that hand, alternating each time with the thumb. When through, go away and do not look back at the tea kettle." [2]

Many healers can cure a sore or a boil by drawing a circle around it with a burnt stick, and marking a cross in the middle of it. Others do the job by sprinkling a little line of dust to form the circle and the cross. Some people charm off a corn by spitting on the forefinger of the left hand and marking a cross on the corn three times. Sometimes they mutter something as they do this, but what magic phrase they use I do not know.

A family near Noel, Missouri, has inherited an "old sayin' " which is guaranteed to cure boils, old sores, pimples, and even blood poisoning. Just cross your hands behind your back and repeat three times: "Bozz bozzer, mozz mozzer, kozz kozzer!" The old woman who told me this said that originally her kinfolk knew what the words meant, and they were supposed to be Dutch. But somewhere along the line, an ancestor of hers got the idea that the meaning must be kept secret, and therefore died without revealing it. "And now," said the old woman, "there aint nobody livin' that knows, 'less'n it would be in one o' them Dutch countries across the water!"

The best way to cure a bunion is to rub it three times with a stone and repeat: "Bunion, bunion, if you be one, leave my foot and take to this stone." Then bury the stone in the dust of a

[2] *Ozark Country*, p. 259.

main-traveled road, not too deep. As soon as the dust is washed away by rain, or blown away by wind, or worn away by traffic, so that the stone is fully exposed, your bunion will disappear. An old man at Harrison, Arkansas, told me that this might work, all right, but that he had cured his own bunions simply but turning his shoes upside down every night.

For a pain in the side, pick up a flat rock, spit under it, and put the rock back exactly where you found it. Some say you must walk away without looking back; if you ever see that rock again and recognize it, the sideache will return.

A persistent headache may be "conjured off" by putting a lock of one's hair under a stone and not mentioning either the hair or the treatment for seven days. I met a witch doctor in Little Rock, Arkansas, who cured headaches and eyestrain simply by writing MOTTER FOTTER on a piece of paper and letting the patient burn the paper in the presence of three witnesses. For a "misery in the back" a friend of mine just waits till he hears the first whippoorwill call in the evening, then lies down on the ground and rolls over three times. To remove a "j'int felon" one goes out on a cold night, draws a deep breath, and runs seven times round the house without exhaling. It's a good trick if you can do it.

I have been told that a bath in a flowing stream before daybreak on Easter morning will relieve the most stubborn case of rheumatism, but none of my neighbors have ever tried this remedy, so far as I can find out.

To cure malaria, chills, fever, and ague all you need is a hickory peg about a foot long. Drive it into the ground in some secluded place, where you can visit it unseen. Do not tell anyone about this business. Go there every day, pull up the peg, blow seven times into the hole, and replace the peg. After you have done this for twelve successive days, drive the peg deep into the earth so that it cannot be seen, and leave it there. You'll have no more chills and fever that season. If the cure doesn't work, it means that you have been seen blowing into the hole, or that you have inadvertently mentioned it to somebody.

Here is another way to cure chills: take a piece of silk thread, tie a knot for each chill that the patient has had, and bury the string under the drip from the roof of a barn. This must be done secretly, and the healer must not be a blood relative of the patient, or of the same sex. If the patient has another chill after the string is buried, somebody must dig it up and tie another knot. Some healers make a great show of using a silk string for infants but claim that a piece of woolen yarn is better for grown-ups. Others tie the knotted string around a persimmon tree, instead of burying it.

"Tying off chills" was still practiced in Christian county, Missouri, as late as 1934. You take a string and measure the patient's girth at the chest, then go into the woods alone, never looking back, and find a tree of exactly the same measurement. First tying one knot in the string for each chill that the patient has had, you fasten the string about the tree at the height of the patient's chest. Do not look back at the string after it is tied around the tree, and do not tell anybody about the matter until you are sure that the patient has fully recovered.

If a child does not grow fast enough, back him up against a tree and cut a notch in the bark, on a level with the top of his head. Put some of the child's hair in the notch. On two occasions I have seen this tried, and one of the children *did* appear to grow very rapidly thereafter.

Three drops of cat's blood, in a jigger of whiskey, is said to cure malarial fever quite as well as any of this complicated tree magic, but the patient mustn't know that there's anything unusual in the whiskey, or it won't work. Mrs. May Kennedy McCord, of Springfield, Missouri, says that some people gather dirt from the nest of a mockingbird that is setting on three eggs —no more, no less. They dissolve this dirt in lukewarm water for a gargle, which is supposed to relieve any sort of throat trouble.

To cure asthma, bore a hole in a black-oak tree, at the height of the patient's head. Drive a little wooden peg into the hole, so as to hold a lock of his hair. Cut the hair and peg off flush with the trunk. When the bark grows over the hole so that the peg is no longer visible, and the patient's hair grows out to replace the missing lock, the asthma will be gone forever.

Otto Ernest Rayburn reports a case in which asthma was cured by tying a live frog on the patient's throat. The frog "completely absorbed the disease" and was left in position until it died.[3] Rayburn says also that some hillfolk treat asthma by killing a steer, cutting it open and thrusting the patient's bare feet into the warm body cavity, and keeping them there until the entrails cool.

What the hillman calls "sun pain" is a terrible headache which lasts all day but doesn't keep the patient awake at night. It must be some sort of sinus trouble, which is relieved in the prone position. Sometimes the pain persists for many days and is so severe that the country M.D.'s, usually conservative in prescribing narcotics, administer large doses of morphine or codein. Mrs. Coral Almy Wilson, of Zinc, Arkansas, tells me that people in her neighborhood treat sun pain by bathing their heads in a stream which flows toward the east. The old-timers used to stir up a certain kind of fungi or green mold and "breathe the stink" in nine deep inhalations, on nine successive days; this was supposed to relieve head catarrh, which we call sinusitis nowadays.

The body of a buzzard is somehow used to treat cancer, but this must be done secretly, for the killing of a buzzard means seven years of crop failure for the whole countryside, and the man who shoots one of these birds is naturally unpopular. Dr. Oakley St. John, of Pineville, Missouri, tells me that a farmer who killed a buzzard some years ago, to treat his daughter's cancer, so enraged his neighbors that they threatened him with bodily harm, and several people came into town to see if he could not be punished by the county officers.

[3] *Ozark Country*, p. 258.

I have copied the following *literatim* from an old letter, dated 1869, belonging to Miss Jewell Perriman, Jenkins, Missouri.

A RESEPT TO CURE CANCERS

Git up soon and dont speak tell you git to a bush and ef hit is a post oak or aney othor kinde of oak you must say Good morning Mr post oak and then say Good morning Sir then say I have came to git you to cure a cancer on my ——. And take your rite hand and brake off a lim and then turn your back to the bush and thro the lim over your left sholder and don't look back. . . . And you must go before sun up and not speak tell you git to the bush.

Any posthumous child can cure the croup simply by blowing in the patient's mouth; one of my neighbors happened to be born several weeks after his father's death, and although he ridicules the healing power himself, he is frequently called out of his bed at night by distracted parents who want him to save their children. The same treatment is used for sore mouth in babies, a white, cotton-like eruption which is called thrash or thresh.

In certain backwoods settlements in Arkansas it is believed that all one need do to cure thrash is to have a preacher blow in the child's mouth. A preacher I know tells me he has done this hundreds of times, although he has little faith in the remedy. "They git well, all right," he said, "but I can't see as they git well any quicker'n them which I *don't* blow in their mouth. But there aint no harm in it, an' I aim to 'commodate folks whenever I can."

Some power doctors cure thrash without blowing into the child's mouth; they even profess to do it at a great distance, by mail or over the telephone. But it appears that the healer always wants to know the child's full name. In one case the baby's name had not been fully decided upon, but the man would do nothing about the thrash until the baby's parents had agreed about the name. A granny-woman of my acquaintance must have not only the full name but also the date of the child's birth; she goes outdoors and repeats the magic words three mornings in succession, before sunup, and the thrash is gone. She would not tell me the formula, but said that it had nothing to do with the Bible, and that God was not mentioned in it.

Dr. W. O. Cralle tells of a woman at Theodosia, Missouri, who treated thrash by holding the child extended in her arms while she repeated: "In the name of the Father, the Son and the Holy Ghost, I command you to leave this child's mouth and enter the mouth of some dumb beast!"

An old woman in Washington county, Arkansas, told me that all these spells and charms are "just ignorant foolishment," adding that she had reared eleven children and never had any difficulty in keepin' 'em clear o' thresh. "An' no monkey business, neither. All I ever done was to make 'em drink rain water out of an old shoe. The only thing is, you got to make *sure* that the shoe aint never been wore by any o' the baby's kinfolks."

A granny-woman in the Cookson Hill country of eastern Oklahoma treated thrash simply by putting crushed green oak leaves in the child's mouth every three hours, and the babes in her charge recovered about as quickly as those submitted to supernatural spells. If no green leaves were handy, she used sage tea, with some honey and a little alum in it, which seemed to work about as well as the oak leaves.

There is no excuse for a properly reared mountain baby ever having thrash anyhow, since it can be prevented by carrying the newborn babe to a small hole in the wall or chinking and allowing the sunlight which streams through to enter the child's mouth.

A woman at Noel, Missouri, told me that an old charm to kill intestinal worms had been passed down in her family for at least three generations. All you have to do is look the patient in the eye, cross your fingers behind your back and say:

> God's mother Mary walked the land,
> She held three worms all in her hand,
> One white, one black, an' t'other'n red,
> For Jesus' sake the worms are dead!

Trachoma is very common in the Ozark country, and there are many superstitions about sore eyes, granulated lids, and other "eye troubles." The tail of a black cat, drawn across the eye every day, is the prime remedy for granulated eyelids; some healers even claim to have cured cataract with this simple remedy, reinforced by a few "old sayin's." In treating what is known as a sty, it is necessary to cut the end of the cat's tail a bit and apply a few drops of the blood to the sty itself, repeating this performance daily until relief is obtained. Another method is for the sufferer to go alone to a crossroads, exactly at midnight in the dark of the moon, and cry:

> Sty, sty, leave my eye,
> Go to the next feller passin' by!

Certain minor eye troubles are treated with a weed called eyebright, but I have not been able to learn just how this plant is used. If a baby's eyes are sore, the mother's milk is regarded as the best possible lotion. Sassafras tea, not too strong, is also regarded as a good eye wash. Young girls often rub sweet cream into their eyes, but I am not sure if this is a medicine or a cosmetic.

The hillfolk try to avoid looking directly at a person who has sore eyes, fearing that their own eyes may be affected. They do not realize that trachoma is infectious, however, and use towels, wash basins, and the like without any fear of contracting the disease. I have heard a highschool teacher insist that girls with "pinkeye" should wear colored glasses, not for the sake of their own eyes, but to keep other students from catching the disease. When the schools at Blue Eye, Missouri, were closed because of an epidemic of pinkeye the fact was mentioned by newspapers all over the country. The citizens of Blue Eye were not pleased, since they think pinkeye is caused by uncleanliness.

A girl from Cape Fair, Missouri, once told me that a woman can peel or cut up raw onions without making her eyes smart, simply by holding a needle in her mouth while she does the job. And in other backwoods towns I have heard that a needle in the mouth is generally believed to be good for sore or watery eyes, no matter what the cause of the irritation. Akin to this perhaps is the idea that an object held in the mouth somehow affects the inner ear and the organs of equilibrium. A sober and educated woman, the wife of a preacher in Yell county, Arkansas, told me that she could never walk a certain difficult footlog until some "peckerwood gals" showed her how. "All you have to do," she told me, "is to hold a little stick crosswise in your mouth!"

I have known old people who went to a great deal of trouble to obtain pieces of hornets' nests, which they used to wipe their spectacles. Not only does this stuff clean the lenses better than the finest cloth or paper, they say, but it is somehow good for sore and tired eyes.

Many backwoods people believe that a man with weak eyes should always grow a mustache, as hair on the upper lip strengthens the eyes. One man told me that when one of his eyes was injured, the pain in his upper lip was worse than that in the eye itself, so that it was quite impossible for him to shave the upper lip for several weeks.

Wearing a green ring is good for people who have weak or defective eyesight. I once met a blind street singer in Little Rock, Arkansas, who wore two rings with large green stones in them. Asked if he expected these rings to restore his sight, he said "No, but I got the damn' things before I went blind, figgerin' they might strengthen my eyes. It didn't do me no good, but I got 'em, so I might as well wear 'em."

Piercing the ears is supposed to prevent or cure certain types of eye disease. Even little boys' ears are sometimes pierced for this reason, although I have never seen an Ozark boy wearing earrings. It is said that the child who can spit on a lightning bug in full flight will enjoy good vision all his life.

When a foreign body gets into the eye, just press a big white button against the eyelid and wink repeatedly; the object which is causing the trouble will pass out through one of the holes in the button. Near Day, Missouri, a small boy got some sawdust in his eye. A friend cut a small pearl button off his shirt, washed it carefully, and somehow placed it *under* the boy's eyelid. I was told that the poor chap walked about for several minutes, with the big bulge in his eyelid plainly visible. It must have been terribly painful, but he stuck with it until the tears washed the sawdust away.

I have heard some talk in Searcy county, Arkansas, of an eye-stone. This thing is said to work like a madstone, except that it is very small, no larger than a BB shot. One man told me that he had seen several of these eyestones, and that they looked like opals. You just wet the stone and slip it under the eyelid; in a few minutes it is supposed to draw any foreign substance out of the eye.

The madstone treatment for rabies was once popular in many parts of the United States and is still well known in the Ozarks. The madstones I have seen are porous and resemble some sort of volcanic ash, but the natives all claim that they were taken from the entrails of deer. These stones are rare now, and they are handed down from father to son, never sold. No charge is made for using the stone, although the patient may make the owner a present if he likes. I have never seen the madstone in actual use, but they tell me that if the dog was really mad the stone sticks fast to the wound and draws the "pizen" out. After awhile the stone falls off, and is placed in a vessel of warm milk, which immediately turns green. The stone is then applied to the wound again, and so on until it no longer imparts a green color to the fresh milk. Virtually every old-time hillman believes that if the madstone is applied soon enough and sticks properly, the patient will never suffer from rabies, even if the dog was mad.

J. J. Hibler, veteran real-estate dealer in Springfield, Missouri, kept a madstone in his office for many years; it was famous in the nineties, and people came from all over southwest Missouri to use it.

Homer Davis, of Monett, Missouri, used to have a madstone, shaped like a half-moon. The old-timers say that it was always dipped in hot milk before applying it to a wound. It was a porous stone, said to have been taken from the stomach of an albino deer more than seventy-five years ago.

Many old people allege that the madstone in a deer is always found in the stomach, while others place it in the intestines or the bladder, or in the udder of a doe, or even "betwixt the windpipe and the lights." Uncle Lum Booth, of Taney county, Missouri, who had given the matter considerable thought, said that so long as the deer was *white* it made no difference in what part of the body the stone appeared.

Even in Kansas City, Missouri, madstones were still in use as late as 1931, according to the Kansas City *Journal-Post*, Aug. 4, 1935. A stone belonging to Mr. Noel E. Jackson, aged pioneer, is said to have been brought from Scotland in the early days by a man named Bates. It looks like whitish limestone, about an inch and a half long, with a sort of honeycomb structure; it has the appearance of a fossil, though Mr. Jackson thinks it came from the stomach of a deer. He says he has seen this stone used hundreds of times and has never known it to fail. He has never charged a cent for the use of it. In 1931 Mr. S. T. Dailey of Strasburg, Missouri, was bitten by a rabid mule. The stone adhered to Dailey's wound for nine hours. Jackson says the stone is often applied to the same patient several times. In the case of a little girl from Independence, Missouri, it stuck for fifty-five minutes and then fell off. Jackson cleaned the thing in sweet milk, dried it carefully, and two days later he applied it again. This second time the stone adhered for thirty-five minutes. Several days later it was tried again, but failed to stick at all, which the neighbors regarded as evidence that the child was safe from rabies.

Miss Naomi Clarke, of Winslow, Arkansas, writes me that madstones are applied to the bites of poisonous snakes as well as dog bites in her neighborhood. I have seen nothing of this

myself and have so far been unable to learn anything definite
about it.

"A hair of the dog that bit you," in the Ozarks, does not
mean simply a morning shot of whiskey to repair a hangover.
People actually do swallow hair from a dog that has bitten
them. I once knew a man who was in some doubt as to which of
two dogs had bitten his little girl; finally he killed both of the
animals, and forced the child to eat a few hairs from each dog's
tail. This man would not admit that he believed such a procedure would prevent rabies. He said that the dogs ought to
be killed anyhow, and that the business of swallowing the hairs
was a very old custom, and there *might* be something in it.

The idea that rabies is especially prevalent during the "dog
days" of late summer, under the influence of Sirius the dog star,
is pretty well exploded in most sections of the United States.
But it is still widely accepted in the Ozarks, and I am told that
some towns, in both Missouri and Arkansas, have passed ordi-
nances forcing the citizens to confine their dogs at this season.
Many hillfolk believe that it is dangerous to go swimming in
"dog days," especially if one has cuts or open wounds in the
skin, since the water is poisonous and may produce an infection
akin to rabies. A lot of intelligent people in Sebastian county,
Arkansas, are convinced that the green scum which appears on
ponds in summer has something to do with rabies. "I know the
doctors don't believe it," an old farmer told me, "but the doctors aint *always* right."

Some woodcutters who live on Sugar Creek, in Benton county,
Arkansas, believe that a mad dog never bites a man who carries
a piece of dogwood in his pocket, according to an old gentleman
I met in Bentonville. "The folks up that way are all damn' fools,
though," he added thoughtfully, "an' maybe there aint nothing
to it." Another Benton county man told me that sensible people are seldom bitten by rabid dogs anyhow. "If you just hold
your breath," said he, "a dog caint bite you, whether he's mad
or not."

To stop a toothache, one has only to walk into the woods with a friend of the opposite sex, not a blood relation. Stand up against the biggest ironwood tree you can find, while your friend drives a little wooden peg into the tree at the exact height of the aching tooth. I have seen many of these "toothache pegs," and when I pulled one out invariably found some brown gummy substance in the hole. But people who do this trick tell me that the peg is perfectly clean when it is driven into the tree. To check this matter I drove some pegs into an ironwood tree myself, without any toothache or magical mumbo jumbo; I pulled these out later, at intervals varying from a few weeks to a year, but never found any gummy stuff on *my* pegs. There may be more to this toothache-peg business than I have been told, but I am setting down such information as I have, for the sake of the record.

Another way to cure toothache is to find the skeleton of a horse or mule. Be sure that nobody is watching you. Pick up the jawbone with your teeth and walk backward nine steps, being careful not to touch the thing with your hands, and then let it fall to the ground. This done, walk away without looking back, and do not mention the matter to anybody. If the pain doesn't stop within thirty minutes or so, it means that somebody *did* see you with the mule's jaw in your mouth. In that case, the only thing you can do is to hunt up another skeleton and go through the whole business again.

A man in McDonald county, Missouri, showed me a big tooth fastened to a leathern string, hanging over the fireplace. "That there," he said solemnly, "is the blind tooth of a big boar hog. Whenever one o' the childern gits the toothache, I make 'em wear that tooth round their neck till the ache's plumb gone." The blind tooth, I found out later, is the hindmost upper molar, but why this particular tooth is required for a cure I do not know. A boar's tusk, which is the canine or eye-tooth, carried in the pocket is said to relieve toothache. If the aching tooth is on the right side, carry the tusk in the right-hand pocket; if on the left, carry it in the left-hand pocket. The tusk treatment serves a double purpose, since the carrying of a boar's tusk is also believed to protect the carrier against venereal disease.

Some people believe that a man who always puts his left shoe on first will never have a toothache; it appears that most men put on the right shoe before the left. I know several families who always keep a supply of toothpicks made from a lightnin'-struck tree; the use of these splinters is believed to stop the teeth from aching, and prevent decay. The hillfolk sometimes deaden an aching tooth by filling the cavity with gunpowder—they say it's very painful for a minute or so, and then the tooth feels fine for several hours. Aunt Mary Johnson, of Theodosia, Missouri, is quoted as saying that the best plug for a holler tooth is a bit of wax from the patient's ear. Another method of treating toothache is to tie knots in a string, one knot for every tooth which *doesn't* ache. If all else fails, the tooth is extracted, either by a regular dentist or an old-time "tooth jumper" who does the job with a specially made punch and mallet.

Some say that it is good luck to place one of your own teeth under your pillow at night—this is supposed to prevent further dental decay. But to lose such a tooth, or have it fall into the hands of an unfriendly person, may bring disaster to the whole family.

To make teething easier, backwoods babies often wear necklaces of elder twigs, cut into short sections and dyed brown; a woman told me that the twigs were brown because they had been boiled in possum grease, but it looked more like walnut stain to me. A silver coin hung round the child's neck is said to help in cutting teeth. Some people think that a string of dried berries is better for teething babies, and that a necklace made of Job's-tears is best of all. Job's-tears are the seeds of *Coix lachryma* and used to be sold in country drugstores.

In some parts of Arkansas, when a babe has a hard time in cutting its teeth, they kill a rabbit and rub the fresh brains on the child's gums. Another way to make teeth come easier is to give the child a mole's foot to play with. The old tradition is that it should be the left hind foot, but the big fleshy front paws are the only ones I have actually seen given to babies. I have heard hillfolk say that the best thing for a teething baby is to put butterfly eggs on its throat, but am not sure that this is meant to be taken literally.

Parents sometimes collect a child's milk teeth as they are shed and bury each one separately under a stone; they believe that this will prevent dental decay in later life. "Whatever you do," an old woman told me, "don't *never* leave a child's baby tooth lay around where the hogs can git at it. If a hog swallers one o' them teeth, a great big *tush* will grow in its place!" When a child's tooth is extracted, he is told that a fine new gold tooth will replace it within a week, provided that he refrains in the meantime from probing the cavity with his tongue.

A bright new dime, placed inside the upper lip in front of the teeth, will often cure bleeding gums or even stop nosebleed. People in Stone county, Missouri, use a folded bit of brown paper instead of the coin. A white bone button, held in the mouth, is recommended for any pain above the tongue, especially headaches and earaches.

Some mountain folk cure the earache, it is said, by putting a brass button in the patient's mouth and then unexpectedly discharging a gun behind his back. There are several more or less funny stories about this treatment, one in particular about a boy who swallowed the button when the gun went off. The earache was cured, but he had a terrible pain in his throat. Later on he complained of cramps in the stomach and was dosed with May-apple root, which is a drastic purgative. Still later came a severe pain in the bowels, and finally he screamed with agony as the big button was discharged from the rectum. The boy sighed with relief for a moment, just after the button was expelled. Then he sprang to his feet and howled again—the earache was just as bad as ever.

Another common treatment for earache is to prick a betsey

bug with a pin and put a drop of its blood into the ear. There
seem to be several species of insects called betsey bugs or bessy
bugs; one is a big black beetle, nearly two inches long, found in
old stumps and rotten wood. People subject to earache sometimes keep several of these betsey bugs alive in a glass jar, to
be used as needed.

Some families are accustomed to treat chills-an'-fever by
placing an ax under the patient's bed. Since this procedure is
also used in "granny-cases" to relieve the pains of childbirth,
there are many jokes and wisecracks about it. I once went to
see a very fat man, who had malarial fever. He stayed in bed
as the doctor ordered and took the doctor's medicine, but his
wife held to the old superstition and insisted on putting an ax
under the bed. I noticed this when I came into the room, and
asked: "What's that ax doing there? You expecting burglars?"
He laughed and clasped both hands over his great paunch, twisting his face in a ghastly imitation of a woman in labor. "Naw,"
he answered, "just expectin'!"

Many people think it is a good idea to burn feathers from a
black hen under the bed of a fever patient. I have seen the
feathers of black chickens dried and saved in little paper bags
for this purpose. For night sweats some hillfolk put a pan of
water under the bed; I have known the wife of an M.D. to do this
in her own home, without the doctor's knowledge. May Stafford
Hilburn says that "if the case was persistent we sprinkled black
pepper in the water. Usually in three nights an improvement
could be noticed, but in some cases it might take a week. This
remedy seldom failed. In fact, I do not know of a case where
it did fail." [4]

Most Ozarkers are much afraid of the painful disease called
shingles, since it is commonly believed if the inflamed area ever
completely encircles the body, the patient will die. Regular
physicians say that this never happens, since shingles always
follows certain nerve sheaths, which do not quite come together

[4] *Missouri Magazine* (September, 1933), p. 21.

in front. The old-timers insist that they have *seen* men die of the shingles, and they continue to fear this ailment above many more serious diseases. A lawyer in Joplin, Missouri, tells of being awakened in the middle of the night and induced to drive forty miles into the country to make a will for a dying man. When he got there he found that his client had shingles, and since the red spots came near meeting in front, the poor fellow was convinced that he had only a few hours to live.

A power doctor near Fayetteville, Arkansas, says that in order to cure shingles one has only to cut off the head of a black chicken and smear the blood thickly over the affected parts. Wrap the patient in sheets and let the whole mess dry. Next morning you just soak the wrappings off, and the shingles will be gone.

Miss Jewell Perriman, of Jenkins, Missouri, reports that in her neighborhood a black cat is sacrificed to treat shingles. She knew a man whose shingles had "nearly gone around" him, but the power doctors cured him by killing a black cat and applying the blood.

In some places one finds people who believe that the blood of black birds or animals has some special virtue as a treatment for any sort of skin eruption. Only a few miles from the city of Hot Springs, Arkansas, two young girls stole a black dog and killed it, in order to use the blood as a remedy for smallpox; they believed that by smearing their faces with the dog's blood they could avoid being pitted or scarred by the disease.

At many points in Missouri and Arkansas country folk treat chickenpox by bringing a black hen and chickens into the sickroom and making them walk over the patient's body as he lies in bed. Near Bentonville, Arkansas, I knew a woman who brought a black rooster into her house and placed it again and again upon the bed where a little boy lay sick with chickenpox. I asked a local M.D. what he thought of this tre .tment. "Well, it can't do any harm," he said, "the bed was dirty anyhow." There are several funny stories about the black-chicken-on-the-bed

business, and it may be supposed to accomplish something beyond the cure of chickenpox.

Mrs. C. P. Mahnkey, of Mincy, Missouri, tells me that one of
her neighbors treated a goiter by baking a toad in the oven till
the oil ran out of it and putting a little of this toad oil on the
goiter every day. It got better, too, says Mrs. Mahnkey. Another goiter treatment is to wear a little packet of salt on a
string round the neck. The salt is renewed every day, and the
used salt buried in the ground each night. Some people believe
that the only way to cure a goiter is to rub it with a dead
man's hand. A small-town undertaker tells me that an old woman
in the neighborhood is always coming to his place, wanting to
try this. A goiter is said to be reduced by applying the two
halves of an apple, after which the patient eats one half and
buries the other half in a cemetery. Some old-timers contend
that the part buried must be put into the coffin of a friend of
the opposite sex, with whom the patient had been intimate.

It is said that a tongue-tied child may be cured by making
him drink rain water out of a new bell. I know of several families
who actually tried this, but without any benefit so far as I can
see.

Grease from the mountings of a church bell, put into the ears
at intervals, is believed to cure deafness. In answer to my question, two old ladies told me plainly that the grease from a school
bell would *not* do. Well, I persisted, what about the Fair Grove
bell? Everybody knows that Fair Grove is a schoolhouse on
weekdays, and a church house on Sundays, and they have
only one bell. This disturbed the old folks for a moment, but
then they answered that the bell at Fair Grove was a school
bell, and the "meetin'ers" used it on Sundays only because
they *didn't have no church bell.* It served the purpose of calling
the worshipers together, but it was not a church bell, and grease
from its mountings would *not* cure deafness.

The best way to stop hiccoughs is to run around the house

seven times without drawing one's breath. Or you can just stand on one leg and cry "Hick-up, stick-up, lick-up, hick-up" three times without pausing for breath. Some healers claim to cure hiccoughs by rubbing a rabbit's foot on the back of the patient's neck—unexpectedly. If all else fails, just stick your fingers in your ears, and have a person of the opposite sex pour nine cups of rain water down your throat.

As recently as 1942, in a modern hospital at Springfield, Missouri, a patient insist_d upon treating his hiccoughs by naming three grains of corn for three friends, and then putting the corn into a vessel of water which was to be suspended above his head.

A woman in Greene county, Missouri, used to tell her family that, in the early 1880's, she saw a child "ground in the hopper" to cure some sort of paralysis. The whole family went to a primitive neighborhood grist mill, and the miller placed the sick girl in some part of the machinery. The thing spun round and round, and when the little patient was lifted out and placed upon the floor, she became dizzy and vomited. The others stood and watched in silence. There were no comments and no questions. It was a solemn occasion. The miller took it all quite seriously too and had evidently been called upon for the same service before.

Mrs. May Kennedy McCord, of Springfield, Missouri, tells of a novel treatment for colic in infants. You just take nine honeybees, alive in a tin can, and roast them in a hot oven. When the bees are absolutely dry, grind them up into a fine powder and feed it to the baby in syrup. Mrs. McCord learned of this "cure" from Mrs. George Roebuck, of Morrisville, Missouri, and Mrs. Roebuck had it from some elderly people in the Boston range of the Arkansas Ozarks.

Another way of curing colic is for the mother to hold the baby upright, walk three steps backward without speaking, and then give the child a drink of water from a brass thimble. If the child has convulsions or "spasms," they may be relieved temporarily at least by wiping the child's face with a greasy dishrag.

Fred Starr, of Greenland, Arkansas, has a sure cure for leg cramps, learned from a granny-woman in Washington county, Arkansas. All you have to do, he says, is to stick the toe of one shoe inside the other when you go to bed, and leave 'em that way all night. An old gentleman who lives in Hickory county, Missouri, tells me that he wards off cramps and leg pains by carrying a dried puffball in his pocket.

To relieve neuralgia or neuritis, especially if the pain is in the back or the legs, one has only to walk around the room three times every morning, without a stitch on but the left sock and shoe. A lady in Little Rock, Arkansas, told me that this had been known in her family for at least four generations and was taken very seriously by the older people.

There are several very strange notions about venereal disease in the hill country. Nearly all of the old-timers are convinced that gonorrhea and syphilis are simply two different stages of the same ailment, and that gonorrhea will invariably turn into syphilis if not properly treated. It is generally believed that all prostitutes are diseased, and that any woman who has sexual intercourse with seven different men will acquire a "bad sickness," even though all the men are free from venereal infection. Many country folk believe that venereal disease is much less likely to be contracted when the moon is in its last quarter than at any other time. Some hill people think that the best way to cure a "dose" of syphilis or gonorrhea is by communicating it to as many other persons as possible—a theory that is responsible for untold misery in the Ozark country.

Every old woman has heard that owls' eggs are a sure cure for alcoholism. Owls lay their eggs in March, and it is said that many Ozark children are kept out of school and sent by their mothers to search for owls' nests in the tall timber. Many a hillman has been fed owls' eggs, scrambled or disguised in one way and another, without knowing what he was eating.

Another way of curing drunkards is to put a live minnow in whiskey and let it die there. The poor chap who drinks this contaminated whiskey doesn't notice anything wrong with the taste, but it is supposed to destroy his appetite for liquor.

It is said that some Ozark temperance workers have advocated placing a pawpaw in the hand of a dying person; if a drunkard, not knowing of the "cunjure," can be persuaded to eat this pawpaw, he will quit drinking in spite of himself. My wife and I knew an old woman who, when the doctor told her she was dying, called for a pawpaw. She held the fruit for a moment, then asked that it be fed to her youngest son after her death. This was done, but the boy was still a booze fighter the last I heard of him.

The hill people have singular notions of the best means of preventing disease, and many of them carry charms or amulets of one sort or another. A prostitute in Little Rock, Arkansas, always wore two or three turns of fine wire around her leg; she said this was a protection against venereal disease. I observed, however, that she also used the conventional prophylactic measures favored by the girls who do not wear wires round their ankles.

Dr. Hershel Shockey, an osteopath who practiced in Stone county, Missouri, during the Second World War, told me that he saw a young man with some rare skin disease brought into an osteopathic clinic in Kansas City. This patient was a hillbilly from southwest Missouri. Told to strip, he took off everything but a piece of copper wire wound about his arm. Jokingly one of the physicians tried to remove this wire, but the patient wouldn't have it—offered to fight the whole hospital staff rather than take off that little twist of wire.

A copper ring, or a piece of sheet copper carried next the skin, is believed to ward off attacks of rheumatism as well as venereal infection. I have seen old men in Arkansas with long pieces of copper wire wound round their ankles, under their socks. In the early days it is said that the telegraph companies had considerable difficulty with hillfolk who cut off pieces of telegraph wire for this purpose. Some young people now contend that an ordinary brass finger ring works just as well as pure copper, but the old-timers still cling to their wire anklets.

Nails taken from a gallows are supposed to protect a man against venereal disease and death by violence. Country blacksmiths used to secure these nails and hammer them out into finger rings. As recently as 1943 there were boys in the Army wearing rings of metal taken from a gallows at Galena, Missouri, where "Red" Jackson was hanged for murder in 1936.

I have known hillmen to spend hours and even days searching the rivers for very large crawpappies in order to get the two circular lucky-bones found in their bodies. These are carried in the pockets to ward off syphilis. The bigger the bones the better, and really large lucky-bones are rare.

Some mountain men wear wide leather cartridge belts, not to carry cartridges in, but because they believe that the wearing of such belts prevents rheumatism and arthritis. One school contends that a potato carried on the person keeps off rheumatism as well as anything. Others think that a buzzard's feather is best of all, a belief attributed to the Cherokees; an old woman near Southwest City, Missouri, painfully bent and twisted by rheumatism, assured me that the black feather she always wore in her hair "had done more good than twenty year o' doctorin'!" A man in Washington county, Arkansas, credited his freedom from rheumatiz and neuralgy to a nutmeg which he carried for many years; he had induced a jeweler to drill a hole through the thing and wore it on a black shoestring round his neck. "In central Missouri," says Fanny D. Bergen, "rheumatism is prevented by carrying in the pocket a nutmeg or a walnut, *Juglans nigra*." [5] I have inquired about this, but have never found an Ozarker who used a black walnut as a pocket piece.

[5] *Journal of American Folklore*, V (1892), 20.

Many Ozark hillmen carry buckeyes in their pockets, and this practice is not confined to the backwoods districts. The two most important bankers in Springfield, Missouri, are buckeye carriers; so is the head of one of the biggest corporations in St. Louis, and also a recent mayor of Kansas City, Missouri. At least one governor of Arkansas not only carried a buckeye but was also known to flourish it publicly on occasions of great emotional stress.

There is an old saying that no man was ever found dead with a buckeye in his pocket, but this is not to be taken seriously. Most people who carry buckeyes regard them as a protection against rheumatism, or hemorrhoids. One of the most successful physicians in southwest Missouri always carries a buckeye; when it was mislaid once he was very much disturbed and let an officeful of patients wait until his pocket piece was recovered. It is very bad luck to lose a buckeye. I asked this doctor about it once. "No, I'm not superstitious," he said grinning, "I just don't want to get the rheumatism!"

To some people the buckeye means more than mere protection from piles and rheumatism. I once saw a young fellow with a very old truck, about to attempt the crossing of Bear Creek, in Taney county, Missouri. The water was high, and the ford was very bad. The boy looked the situation over carefully, then set his jaw and climbed into the driver's seat. "Well, I've got a buckeye in my pocket," he said quite seriously. "I believe I can make it!"

There is a persistent story that the custom of carrying buckeyes came from the Osage Indians, who used them in poisoning fish. But the Osages tell me that it was the *root* of the buckeye tree, not the nut, that they used to kill fish. And I have never found an Osage who would admit that he carried a buckeye for luck.

Wearing a green penny in a sack round the neck is supposed to prevent "lung trouble"—which usually means tuberculosis. A large bullet hung at the throat wards off catarrh, but it must be an old-fashioned bullet of solid lead; the modern bullets with copper or steel jackets are worthless for this purpose. A piece of rhubarb root, worn on a string round the neck, will protect the wearer against the bellyache. It is said that a pair of crawpappy pincers sewed into a man's clothing has the same effect.

Dr. C. T. Ryland, of Lexington, Missouri, told me that he was called to see a sick infant in a family from south Missouri. The child had what was called "summer complaint," with a high temperature. Noticing a string of yellow wooden beads around the baby's neck, Dr. Ryland was told that "them's bodark, to keep fever away from the brain."

I once met a very old man on the road near Sylamore, Arkansas, wearing a string of large red glass beads. I asked five or six of his neighbors about it, and they all told me that he wore the beads as a remedy for nosebleed. "Oh yes, I reckon it works all right," said one young fellow in answer to my question, "but I'd ruther *have* nosebleed as to pack them fool beads all the time!"

Some Ozarkers believe that epileptic fits may be prevented, or at least made less violent, if the afflicted person carries a human tooth in his pocket, but the tooth must be that of a person not related to the patient by ties of blood. It is believed in some quarters that an epileptic may postpone his attacks by "packin' a flintrock," especially if he can find a lucky flint with a hole in it.

Ozark children, in many isolated sections, still wear little packets of asafetida all winter to protect them from the common diseases of childhood. When spring comes, with sassafras tea and other internal prophylactics, the child is permitted to discard the asafetida. Small boys are sometimes forced to wear little bags of camphor sewed to their shirts, to prevent their catching meningitis or infantile paralysis. Others have flat leather bands or red woolen strings round their necks, or even dirty socks under their collars to ward off colds and influenza.

A little iron wire worn as a necklace, according to some power doctors, will protect a child from whooping cough. A piece of black silk around the neck is regarded as "liable to keep off croup."

Otto Ernest Rayburn says that "in grandmother's day a mouse's head tied around the baby's neck prevented certain ills," [6] but I have never been able to learn just what these ills were, or to get any definite information about this matter. In one settlement I found the children coming to school with little round pieces of porous stone sewed into their garments; it is said that these stones are taken from the bladders of deer, and are supposed to protect the wearer against violence and financial loss as well as diseases.

Many backwoods women wear red yarn strings about their abdomens. Some say that this is in order to prevent cramps. I am not sure that this is the true explanation, but it is a fact that red woolen strings are worn, particularly by young unmarried women.

Some say that the dried skin of a mole, stuck fast to the chest with honey, will prevent or even cure asthma. I once persuaded one of my neighbors to try this, but it didn't seem to do him any good. Women sometimes wear a mole skin, or the dried foot of a mole, between their breasts in the belief that it prevents cancer.

The best way to avoid getting the mumps is to cut a chip off an old hog trough, carry it in your pocket, and rub it over your jaws and throat every day. The adult male Ozarker is afraid of mumps, because he fears that the disease may "go down" on him and damage his testicles. Some men think they can prevent this calamity by smearing the parts with marrow from a hog's jaw. Other hillmen wear a little sack of salt, tied around the waist with a string. A country lawyer told me, in all seriousness, "I never knew a man who carried salt to have the mumps go down on him. Probably it's just a coincidence, but just the

[6] *Ozark Country*, pp. 253–254.

same—" he unbuckled his belt, pulled up his shirt, and showed me the little package fastened around his middle with a neat cotton band. It is said that when a hillman actually *gets* the mumps he may still prevent the disease from "going down" by soaking a woolen string with hog manure and tying it round his neck. But a man in Siloam Springs, Arkansas, tells me that he gave this measure a fair trial, and "there aint nothin' to it."

In some parts of eastern Oklahoma, when a man comes to the place where a horse has just been rolling on the ground, he spits —this is supposed to ward off backache or lumbago. I knew a farmer near Harrison, Arkansas, who was careful to spit in the road whenever he saw a big woolly worm or caterpillar; he said that failure to do this always caused him to have a chill within twenty-four hours. Mrs. May Kennedy McCord, of Springfield, Missouri, used to say "kiss a mule, cure a cold," but I'm not certain that she meant it to be taken literally.

A big red onion tied to a bedpost is said to prevent the occupants of the bed from catching cold. A famous politician in Arkansas had an onion fastened to his bedpost as recently as 1937. When I asked him about this he laughed rather sheepishly. "That's just one of Maw's notions," he said, referring to his mother-in-law. "She lives with us, and she's getting old, and we try to humor her. Of course, I don't believe in such things myself."

One often hears hillfolk say that wearing a piece of dog fennel in the left shoe will prevent the wood ticks from biting your legs.

A great many Ozarkers believe that a live minnow swallowed by a baby will prevent it from ever having the whooping cough. Miss Jewell Perriman, Jenkins, Missouri, tells me that this is not a superstition but a well-known fact, and she has seen it demonstrated several times. Other hillfolk think that it isn't necessary for the child to swallow the minnow; they just put it inside the infant's mouth and pull it out again by a string attached for that purpose. Once, in Washington county, Arkansas, I saw a power doctor put a live minnow into a baby's mouth; his purpose in doing this was not made clear to me, but the child did not catch whooping cough. It died about four months later from some other ailment, which the parents diagnosed as "summer complaint."

Most backwoods healers believe that night air is poisonous and advise their patients to shut every door and window tight, although a large family sleeps in a small cabin. If it were not for the chinks in their clumsily built shanties, and the draught of their great chimneys, some of these folk might easily be suffocated. Many old-timers are convinced that malaria is somehow caused by stagnant water, but nearly all of them laugh at the idea that mosquitoes have anything to do with it.

It is generally believed that chills are caused by eating watermelons or muskmelons or cucumbers too late in the autumn, and that it is dangerous to eat any sort of fruit or vegetables out of season. In one southern Missouri county the relief agency distributed fine shipped-in carrots in the winter of 1940; the people were hungry, too, but I saw bunches of these carrots in the ditches along the road, where my neighbors had thrown them away. One farmer gathered up a lot of carrots and fed them to his pigs, "so's to be sure the childern wouldn't git a-holt of 'em!" The relief office in the same village gave away a lot of grapefruit also, but many of the people had never seen grapefruit before, and some of them threw the stuff to the pigs rather than take a chance with it. Several families boiled their grapefruit, since it never occurred to them that fruit could be eaten raw in the wintertime.

There is a very general notion in the hill country that the instrument which caused a wound is still a part of the situation and must be somehow included in the treatment given the wound itself. Thus when a mountain man cuts himself accidentally, he hastens to thrust the offending knife or ax deep into the soil, believing that this will stop excessive bleeding and make the wound heal faster.

A boy at Harrison, Arkansas, stepped on a nail which passed entirely through his foot. After his father had dressed the wound with vinegar he took the boy on a horse and went back to the place where the accident occurred in order to *find the nail*. The father wanted to take the nail home, wash it in kerosene and put it away in a dry place. "If the nail rusts," said he, "the wound will fester."

Miss Jewell Perriman, Jenkins, Missouri, tells me that the people in her neighborhood, if injured by a rusty nail, apply turpentine to the nail before they put it on the wound. Boys in some parts of Arkansas carry the nail home and thrust it into a bar of soap, to the same depth that it was accidentally stuck into the foot; it is not clear exactly why they do this, but it is evidently connected with the idea of preventing rust, which is associated in the hillman's mind with tetanus, or lockjaw.

In dressing gunshot wounds, doctors are often requested by the patient to put a little salve or antiseptic on the bullet which caused the injury, in order to prevent blood poisoning. I knew one man who always carried the bullet which had been cut out of his leg; whenever he felt a twinge of pain, he would take the bullet out of his wallet and put a drop of skunk oil on it. He laughed a little every time he did this, and never admitted that he believed in the efficacy of such a procedure.

Something of the same sort is shown in the treatment of snake bites. Several miles west of Hot Springs, Arkansas, I came upon some small boys. They had built a rousing fire by the roadside and were burning a large copperhead. This snake had bitten one of the boys, whose leg was already badly swollen. I asked why they didn't do something for the boy, but they replied that their chief concern was to burn the snake "plumb to ashes." As soon as the body of the snake was entirely consumed, the boys told me, they were going to take the injured lad to the doctor in a nearby village.

I have known educated hillfolk, who depend upon regular physicians for ordinary ailments, surreptitiously to consult a backwoods magician when bitten by a poisonous serpent. Dr. W. O. Cralle, Springfield, Missouri, tells of an old woman who warned him never to go to an m.d. in case of snake bite. The doctor might fix it up temporarily, she said, but the bite would always hurt on the anniversary of the day it occurred, so long as the patient lived. An old-time healer, on the other hand, would cure it in his own fashion, and it would never cause any further trouble.

Miss Jewell Perriman, of Jenkins, Missouri, tells me that her Uncle Bill had a secret method of curing snake bite, and people came from miles around for treatment. Uncle Bill belonged to a family of which it was said "them folks don't kill snakes." This is very unusual in the Ozarks, where most people do kill every snake they see. When a large copperhead was found in the Perriman house, Uncle Bill caught it with the tongs, carried it out into the orchard, and released it unharmed. His cure for snake bite was known in the family for at least a hundred years. Uncle Bill had it from his father and told it to his eldest son. The son was an educated fellow, an m.d. from a great university, and he did not believe in this magic stuff. So the young doctor never used the family treatment, but he did not laugh at it, and he never told it to anybody, so far as is known. The secret is lost now, for Uncle Bill is long dead, and his son died suddenly without issue. All that Miss Perriman knows of the snake-bite cure is that the snake must not be injured, and that Uncle Bill had a strip of ancient buckskin in which he tied certain knots as part of the treatment. She showed me the buckskin. It was about half an inch wide, perhaps twelve inches long, carefully rounded at the ends. Three knots had been tied in it, one in the middle and one at either end.

Another Ozark youth, a member of a clan which doesn't kill snakes, was startled into shooting a water moccasin one day, when he was fishing. Immediately the boy began to see moccasins everywhere. He shot and killed about thirty in two hours and then became a little frightened, as there seemed to be something supernatural in the sudden appearance of so many poisonous serpents. When he told his father what had occurred, the old man just looked at him solemnly and said nothing at all. That boy was terribly nervous for several weeks, and he never killed another snake as long as he lived. He would not admit that he was in any degree superstitious but said several times that there was "something funny" about his family when it came to "messin' with snakes."

Some backwoods Christians of the wilder Holy Roller cults —adherents of the so-called "new ground religion," "pokeweed gospel," or "lightnin'-bug churches"—do not believe in doctors and will not take any sort of medicine. Their preachers say that the Word is ag'in physicians, and quote James 5:14-15: "Is any sick among you? Let him call for the elders of the church; and let them pray over him, anointing him with oil in the name of the Lord; and the prayer of faith shall save the sick."

I have seen seven or eight backwoods preachers kneeling about a sick man's bed, shouting the gibberish they call "the unknown tongue." As soon as these fellows knew that I was present they stopped yelling, since they believe that the presence of an unbeliever breaks the charm. They claim some remarkable cures of inoperable cancer and the like. I know personally of cases where they have attempted to raise the dead; in one instance they "wooled the corpse around" for several hours, even pulling the body off the bed by their frenzied "laying on of hands."

In Taney county, Missouri, I knew an old woman who was very ill and sent word to the nearest meetin' that she wanted the preachers to pray for her, but did not want them to come to her house because the family was opposed to the "pokeberry religion." Several of the preachers knelt down in the church, took bottles of holy oil from their pockets, poured a little of the stuff on a handkerchief, and prayed over it in the unknown tongue. The old woman applied the handkerchief to her abdomen next the skin and wore it for several days; then she announced that she was miraculously healed, and the preachers claimed to have effected the cure at a distance of two and one-half miles, without even seeing the patient. The woman died a few weeks later.

In cases of difficult childbirth the "buck-brush parsons" sometimes try to help, and their prayers are so loud as to drown out the screams of the wretched woman; this scandalizes the conventional midwives, who feel that men should not be present at such times.

Rex Thomas, newspaperman of Lamar, Missouri, told me about the Rev. A. D. Etterman, an evangelist who was "run out" of Newport, Missouri, in October, 1934. The villagers claimed that Etterman's family spread the itch through the whole community, so that the public school had to be closed for two weeks. It was said that Etterman could cure leprosy by supernatural means, but the lowly scabies was apparently beyond his powers.

These Pentecostal fanatics do not patronize the backwoods herbalists or power doctors or granny-women, at least not openly. Sometimes it may be that a Holy Roller weakens under the lash of pain and visits a nonreligious healer in secret. But when a "new ground" religionist calls a doctor he generally insists upon a licensed m.d. from town. Physicians in the Ozark communities tell me that when they are called to a Holy Roller cabin they usually find somebody at the point of death. "Such people don't want treatment," one doctor said grimly, "they just want me to examine the patient, so that I can sign a death certificate!"

8. Courtship and Marriage

In pioneer days it appears that a woman's least attempt to make herself attractive by artificial means was regarded with suspicion. There are places in the Ozarks even now where a married woman who uses "face whitenin' " is looked down upon by her respectable neighbors. In the remotest settlements nowadays, however, young girls manage to get "store-boughten" cosmetics—cheap powder, lipstick, and perfume. A few years ago the mothers of these girls used flour or corn-starch for face-whitenin', and I have seen a woman take an artificial rose off an old hat, dampen it with her tongue, and rub the dye on her cheeks by way of rouge. The old-timers tell of a weed called cow slobber, too, with a red sap which gave color to many a hill-country belle's cheek.

There are many odd folk beliefs connected with backwoods beauty treatments. Dew, or dew and buttermilk, or various mixtures of honey and buttermilk are recognized remedies for roughened skin and pimples on the face and neck. Rain water caught on the first day of June is supposed to clear up muddy complexions and eliminate freckles. The fresh blood of a chicken —that of a black pullet in particular—is also said to remove freckles and make the skin white and creamy. Fresh tomato juice is a very fine bleach for darkened skins, although some girls prefer to rub their arms and faces with cucumber pulp just before going to bed. Mrs. Addah Matthews, of Monett, Missouri, says that Ozark girls used to apply sassafras tea to their faces, in the belief that it would benefit their complexions.

A few years ago, girls came to believe that a poultice of

fresh cow dung removes freckles, makes the skin soft and fresh, and greatly improves the feminine complexion. A pretty woman in Crane, Missouri, told me that she and her chum made thick masks of cow dung and wore them for hours at a time. "It drawed up my face," she said, "till I couldn't hardly move a eye-winker!"

The dirty water from a blacksmith's tub, in which hot horse-shoes have been tempered, is famous as a lotion for a spotted or muddy complexion. Many girls try to remove freckles by rub-bing the face with a boy baby's diaper, wet with fresh urine. Some of the most popular treatments are kept secret. Once I made some complimentary remark to a girl about her com-plexion, and she started to sing the praises of a new cosmetic she had brewed out of beet tops, when suddenly she stopped short with the remark that if she *told* anybody the spell would be broken and the charm wouldn't work.

It is proverbial that the winds of March are bad for the complexion:

> March winds and May sun
> Make clothes white and maids dun.

Many mountain women say that to eat chicken hearts, espe-cially *raw* chicken hearts, will make any girl good looking; I know one poor damsel who ate them for years, but without any benefit so far as I could see. May Stafford Hilburn says that in her section of the Ozarks the girl must swallow the chicken heart not only raw but *whole!* [1] In Cassville, Missouri, a woman told me that to swallow a raw chicken heart at one gulp may not make a girl beautiful, but it will render her sexually attractive, so that "she can git whoever she wants."

The touch of a dead man's hand is popularly supposed to dis-courage moles, blackheads, enlarged pores, and other facial blemishes. I have seen a little girl, perhaps three years old, dragged into a village undertaking parlor and "tetched," in

[1] *Missouri Magazine* (September, 1933), p. 21.

the belief that a large red birthmark on the child's face might thus be removed.

A girl can cure her chapped or roughened lips by kissing the middle bar of a five-rail fence, but it is well to put a bit of lard or tallow on the lips also, according to my informants.

Most country girls have their ears pierced for earrings, but this should be done when peach trees are in bloom, and when "the sign is right." If the ears are pierced at any other time, the openings are likely to become infected; one girl told me her ears got so sore she "couldn't hardly pull the strings through without hollerin'!"

The Ozark women have several outlandish treatments for falling hair, but the details of these are supposed to be kept secret, as to tell anybody will break the charm. I have been unable to learn anything definite about this business, beyond the fact that one course of treatment takes forty-nine days and requires large amounts of fresh urine, which is carried in bottles and buckets from all over the neighborhood to the house of the woman undergoing the treatment.

In Washington county, Arkansas, there are women who claim to cure baldness, or at least to arrest falling hair, with a salve made from tallow mixed with the scrapings of old harness, preferably that which has been worn by a white mule. Wild-cherry bark makes a fine hair tonic and hair restorer. Sage tea is not only popular as a hair dressing but is also said to restore the natural color of hair which is turning gray. A tea made from peach-tree leaves, with a little sulphur added, is said to be a sure cure for dandruff. Sap from wild grape vines is highly recommended as a hair tonic.

I am told that in pioneer days some women made a curling fluid by steeping flaxseed in hot water, but just how this was supposed to work I do not know. Some say that it was applied to the hair just before the rag curlers were put on. "We didn't have no curlin'-irons in them days," an old woman told me.

The girl who cuts her hair at the time of the new moon will

see it grow rapidly and luxuriantly. Hair cut in the dark of
the moon is likely to lose its luster, or even to become gray prematurely. A woman's hair should never be cut in March—this
makes it dull and lifeless and sometimes causes headaches which
persist until midnight on March 31.

A mountain girl of my acquaintance placed a lock of her
hair under a stone in a running stream, believing that the water
would make her hair glossy and attractive. Another way to
promote the growth of hair is to bury a "twist" of it under the
roots of a white walnut tree, in the light of the moon.

To burn combings, or hair which has been cut off, is forbid-
den to Ozark girls, as it would make their hair brittle. Combings
should be buried in the ground. Mrs. Mary Elizabeth Mahnkey,
of Mincy, Missouri, tells me that one must never throw combings out of doors—if a bird should use even one hair in building
a nest, the original owner of the hair is likely to go insane.
Others say that to have your hair in a bird's nest won't neces-
sarily drive you crazy, but it will cause a series of terrible
headaches.

Children are often told that eating bread crusts makes the
hair curly, and some parents contend that a diet of carrots also
causes hair to curl. Most mountain folk feel that curly hair is
somehow more attractive than straight, so it may be that these
sayings are intended primarily to induce children to eat bread
crusts and carrots. One often hears that if a straight-haired
girl shaves her head, the new hair will "come in curly," but I
have never known anybody to give it a trial.

It is always bad luck to part one's hair with a comb that has
touched the head of a corpse; to do so may cause the hair to
fall out.

Country women in the Ozarks seldom put water on their hair
—they prefer to dry-clean it with cornmeal. But when it is
necessary to wet one's hair, it is best not to use a comb until
the hair is perfectly dry. To comb wet hair always makes it
coarse, according to the granny-women.

Nearly all of the old-timers disliked to comb their hair by artificial light. I have seen a man at least seventy years old hobble out into his back yard and stand in the moonlight while he combed his long white hair, rather than comb it in front of a mirror in the kitchen illuminated by a kerosene lamp.

A young woman should *never* comb her hair at night, under any condition, since to do this is said to "lower a gal's nature" —that is, make her less passionate sexually. That is the meaning of the old sayin':

> Comb your hair after dark,
> Comb sorry into your old man's heart.

Many hillmen still believe in love powders and potions, and this belief is encouraged by the country druggists, who sell a perfumed mixture of milk sugar and flake whiting at enormous profits. This stuff is dissolved in a girl's coffee or fed to her in candy and ìs said to be quite efficacious. Many mountain damsels carry love charms consisting of some pinkish, soaplike material, the composition of which I have been unable to discover; the thing is usually enclosed in a carved peach stone or cherry pit and worn on a string round the neck, or attached to an elastic garter. I recall a girl near Lanagan, Missouri, who wore a peach stone love-charm on one garter and a rabbit's foot fastened to the other.

Surreptitiously touching the back of a man's head is said to be a sure way of arousing his sexual passions, and every mountain girl knows that if she puts a drop of her menstrual fluid into a man's liquor he is certain to fall madly in love with her. Whiskey in which her fingernail trimmings have been soaked is said to have a very similar effect. These beliefs are taken so seriously in the Ozarks that the victim of a love-charm or philter is not held morally responsible for his actions, and many a deserted wife is comforted by the reflection that her man did not leave of his own free will but was "cunjured off."

Ozark girls sometimes carry little wasp nests in the belief

that they somehow attract men. These objects are usually pinned to the lady's undergarments—if she wears any undergarments. It is said that if a girl steals the band from a man's hat and makes a garter of it, the original owner will fall in love with her at once. Yellow garters are very popular, as they attract men to the wearer and even render her lovers faithful. For a married woman to wear yellow garters is not so good, however—it indicates that she is interested in men other than her husband. Many a mountain girl conceals dried turkey bones about the room in which she meets her lover, or even secretes them in her clothing, in the belief that they will render him more amorous. I once heard some village loafers "greening" a young chap because some turkey bones had been found behind the cushions of his Ford, the supposition being that they had been placed there by women who had ridden with him.

Mountain girls sometimes carry the beard of a wild turkey gobbler concealed about their clothing. Rose O'Neill, of Day, Missouri, asked a neighbor about this once and was told that "we use it to clean the comb with." Probably the gobbler's beard does make a satisfactory comb cleaner, but there is no doubt whatever that some backwoods damsels regard it as a love charm.

A plant called yarrow, or milfoil (*Achillea millefolium*), is used in making love potions. The same is said to be true of dodder, also called love vine or angel's hair. Women in northwest Arkansas tell me that the roots of the lady's-slipper or moccasin flower (*Cypripedium*) contain a powerful aphrodisiac. The leaves and stems of mistletoe are made into some kind of "love medicine," but the whole matter is very secret. I have on two occasions seen women boiling big kettles of mistletoe out of doors but was unable to get any details of the procedure.

If a girl has quarreled with her lover, she may get him back by taking a needle and drawing a little blood from the third finger of her left hand. Using the needle as a pen, she writes her initials and his in blood on an ironwood chip, draws three circles around the letters, and buries the chip in the ground. The recreant boy friend will be hangin' round again in three days, or less.

The boys in northwestern Arkansas make a love medicine from the web of a wild gander's foot, dried and reduced to powder. Put a pinch of this in a girl's coffee, and she will not only fall in love with you at once but will be faithful to you as long as she lives. This is somehow connected, in the hillman's mind, with the belief that wild geese mate but once.

By cleaning her fingernails on Saturday, and muttering a mysterious old sayin' at the same time, a girl can *force* her lover to visit her on Sunday. When a boy says "my gal fixed her fingernails yesterday," he means that he is going to see her and implies that he does so rather reluctantly.

If a girl puts salt on the fire for seven consecutive mornings it will bring her absent lover home, whether he wants to come or not. Or she may place her shoes together on the floor at right angles, so that the toe of one touches the middle of the other, and recite:

> When I my true love want to see
> I put my shoes in the shape of a T.

This is said to be especially effective when the errant swain is married or has become entangled with a married woman.

I once knew two sisters in Jasper county, Missouri, who went far out in the woods and bent several twigs on a pawpaw tree, tying them fast in the bent position with twisted locks of their own hair. Relatives of these girls told me that this had something to do with an unsatisfactory love affair in which both girls were involved, but I was unable to learn anything definite about the matter. It was not the sort of thing that a mere acquaintance could safely investigate.

In rural Arkansas the backwoods girls tie little pieces of cloth to the branches of certain trees—usually pawpaw or hawthorn, sometimes redbud or ironwood. I have seen five of these little bundles in a single pawpaw tree. I have untied several and examined them carefully; there was nothing in them that I could see, just little pieces of cloth, doubtless torn from old dresses or petticoats. The natives say they are love charms, but just how they work I do not know. No woodsman that I have ever known would think of touching one of these objects, and I have often been warned that it is very bad luck to "monkey with such as that."

In some localities it is said that a man hides the dried tongue of a turtle dove in a girl's cabin—this makes her fall madly in love with him, and she can't deny him anything. I was told of a case in which a girl's superstitious parents searched the cabin for days, trying to find the tongue which they believed must be hidden there. The neighbors laughed about this, and the girl herself said that turtle doves' tongues had nothing to do with the case, but the parents still believed the old story. They never did find the dove's tongue, however.

A girl can take a needle which has been stuck into a dead body, cover it with dirt in which a corpse has been laid, and wrap the whole thing in a cloth cut from a winding sheet; this is supposed to be a very powerful love charm, and a woman who owns such a thing can make any man fall in love with her. A needle which has been used to make a shroud is useful, too. If a girl thrusts such a needle into her lover's footprint in her own dooryard, he is forced to remain with her whether he wants to or not. If he leaves the neighborhood he will get sick, and if he stays away long enough he will die.

Girls in love are supposed to have an inordinate appetite for cucumber pickles. In the eighties boys used to leave little boxes of fruit and candies at their sweethearts' doorsteps on the eve of February 14. For a boy to include a pickle was considered very daring, and the old folks said that a girl who ate one of these Valentine pickles was henceforth unable to resist the boy who gave it to her. Some old-timers, however, insist that pickles were traditionally regarded as a *cure* for love sickness rather than a love charm or an aphrodisiac. According to this interpretation, the pickle in a Valentine box was no more than a humorous reference to a rival, or to some previous love affair.

Negroes in Arkansas make and sell charms to keep husbands constant, to bring back wandering lovers, to help in seducing girls, and so on. They are little cloth bags containing feathers, hair, blood, graveyard dirt, salt, and sometimes human bones. Some low-class white people buy these and carry them. They are called *charms, conjures, hands, jacks* or *jujus.* Many white people laugh at this "nigger business," but I have known educated white men who were careful to avoid touching these charms. It was a dealer in jujus, in Little Rock, Arkansas, who told me that a man infatuated with an unworthy woman could cure himself by smearing the fresh blood of a male deer over his genitals.

A hillman whose wife is "triflin' on him" is sometimes persuaded that he can make everything right by going into the woods at midnight and boring a hole in the crotch of a pawpaw tree. This done, he mutters a secret Biblical quotation, drives a stout wooden peg into the auger hole, and walks away without looking back at the tree. The hole behind the peg may contain a wad of human hair, dried blood, fingernail parings, a piece of a woman's undergarment, and some unidentified material resembling beeswax. This method of curbing marital infidelity is known as the "pawpaw conjure" and is said to be of Negro origin.

It is generally believed that a man who seduces little girls is likely to have a curse laid upon his family, and his own children are particularly liable to the same outrage that he has perpetrated upon the daughters of others.

Marriage is still regarded as a serious matter in the Ozarks, and there are many singular superstitions connected with the choice of a mate. The typical hillman is determined to marry a virgin at any cost, and is firmly convinced that he can detect virginity at a glance. The theory is that every female child has a tiny cleft or depression in the end of her nose, and that this depression immediately disappears after sexual intercourse is effected.

There are several strange old notions about the use of mirrors in testing female virtue. One of these is reflected in a song still popular in the backwoods:

> Mamma, mamma, have you heard?
> Papa's goin' to buy me a mockin'-bird!
>
> If the mockin'-bird won't sing
> Papa's goin' to buy me a golden ring.
>
> If the golden ring is brass
> Papa's goin' to buy me a lookin'-glass.
>
> If the lookin'-glass don't shine
> Papa's goin' to shoot that beau of mine!

A young woman near Mena, Arkansas, who repeated these verses, explained the final stanza by saying that the lookin'-glass "shines" only for virgins and virtuous wives.

Many hill women are firmly convinced that a man's penis is exactly three times as long as his nose, and a girl who "keeps company" with a very long-nosed man is subjected to the good-natured raillery of her friends. There is an old saying to the effect that a girl with a small mouth has a small, tight vagina. Teeth set wide apart indicate a passionate, sensual nature. Cold hands are believed to be associated with a warm heart and are often regarded as a sure sign that one is in love. A woman with very small ears is likely to be miserly and petulant. If a girl's second toe is longer than the big one, she will try to bully her lover. When a woman has the habit of resting her thumb inside her clenched hand, everybody knows that she will be ruled absolutely by her husband, while if her thumb is habitually extruded the man who marries her will probably be henpecked.

To tell if a person is jealous, hold a buttercup under his chin;

if the yellow color of the flower is reflected, so that the skin looks yellow, he's jealous. There is some trick of detecting jealousy by holding a red-hot poker near the face; a little boy lost one of his eyes because of this foolishness at the Cherry Grove schoolhouse near Lamar, Missouri, in 1938.

To speak of a person as white-livered, in some parts of America, is to call him a coward. In the Ozarks, however, white-livered generally means oversexed. When a lively, buxom, good-looking woman loses several husbands by death, it is often said that her inordinate sexual passion has killed 'em off, and she is referred to as a white-livered widder. Usually it is only a figure of speech, but there are people who actually believe that a "high nature" is correlated with white spots on the liver, and that this condition has often been revealed by postmortem examination.

There are many ways of determining whether or not one's sweetheart is faithful. If the fire which a man kindles burns brightly, he knows that his sweetheart is true to him, but if it smolders, she is likely to prove unfaithful. As a further test, he may go into a clearing and bend down a mullein stalk so that it points toward her cabin; if she loves him the stalk grows up again, but if she loves another it will die. Mrs. Addah Matthews, Monett, Missouri, says that "a girl used to name a mullein stalk, then bend the stalk toward her fellow's house; if it grew bent in that direction he loved her." Sometimes the girl puts a bit of dodder or love vine on a growing weed; if it flourishes, her lover is faithful, and if it withers he is not to be trusted. Or she may pluck a hair from her head and draw it between her fingers—if it curls he loves her, if it remains straight he does not. Another girl picks a cocklebur, names it for her lover, and throws it against her skirt; if it sticks, she knows that her lover is true to her, if it doesn't stick she thinks he is false.

A hill girl often names a match for a boy whom she admires and then lights the match; if it burns to the end without breaking, she is assured that the boy loves her. My neighbor's daughters once used up half a box of matches in this search for knowledge, an extravagance which was harshly rebuked by the frugal parents. Another common trick is for a girl to light a match and hold it straight up; if the blackened head turns toward her boy friend or her boy friend's home, it is a sign that he loves her. But if the match points in some other direction, she has reason to doubt his fidelity.

If a ring suddenly breaks upon a person's finger, without any obvious reason for its breaking, it means that his or her loved one is unfaithful; some say that it means the absent one has committed an act of infidelity at the exact moment when the ring cracks.

To find out if her sweetheart loves her, a girl hangs a Bible up with a string and repeats aloud: "Whither thou goest, I will go. Where thou lodgest, I will lodge. Thy people shall be my people, thy God my God." Then she shouts the name of her boy friend—Jim or Bill or Alec or whatever it is. If the Bible turns on the string so that the edge points toward the speaker, it is a sign that the boy loves her. Some say it means that they will marry.

There are many ways in which a mountain girl may learn the identity and characteristics of her future husband. She may put a live snail in a glass fruit jar over night; the initials of the man she is to marry will be outlined in the snail's slimy track. An old woman once told me that if a girl counts nine stars each night for nine consecutive nights, on the ninth night she will inevitably dream of her husband-to-be. A simpler method is to stare very hard at the brightest star in sight and wink three times; this produces the dream on the first night and gets the same result with much less expenditure of time and energy. Some girls divine their future marital adventures by what is called cancellation; they write down their own names with those of their boy friends, and cancel out identical letters, shouting "false, true, false, true" the while. This cancellation business is a bit more complicated than appears at first sight, and I have never been able to understand exactly how it works.

Down south of Hot Springs, Arkansas, they tell me that a girl goes out in the woods after a rain and "repeats a verse"—meaning a passage from the Bible. Then she reaches behind her without looking and lifts up a flat stone. Under the stone she'll find a hair, and it will be the same color as that of the man she is destined to marry.

A woman at Zinc, Arkansas, says that when a girl hears a dove and sees the new moon at the same instant, she repeats this verse:

> Bright moon, clear moon,
> Bright and fair,
> Lift up your right foot
> There'll be a hair.

Then she takes off her right shoe and finds in it a hair like that of her future husband.

Mrs. Effa M. Wilson, Verona, Missouri, has a slightly different version. She says that when you hear the first dove coo in the spring, sit down wherever you are and take off your right stocking. In the heel of the stocking you'll find the hair, and it will be exactly the color of your future husband's hair. A lady in Marshfield, Missouri, tried this, and to her amazement she did find a hair in her stocking. It was a blond hair, though, and she married a black-haired man.

Sometimes a mountain damsel boils an egg very hard, then removes the yolk and fills the cavity with salt. Just before bedtime she eats this salted egg. In the night, according to the old story, she will dream that somebody fetches her a gourd filled with water. The man who brings her the water is destined to be her husband. It is surprising how many young women have tried this, and how many feel that there may be something in it.

A girl near Clinton, Arkansas, tells me that she has only to write the names of nine boys on a slip of paper and put the paper between her breasts at bedtime; she is sure to dream of the one who will be her husband.

The girl who looks at the new moon over her right shoulder and repeats:

> New moon, new moon, do tell me
> Who my own true lover will be,
> The color of his hair, the clothes that he will wear
> And the happy day he will wed me,

will dream of her future mate that night.

They tell me that sometimes a girl writes the names of six boys on six slips of paper and puts them under her pillow. When she awakes in the night, she pulls out one at random and throws it on the floor. She does not look at it until daylight, when it will be found to bear the name of her future husband. The girl who lights a lamp to look at the slip before morning will have very bad luck and perhaps get no husband at all.

If a girl finds a pod containing nine peas, she hangs it up over the door. The first eligible man to walk under the pod will be her future husband.

The first time a country girl sleeps in a strange room, she names the four corners for four boys of her acquaintance. The first corner that she looks into when she awakes bears the name of the boy she will marry.

In some sections, when a backwoods girl sees the new moon, she *names* a boy—pronounces his name aloud. Then she watches for the boy, day after day. If he happens to have his face toward her, the first time she sees him, she thinks that they will someday be sweethearts. If his back is toward her, she feels that there is nothing to do but forget him.

The first day of May is important to girls who are looking for information about their future mates. If a girl gets up early on the morning of May 1, goes to the spring, and breaks a guinea's egg into a cup, she'll see the face or the initials of her husband-to-be in the water. A girl who looks obliquely into a mirror when she first wakes up on May Day will see the re-

flection, or at least initials or letters forming the name, of the
man who is to be her mate.

A maiden lady who wants to see her future husband goes to
a well at noon on May 1 and holds a mirror so as to reflect the
light down into the darkness. Some girls say that they have
actually seen their mates-to-be in the water. Others are afraid
to try this stunt, because sometimes a girl doesn't see any man,
but an image of herself in a coffin, which means that she'll die
before another May Day. If a girl sees nothing at all in the
water, she is very likely to be an old maid.

A woman in Christian county, Missouri, used to do the same
trick with a gold ring in a glass of water. She set the glass in
front of a mirror and gazed fixedly at the reflection of the ring.
I was told of another maiden who looked into this ring-mirror
gadget and saw a new-made grave by the river; everybody
thought it meant that the poor girl would die soon, but she lived
to be nearly seventy.

On the last night of April, a girl may wet a handkerchief
and hang it out in a cornfield. Next morning the May sun dries
it, and the wrinkles are supposed to show the initial of the man
she is to marry. Or she may hold a bottle of water up to the
light on the morning of May 1, just at sunrise, and see a picture
or outline of the boy who is to be her husband.

Sometimes a widow gets up before dawn on May Day and
hangs a horseshoe over her door. The first creature to enter
will have a complexion and hair color like that of her future
mate. There is a whole cycle of funny stories based on this
belief, tales of possums, rats, snakes, or even skunks wandering
in, and so on.

Some girls hunt birds' nests on May 1. If the first nest a girl
finds on that day has eggs in it, she'll be married soon; if the
nest is empty, she will be an old maid. "But what if there are
young birds in the nest?" I asked the girl who told me about
this. She cast down her eyes, blushed, and made no answer. Her
mother overheard the question, and called the girl into the

house at once. I have never been able to learn what happens
to the girl who finds young birds in the nest.

Here is another way of looking into a mountain maiden's
future: take three bowls, one containing clean water, one full
of dirty water, one empty. Blindfold the girl, lead her into the
room, and ask her to select one of the bowls. If she picks the
clean water, she'll be happily married; if she picks the dirty
water, she will soon be a widow; if she picks the empty bowl,
she'll be an old maid.

One may always ascertain the future bridegroom's occupa-
tion by counting the buttons on a girl's new dress—rich man,
poor man, beggarman, thief, doctor, lawyer, merchant, chief—
but this does not seem to be taken seriously except by very small
girls. If a little girl is always getting her apron wet, when she
washes the dishes, it is a sign that she'll marry a drunkard.
The woman who finds a broken feather or a crooked twig in
her hair will marry a most unsatisfactory man—some say that
her husband will be a cripple.

If a girls wets her nightdress, hangs it before the fireplace
to dry, and goes to bed stark naked in a room by herself, she
is sure to see her future mate before morning. The story is that
his image appears as soon as the nightdress is dry enough to
be turned; he walks into the room, turns the nightdress around,
and walks out again. There are many stories about this "conjure," some of them a bit ribald.

Or a girl may urinate on the sleeve of a man's shirt and hang
it up between her bed and the fireplace. In this case her future
husband is forced to appear in the night and move the shirt
so that it will not burn. "He aint really there, of course," one
woman told me. "She just *dreams* it."

Some hillfolk say that a girl can call up a phantom of the
man she is to marry by wrapping a lock of hair with some of
her fingernail clippings in a green leaf and thrusting them into
the ashes in the fireplace. Then she sits down before the fire.
When the hair and fingernails begin to get warm, the ghostly

appearance of her future husband is supposed to rescue them from the fire. Sometimes several girls try this at once. The door must be left open, and everyone must maintain absolute silence.

In some sections of Arkansas, the girls "set a dumb supper," by making a pone of cornmeal and salt, in complete silence. Each girl must take her turn at stirring the meal, each must shift the pone as it bakes; each must place a piece of the bread on her own plate, and another on the plate next hers at the table. When this is done, the girls open the doors and windows, then sit down silently and bow their heads. All during the baking, the wind has grown stronger, and by this time there should be a regular gale blowing through the house. Often the lights are blown out. The phantom husbands are supposed to enter in silence. Each girl is supposed to recognize the man who sits down beside her. If she sees nobody, it means she will never marry. If she sees a black figure, without recognizable features, it means that she will die within a year. Many people still take this business seriously enough to forbid their daughters to trifle with it. Some parents say it aint Christian and smells of witchcraft, while others object to such foolishness because it sometimes frightens nervous girls into hysteria.

An old woman in Washington county, Arkansas, told me that when she was a girl they always walked backward while cooking and serving a dumb supper, and measured everything by thimblefuls instead of by spoonfuls or cupfuls. According to this version of the tale, nobody expects to see an apparition enter the room, no extra plates are set for ghostly visitors, and there is no supernatural wind to blow out the lights. Each girl sits down in silence and eats her tiny portion of food, then bows her head over the empty plate. If all goes well, she sees the outline of her future husband's face *in the plate*, comparable to the figures seen by crystal gazers and the like.

Otto Ernest Rayburn, of Eureka Springs, Arkansas, says that in his neighborhood early May was the only proper season for a dumb supper; Rayburn's informants seemed to regard the ritual as more or less of a joke, but the old-timers that I have interviewed were very serious about it, even a little frightened. May Stafford Hilburn, apparently referring to the region about Jefferson City, Missouri, mentions the dumb supper as an old-fashioned custom "to hasten the culmination of a budding romance through the mystic rites thus performed." [2] I am not certain just what this means, but Mrs. Hilburn's description calls for midnight, absolute silence, walking backward and so on, just like the dumb-supper ritual in other sections.

In Cedar county, Missouri, the same sort of function was called a "dummy" supper. Working in absolute silence, walking backward and looking over her left shoulder, each girl placed a chair at the table and set out dishes, knives, and forks as if for a meal, except that the dishes were empty. This done, the girls took their places behind the chairs and stood with bowed heads. The idea was that after a short period of silent concentration the wraith or spirit of each girl's husband-to-be would appear for a moment in the chair she had prepared for him. One spoken word, a laugh, a smile, or even a frivolous thought on this solemn occasion was supposed to break the charm. There have been cases in which overwrought damsels persuaded themselves that they really saw ghostly figures seated at the "dummy table." One old woman assured me that the phantom husband was visible to all of the girls about the table, but the general opinion is that he appeared only to the damsel who stood directly behind his chair, and who was destined to become his wife.

Mrs. C. P. Mahnkey, of Mincy, Missouri, tells a good story about the dumb-supper ceremony. She says that it is not fiction, but a tale that was told and believed in Taney county, Missouri, when she was a girl. Here is the story in Mrs. Mahnkey's own words, as published in the *White River Leader*, Branson, Missouri, Jan. 4, 1934:

[2] *Missouri Magazine* (October, 1933), p. 14.

A dear friend of mother's, a plump and jolly woman, comforting and reposeful, not one capable of harboring such strange and weird beliefs, told the story of the dumb supper, so vividly, so impressively, that I never forgot. She and mother were quilting and as the story progressed, and she would bend her face to bite off her thread, she got in the way of giving a cautious glance over her shoulder, and before the tale had ended, I, too, was giving rather awed glances out into the long, darksome hall.

She was talking as if she had been present, or as if she had intimately known the parties engaged in this supernatural feast. It seemed the family were away for the night, and the grown girls, left in charge of the home, had invited in some neighbor girls to keep them company, so a dumb supper was proposed. This meant, that in utter silence, and every step taken, to be made backwards, the table was to be laid for a guest, who would come in at midnight, and who was to be the future husband of the girl at whose plate he sat down. The table was only set for one, as it seemed at the test, only one girl was brave enough to thus put her fortune to the trial.

The others watched her in fascinated silence, as she stepped quickly, if awkwardly, about her task, in the big low ceilinged kitchen. She placed a peculiar knife at the side of the mysterious guest's plate, with a roguish smile at her friends. A sharpbladed knife, set into a piece of deer horn, for one handle.

In utter silence they waited, until the old clock slowly droned out the 12 strokes of midnight, when to their terror, the door was dashed open, a tall form advanced, with swift noiseless steps, and then—an icy wind blew out the light, and one of the horrified girls screamed. But one braver than the rest, closed the door and lighted the lamp. No spectral visitor, they were alone, but the maiden who had set the table, pointed with white face and shaking hands, the peculiar old knife was not there.

Later, this girl did marry a stranger, who had come, as a visiting cousin, to the home of a nearby neighbor. And they seemed to be very happy, although the man was very quiet, even taciturn.

One day the girl's mother, going across the ridge to visit her, found the little cabin strangely cold and forbidding, and hurried in, to find her daughter lying as if dead, with a knife thrust into her breast.

When at last help had been summoned, and the old backwoods doctor, able surgeon was he, too, brought her back to consciousness, shudderingly she told the story.

In a moment of girlish confidence she had told the story of the dumb supper, and the strange guest, "as tall as you," she had said, and he had listened, in sinister silence. Then he went to an old leather valise he always kept locked, unlocked it, took something in his hand and said to her coldly, "And you are the one. You are that witch. That night I walked through hell," and thrust the knife into her breast, and ran from the house. He was never seen again, and the knife was the same old peculiar knife with the deer horn handle and the keen blade, that the thoughtless girl had laid when so careless and gay, she had set the dumb supper.

When a man has asked a girl to marry him, and she cannot decide whether to have the fellow or not, the old women sometimes advise her to "leave it to the cat." In this procedure she takes three hairs from a cat's tail, wraps them in white paper, and puts the package under her doorstep. Next morning she unfolds the paper very carefully, so as not to shake up the three hairs. If they have arranged themselves in the approximate form of the letter *Y*, the answer is *yes;* if they fall into the shape of an *N*, she will do well not to marry the young man.

There are some things—such as kissing over a gate—that lovers must never do, under any condition, though it is not clear just what would happen to them if they disobeyed this injunction. Neither must a man kiss a girl while he is standing and she is sitting in a chair, since to do so would cause a violent quarrel or "fraction" at once, and perhaps some more serious calamity.

The girl who kisses a man, or even winks at a man, while she is menstruating will ultimately be "ruint" and probably have an illegitimate child. The same fate will come to a menstruating girl who sits in a chair that has just been vacated by a boy. Many mountain girls who do not really believe these things are still careful about this chair business. "There's nothing to those old sayin's, of course," one young woman told me, "but everybody *knows* about 'em, so it don't look modest for a girl in that shape to go round settin' in boys' chairs. And some of these old grannies always notice it. They've got an eagle eye for things like that."

It is said that if a family keeps black cats about, all the daughters will be old maids. Young girls are told that if they trim their fingernails on Sunday they will be slow in finding husbands. A girl who rides a mule will never get a man. If a woman sits on a table, or lets anyone sweep under her chair or across her feet with a broom, she will not get married for a long time. A girl who inadvertently steps over a broom will either not marry at all, or she will be unhappy in her married life. If a country girl accidentally upsets a chair, she will remain single for at least a year; when a young girl knocks over a chair in the presence of persons not friendly to her, she abandons all decorum and leaps wildly to set it up again, because any malicious individual may begin to count inaudibly as the chair falls, and the number of counts made before the chair is picked up represents the number of years which must elapse before the poor girl's marriage.

There is an old saying that a girl who takes the last biscuit from the plate at the table will be an old maid, and there are some people in Missouri and Arkansas who take this very seriously. If a *man* happens to take the last biscuit it is said that he will soon kiss the cook—but this latter notion is only a joke, a cause for polite laughter.

If a boy meets a girl with whom he has been intimate and doesn't recognize her because she is dressed up, it means that one or both of them will marry very soon. If a dog who knows you well suddenly acts as if you were a stranger, it is a sign that you will soon be married. If the first corn silk you see in the summer is red, you will attend more weddings than funerals that year.

When one sees two snakes in a house at once, it means that there will be a wedding there before long. If two crows persistently circle over a cabin, it is a sign that a daughter of the house is about to marry. A girl who accidentally steps on a cat's tail will be married before the year is out. If a girl's skirt is always catching on briars, it is said that she will soon catch a husband.

When three candles or lamps are accidentally placed in a row, it means that there will soon be a marriage in the family. If four people happen to "shake hands crossways" a wedding is also to be expected. A butterfly in the house, or a bee in a woman's shoe, or the accidental dropping of three pans at once are also wedding signs. When a woman inadvertently puts two knives or two forks together at one plate, she knows that someone who sits at the table that day will be married before the year is out. If the coffee grounds in the bottom of a cup form a ring, it means that somebody in the family will be married soon.

Some backwoods girls cross their fingers and then listen for the whippoorwill, every repetition of the bird's cry representing a year which must pass before the listener can get a husband. When an Ozark girl finds a jointsnake she hits it with a stick and carefully counts the pieces; as many segments as the snake breaks into, so many years will elapse before her wedding. If she hears a mockingbird sing after dark she often hastens to put a man's hat on her head, since this means that she will soon be happily married.

I knew a young schoolmarm in Missouri who scorned most of the backwoods superstitions, but who always kissed her thumb when she stumbled, in obedience to the old rhyme:

> Stump your toe,
> Kiss your thumb,
> You'll see your beau
> 'Fore bedtime comes.

If a girl inadvertently speaks in rhyme, it is a sign that she will meet her lover that night:

> Make a rhyme, make a rhyme,
> See your beau before bedtime!

It sometimes happens that a girl has a spot of dirt on her face, without knowing it. Somebody sees the spot and cries: "You got a beauty spot!" Thereupon the girl kisses the back of her hand, certain that she will see her lover in a few hours.

If a redbird flies across a girl's path, she is sure to be kissed twice before nightfall. When a boy and girl accidentally bump their heads together, ribald old men say it's a sign that they will sleep together soon—perhaps that very night.

When a girl's apron is unfastened accidentally, or her skirt turns up, or her stocking falls down, or her shoe comes untied, she believes that her lover is thinking of her. The woman who inadvertently addresses one person by another person's name knows that the second individual is thinking of her at the moment the name is pronounced. But when a girl burns the corn-bread it means that her sweetheart is angry, and if she finds cobwebs in the cabin she fears that he will never visit her again.

Some folk name two apple seeds for a boy and a girl, and drop them on a hot fire shovel; if the seeds move closer together, the boy and girl will marry, but if the seeds spring apart, the boy and girl will separate. Apple seeds are also used by a girl to see which of her suitors she should accept; she names a seed for each lover, moistens the whole lot and sticks them on her forehead. The seed which adheres longest represents the most ardent and persistent of her admirers, and the one who will make the most satisfactory husband.

Many hillfolk tell fortunes and predict marriages by means of certain quotations from the Bible. For example, the twenty-first and thirty-first chapters of Proverbs have thirty-one verses each. Chapter 21 is man's birthday chapter; chapter 31 is woman's birthday chapter. A boy looks up his proper verse in the man's chapter, according to the date of his birth. A man born on the twenty-third of any month, for example, reads Proverbs 21:23—the content of this verse is supposed to be especially significant to him.

There are few professional fortunetellers in the Ozarks, although many of the backwoods seers are accustomed to take money for their services. They always point out, however, that the "power" is not for sale, but that the client may make them a small gift if he likes. So far as I can see, the methods of these women do not differ greatly from those used in other sections of the country—cards, tea leaves, crystal gazing, palmistry, and the like. Mrs. Angie Paxton, of Green Forest, Arkansas, perhaps the most famous of the Ozark fortunetellers, generally made use of coffee grounds, in a cup which was "shuck up" by the customer. Mrs. Josie Forbes, of Wayne county, Missouri, whom the newspapers always called "The Witch of Taskee," used to sit at a table with the client and make four dots with a pencil on a piece of paper. She marked one *N*, one *E*, one *S* and one *W*. "Them's the four directions," she said solemnly. Around these four characters she traced random curving lines, until the whole thing looked like a conventionalized Arabic inscription. Then she began to talk, glancing carelessly down at the paper from time to time as if for confirmation. Her "readings" were the usual stuff, except that she rather specialized in the diagnosis of obscure diseases, for which she recommended various herbs and proprietary medicines. Both Angie Paxton and Josie Forbes talked a good deal about love and marriage, whenever the customer was not too old or decrepit.

Groups of unmarried women at quilting bees used to shake up a cat in the newly completed quilt and then stand around in a big circle as the animal was suddenly released. The theory was that the girl toward whom the cat jumped would be the first of the company to catch a husband. At other times the quilters would wrap an engaged girl up in the new quilt and roll her under the bed, but the exact significance of this procedure has never been explained to me.

When a lot of sparks are seen to fly from a chimney late at night, passers-by say it is a sign that "young folks are a-courtin' " in the cabin. If a bachelor sits between a man and wife at the dinner table, it means that he will be married before the year is out. The girl who washes her face in dew, just at sunup on May 1, will marry the man she loves best. When a butterfly alights on a young woman's head, it is a sign that she may change her old beau for a new one "before snow flies." I once knew a widow who liked to put a four-leaf clover in her shoe before going to town; she said it might bring her a rich suitor.

In some localities, when a girl sleeps with her legs crossed it means only that she is dreaming of her sweetheart, but several old-timers in Scott county, Arkansas, and Jasper county, Missouri, tell me it is a sign that she is destined to have many children.

A schoolmarm in Fayetteville, Arkansas, says that a girl who looks into a spring before breakfast on May 1 will see, not only her future husband, but also the children she is to have by him. A young woman may check this latter information by skipping flat stones on the surface of a stream, believing that the largest number of skips represents the largest number of children it is possible for her to bear.

In the hills near Mena, Arkansas, I met a woman who carefully counted the little branches on a brier that stuck to the front of her dress. She said that the number of branches was supposed to equal the number of children she might expect to bear. Perhaps this brier-counting is not taken very seriously, but it is certainly known to many young women in the backwoods sections of Arkansas and Missouri.

The signs and omens connected with the marriage ceremony are numerous and conflicting, but there is a general feeling that long engagements and postponed weddings do not augur any good. The old sayin' "happy the wooin' not long a-doin' " expresses the Ozarker's attitude.

The best dates and seasons for weddings are determined in part by the changes of the moon and the signs of the zodiac, but the interpretation of this material varies widely. Many old-timers believe that marriages consummated at the full moon, or when the moon is waxing and near the full, are the happiest and most prosperous. In this connection, mountain boys declare that "tomcattin' " is always best in the moonlight, especially when the moon is full, contending that at this time a man does not acquire any venereal disease and is refreshed rather than exhausted by his efforts.

The Clinton (Missouri) *Eye*, in reviewing old-time Missouri superstitions, says cryptically that "it is bad luck to marry in the wrong sign of the moon." [3] Many hillfolk believe that June weddings, consummated when the moon is full, are best of all. However, marriages in January are highly regarded in some quarters, according to the old rhyme:

> Marry when the year is new,
> Your mate will be constant, kind and true.

Weddings in May are said to be unlucky, and so are those celebrated in rainy or snowy weather; bright, warm wedding days are best, and there is an old saying "happy is the bride that the sun shines on." To marry while the wild hawthorn or red-haw is in bloom would be very bad luck indeed. There are some people, however, who say that young folk should marry when the sign's in the loins—in Scorpio, that is—and that nothing else matters.

The wedding day is called the bride's day; if it is bright and pleasant her wedded life will be happy. If the morning is fair and the afternoon rainy, the first part of her married life will be happy, and the latter half unhappy. The day after the wedding, when the "infare" dinner is held at the home of the bridegroom's parents, is known as the man's day, and the same weather signs indicate his future happiness or unhappiness. To postpone a wedding is very bad luck, however, an almost certain sign that one of the contracting parties will die within a year, so that when a certain date is once decided upon the ceremony must be performed, no matter what the weather conditions may be.

It is best to purchase a wedding ring from a mail-order house, because the ordinary "store-boughten" ring may have absorbed

[3] Sept. 7, 1936, p. 5.

bad luck from someone who has tried it on in the store. Once on the bride's finger, the ring should not be removed for seven years.

A couple being married should stand with their feet parallel to the cracks in the floor, as to stand crosswise invites bad luck and evil spirits; this is taken quite seriously in some places. A bride is sometimes audibly reminded to thrust out her right foot as she turns away from the preacher after the ceremony, since it is bad luck to begin one's married life on the left foot. A pinch of mustard seed may be thrown after a newly married couple, by the bride's parents; this is never commented upon, and I have been unable to learn its significance. If newly married people see a toad in the path, immediately after the ceremony, they regard it as a good omen.

Another old-time notion is that the newlywed who falls asleep first after the wedding will be the first of the couple to die; this is widely credited in some sections, although it is rarely mentioned or discussed. Others think that if the number of letters in the couple's given names—both names added together—is divisible by two, it means that the bridegroom will live longer than the bride; if the number is odd, the bride will outlive her husband.

Some mountain girls believe that it is bad luck to marry a man whose surname has the same initial as one's own:

> Change the name an' not the letter,
> Marry for worse an' not for better.

It is a very bad omen for a bride to help cook her own wedding dinner, and some say it means that she will die soon after the ceremony. Many Ozark mothers will not even allow their daughters to go into the kitchen for several days before they are to be married.

It is quite all right, however, for a bride to make her own wedding garments, and considerable thought is given to the old adage that a bride should wear "something old and something new, something gold and something blue."

Mountain girls sometimes conceal a lock of their own hair in the hem of another girl's wedding dress, or thread a fine needle with a single hair which is then sewn into some inconspicuous part of the bride's outfit. Exactly what sort of "conjure" this is I can't say, but it is akin to witchcraft, and somehow benefits the owner of the hair at the poor bride's expense. I know of one girl who borrowed a reading lens and examined her wedding garments very carefully, to make sure that the women who helped make the dress had not surreptitiously sewn some of their hair into it.

The color of a bride's dress is important, of course, and every hill girl knows the little rhyme:

> If when you marry your dress is red,
> You'll wish to God that you was dead;
> If when you marry your dress is white,
> Ever'thing will be all right.

There are similar verses about the other colors, but they seem to be taken less seriously somehow:

> Marry in green,
> Ashamed to be seen.
> Marry in brown,
> Move into town.
> Marry in blue,
> Always be true.
> Marry in yeller,
> Ashamed of her feller.
> Marry in black,
> Very bad luck.

Here is another version as I heard it near Harrison, Arkansas:

> Blue is true,
> Yaller's jealous,
> Green's forsaken,
> Red is brazen,
> White is love
> And black is death.

This is the way they say it at Sallisaw, Oklahoma:

> Marry in white, you have chosen just right,
> Marry in blue, your man will be true,
> Marry in brown, live out of town,
> Marry in green, ashamed to be seen,
> Marry in red, wish yourself dead,
> Marry in black, better turn back,
> Marry in yellow, got the wrong fellow,
> Marry in gray, you'll be a widow some day.

This brings us to another old-time verse, which deals with the significance of eye color in women:

> If a woman's eyes are gray,
> Listen close what she's got to say;
> If a woman's eyes are black,
> Give her room an' plenty o' track;
> If a woman's eyes are brown,
> Never let your own fall down;
> If a woman's eyes are green,
> Whip her with a switch that's keen;
> If a woman's eyes are blue,
> She will always be true to you.

A hill woman is very careful not to exhibit any of her wedding garments until she has worn them, or at least tried them on. I recall a girl who was about to show her mother the new pink "weddin' slippers" which had just arrived by mail, but caught herself just in time, reminded by her sister's agonized outcry. The entire family trembled over this narrow escape from some nameless calamity.

After the bride is completely dressed for the ceremony, she must not look into a mirror until the preacher has pronounced the fateful words—if she does, the marriage will turn out badly. The bride sometimes dresses before her mirror, but is careful to leave off some small item of attire, such as a bow of ribbon, which is put on at the last minute without looking in the glass.

It is bad luck for a backwoods bridegroom to put away his wedding clothes immediately and resume his workaday overalls. He is always advised to wear his new suit occasionally for several months, whether he goes to town or not. The bride does not seem to observe any such custom; she may not *sell* the dress she was married in, but she is free to wear it, or pack it away as a sort of keepsake, or give it to a younger sister. Ultimately it finds its place in the patchwork quilts of the clan, where it may be pointed out as Gran'ma so-and-so's wedding dress, long after the bride and groom and all the "weddin'ers" are sleeping in the buryin'-ground on the hill.

There seem to be no particular taboos attached to the newly-weds' cooking utensils, except that it is very bad luck to set up housekeeping with a new coffeepot. I have known hillfolk, even educated ones, to borrow a battered old coffeepot and use it for a month or two, before bringing a brand-new one into the house.

Some religious hillfolk, particularly the adherents of certain so-called Holy Roller cults, consider it proper to refrain from sexual intercourse the first night after marriage; some of them are so ostentatious about the taboo that they do not allow the bride and groom to be alone in a room together. This is supposed to show that the union is somehow spiritual, not based upon mere physical attraction. A fourteen-year-old girl in McDonald county, Missouri, was about to be married, and spoke with something like alarm of what might happen on her wedding night. The girl's aunt said to her, in the presence of my wife and several other women: "Don't you be skeerd, honey. You're a-marryin' a Christian gentleman! He won't do *nothin'* the first night, not even if you was to ask him!"

9. Pregnancy and Childbirth

The superstitions connected with pregnancy and childbirth are very numerous, kept alive and promulgated by the backwoods midwives who are known as granny-women. Many hillmen will not allow a physician to attend their wives in childbirth, believing that a granny-woman is better. It is surprising, too, how many women do not want a physician at this time. "Doc Holton's all right, in case o' sickness," the mother of seven children said to me, "but I sure don't want no man-person a-conjurin' round when I'm havin' a baby!" Male yarb doctors and power doctors have many remedies for "female troubles," and some of them try to produce abortions, but they generally leave obstetrics to the granny-women. When a granny-woman gets into difficulties she seldom consults with a yarb doctor or a power doctor, but calls in a regular physician.

Large families are common among the old-timers, and some hillfolk believe that a girl will have the same number of children that her mother had, if she allows nature to take its course. When a woman has her first baby, the granny-woman looks very carefully for any lumps or enlargements in the umbilical cord, since the number of these lumps is supposed to indicate the number of children the woman will bear. There is a general notion among these people that more babies are born in August than in any other month, and when a woman's first child is born in August it is a sign that she will have many more children.

It is said that if a child is conceived in the winter the mother will be subject to chills, and if it is conceived in the summer she will have "hot flashes" and fevers. Some pregnant women sew little pebbles into their garments, or wear pebbles strung around the waist in little cloth sacks; there is something secret about this, something not to be discussed, but it is supposed to prevent future pregnancies.

If a woman does not wish to become pregnant, she is very careful about letting people place babies on her bed. Here is an item from the Springfield (Missouri) *News & Leader*, Dec. 10, 1933: "At a party in Springfield not long ago, a woman started to lay her baby down on the bed. The hostess didn't want a baby right away, so she asked the guest *to lay the baby on a chair.* . . . And if a bride is very anxious to have a baby, her friends may all take their babies to her house and lay them on her bed. It's regarded as a sure sign of the coming stork."

A male visitor should always leave a cabin by the same door he entered; if he fails to do this, it may mean that there'll be an increase in the host's family. Many mountain people take this very seriously, and some women make certain that a visitor *does* go out the same way he came in. There are a lot of bawdy stories on the subject, of course.

Every mountaineer's wife knows that if a baby's diaper is left in her house by some visiting mother, she herself will very shortly become pregnant. I've heard some good stories about that one, too.

Mistletoe is used somehow by women who wish to have children, and some say that it can be administered by the husband, without the wife's knowledge or consent. If a woman cannot conceive, the power doctor may take nine little switches and tie a knot in each. Then he burns them and makes the woman eat the ashes.

A tea made of tansy leaves is a well-known abortifacient. Mrs. May Kennedy McCord says: "Girls used to soak tansy leaves in buttermilk to whiten their skins, but I remember very plainly that when they went to Grandma Melton's to get the tansy . . . they were very particular to tell her what it was for! Camomile tea was another suspicious *character sp'ilin'* tea." [1] Mrs. McCord returns to this subject in the *News*, Aug. 16, 1941, where she remarks: "And I recall that no woman ever drank cedar-berry tea without being 'talked about.' Men might take it for chills, but never women!" Pennyroyal leaves are also supposed to bring about abortions, and so is a tea made from the roots of the cotton plant, though the latter is usually mixed with tansy for the best results. Large doses of turpentine are believed to cause abortions. Any drug used for this purpose should be taken in one of the *odd* months—January, March, May, July, September, or November.

I have known middle-aged women who, at certain times or seasons, mixed pennyroyal leaves with the tobacco which they smoked in their pipes. They were rather secretive about this, implying that it had to do with some female disorder, but I was never able to get any definite information on the subject.

A tea made of black snakeroot (*Cimicifuga*) is also used as a medicine for "female troubles"—which usually means amenorrhea. Squawroot (*Caulophyllum thalictroides*) is highly recommended for "the diseases of women." The blossoms of red clover, dried and powdered, are supposed to "relieve irregularity." A tea brewed from horehound and raspberry leaves is recommended to young girls who complain of a scanty or painful flow, although some yarb doctors think that a strong infusion of red-stemmed smartweed is better in such cases.

Some women in Washington county, Arkansas, are loud in praise of Devil's-shoestring as a remedy for menorrhagia; I am not familiar with this plant, but the name is sometimes applied to goat's-rue, a weed which the Choctaw Indians use in poisoning fish.

Blackhaw bark, according to the old folks, makes a tea that is useful in all sorts of "female complaints." It is good for scanty, irregular, or painful menstruation. Women going through the change of life consume large quantities of blackhaw bark, and

[1] Springfield (Missouri) *News*, Dec. 3, 1940.

this use of the stuff is so well known that there is a whole cycle of allegedly funny stories about it.

Mountain girls are not overfond of bathing at any time, but they are taught *never* to bathe or even wash their hair while they are menstruating. There is an almost universal belief among the hillfolk that to do so causes coughs and colds, leads to pulmonary tuberculosis, or may even induce a paralytic stroke. Pregnant women bathe very seldom, and never in cold water. In some clans it is believed that death is the penalty for an expectant mother who crosses a running stream, and there are tales of women going to great lengths to avoid this danger.

A pregnant woman may go about her household tasks as usual, but she should never try to "put up" fruit—the stuff will spoil every time. She can attend to her chickens, milk cows, work in her garden, and do other farm chores, but she must on no account jump over the endgate of a wagon, or stoop under a horse's neck—if she does, she is certain to miscarry. "That ought to be good news to the gals who *want* to get rid of their babies," I said to the old woman who told me this. "Hit don't work that-a-way, an' you know it," she answered. "You aint serious-minded, Vance, an' it aint no use to tell you 'bout them things."

It is common knowledge that in certain neurotic families the husband falls ill when the wife becomes pregnant. One man told me that his wife had six children, and that during each pregnancy he vomited every morning, and so on. The midwife confirmed his story, as did a local physician who was familiar with the case. This man's wife was much pleased, thinking that her husband's suffering indicated the depth of his affection for her and somehow made her pregnancy easier. "My man he allus does my pukin' for me," she told the neighbors proudly. Such a situation is not rare enough to cause much comment and is referred to as a sort of joke on the husband.

Not many hillfolk practice any sort of magic to determine

the sex of an unborn child, although some granny-women teach that parents may "fetch a boy" by sticking a knife in the mattress, while a woman who wants a girl can get results by placing a skillet under the bed.

There is a rather common idea that the sex of a child is somehow determined by which parent is the more powerful sexually; if the father is most passionate, the children will be mostly girls, while if the mother is more sensual than the father, there will be many boys in the family.

Some peckerwood folk in central Arkansas believe that if a husband sits on his roof for seven hours, near the chimney, his next child will be a boy. I have known several men to try this, but only one stuck it out for the full seven hours. He took a hammer up with him, and when anybody that he knew came along the road, he pretended to be fixing the roof. The next child *was* a boy, too.

Granny-women say that when a pregnant woman's burden seems to be "carried high" the child is likely to be a female, but an unborn babe that is "carried low" is nearly always a boy. A woman who is "big in front" early in her pregnancy expects a boy baby, while one who grows "big in the back" will give birth to a girl.

When a pregnant woman has a craving for some particular article of food, every effort is made to satisfy it, because otherwise the child is very likely to be "marked." I have seen birthmarks which were supposed to resemble strawberries, cherries, sweet potatoes, prunes, eels, and even hams—all of which owed their existence to the mother's unsatisfied craving for these things. Even if the child has no external marks, his mind is likely to be affected, and he is sure to be "a plumb glutton" for the particular food that could not be obtained for his mother.

Children are also said to be marked by some sudden fright or unpleasant experience of the mother, and I have myself seen a pop-eyed, big-mouthed idiot whose condition is ascribed to the fact that his mother stepped on a toad several months before his birth. In another case, a large red mark on a baby's cheek was caused by the mother seeing a man shot down at her side, when the discharge of the gun threw some of the blood and brains into her face. Another woman in my neighborhood saw two large snakes fighting or copulating, and when her babe was born some months later it had two writhing serpents in place of a head, according to local testimony. I recall a young farmer who had been worsted in a drunken fight and appeared in the village all covered with blood and dirt. Instantly everybody sprang to prevent the injured man's pregnant wife from seeing him, and one old man shrilled out: "Git Emmy away, folks —she'll mark that 'ar young-un shore!"

The editor of a newspaper at Pineville, Missouri, told me that during the Civil War some bushwhackers killed a man near that place; they cut off one of his ears and threw it into his wife's lap as she sat on her little front porch. The woman was pregnant at the time, and when her child was born one of his ears "warn't nothin' but a wart." The people in Pineville regarded this as a classic case of "marking"—a positive proof that prenatal influence is a fact.

Mr. J. A. Wasson, of Nixa, Missouri, in the Springfield *News*, Sept. 16, 1941, tells of Uncle Wesley McCullah, who was killed by a bullet which incidentally knocked out two of his front teeth. Shortly afterward McCullah's widow gave birth to a baby girl, "born with two teeth the same as her father lost."

"Babies are certainly marked by their mothers during pregnancy," writes Miss Annie K. Wilson, of Magnolia, Arkansas, "a red spot on my finger attesting to that fact, for didn't Mother dress a cut on my father's knee and get blood on her finger?" [2]

A pregnant woman must not look at a dead body, since this is likely to mark the baby and might cause it to be born dead;

[2] *Arcadian Life* (April, 1937), p. 27.

women in the early months of pregnancy sometimes attend funerals but always take care not to look directly at the corpse, even if it is that of a near relative.

In Lawrence county, Missouri, a woman gave birth to a female child who was said to be "marked for a cat"—the mother having been startled by an unexpected encounter with a trapped wildcat in the fourth month of her pregnancy. This baby looked all right except that its body was unusually hairy, but it never learned to talk or to walk erect. It mewed and growled like a cat, ate like a cat, and slept curled up on a pillow behind the stove. When the cat girl reached the age of thirteen she began to have "wild spells" at regular intervals, like an animal in heat. So the family built a stout cage inside the house, and shut her up while the "spell" lasted—a neighbor said that "you could hear her a-hollerin' an' a-yowlin' half a mile off." I am told that this cat woman was still living near Aurora, Missouri, in 1941, and she must have been more than fifty years old at that time. In recent years, however, she has been very quiet. She sleeps most of the time and does not have to be caged any longer. I asked a physician who knows that neighborhood about the cat woman. "I have never seen this case," he answered, "but I have heard about her for many years. I don't doubt that they have got an idiot in that house, who walks on all fours, and is unable to talk. Doubtless she eats like an animal and behaves like one in other ways. You can see such creatures in any asylum. But all this stuff about her being 'marked' by a cat— that's just backwoods superstition. If the mother of that idiot had been scared by a wolf instead of a wildcat, the child would have been called a 'wolf girl,' and these farmers would imagine that the noises she makes sound exactly like a wolf growling."

Otto Ernest Rayburn, of Eureka Springs, Arkansas, tells of a woman who was frightened by cattle during her pregnancy, and the child had a strange cowlike face, "with two small growths protruding from the head like horns." Not only that, but the creature "emitted low, rumbling sounds like the bellowing of a bull!"

I am told that there are numerous secret things to be done and other equally secret things to be avoided during pregnancy, in order to make the delivery as easy as possible. For example, it is very bad luck to make a cap or any kind of headgear for a baby before the baby is born—to do this nearly always makes the "birthin'" a difficult one. In fact, it is dangerous even to *talk* about the head or headgear of a baby before it is born; above all, it is bad luck to tell anybody *not* to make a cap under such conditions. If some ignorant outsider does give an expectant mother a child's cap she burns it instantly, sometimes right before the donor's eyes.

A woman at Paris, Arkansas, told me that a plant called spikenard was the best thing to make childbirth easy, adding that a woman who had plenty of spikenard didn't need no granny-woman; she bought the dried herb from a traveling yarb doctor and didn't know whether it grew wild near Paris or not. "If you caint git spikenard," she said, "the next best thing is sweet flag" (*Acorus calamus*), which is common in many parts of the Ozark country. People near Paris tell me that spikenard is also known as wild licorice; it may be *Aralia racemosa*, but I'm not sure about this.

An oil made from pigs' feet is often given internally in the belief that it somehow facilitates the bearing of healthy children.

I have met two granny-women who carry old silver coins that were once stolen from a church. It is said that to put one of these coins into a feather bed protects the person who sleeps on the bed from cramps and venereal infections, but above all it is used to ease the pains of childbirth.

There are some old people who always make sure that an empty hornets' nest is hanging in the loft of the cabin where a woman is to be confined. I have heard of granny-women who refused to deliver a child until they saw the hornets' nest for themselves but have never met one who would admit this. It is a fact, however, that there are few really old cabins in which one cannot find a hornets' nest suspended under the eaves, or attached to one of the rafters.

Near Pineville, Missouri, I once sat with a neighbor out in a woodlot, while his wife was giving birth to a child in the house. This man had a regular physician in attendance, but one of the neighborhood granny-women had arrived ahead of the doctor. The patient screamed several times, and then the granny-woman came out to the wood pile and picked up the ax, which she carried into the house. I was horrified at this, but the husband sat unmoved, so I said nothing. After it was all over I asked the doctor privately how on earth the old woman had made use of a five-pound double-bitted ax in her obstetrical practice. The doctor laughed and replied that she just put it under the bed. "A common superstition," he said. "It's supposed to make a difficult birth easier, and she saw that this was going to be a pretty bad one."

Later on I learned that this ax-under-the-bed business is practiced in all parts of the Ozark country. An old granny near Sulphur Springs, Arkansas, told me that an ax used for this purpose must be razor-sharp, since a dull ax may do more harm than good. It appears that some families—I found several near Sylamore, Arkansas—place a sharp plowpoint under the bed, instead of an ax.

In cases of difficult childbirth, many hillfolk burn corncobs on the doorstep, or even under the bed. There is an old story to the effect that red cobs are much more effective than white cobs, but this is not taken seriously. There is some connection, however, in the hillman's mind, between corncobs and childbearing. I once knew a fellow who was outraged because his wife gathered a great many red cobs and burned them in the fireplace at night; he thought that she did this because she was unwilling to have any more children.

Mrs. May Kennedy McCord, of Springfield, Missouri, says

that some granny-women, when things begin to go wrong, snatch up all the blankets in the house, dip 'em in hot water, and hang them up around the woman's bed.

Many of the old midwives still administer gunpowder and water to women in labor, believing that it stimulates the muscular contractions which expel the child.

Dr. J. H. Young, Galena, Missouri, told me of an old-time healer who proposed to "quill" a woman who was having a very difficult delivery. Dr. Young had no idea what "quillin' " meant, but he found out that the old "doc" intended to fill a turkey quill with snuff and blow it in the woman's face. The theory is that the snuff makes the woman sneeze, and the baby is born instanter.

Granny-women in many parts of the Ozark country used to give a tea made of blackberry root to a woman in childbirth; this was supposed to expedite matters but was regarded as much less drastic than the use of the quill.

After the babe is delivered, some hillfolk burn a handful of chicken feathers under the bed, as this is supposed to stop hemorrhage. If the woman has a really bad "bleedin' " they kill a chicken and fasten the warm lining of its gizzard over the affected part, usually burning a few feathers at the same time. Needless to say, one never sweeps under the bed of a woman in childbirth, or she would surely die. So the ashes of corncobs, chicken feathers or anything else that is burned must lie there until the woman is up and about.

When a babe is "born blue" the granny-woman makes "skillet-bark tea" from the soot off'n the bottom of a kettle or frying pan. She feeds a few drops of this to the child every ten minutes or so over a long period of time, perhaps as much as twenty-four hours.

Many granny-women are accustomed to give every newborn babe quantities of onion tea, then wrap it in a blanket and wait till it "breaks out with the hives." If the reddish rash does not appear, they fear that the child will not live long.

A very common idea is that the afterbirth must be buried just outside the house, at the corner of the chimney. Some women say that the particular spot is not important, but they all agree that the afterbirth should be buried; if it is burned or thrown into water, the mother will not make a proper recovery.[3]

There are several strange notions about babes born prematurely. The grannies all insist that while seven-month babies are not uncommon, eight-month babies are almost unknown. Or, as one old woman put it, seven-month babes often live, while eight-month babes are nearly all born dead, or die a few hours after birth. I once asked Dr. Oakley St. John, of Pineville, Missouri, whether seven-months babies ever lived to grow up. "Yes," he said solemnly, "if the parents of a seven-months baby are newly married, the baby generally lives. But when a woman who has been married more than eight months has a seven-months baby, it nearly always dies." An old backwoods midwife who was in the office scowled darkly. The granny-women regard this as a serious question, and they do not like to hear people joking about it.

Nothing can convince some of these women that premature babies ever have fingernails. When a baby is born less than nine months after its parents have been married, the old gossips always look for the nails. "Caint fool me," said one old woman. "Them young-uns planted their corn 'bout six weeks 'fore they built their fences. I *seen* fingernails on that baby!"

Many old-timers believe that women never suffer "after-pains" following the birth of a first baby, but very often have them after subsequent births. So if a woman does experience these pains after the birth of her first child, her reputation is more or less damaged, no matter what the midwives and the

---

[3] The same thing is true of amputated limbs, although here the belief is that the owner will return after death in a mutilated condition and be forced to search for the lost member through all eternity.

doctors say. Everybody thinks she must have given birth to a baby some time previously and kept it secret.

There is a very general notion that a woman loses a tooth every time she has a child. Some say that this goes for abortions or miscarriages as well, so that every pregnancy involves the loss of a tooth, no matter what happens to the fetus.

Multiple births are regarded with something like horror in many localities. "It aint fitten for a woman to shell out young-uns in litters that-a-way, like a brute beast!" said one of our old neighbors at Pineville, Missouri. Twins are always associated with tragedy and misfortune. Mrs. C. P. Mahnkey, Mincy, Missouri, recalls that the wife of a notorious Bald Knobber named Matthews gave birth to twins shortly before her husband was hanged at Ozark, Missouri, in 1889. There was a good deal of talk about this at the time, and it is still remembered and discussed in Matthews' old neighborhood.

If a child is born with a caul or "veil" the membrane is carefully dried and given to the child after it reaches maturity, otherwise the youngster is condemned to a life of perpetual misfortune. The series of calamities which befell one of my neighbors is accounted for by the fact that she was born with a veil, which the granny-woman in attendance very properly hung on a bush to dry; this woman forgot to bring it to the house, however, and a great storm blew the thing away into the hills. In case the afterbirth or the veil falls into the hands of an enemy of the family, the child will be more or less in this person's power always and may be forced into all sorts of evil deeds through no fault of its own. Another important thing to be remembered is that the band which protects the navel of an infant must be turned over three times before it is washed or burned; some people regard this as a safeguard against witchcraft, while others think that it simply prevents the child from having backache later in life.

Many old-timers believe that sexual unions between human beings and domestic animals are sometimes fruitful. Stories of women giving birth to litters of puppies, mares bringing forth colts with human heads, and a great variety of similar phenomena are related and generally believed. I have never been able to locate a hillman who has actually seen any of these monstrosities—"the folks allus puts 'em out o' the way," as one old man told me.

Hillfolk will seldom admit that their children were born crippled or defective, since this might somehow discredit the family. They always say that a defective child was injured shortly after birth, or that its condition is due to smallpox, measles, or scarlet fever. I remember a little boy with a crippled foot—the sort of thing that the doctors say is always congenital. The child's father insisted to me that the boy was perfectly normal until the age of two, when he was sick for a long time and "the fever fell in his leg." Another member of the family told me privately that the child had been crippled from birth, because somebody had "throwed a spell" upon the mother.

The place where a birth occurs is of no great importance in Ozark folklore, although some say that a babe is lucky to be born in a covered wagon, or under a wagon sheet. It is generally thought best, however, that the mother's head should be toward the north. Misfortune would certainly be the portion of a child should the moonlight fall upon the bed at the time of its birth, and even an adult who sleeps much in the moonlight is likely to go blind or crazy, or both.

Most of the old-timers believe that a woman should never be bathed "all over," or her bedding completely changed, for nine days after the child is born. Some say that the palms of a child's hands should not be washed until the child is three days old—to do so washes away the infant's luck, particularly in financial matters. It is always best to bathe a new baby's head with stump water; if ordinary water is used, the child is likely to be prematurely bald when it grows up.

Mrs. May Stafford Hilburn says that it is customary to "wrap a newborn boy baby in his father's shirt, to bring the child good luck. A baby girl is given her mother's petticoat as swaddling clothes, for the same reason." [4]

Backwoods people sometimes carry a baby boy out into the dooryard when he is very small and show him the outside of the house—it is said that this will prevent him from running away from home later on. Many granny-women think it is a good thing to carry any newborn babe three times around the cabin; some say it protects the infant against sore eyes, others that it wards off colic.

In some clans, when a baby boy is born, a sister of the babe's father comes to the house, looks at the child, and then burns the first hat she finds. No matter whose it is, nor how valuable, she just picks up a hat and throws it into the fireplace. Many people laugh at this and pretend to take it lightly, but it is never omitted in certain families. I know of one case where there was some doubt about the child's paternity, and the husband's family were by no means friendly to the young mother, but despite all this one of the sisters came and burned the hat; she did it silently and grudgingly and most ungraciously, but she did it. This practice is never discussed with outsiders, but it is sufficiently known that a series of funny stories has grown up about hats being burned by mistake, strangers' hats missing, doctors leaving their hats at home, and so on.

Medical men say there's nothing to it, but thousands of old women in the Ozark country are firmly convinced that cats must be kept away from new babies; they believe that if a cat gets a chance, it will sit on the baby's chest and suck its breath until the child is suffocated.

When a very young baby cries and seems in pain, the mother looks to see if the wind is in the northeast; if it is, she doesn't worry, since all babies are supposed to be irritable when the wind is in the northeast.

There are numerous old sayin's about the influence of the day of a child's birth upon its character and prospects. Some

[4] *Missouri Magazine* (September, 1933), p. 21.

of these are recorded in a rhyme contributed by Mrs. Marie Wilbur, Pineville, Missouri.

> Monday's child is fair of face,
> Tuesday's child is full of grace,
> Wednesday's child has far to go,
> Thursday's child is full of woe.
> Friday's child is loving and giving,
> Saturday's child must work for a living.
> A child that's born on the Sabbath day
> Is blithe and bonnie and rich and gay.

Here is a variant from an old manuscript book belonging to Miss Miriam Lynch, Notch, Missouri.

> Sunday—never to want,
> Monday—fair in face,
> Tuesday—full of grace,
> Wednesday—woeful and sad,
> Thursday—a long ways to go,
> Friday—loving and giving,
> Saturday—work hard for a living.

A baby born on New Year's will be lucky always, no matter what day of the week it happens to be. A child born at the time of the new moon will be exceptionally strong and muscular.

Children born on Friday the thirteenth will always be unlucky, but a part of this evil may be avoided by falsifying the record; if such a child ever does have any good fortune, it will be after the death of the last person who knows the true date.

Some granny-women claim that a baby born between June 23 and July 23 will be a "natural born failure" all its life, clumsy and unlucky at everything it tries to do. I have known two women, living in widely separated parts of the Ozarks, who took extraordinary precautions to prevent their children being born at this unlucky season. Mr. Booth Campbell, of Cane Hill, Arkansas, told me that the old-timers in his neighborhood always claimed March 21 as the unluckiest birthday in the month, and one of the most unfavorable days in the whole year.

There are several methods of predicting what a child's future life is to be. One of the commonest is to offer a boy baby a bottle, a Bible, and a coin. If he grasps the bottle first, he will be a drunkard; if the Bible, a preacher, or at least a religious man; while if he chooses the coin, he will engage in some mercantile pursuit.

If there are seven sons in a family, and no daughters, the seventh son is clearly intended to be a physician. The seventh son *of a seventh son* is a physician in spite of himself, endowed with healing powers which cannot be denied. Even if such a man does not study or practice medicine, he is very often called "Doc" or "Doctor" by common consent. However, small-time gamblers are often called "Doc" too, just as every backwoods auctioneer becomes a "Colonel."

If there are ten sons in a family, and no daughters, the tenth son must be a preacher. "God meant it to be that-a-way," an old woman once told me. "He knows how many preachers we need in this world." She would not go so far as to say, however, that it is a mistake to call men who are *not* tenth sons into the ministry.

Many hillfolk believe that a third son is more intelligent than his brothers and should therefore be encouraged to "git more book-l'arnin'." Others contend that, other things being equal, the fourth child has the brains of the whole family. It is often said too that a child who is small for his age is unusually bright, while a boy who is large for his age is generally slow or even dull-witted.

One often hears that babies with long hair grow very slowly, since their strength all goes into the hair. Some hillfolk believe that an infant with very long hair, or any other characteristic which makes it appear older than its real age, will not live long. It is very unfortunate for a baby to see his reflection in a mirror; some say that this will cause the child to have bad luck all his life, others think that he will never live to reach maturity.

A boy baby who bites his nails very young will not grow tall and is likely to be in poor health most of his life. It is a bad sign for a child to talk before he walks. Many old folks say that if a baby walks before he crawls, there is not much chance of his getting very far in life; some think that such a baby will become insane, or at least very eccentric, when he grows up. A small child who sticks his head into a gnat ball (a swarm of gnats or other small flying insects) will be unlucky and in poor health for seven years.

It is good luck for a new baby to wear another baby's clothes; but once worn, these must never be returned to the child for whom they were first intended. Never tickle a baby under the chin, as this may make him stammer. I have seen backwoods mothers give children water in a thimble; this is believed to help in their teething and produce strong, pleasant voices in later life.

Some old people say that if you take the first louse ever found on the baby's head and crack it on a bell, the child will be a good singer. Nancy Clemens, of Springfield, Missouri, tells me that she once knew a girl who talked a great deal; the girl's parents said, half seriously, that it was because when she was a baby an old woman found a louse on her head and cracked it on a cowbell.

A blister on a boy's tongue is a sure sign that he will be a liar when he grows up, but a blister on a girl's tongue has no such significance. Little girls are told that if they can touch their elbows with a blister on their tongues, they'll turn into boys. It is very bad luck for a little boy to eat birds' eggs; some of the old-timers think that a boy who does so will never mature sexually or will be somehow abnormal in that regard. Small children of either sex are warned against sitting on rocks, or stone steps, since the old folks say it will make 'em hardhearted. A little boy who persists in wearing a string of beads always comes to a bad end and is very likely to be hanged.

Mrs. Isabel Spradley, Van Buren, Arkansas, tells me that the natural or accidental death of a child's pet kitten is a fine thing for the child, according to the old-timers in her neighborhood. But it is very bad luck for anybody to kill a child's cat intentionally.

Never call a baby "angel," because babies called by that name do not live long. When an infant smiles in its sleep, it may mean that the child is talking to the angels, and this is a bad omen.

Ozark women have some peculiar notions about the proper feeding of nursing mothers. Some women eat great quantities of raw onions, while others drink sorghum-and-water by the gallon, to insure good rich milk for the baby. I know one woman who never touched tobacco ordinarily, but while she was nursing her babe she chewed snuff and "long green" incessantly; she said that this was supposed to purify her milk.

Many Ozark mothers can hardly be induced to wean their children. The doctors say that eight or nine months is long enough for a woman to nurse a child, but thousands of back-country mothers nurse their babes for eighteen months, or even longer. Dr. J. H. Young, Galena, Missouri, tells me that some of his patients don't wean their babes until they are two or even three years of age. I myself have seen children at least five years old run to the mother who was nursing a younger child and beg for "jest a taste, Maw!" The chief reason for all this, I take it, is the belief that a woman who is nursing a child can't become pregnant. I have heard a great many funny stories about this matter of backwoods reluctance to wean children.

One of the more innocent of these tales refers to a sixteen-year-old boy who had never used tobacco. One day he suddenly asked his father for a chaw, and the man expressed some surprise. "Well," said the boy, "Maw's been eatin' onions again, an' I got to have somethin' to take the taste out o' my mouth!"

Many backwoods women say that they are not afraid of any infectious disease so long as they are nursing babes. This applies particularly to measles and scarlet fever; women with babes at their breasts walk fearlessly into houses where people are sick with these diseases, when they would hesitate to do so if their babes were weaned. Some even claim that a nursing mother is temporarily immune to venereal disease, but I do not know how widely this latter idea is accepted.

When a mother is finally persuaded to wean her child, the general opinion is that it should be done in Aquarius, when the sign is in the legs. Others say that either the thighs or the knees are favorable places for the weaning sign. One woman told me that any sign below the heart will do, but that it is absolutely impossible to wean a child when the sign is above the heart, adding that she had seen it tried with most distressing results. May Stafford Hilburn says that "an Ozark mother weans her baby by the sign. If it should be in the head he will be stubborn and refuse food. If it is in the heart he will cry himself sick, and give her much worry. Neither will she disregard the sign if it is in the stomach, for then strange foods will upset his digestion. If she waits until the sign is 'going down' he sleeps like a log, and no bad effects are noticed." [5]

Even after the child is weaned, there are still some difficulties about feeding. I have seen a woman sitting at a table, with the whole family present, also several strangers who had been invited to dinner. Sitting there with the babe on her lap, she chewed up bits of meat and other food, removed it from her own mouth, and fed it to the child with a little wooden spoon. This performance may be good for the child, but it's pretty tough on the spectators.

[5] *Missouri Magazine* (September, 1933), p. 20.

10. Ghost Stories

Nearly all of the old-time hillfolk are firm believers in ghosts and wandering spirits, although few adult males will admit this belief to outsiders nowadays. But in the childhood of men and women still living, the telling of ghost stories was much more common than it is today. The pioneers used to invite people to their cabins for the express purpose of swapping supernatural tales. It was a recognized form of social entertainment, especially favored by people who did not hold with dancing or card playing.

Mrs. May Kennedy McCord, of Springfield, Missouri, thinks that the decay of ghost stories in the Ozarks is due to the fact that there are so few really *lonesome* places nowadays. In order to raise a good crop of ghosts, she says, we must have a lot of old mills and deserted houses and covered bridges—and these romantic spots are not so common as they used to be.

It seems to me that the Ozark ghost stories do not differ greatly from those that are told in other sections of the United States. An account of Ozark superstition, however, would be incomplete without any mention of these tales, so I record some of them here for what they may be worth.

There are many humorous cracks about the hillman's belief in ghosts. One ancient wheeze refers to a superstitious fellow who was afraid to walk past the graveyard at night. His friends tried to build up his morale, assuring him that ghosts have never been known to hurt anybody. "Maybe not," said the hillman, "but I just don't want 'em a-follerin' me around!"

Mr. Lewis Kelley, Cyclone, Missouri, told me a kind of comic

ghost story he had heard near Cyclone in the eighties. It seems
that old lady Jones and her two sons were stealing sheep from
Jim Bray, a rich old man who had not walked for years because of his rheumatism. The old woman would wait in the
graveyard by the road, while her two boys went into a field and
got one of Bray's sheep. She always examined the animal they
carried out, and if it wasn't fat enough she'd make the boys
turn it loose and go back after another. One dark night she sat
in the graveyard and waited impatiently. The boys were a little
slower than usual. Meanwhile Jim Bray was talking to his family, upbraiding them because they didn't catch the sheep thieves.
"If I could walk," he cried, "I'd go over an' lay for 'em in the
old graveyard, an' I'd stay thar till I *did* ketch 'em." Finally
two of the Bray boys said "All right, Pappy, we'll jest pack
you over thar," so they picked up the old man and carried him
across the pasture. It was a very dark night, but they knew
the path. When the two boys carried their father into the graveyard, old Mis' Jones saw them dimly and thought that it was
her boys returning with the sheep. " 'Bout time you-uns was
a-comin'," she croaked hoarsely. "Is he fat?" and she pinched
the old man's leg! With wild yells of terror the Bray boys
dropped their Pappy and "tuck out" for home, but the old man
was right at their heels when they reached the cabin. Mr. Bray
never doubted that the Devil himself had been waiting for him
in the graveyard. All the rest of his life he boasted that the Old
Boy had riz up out of hell to cure his rheumatism, after the
doctors had plumb give up the case.

Another old tale of the same general type was about two men
who heard that the Devil had been visiting a certain buryin'
ground, so they went and hid behind a stone wall to see what
they could see. This was just before dusk. Two little boys came
along, with a sack of pawpaws they had gathered. They spread
the pawpaws out on the ground, on the opposite side of the
wall from where the two men were hiding, and began to divide
them. "You take this one, I'll take that one; you take this one,

I'll take that one," one of the boys chanted, as he placed the pawpaws in two separate heaps. Finally the other boy said: "Well, that's all, except them two big ones over there. You take the dried-up one, and I'll take the fat one." This described the two men pretty well, and they broke out of hiding and ran yelling for home. They thought that some Evil Spirits were dividing up the dead, and that they had been counted in with the others.

One of my friends at Mena, Arkansas, told of a young man who was notoriously afraid of the supernatural, and some of his comrades planned to play a joke on him. They dressed in white garments and hid near an old graveyard. When the "skeery" fellow came along the road they sprang out with loud groans and shrieks. The young man was frightened almost to the point of madness. He gave one great leap and ran blindly until he was stopped by a wire fence. Screaming at the top of his voice he snatched out an old revolver and emptied it at his tormentors. Two of the masqueraders were hit, one of them being quite seriously wounded. There has been no more "playin' ghost" in that neighborhood.

A woman near Sparta, in Christian county, Missouri, tells a story she learned from her grandmother. A young man had been visiting his sweetheart, and as he rode away from her gate at midnight she called out "I'll be with you all the way home." Soon he noticed something white floating in the air behind him. He put spurs to his horse but the white thing stayed close. Just before he reached home the young man's hat blew off, and he did not stop to look for it. Next morning he told his mother that the girl was a witch, and that he would never go to see her again, or have anything to do with her. The girl had no idea what was wrong; she wrote several letters to the young man, but he did not answer them, and a few months later she married and moved to Oklahoma. Our young man never saw her again, but that fall he walked out in the woods one day and found the lost hat in a patch of brambles. A roll of cotton was attached to it. The girl and her mother had been carding cotton on the night of his last visit, and some of the stuff had caught under his snakeskin hatband. The long roll of cotton, streaming from the hat, was the "white thing" that had floated behind as he rode homeward.

In Jackson county, Missouri, the old folks tell of two loafers who were employed to transport a corpse secretly from a village graveyard to a medical school in Kansas City. This was in the eighties, and they had the body wrapped in canvas and covered with straw in the back of a wagon. It was a dark, cold night, and the ground was covered with snow. They stopped for a toddy at a roadside tavern, and while they were inside a drunken country boy, knowing nothing of the corpse under the straw, crawled into the wagon box and went to sleep. When the grave robbers started on again they had a bottle of whiskey and became gradually more jovial. Finally, as they were taking a drink out of the bottle, one of them turned around and shouted to the corpse: "Git up, old stiff, and have a snifter!" This aroused the country boy, who sat up with a jerk. "Don't keer if I do," he answered loudly. The boy was astounded when both men screamed wildly, leaped out of the wagon, and fled into the woods. "I could hear them fellers a-hollerin' for a long time," he said later on. "They kept a-gettin' fainter an' fainter, but they was still a-hollerin'," he added.

Some of the tales that the hillfolk call ghost stories are not very startling, but simply accounts of sights or sounds commonplace enough, except that the usual causes of these sensations are apparently lacking. Some people named Criger, for example, drove up to a house near Rogersville, Missouri. This house had long been vacant, and the villagers said it was ha'nted. The Crigers stopped because they saw smoke coming out of the chimney. They entered the house and found it empty, everything covered with dust. They examined the chimney, and made certain that there had been no fire there for a long time. There were no birds' nests in the chimney, no chimney swallows to stir up dust. So the Crigers, unable to explain the smoke other-wise, reluctantly decided that perhaps the house *was* ha'nted.

In many parts of the Ozark country one hears of a cabin which is haunted by a wood-chopping ghost. People who try to camp there are kept awake by somebody chopping wood all night. At intervals one can hear a grindstone being turned slowly to sharpen an ax, and even detect a change in the sound every few minutes, as if water were being poured on the stone. But there is no grindstone in the vicinity, and nobody has lived there for more than twenty years.

An old lady in McDonald county, Missouri, told me that she once sat alone in her two-room cabin, with the door bolted and the windows fastened on the inside. Suddenly she heard the latch on the door move, and the sound of a heavy man walking across the floor. "I could hear one of his boots squeak at every step," she said, "and then I heard the dipper rattle in the water bucket, like somebody was a-gittin' a drink." The old woman jumped up and ran into the kitchen, but there was nobody there. The door was still bolted, and the windows were still fastened on the inside.

Tom Moore, of Ozark, Missouri, tells the story of a "Squire Reardon" who went out with some other lawyers to visit a farmer in Taney county, Missouri. This farmer claimed that he could hear his daughter singing out in the woods every afternoon, although the girl had been dead for several months. They heard "a woman's voice, gradually increasing in volume until some of the words were reasonably plain . . . as if it were traveling along the pathway . . . loud enough for the yodeling to be heard at the end of each verse." Two lawyers hurried toward the sound and watched the pathway along which the ghost was supposed to walk, but they could see nothing of the singer.[1] The "Squire Reardon" of Moore's story was easily identified as Lou Beardon, a lawyer who lived in Branson, Missouri. I knew Beardon well and asked him about this ghost-story. Beardon

[1] *Mysterious Tales and Legends of the Ozarks,* pp. 116–121.

said that he did not believe in ghosts but admitted that he heard a strange sound in the woods that day, adding that Judge Moore and others professed to believe it was the voice of a girl who had died some time before. "We all heard something," said Beardon. "I never heard anything quite like it in the woods before, but I reckon it must have been some kind of a varmint, or maybe a bird. It sounded like a girl singing, but there wasn't no girl there. . . . I don't know what it was," Beardon ended slowly.

Mrs. Coral Almy Wilson, of Zinc, Arkansas, tells of a couple who tried to sleep all night in a haunted house. They barred the door with a hickory stick, thick as a man's arm. The ghost burst in the door at one blow, but there was nothing to be seen. A moment later they heard something like big marbles or billiard balls rolling over the floor. They got up and lit a candle but saw nothing out of the ordinary. The man barred the door again, and he and his wife were about to lie down again when the ghost resumed its labors. The door burst open for the second time, and as the man sprang to his feet the sound of the big marbles rolling was heard again. "Once is a God's plenty, and twice is too much," so the couple gave up the project and rushed out into the night.

Miss Emma Galbraith, Springfield, Missouri, got this tale in 1934 from an aged Negro: A yellow woman was entertaining another man in the cabin, while her husband was away. She was parching corn at the fireplace. The husband came home unexpectedly, and she braced herself against the door, so as to give the man a chance to escape by a window in the rear. The enraged husband fired through the door, and the woman was instantly killed. Neighbors both white and black declared that they could smell corn parching whenever they passed the cabin in the evening, even after the place had been vacant and dilapidated for many years.

Around Cape Girardeau, Missouri, they tell of a Yankee spy who was captured in the vicinity during the Civil War. Awaiting execution, he danced and sang and "carried on" so that many

people were disgusted. They thought that a man about to die
should not sing dirty songs or shout ribald jokes at everybody
who came within sound of his voice. But the spy took nothing
seriously, laughed at the good priest who visited him, and even
made fun of his own relatives when they came to bid him good-
bye. Finally he was hanged at the big gate of St. Francis Hospital and buried in Lorimer Cemetery. To mark his grave they
put up a stick about three feet high and hung the dead man's
army hat on top of the stick. When anybody approached the
grave at dusk, the ragged old hat would wiggle and dance about,
even when there was not a breath of wind stirring.

Mrs. C. P. Mahnkey once saw clearly a little cabin on a ridge
in the old McCann game park, near her home at Mincy, Missouri. Never having noticed the building before, she got down
the big field glasses and scrutinized it very carefully, remarking
that there was smoke coming out of the chimney. But the next
day the cabin was gone. And the neighbors told her that there
had never been any cabin at that place, so far as any of them
could remember.

There are many ghost stories concerned with Breadtray
Mountain, in Stone county, Missouri. Otto Ernest Rayburn
repeats a number of these legends, which are largely concerned
with buried treasure. "Breadtray Mountain has a legendary
reputation seldom paralleled," says Rayburn. "It is a landmark of strange incident, and hillfolks carefully avoid it." [2]
Many old-timers firmly believe that Spaniards, at some time or
other, buried a great store of gold on Breadtray Mountain just
before they were all killed by the Indians. This seems to be a
variant of the well-known "Lost Louisiana" treasure story.
Tom Moore says that people who visit Breadtray Mountain at
night hear sobs and groans and smothered screams; they believe that these noises are made by the ghosts of Spanish soldiers who were massacred by Indians. Judge Moore intimates
that he has heard these sobs and groans himself, as he says that

[2] *Ozark Country*, pp. 304–306.

his tale "does not come from second-hand information, nor is it based upon hearsay." [3] Mrs. C. P. Mahnkey also refers to mysterious sounds heard by many hillfolk at night on Breadtray Mountain.[4]

The following tale is told about one of my neighbors near Pineville, Missouri, and believed by practically everybody in the settlement. This woman was unkind to her stepchildren, and one day, as she sat alone in the cabin, a violent blow knocked her flat on the floor, while a loud voice cried out: "Be good to my children!" This story is confirmed by the woman herself, who certainly had some sort of a stroke or seizure at the time. Several of her neighbors swear that they visited her later in the day and saw the print of an invisible hand on her face several hours after the attack.

Not far from my old home in McDonald county, Missouri, according to the old-timers, a man was captured years ago by a band of night riders, who hanged him with his own knitted "galluses" until these broke and then finished the hanging with a hickory withe. Some women living nearby buried the body, but it was dug up later by dogs. Not liking the spectacle of human remains being gnawed by dogs, the ladies gathered up the bones and dropped them into a big hollow tree. Serious-minded, sober men and women assure me that they have seen strange lights about this tree and heard groans, and something like old-fashioned gun caps exploding all about.

Some fifty miles south of Springfield, Missouri, on the old Wire Road, the Oak Grove schoolhouse was supposed to be haunted by the ghost of a man hanged there by bushwhackers during the Civil War. Only a few years ago four men rode by the schoolhouse on the way home from a dance and saw a grinning, bald-headed fellow peering out through the window. Coming closer, they noticed that the stranger had no eyebrows or eyelashes. The hillmen addressed the man politely at first, but he made no answer. Finally one of the boys drew his six-shooter and fired six shots which smashed the glass of the window, but the stranger grinned on unmoved. Then two of the boys kicked in the door and searched the schoolhouse, but the room was empty. The two boys who remained outside, however, could still see the stranger sitting just inside the broken windowpane. There are several versions of this tale. Judge Tom Moore, of Ozark, Missouri, who says he is not superstitious, writes the whole thing up in his book *Mysterious Tales and Legends of the Ozarks.*[5]

Mrs. Carrie George, of Toronto, Missouri, says that a cabin on Old Brushy creek, in the Glaize Park area overlooking the Lake of the Ozarks, was regarded as haunted for more than fifty years. The story is that the people who lived there had murdered a peddler for the sake of his pack and buried the body under the kitchen. The peddler's ghost returned almost every night and disturbed people so that the farm changed hands often. One owner tore down the shed kitchen and dug in the earth underneath, but did not find the peddler's bones. The ghost kept coming back as before and frightening people. For a long time the house stood empty and was still unoccupied the last I heard of the matter.

There are many tales about ghosts who speak to people, telling them to dig at such-and-such a place to find a buried treasure. The ghost is usually that of some fellow who died without being able to tell anybody where his treasure was concealed, and who cannot rest quietly until someone gets the money and enjoys it. I met one man who had a persistent vision in which his grandfather, dead for many years, appeared and told him such a tale. After having this dream three nights a-runnin', he dug at the place indicated. He found no treasure but left the hole open, so the ghost could see that his instructions had been carried out. Apparently the grandfather's spirit was satisfied, since the man had no more of these disturbing dreams.

[5] Pages 14–22.

People in Wayne county, Missouri, say that somewhere near Taskee an old man was murdered in a farmhouse, supposedly for his money. For many years after that the old man's ghost was seen there at intervals and nobody would live in the house. Finally a traveler who was not afraid of ghosts went to bed there, after building a rousing fire on the hearth. In the night he awoke to see the ghost of an old man sitting in front of the fireplace. "Follow me," said the ghost, "and I'll show you where the money is. I caint get no rest until somebody finds the stuff and spends it for something useful." They went outside, where the ghost pulled out some small stones at the base of the chimney. Reaching his hand into the hole, the traveler found quite a sum of money wrapped in an old newspaper. The ghost was never seen again.

In Benton county, Arkansas, one hears of a family who have become accustomed to the presence of a ghost, named Sissy. Sissy was an old maid relative, who wore a peculiar slat bonnet and a sort of cape, easily recognized at a distance. Very often members of the family catch a glimpse of Sissy in the orchard, or near some of the outbuildings. She never comes into the house and never makes any noise or other disturbance. Sissy died about the time of the Spanish-American War and was still seen as late as 1940. The children are told never to laugh at her or to bother her in any way. It is said that strangers have come to the farm and seen Sissy, always at a little distance, without suspecting that she is not a living person. One member of the family even tried to photograph Sissy but never caught sight of her while he had the camera in his hands.

I personally knew a young woman, a distant connection of my family, who died under most unhappy circumstances. On her deathbed she tried to tell her parents and her brothers something—they thought it was the identity of the man who had betrayed her. But she was unable to make herself understood. The whole neighborhood believes that this girl's spirit came back and haunted the house for many years. The family consulted mediums and planchettes but could never get in touch with her, although the ghost could be heard walking about and opening drawers in an old bureau almost every night.

In November, 1934, the Associated Press carried a long story about "The Ghost of Paris"—a specter which has been seen at intervals in Paris, Missouri, for more than seventy years. The "Ghost of Paris" was a woman, tall, dressed in black, carrying some sort of wand or cane in her hand. She appeared every year about the middle of October and was seen now and then about the town until spring. The story identified this ghost as the jilted sweetheart of a Confederate soldier; on her deathbed she swore to haunt her faithless lover and the whole town forever. The "Ghost of Paris" was never known to injure anybody, but she frightened children into hysterics. Even grown men, in several cases, had been known to run down the middle of the street, yelling for help. It seems that the ghost has not been seen in Paris since 1934, and some people have suggested that the newspaper publicity somehow exorcised it.

It was in 1932, I think, that an odd story went the rounds in Madison county, Missouri. A party of local people coming along Highway 61 noticed that a certain house had burned down. Nothing was left but the chimney, with the remains of a cookstove and two iron beds standing upright in the ashes. Several days later, having told their friends about the house being burned, they passed the same way again. They were astounded to see the house intact, and the people who lived nearby said that there had been no fire. Most persons regarded all this as a sign that the house *would* burn down in the near future, but it was still standing when I drove by the place in 1940.

About three miles west of Reeds Spring, Missouri, is a little hog wallow known as Dead Man's Pond, so called because two bank robbers were killed there not long after the Civil War. About 1886 Mr. Will Sharp, of Reeds Spring, found a skull and some other human bones in the mud. He picked them up and put them in an old hollow stump nearby. The neighborhood of Dead Man's Pond has long been supposed to be haunted, and many persons have reported strange doings in the vicinity. Will Sharp, who still lives near the place, refuses to admit that *he* ever saw a ghost there, but says that his brother, Palmer E. Sharp, had a peculiar experience. "Palmer had been to take his girl home," writes Will Sharp. "They had attended a party, riding a horse apiece, and he was leading her horse in the old-fashioned way. As he went back home alone it was a nice starry night. Just as he was passing the Pond, the horse he was leading slowed up and caused Palmer to look around. He said he would have sworn there was a man in the saddle of the horse he was leading. The man just seemed to disappear right before his eyes, and Palmer always tried to beat the dark after that. Now, my brother was not afraid of ghosts, but what did he see?" Mrs. May Kennedy McCord, of Springfield, Missouri, refers to the ghost stories about Dead Man's Pond and tells of one Willie Webber, who saw a woman in black "with a red apron, and her hands rolled in the apron" coming along a path near the pond. Suddenly the woman's figure vanished, though it was "late evening" (which means late afternoon, before sundown) and Webber could see plainly for several hundred yards in all directions. There was no way that the figure could have disappeared so suddenly, but it *did* so disappear. Mrs. McCord lived not far from Dead Man's Pond as a child and often heard stories of its being haunted. She says that even now she would be afraid to go there alone, after nightfall.

In several widely separated localities I have heard the story of a savage, ill-tempered woman who was always fighting with her husband. She died suddenly, and some people thought the man must have poisoned her, but the doctors found no evidence of poison. After her death, the widower continued to live in the old house. Neighbors heard noises, as if he was still fighting with his wife. Dishes breaking, shouts and curses, furniture being thrown around, and so on. One neighbor rushed over there, and found the man sitting quietly in front of the fire. All the racket seemed to be in the lean-to kitchen. The neighbor could plainly hear the woman cursing; he recognized her voice as well as certain unusual cuss words and obscene phrases to which she had been partial in life. "Don't get excited," said the widower quietly. "She ain't mad at nobody but me."

There is an old story of two villagers who had to pass a buryin' ground on their way home from sparkin' some country girls. On several occasions they saw a gigantic white bird flopping about among the tombstones—like a swan, or maybe a pelican, but much larger than either. Finally one of the boys decided that it was a ha'nt, and called out loudly: "In the name of the Father, Son, and Holy Ghost, what's the matter with you?" The great bird croaked a reply: "I'm lost and tortured in hell! I'm lost and tortured in hell!" Having said this, it flew away toward the south, and was not seen again.

Otto Ernest Rayburn quotes an old-time hillman who remarked: "If a white moth lingered about us, we thought it was the spirit of one of our deceased grandparents hovering over us." [6] I have mentioned this to many Ozarkers but have never found anybody who had heard of such a belief. The general feeling is that while demons or perhaps lost souls might assume the forms of birds or animals, the idea of one's grandparents turning into *insects* is an alien notion. "It must be that feller has got some Injun in him," one old man observed. "An Injun will believe any kind of foolishment," he added solemnly.

A very common backwoods tale concerns a cabin where a peddler or a traveler is supposed to have been murdered many years ago. There was a big blood spot on the floor, and this became wet with fresh blood every year on February 2, the date of the peddler's death. A man sitting in this house on February 2 would see weasels, skunks, minks, wolves, or even deer dash in at the open door, plunge into the big fireplace and vanish up the chimney. I have heard this story perhaps twenty-five times,

[6] *Ozark Country*, p. 157.

in Missouri, Arkansas, and Oklahoma, but I have never yet found anybody who could tell me just where the cabin was located.

There are many tales of great ghost dogs, and other monstrous animals. One of my best friends told me seriously that as a little boy in McDonald county, Missouri, he once met a spotted hound that was bigger than a cow, and made tracks in the snow nearly two feet across. At the time he was astounded that a dog should attain such a size, but it never entered his head that there was anything supernatural about the animal. It was years later, when he came to realize that there were no such dogs anywhere in the world, he knew that he had seen a "booger dog." When I first heard this tale I suspected that the man had invented it for my especial benefit, but on checking with his relatives I learned that he had told the same story more than twenty years previously, and that it was known to everybody in the neighborhood.

Around the town of Bunker, in Reynolds county, Missouri, they still tell of the ghost dog that Dr. J. Gordon encountered years ago. Crossing a little stream on horseback, near the Bay Cemetery about nine miles west of Bunker, late at night, he saw a figure like a dog, but very much larger. This thing apparently walked on the water without a sound or a ripple. Dr. Gordon saw it many times, once in bright moonlight. Sometimes it crossed ahead of him. Once it jumped on the horse behind the doctor. The animal plunged wildly, and the doctor fired his derringer into the ghost dog twice, but it was not dislodged. He struck at the beast with his fist, the gun still in his hand, but could feel nothing, and his arm slashed right through the figure as if there was nothing there.

Some night hunters in Pemiscot county, Missouri, swore they saw an enormous black dog, fully eight feet long, without any head. They came close to the creature, and one man threw his ax at it, but the ax passed right through the body of the booger dog and stuck fast in a tree. The coon hounds which accompanied the men paid no attention but acted as if they didn't see the big varmint at all. One member of the party had been drinking, but the rest of the hunters were quite sober. And every one of them saw the headless ghost. The fact that the dogs paid no attention somehow reassured them, and they were not panic-stricken as might be expected.

Mrs. Mary Elizabeth Mahnkey tells how a fiddler named Jake Lakey was killed at a dance in Taney county, Missouri, about 1900. Her neighbor young Lewis Blair and another boy were sent on horseback to break the news to Jake's wife, who lived several miles away. Blair told Mrs. Mahnkey that a great black dog ran beside their horses all the way, and when one of the riders struck at the creature with a quirt, the quirt slashed right through it. And when they got to their destination, Mrs. Lakey said calmly: "You'ens have come to tell me that Jake is dead." [7]

A young man near Alma, Arkansas, was passing a deserted house one night, when he saw a strange woman in a long white robe standing at the gate. A little fuzzy white dog ran out in front of him, and it seemed to be barking, although he heard no sound. The boy threw a stone at the dog and was astounded to see the animal separate into two parts, let the stone pass through, and then go back together again. He talked the matter over with his parents, and they agreed that it was evidently a warning of some impending evil, probably an early death. The young fellow lived for many years, however, and I believe he is still alive. But about a month after he saw the ghost dog, he had one of his eyes gouged out.

Farmers near Braggadocio, Dunklin county, Missouri, tell of a headless dog supposed to live in a hollow elm tree just outside the town. At night this phantom runs through the village streets. It behaves just like any other dog, but it is clearly headless. Many people have seen it on moonlight nights, usually at a distance of about twenty yards. The town dogs always get

[7] *Ozark Life* (June, 1930), p. 31.

out of its way but do not seem panic-stricken or unduly alarmed.

Tom Moore tells of an old woman who lived alone in a shanty near Galena, Missouri. Each evening passers-by heard her talking animatedly, although they could see that she was alone. People who heard her talk said that she spoke as if to a man and often referred to a dog which accompanied the man, though neither man nor dog was visible. Finally the old woman became ill and was taken to the poorhouse where she died. After her death several residents of Galena saw a whiskered stranger with a big dog near the old woman's cabin. This man and dog were seen by different people on several occasions but disappeared suddenly at the edge of a cliff. Because of this unexplained disappearance, apparently, Judge Moore and others decided that the stranger and his dog were somehow supernatural.[8]

People near Pevely, in Jefferson county, Missouri, tell of a ghostly white fox which has been seen by many farmers, and even by motorists on Highway 61, as recently as 1932. Albino foxes are not unknown in the Ozarks, but there was something very special about this one. It was quite tame and had been fired on many times at close range, but without result. Foxhounds seemed aware of its existence, but they would not chase it. Several persons believe that it could transform itself into a skunk at will; others say that they actually saw it turn into a short-haired black and white dog, with a stump tail.

In southeast Missouri old soldiers claimed that during the War between the States some men used to see the specter of a monstrous black hog just before a battle. This was recognized as a sign that the man who saw the thing would be killed in action. He told his comrades, made arrangements for letters and keepsakes to be sent home, and so on. It is said that a man who saw the black boar never lived more than seven days. They tell of one trooper who saw the death sign just before a major engagement but came through the battle unhurt. He laughed at "superstition" and bragged about his escape, but was killed the

8 *Mysterious Tales and Legends of the Ozarks*, pp. 142–148.

next evening by the accidental discharge of a comrade's revolver. It was a Yankee pistol captured in the battle, one of the new double-action or self-cocking kind, with which the boys were not familiar. While the new owner was fiddling with the lock of the weapon, it was somehow discharged. The bullet smashed through the brain of the cavalryman who had seen the great black boar.

In Stoddard county, Missouri, near Bloomfield, stood the ruin of an old house, so dilapidated that there was not much left save the big stone chimney. There was a neighborhood story that gold and silver were buried somewhere about the place. People who tried to dig for the treasure were all driven away by pigs—dozens of wild pigs which came squealing and dashing back and forth over the site of the old building. They were ghost pigs, not affected by stones or bullets. One man fired repeatedly with a shotgun at very close range, but the animals paid no attention. The general impression was that the phantom swine were somehow stationed there to drive off treasure hunters.

A very similar story used to be told in the vicinity of Jane, Missouri, near the Missouri-Arkansas line. In this case the pigs were said to be guarding the place where a murdered woman was buried many years ago. The woman had some valuable jewelry concealed on her person, and it is said that her own half-wild pigs prevented the murderer from exhuming the body and getting the valuables which he overlooked at the time of the killing. This all happened long ago, of course; the pigs which guard the spot nowadays are not living animals, but ghost pigs.

The children near Southwest City, Missouri, a few years ago, were afraid to go near an old slaughterhouse. The story is that the place was full of ghost cattle, some of them headless. A prominent citizen told me that he himself had seen the shadowy figures of "little bulls" with great spreading horns, often seven feet from tip to tip. He mentioned this as showing that the cattle ghosts somehow derived from pioneer days, as there have been no long-horned cattle in the Ozarks for many years.

Much has been written about the "headless ghost of Nicker-son Ridge," but I have been unable to get much information beyond that published by my old friend Otto Ernest Rayburn, the author of *Ozark Country*. It appears that Tomp Turner, who lives near Kimberling Bridge on White River, in the southern part of Stone county, Missouri, is not a superstitious man. He did not believe the headless ghost story until about 1915, when he saw the thing himself. Highway 13 follows the old Wilderness Road, where the headless specter had been reported by the settlers in pioneer days. One night Tomp was riding south on the highway, when his horse suddenly became very nervous. He saw the figure of a headless man approaching slowly —not walking, but gliding along as if on roller skates. When the thing came within thirty steps, Tomp's horse became unmanageable and bolted into the brush. Tomp finally forced it back into the road again, some fifty feet beyond, but the ghost was nowhere in sight. And, as Tomp himself remarked, he didn't go back to look for it. Several other people have caught glimpses of the thing in recent years. On wet nights it is said that the ghost keeps to the brush along the roadside, and groans and cries are heard from among the bushes. It seems that the headless ghost is never seen or heard except on a particular stretch of road, not more than two or three hundred yards in length. I met Tomp Turner myself at his home in July, 1932, when Otto Ernest Rayburn and I went down White River. It was Rayburn who told me the story in the first place, and he has never been able to find any legend or history of a murder at this place which might explain the apparition.

Another headless ghost has been seen in Morgan county, Missouri, since the Civil War. Some claim that it was on the job even before the War, as early as 1850. John A. Hannay, formerly of Versailles, Missouri, says that he saw this ghost sitting on top of a strawstack in the moonlight. It was plainly headless, but was called "Old Raw Head" by the natives. When Mr. Hannay saw the thing it was about forty yards distant, but as he approached the ghost slid down the opposite side of the stack and was gone. Hannay's grandparents had seen the same specter many years before, according to the family tradition; they were riding along a country road, and this headless thing ran right between their horses, frightening the lady almost into hysterics. Some people claim to have heard "Old Raw Head" scream and even pronounce words distinctly, but I have never been able to find out just what the headless specter said. Some people have thought that it must be the ghost of someone who was murdered in the vicinity. Mr. Hannay says that there were plenty of cold-blooded murders committed here in the years following the Civil War, and that he knows the names of many people involved in these killings; however, he thinks that it is best not to mention these people now, because their relatives and descendants are still living in Morgan county.

Some farmers tell of a headless ghost in St. Francois county, Missouri, at a house on Back Creek, near Highway 61 south of Farmington. This ghost appears at upstairs windows of the old house and rattles chains to frighten campers and tourists away. They say that a family named Griffin once lived there, and that the Griffins used to give semipublic dances in the building. One night there was a big fight, and a fiddler cut off Johnny Griffin's head with his bowie knife. Griffin was short of stature, while the ghost appears very tall even without his head. Nevertheless, many people believe that the headless specter is the ghost of Johnny Griffin, doomed to haunt forever the scene of his decapitation.

There are men and women still living who recall the excitement that swept the village of Fair Grove, Missouri, in 1895, when a picture of the Devil suddenly appeared upon the wall of the Methodist church. The following account is clipped from the Springfield (Missouri) *Republican*, dated Jan. 5, 1896.

If anyone should entertain the idea that superstition is forever banished from the minds of the American people, he should visit just now the little town of Fair Grove in Greene county. The appearance of a face upon the Methodist church wall has aroused the whole community and many are speculating upon its origin. During the prayer meeting on the night of December 19th someone made a discovery. On the north side of the cupola, in the church room facing the pulpit, appears a curious looking picture. How, when, or from what source it came is a mystery and will perhaps never be solved. The picture is about life size and the most hideous looking thing that can be imagined. The face has the appearance of Satan with fearful eyes, wide open mouth and a terrifying look. The next morning after the discovery people all around town began flocking to the church to see the strange picture. Some were quite sure it was the work of the devil; others believed it the work of God. Some thought it the work of human hands, and some thought it had been caused by a leak in the roof. It was plain to see that the likeness had not been placed there by a human hand, as there was no paint used, and it was perfectly dry when found, and could not be erased. The theory that it had been caused by the rain appeared to be contradicted by the fact that the top of the picture was three feet from the ceiling, and all above it was perfectly dry. The rain could not have come through the building wall as that wall was on the inside and some eight feet from the outside of the church. Many people in and around Fair Grove are much wrought up over the matter. Like the handwriting on the wall at the feast of Belshazzar it stands. It is said that a few days prior to this strange appearance, Rev. John Morgan and Rev. E. Plummer were conducting a revival and little interest was manifest. After preaching an eloquent sermon on the righteous life, the minister requested those who wanted to live this life, and go to heaven, to stand up. Finding no one who responded, the minister then asked if there was anyone who deliberately chose to go to hell, and if so to stand up. One young man promptly arose to his feet, much to the surprise of all present. It is claimed by some that the young man did not understand the minister's proposition, and stood up by mistake. At any rate he is of good family and stands well in that community. Those who are superstitious about the strange picture which has appeared on the wall of the church, think it was sent there as a rebuke to the young man who arose to his feet on that occasion.

Mrs. C. P. Mahnkey, of Mincy, Missouri, tells of several local people who thought they heard a baby crying in a certain deserted log house. But there was no baby there. After some puzzled talk about this, it was remembered that "a family had formerly lived there who had a feeble-minded girl. This girl was known to be an expectant mother, but no one ever saw the infant and after a time the family left the country." Mrs. Mahnkey was content to leave it at that, but local opinion is that the baby was born and was killed by one of the girl's brothers, who probably buried the little body somewhere about the cabin.

Another of Mrs. Mahnkey's stories of the supernatural concerns the death of a certain "old man Cook," head of one of the great clans of the Swan Creek neighborhood, in Taney county, Missouri. "One of the women told me a curious tale of the night Gran'pap died," writes Mrs. Mahnkey. "Some of the watchers were out in the yard. They knew that the end was very near. Suddenly they were startled to see a solitary horseman ride up to the front gate, a military figure on a great white horse. Phantom-like and eerie, as there was not a sound. And just then someone came out from the house, and said the old man had died, and the silent rider and the big white horse disappeared."

Tom Moore tells of an old building at Sand Springs, on the road between Rolla and Springfield, Missouri, where during the Civil War a preacher used to hold forth against the Southern cause. One Sunday night a Confederate officer threatened the preacher, then rode his horse right into the meetinghouse, and had almost reached the pulpit when he was shot dead. The officer's body fell to the floor near the pulpit, and his horse turned and walked slowly out of the building. In recent years, according to Judge Moore's version of the tale, people who visit the place at night have heard the horse walk into the building. A moment later they hear the thump of a falling body on the dirt floor, then the sound of the horse walking slowly out of the place. Several persons have followed the sound of the horse's hooves with flashlights but have seen nothing.[9]

Miss Mae Traller, schoolteacher at Everton, Missouri, reports her investigation of a ghost which frightened the country

9 *Mysterious Tales and Legends of the Ozarks*, pp. 35-51.

folk near the town. Many persons in the neighborhood had seen this ha'nt near the old Payne orchard. Usually a vague, gaseous shape would rise in front of some startled pedestrian, float along ahead of him for a bit, and then sail slowly away into the tree-tops. Miss Traller and another teacher drove out to the haunted orchard at twilight and loitered about waiting for the ghost to appear. Suddenly they both saw it—"a strange luminous object, something like a fog, but I shall always declare it had a human shape," writes Miss Traller. "The thing wavered and started toward us, then with a faint breathlike sigh it drifted off above the orchard and away." Oddly enough, this seems to have been the ghost's final appearance—Miss Traller never heard of its being seen again.

People around Nixa, Missouri, still talk about the mysterious motor car that forced Sheriff Frank Jones off the road and caused his death in the spring of 1932. Several prominent citizens have seen this phantom car on the highway between Nixa and Ozark, and Fred McCoy, manager of the local telephone system, narrowly escaped being wrecked at the exact spot where Sheriff Jones was killed.

A spectral horseman has been reported occasionally for many years at a certain point on what is now Highway 13, in Polk county, Missouri, not far from Bolivar. A little knoll about a hundred yards east of the highway is called Dead Man's Hill, and there is an old story about a horse thief who was shot to death here and buried on top of the knoll. A rude headstone may still be seen, but there is no inscription, since the man was a stranger. Flowers were found on this grave at intervals for many years, so it was believed that the thief's identity was known to somebody who lived nearby, but who did not reveal the secret. Men who have seen the ghostly rider have remarked particularly his neat homespun garments, dyed brown with butternut juice, his cowhide boots, and the two big Colt revolvers swinging at his side. There is nothing in this to identify

the ghost, however, since many figures similarly attired rode
the Missouri trails in the early days.

Members of the McDowell family, pioneers in Stone county,
Missouri, tell of a ha'nt that used to live in a big black-oak
tree, just across the James River from Galena, near the Fred
McCord farm. The McDowell children would slip down the road
sometimes just at dusk and stand well back from the haunted
tree, keeping an eye out for the ghost to appear. Soon or late
one of them would see "something white a-risin' " in the underbrush, upon which they all screamed and lit out for home at top
speed. Nobody ever stopped for a second look, and therefore no
detailed description of the "black-oak ghost" is available, but
at least two generations of the McDowell clan were firm believers in it.

In the northeastern corner of Oklahoma, some fourteen miles
from Joplin, Missouri, is a lonesome stretch of country road
called the "Devil's Promenade." Some mighty strange people
have lived along this road, and some very strange things have
happened there. The best of the "ha'nted road" stories cannot
be told at this time, but there is no longer any secret about the
phenomena of the "Indian lights," which have been seen by thousands of tourists and discussed in newspapers as far off as St.
Louis and Kansas City. One has only to drive slowly along
the road any night after dark to see the "jack-o'-lantern" come
bobbing along, always traveling in an easterly direction. Sometimes it swings from one side of the road to another, sometimes
it seems to roll on the ground, sometimes it rises to the tops of
the scrubby oak trees at the roadside, but it never gets more
than a few feet from the road on either side. I have seen this
light myself, on three occasions. It first appeared about the size
of an egg but varied until sometimes it looked as big as a washtub. It is hard to judge the distance, but the light seemed about
a quarter of a mile off when I first saw it and disappeared when
it approached to a distance of perhaps seventy-five yards. I saw

only a single glow, but other witnesses have seen it split into two, three, or four smaller lights. The thing looked yellowish to me, but some observers describe it as red, green, blue, or even purple in color. One man swore that it passed so close to him that he could "plainly feel the heat," and a woman saw it "burst like a bubble, scattering sparks in all directions." A fellow who drove his car straight at the dancing phantom lost sight of it, but others standing a little way off said that they saw the light hovering impishly above the pursuer's car, out of his sight but plainly visible to everybody else in the neighborhood.

Some people think that the light at the "Devil's Promenade" is the ghost of an Osage chief who was murdered near this spot; others say it is the spirit of a Quapaw maiden who drowned herself in the river when her warrior was killed in battle. Others have suggested that the effect is produced somehow by electrical action of the mineral deposits in the ground, or by marsh gas. Mr. Logan Smith, of Neosho, Missouri, always contended that the mysterious lights are those of automobiles driving east on Highway 66, some five miles away. F. H. Darnell of Neosho, and a group of surveyors from Joplin, also incline to the view that cars on the distant highway are responsible for the mysterious lights. A. B. MacDonald, of the Kansas City *Star*, who came down to investigate the matter in January, 1936, is another convert to the Logan Smith theory. William Shears, who lives near the Promenade and has studied the phenomena, thinks that the lights may derive from the beacons at the Quapaw airport some six miles away. But the old-timers laugh at all such explanations, claiming that the Indian lights were seen at the same spot in the deep woods, fifty years before the "Devil's Promenade" road was built. Fred C. Reynolds of Kansas City says that his grandfather, a pioneer doctor at Baxter, Kansas, observed these lights "long before there was any such thing as a motor car," adding that he himself saw the "jack-o'-lantern" as a boy. Bob Hill of Joplin, Missouri, observes that the phantom was seen by many persons in this vicinity before there was a Highway 66, and certainly long before the airport was established at Quapaw, Oklahoma.

In many parts of the Ozark country one hears tales of moving lights, which usually appear in cemeteries. These "graveyard lights" are seldom seen at regular intervals or by large numbers of witnesses, but reports of them are fairly common nevertheless. People who live near a little buryin' ground on Highway 123, between Spokane and Walnut Shade, in Taney county, Missouri, have talked about such "fox-fire lights" for many years. A bluish light, they say, apparently about as high as a man's head, first appears among the gravestones and then slowly crosses the road. It moves about as fast as a man walking, I was told. After listening to these tales I went to this graveyard myself and waited in the dark for hours on three consecutive nights but saw nothing out of the ordinary.

May Kennedy McCord, of Springfield, Missouri, printed several tales of local ghosts and spirits in the Springfield *News & Leader* (Feb. 2, 1936). Here is a letter which she received a few days later, from a minister of the gospel:

Dear Madam—I read your ghost stories with interest, and I will add a modern daylight story. Two days before Christmas 1925, four of us were sitting in plain view of Little Creek cemetery, and there appeared a pillar of fire, about ten feet high with a flaming star at the top of it. It occurred at 4:15 P.M., and was there at the same time three days later. It appeared four times. I have lived here fourteen years and have lived in sight of other cemeteries, but that is the first ghost I ever saw and I am 75 years old. I have been a preacher 55 years. A man went to the cemetery to watch for it and be there when it came; said he would throw his coat over it. Well, it came, but *he run like a turkey.* Yours in Jesus' name, A. J. Graves, Hartville, Mo.

There is an old tale often told to children about a family that had just finished butchering hogs. That night, after they had all gone to bed, they heard a voice cry out: "Where's my hog's feet at?" The old man got out of bed but saw nothing. Pretty soon the voice was heard again: "I want my hog's feet!" The man jumped up again, and the old woman told him to keep a-lookin' till he found the intruder. Finally he peered up the chimney and sprang back as though amazed. "God-a-mighty!" he cried. "What's them big eyes for?" A long pause, and then came the deep-voiced answer: "To see you with." The old man turned away from the fireplace, but came back in a moment to ask: "What's them big claws for?" There was a hollow groan from the chimney, then the strange voice boomed: "To dig your grave with!" This quieted the old fellow for awhile, but a few minutes later he quavered: "What's that big bushy tail for?" A long silence, then the reply: "To sweep off your grave with." No more questions were put for some time, but finally the old gentleman couldn't stand the suspense any longer. "What's them big teeth for?" he cried. "TO EAT YOU UP WITH!"—At this point the story-teller's voice rises to a scream, and he jumps at the listening child with a great show of teeth. This story is sometimes called "Raw Head and Bloody Bones" or "Raw Bones and Bloody Meat."

Another backwoods bedtime story, told to children around the fire at night, relates the troubles of a woman who killed her baby and cooked it and served it to her husband. Not knowing what sort of meat it was, the man ate the stuff without comment. Later in the night came the little ghost crying: "Pennywinkle! Pennywinkle! My maw kilt me, my paw et me, my sister buried my bones under a marble stone. I want my liver an' lights an' wi-i-i-ney pipes! Pennywinkle! Pennywinkle!"

Here's a fragment of another juvenile tale, salvaged in Christian county, Missouri, some years ago: A traveler was a-ridin' along and he come to a ha'nted house. It was plumb full of cats. There was cats runnin' all over the place, and even up on the roof. A great big cat come up to the traveler and says: "When you git to the next house, you stop and tell 'em that old Kitty Rollins is dead." So the next house he come to, the traveler got down and went in. The house was empty except for an old bedraggled-lookin' cat settin' in the corner by the fireplace. "Well," says the traveler, "I come to tell you that old Kitty

Rollins is dead." The old cat jumped up and says "By God, I'll be king yet!" and out of the door he run.

A man once interrupted my lecture on Ozark folklore to ask how many people in the Ozark country really believe in ghosts and witches. I am unable to answer such a question, of course. Mr. H. L. Mencken, who lives in Baltimore, once announced his conviction that 92 percent of the people in Maryland believe in ghosts, and that 74 percent also believe in witchcraft. I have no idea how Mencken arrived at these figures, and I do not claim to know whether or not they are correct. I have some acquaintance with Maryland, however, both the cities and the rural districts, and I do not for a moment believe that people in Maryland are more superstitious than those who live in the backwoods sections of Missouri and Arkansas.

Sometimes one encounters an outspoken skeptic, even in the Ozarks. An old man in Morgan county, Missouri, said: "I have heard talk about a ghost around here for fifty years, but I never seen it. I would walk ten miles to see a ghost any time. But I don't believe there is no such thing. The people here aint got much sense. One of my neighbors thinks a man who has been dead four years comes and steals cream out of his springhouse every night!"

There is a rather general idea that departed spirits, when they return to earth, prefer to appear in the dark of the moon. It is also believed that the dead, if they can't rest in their graves, are somehow inclined to loiter about redbuds, pawpaw trees, and haw bushes—though why they should be attracted to these particular plants nobody seems to know. Another common notion is that persons born on Hallowe'en are more likely to see ghosts and talk with them than are persons whose birthdays fall on other dates.

Some people say that a rider can often see a ghost, ordinarily invisible, by looking at it from between his horse's ears. "You just sight down the horse's nose like it was a rifle bar'l," a farmer told me. It is widely believed that dogs and horses see all the ghosts that men do, and many more which are invisible to the human eye. So one may be sure that if there is a ghost anywhere about, the horse's head will be pointed at it. I used to try this trick, whenever my horse showed alarm without any apparent cause, but I was never able to see anything supernatural.

Several old-timers have told me that if one addresses a ghost with the words "in the name of God," the apparition will be powerless to do any harm. Other people think it's safer to cry out "In the name of the Father, Son, and Holy Ghost, what do you want?" If the thing is a witch or a demon it will vanish when the sacred names are pronounced; if it is simply a restless unhappy spirit it will return a civil answer in plain English and depart.

I have heard many stories of backwoods preachers who claim the power to quiet wandering spirits and drive ghosts or demons out of haunted houses, but I have never been able to trace one of these tales to its source. I know several Holy Roller preachers who say they are willing to attempt the exorcising of a specter, but I have never found one who would affirm that he had actually done so.

Some old folk pretend to lay a ghost by putting a stone on the dead person's grave. A very small pebble, or a handful of gravel, will do as well as a large stone. I have myself seen graves which were conspicuous because of the large number of pebbles which had been placed on them. And I have seen apparently intelligent adults—always half-jokingly, or with some humorous apology—toss little pebbles on such graves.

The Ozark hillman frequently entertains a wry humor in connection with his folk beliefs—humor of a sort not often encountered elsewhere. An old gentleman in Eureka Springs, Arkansas, talked freely about pioneer customs, folksongs, play parties, and even feuds, but when asked for local ghost stories he had nothing to contribute. "There's ghosts in Texas," he said soberly, "and maybe in Oklahoma, but not here." I waited for a long moment, without any comment. "This country is just naturally *too rough* for ghosts," he said finally. And anybody who has visited Eureka Springs will understand exactly what the old gentleman meant.

11. Animals and Plants

There are numerous miscellaneous superstitions regarding animals and plants, which do not fall conveniently into any of the classes hitherto discussed. For example, there is the notion that roosters always crow at midnight, and again about 5 A.M., but that on Christmas morning they all sound off exactly at three o'clock. In some sections, farmers insist that snake doctors (*Odonata*) are never seen over the fields before 10 A.M. or after 4 P.M. The harvest fly or summer locust, a big yellow cicada, is supposed to begin its song precisely at high noon; I have seen a farmer stop work in the field and set his watch by the harvest fly's note.

Many backwoods folk are convinced that there is a mutual understanding between squirrels and mosquitoes, so that the latter protect the former from hunters. In early June, when the squirrels are feeding on mulberries, mosquitoes sometimes appear in such numbers that a hunter cannot remain quiet long enough to stalk a squirrel.

My ridge-runner friends nearly all insist that the big Ozark fox squirrels castrate the smaller gray squirrels; the male fox squirrels and the male gray squirrels do fight savagely sometimes, and it is true that many male grays in this region are without visible testes.

A great many hillmen believe that the male opossum ejects his sperm into the nose of the female, which then blows the spermatic fluid into the vagina—a belief wholly without foundation, which doubtless had its origin in the peculiar bifurcate form of the opossum's penis, and to the female's habit of nosing the vulva.

Very few Ozark hunters accept the ordinary opinion that deer shed their horns annually. Each year, the hillfolk say, the horns soften and velvet shows on them; evidently they itch, too, as the animals are often seen rubbing them against bushes. This rubbing causes the soft ends of the horn to split open, and sometimes to bleed. Then the horns grow a bit, and turn hard again; as the ends are split, there are two points where one grew before. Sometimes one tip splits into three parts instead of two, so that the right and left antlers differ in the number of points. If deer really shed their horns every year, as the government game wardens say, how is it that we don't find them lying about on the ground?

It is very generally believed that the appearance of an albino deer is a bad sign; some hillfolk think it has something to do with witches' work, others that it is an indication of disease among the deer, and that venison will be unwholesome for seven years. In 1939 a white deer was seen in Taney county, Missouri, and many natives were pretty much upset about it. Mrs. C. P. Mahnkey, of Mincy, Missouri, wrote to a local newspaper: "I cannot overcome a subtle uneasy feeling that this may be a *token*. In other words an omen, or warning, but old-timers use the old words."

The old folks at Thomasville, in Oregon county, Missouri, say that the early settlers often saw a white buck in the woods, but nobody would shoot it for fear of some bad luck. It was seen at intervals for about fifteen years, and when it finally disappeared people said that it must have died of old age.

Many old-time hunters believe it is a mistake to kill deer on Sunday. Not only sinful, but also unlucky; some say a man who bags a deer on the Sabbath will not get another for seven weeks, even if he goes hunting every day. A well-known hunter in Missouri saw a small doe almost in his front yard one Sunday and refrained from shooting it, although he was badly in need of meat. Early next morning he looked out to see two fine bucks in the same place and killed them both. This man was firmly

convinced that the two big deer were somehow *sent* to him on
Monday, because he had resisted the temptation to shoot the
little deer on Sunday.

Woodsmen say that the fox sometimes "charms" squirrels
out of the trees, simply by rolling about on the ground until
the squirrel becomes "dizzy like" and gradually descends to
see what is going on. Finally, when the distance is short enough,
the fox suddenly recovers, makes a great spring and catches its
prey. Three old hunters, sober and ordinarily trustworthy men,
assure me that they have witnessed this performance. A great
many others have heard of it, and seem to believe that foxes
really do charm squirrels and even wild turkeys in this manner.
Dr. J. H. Young, of Galena, Missouri, told me that he once saw
a red fox rolling wildly about beneath a tree in which two squirrels sat watching the fox's antics. Dr. Young waited a long
time, but the squirrels did not come down.

When a female fox is pregnant, or is nursing her young,
many hillmen believe that something changes about the odor
of her body, so that even the best hounds can't follow her trail.
Frank Payne, of Stone county, Missouri, in the midst of an
argument about religion, once mentioned this as evidence that
there is a God who takes care of foxes at such times, in order
that they shall not be exterminated.

In many parts of the Ozark country one hears of enormous
wildcats; there are men who swear they have killed cats four
feet high, weighing 150 pounds! A bobcat shot by Del Taylor,
near Galena, Missouri, in January, 1945, was the biggest I
ever saw in the Ozarks. But it was very thin and probably
weighed less than forty pounds.

Marvel Cave, near Notch, Missouri, was regarded with superstitious awe by many of the old-timers, who used to warn tourists away from the place. A schoolteacher in Walnut Grove,
Missouri, declared that one subterranean room was literally
full of the bones of panthers and bobcats. All of these animals
for miles around, according to the old story, made their way

into the cavern before they died, to leave their bodies with those of their ancestors in the "cat room." It is true that the bones of panthers and wildcats, along with those of deer, elk, bears, and other animals, have been found in Marvel Cave. But the "cat room" story is obviously a myth.

Many of the old settlers believe that panthers or "painters" have a great appetite for human infants and will go to almost any length to obtain one. It is said that they locate babies by smelling the mother's milk as the babe is fed. Wayman Hogue tells several stories of panthers devouring babies. At Hogue's own home, in Van Buren county, Arkansas, a painter fought their dog to a standstill and came down the chimney after a five-day-old infant. The beast was driven off by Hogue's mother, who tore open a straw mattress and threw the straw on the fire, producing a great blaze through which the painter could not descend.[1]

Farm boys always tell the city feller that a skunk cannot discharge his stinking liquid without raising his tail, and that one has only to hold the tail down to render a polecat harmless. They say also that if a skunk or civet is suspended by the tail, so that its feet do not touch any solid object, the animal is unable to throw a single drop of perfume.

Groundhogs are hunted by boys with dogs, and young groundhogs are very good eating. But some of the old-timers frown on the modern practice of shooting groundhogs. They don't mind if city sportsmen do it but often forbid their own children to shoot groundhogs, because it is supposed to bring bad luck.

There are persistent tales of a fine-haired, golden-yellow, red-eyed groundhog, much larger than the ordinary kind. Harold Wales refers to this as the "yellow-bellied marmot." [2] I have met old hunters in Arkansas who claim to have shot these "big goldy groundhogs" but have never seen such an animal myself.

The old folks are all agreed that it is bad luck for a hunter

[1] *Back Yonder,* 1932, pp. 170–181.
[2] *Arkansas Gazette,* July 3, 1938.

to return home with an empty gun—this entirely apart from the immediate advantages of personal protection and the like. I have been told of cases in which whole families have gone supperless because of a hillman's reluctance to use his last cartridge.

There is a very general notion in southwest Missouri that there were no rats in the Ozarks in the early days, until they were brought in by settlers from the east. One John Cooper, who lived in Springfield, Missouri, in the early 1900's, always contended that there were no rats until the Frisco railroad came in. The rats arrived in boxcars, he said, and later took to the woods and became common everywhere as they are today.

It is bad luck for a rabbit to cross your path from left to right; you can take the curse off, however, by tearing some article of clothing just a little. If the same rabbit crosses your path *twice*, it means that you are needed at home immediately.

One often hears that it is a bad sign for a flying squirrel to get into an automobile, and people who have closed cars are careful to run up the glass at night. There is a good practical reason for this, however, since flying squirrels have been known to gnaw big holes in the upholstery.

Some hillmen claim they can prevent wolves from howling, or hounds from baying, simply by muttering some gibberish. I have seen this tried, but with no great success. Some men can make an owl cease hooting, it is said, merely by pulling their trousers pockets inside out, and others pretend to stop the noises of crickets, katydids, tree toads and even bullfrogs by the same procedure.

I was once tramping through the woods at dusk, hunting the cows with a farm boy. We stopped at intervals and strained our ears for the distant bells but could hear nothing save the clamor of tree frogs and katydids. Finally we rested under a big tree which seemed to be full of these noisy creatures. "Watch me make 'em shut up," said the boy, and slapped the trunk lightly with his hand. Instantly all was silence. I have since tried this trick myself, and it seems to work under certain conditions. But I don't think there's any magic about it.

The Ozarker does not like to hear a screech owl near his cabin, since it is always an unfavorable sign and may indicate sickness or approaching death. But above all he cautions his children never to *imitate* the call of such a bird under these conditions. If an owl hears its cry answered from within the cabin, it will return again and again and sooner or later descend the chimney and scatter the fire out on the floor, so as to burn the whole place down.

One often hears children say that whoever hears the first dove coo in the spring will soon take a trip in the direction from which the sound came. Some older hillfolk really seem to believe that whatever a man is doing when he hears the first dove of the season, that's what he'll have to do all summer. In Taney county, Missouri, they tell me that the ruling bird is the whippoorwill rather than the turtle dove, but the idea is the same.

Various sorts of birds are believed to carry warnings. A woman in my neighborhood whipped her grown daughters unmercifully, until one day "the redbirds come an' ha'nted her" by tapping on the windowpane, which gave the woman a terrible fright and caused her to mend her ways. Another of my mountaineer friends was greatly disturbed when a "rooster redbird" hovered about his door; he said that it was a warning of death, and sure enough, one of his daughters died within a few weeks.

If a bird defecates on a girl's hat or bonnet, it is regarded as positive evidence that her parents are stingy; some say it's a sign that the parents do not approve of the girl's suitor.

Buzzards are supposed to seek out and vomit upon persons guilty of incest. It is said that a certain man near Siloam Springs, Arkansas, never ventures out into the open if a buzzard is anywhere in sight. There are persons who have a pathological horror of buzzards, just as some otherwise normal individuals hate and fear cats.

I have met men who contend that when the buzzards disappear in the fall they do not fly south but hibernate in caves like bears, bats, and groundhogs. Lennis L. Broadfoot quotes Ed Lehman, Carter county, Missouri, as follows: "I go in some caves where there's great flocks of buzzards. There's lots of people that don't know where the buzzard goes for the winter, but they live in the caves here in the Ozarks all winter long." [3]

There is an old story that when a crow fails in his duty as a sentry—I believe it is true that some crows watch while others feed—all the crows in the neighborhood meet to "try" the offender. If the culprit is found guilty the rest attack him and kill him at once. An old man in Southwest City, Missouri, told me that he had twice "heard the crows a-caucassin' " in the tall trees near his home and had on both occasions seen the guilty bird pecked to death by his fellows. The noise made by crows at a trial, he said in all seriousness, is very different from that which they make when they are tormenting a hawk or an owl.

It is said to be very bad luck to count the birds in a flock. Nevertheless, Ozark children have a little jingle to sing when they see crows flying:

> One's unlucky,
> Two's lucky,
> Three's health,
> Four's wealth,
> Five's sickness,
> Six is death.

I have heard this used in Newton county, Arkansas, as a counting-out rhyme, in connection with some childish game.

To find a dead crow in the road is always lucky, but a dead "carr'n crow" is a sign of superlative good fortune. Just what "carrion crow" means in the Ozarks is not clear to me, as I have never examined one of these birds. Some old hunters say that the carrion crow is just a little larger than an ordinary crow, dead black rather than glossy, and that it croaks or

[3] *Pioneers of the Ozarks*, p. 146.

squalls rather than caws. But other Ozark woodsmen tell me that the real carrion crow is as big as a buzzard, but a bit darker in color, and its head is feathered while the buzzard's head is bare. It is said also that the tips of the carrion crow's wings are whitish and much more rounded than the buzzard's wing tips. These birds are said to fly with buzzards, and nearly all of the old folks believe that they mate with buzzards. Several river guides have pointed out flocks containing both buzzards and carrion crows on the shores of Lake Taneycomo, but they all looked pretty much alike to me, and I could never get close enough to see the difference in heads and wing tips.

There is a good deal of confusion in the Ozarks about the whippoorwill, a crepuscular or nocturnal bird which is often heard but seldom seen. A great many hillfolk believe that the whippoorwill is identical with the night hawk or bullbat, often seen flying about in the late afternoon. Some Ozarkers apparently believe that the bullbat somehow changes into a whippoorwill, or vice versa. Charles Cummins, a veteran newspaperman of Springfield, Missouri, defends this belief in the Springfield *Leader & Press*, Sept. 25, 1933:

Coincident with the appearance of the Harvest Moon, Ozark bullbats are turning to whippoorwills. You are leary of that? Skeptical, also, that tadpoles turn to frogs, wiggletails to mosquitoes? The bullbat, which came off the nest early and has awkwardly, like the young martin, clung fast to a tree limb all Summer, soon will be seeking a barrage in low growth trees, where at evening tide it will begin that familiar and lonesome call.

The truth is, of course, that the bullbat and the whippoorwill are two distinct species, which differ widely in appearance and habits. Neither bullbats nor whippoorwills "come off the nest," because they do not build nests but deposit their eggs on bare rocks or on the ground. I have seen both birds incubating, and found bullbats' eggs on a gravel roof in Joplin, Missouri.

There are people at Thayer, Missouri, and at Mammoth Springs, Arkansas, who claim that the bullbat, the whippoorwill, and the rain crow are one and the same bird—which presumably gives the rain crow "holler" at midday, the bullbat cry in the afternoon, and the whippoorwill call at night. The rain crow of the Ozarks is the yellow-billed cuckoo, which has nothing much in common with either the bullbat or the whippoorwill. Some Ozark natives have told me that the rain crow is merely a variant of the turtle dove, hatched by the same parents, so that the rain crow and the turtle dove are comparable to the red and gray phases of the screech owl. This confusion of rain crow and turtle dove is understandable, since the two are somewhat similar in appearance at a little distance. According to W. S. White, of Bolivar, Missouri, most of his neighbors believe that the rain crow lays its eggs in other birds' nests as the cowbird does; this belief seems very odd, since any sharp-eyed country boy can find the rain crow sitting on its nest, and the large pale-green eggs are common in Ozark collections.

It is said that all hawks are blind in dog days, which is obviously not true. Many farmers think that hawks call chickens to their doom by imitating the cry of a young chick in distress, and this may be a fact for all I know.

Blue jays are supposed to be very rare on weekends, and children are told that these birds go to hell every Friday to help the Devil gather kindling. Another story is that the blue jay spends Friday breaking off twigs to be burned by wicked people here on earth. There is an old song with the chorus:

> Don't you hear that jaybird call?
> Don't you hear them dead sticks fall?
> He's a-throwin' down firewood for we-all,
> All on a Friday mornin'.

The great pileated woodpecker, rare in most sections of the country, is still fairly common in the Ozarks. Most Ozarkers call it a woodhen, but it is also known as "God Almighty" or "Lord God Peckerwood," doubtless because of its large size; it looks as big as a teal duck, or a crow. This bird is supposed to have some supernatural powers, and I am told that various portions of its body are highly prized by witches and goomer doctors.

It appears that many old settlers have a peculiar feeling about the wren; some of them really believe it is different from all other birds, and that there is something supernaturally evil in its habits. The bite of a wren is supposed to be deadly poison, perhaps because wrens eat so many spiders. I have known country boys who were accustomed to rob every birds' nest they could find, but had never even seen a wren's egg, much less touched one, although wrens were nesting all over the place. Several of these fellows told me that it is very bad luck to kill wrens, the best course being to let them severely alone.

I have heard experienced woodsmen insist that young crows, before they leave the nest, are white. Why they say this I have no idea, since one has only to look into a crow's nest in the spring to see that it isn't true.

There are numerous old sayings and proverbs about the dates when certain birds first deposit their eggs. One often hears it said that guinea hens never lay until the first week of "buck-berry swell." The buckberry swell is the season when the buds on buckbrush begin to enlarge, usually about the middle of March, I think.

Many turkey hunters claim that loud thunder really does kill young birds in the egg, especially birds that nest on the ground such as turkey, quail, ducks, geese, and the like. They insist that it is the thunder that does the damage, not the lightning or the rain. One veteran hunter says that hen turkeys usually desert their nests about twelve hours after a severe thunderstorm; he thinks they can tell somehow that the eggs are dead and realize that it's no use to fool with 'em any longer. Some of these Ozark bird hunters tell a story about the time the powder works blew up, over in Jasper county, Missouri, and no quail were hatched that year for seven or eight miles around.

Old fishermen have told me that the redhorse and white suckers will not spawn until they see dogwood blossoms on the banks of White River. It is true that these fish shoal about the same time that the dogwood blooms, but it is doubtless a matter of temperature; certainly there is no evidence that any fish can see flowers on the shore, or distinguish between dogwood bloom and other flowers.

Harold Wales, of Mammoth Springs, Arkansas, mentions the hillman's belief that the eel is a *male catfish.*[4] Many hillfolk believe there is something supernatural about the reproduction of eels. This is doubtless because no little eels are seen in the streams, and eels are never found to contain spawn. The Ozarker does not for one moment accept the scientists' tale that eels reproduce only in salt water.

Another odd notion is that if you leave a fried eel alone, the flesh will be "blood raw" in a few hours, just as if it had never been cooked at all. This is not true, as anybody with a piece of fried eel can demonstrate. But I have heard the story all over the Ozark country, and have met a score of men and women who declared that they fried eels at night and saw the same fish dripping with blood next morning.

Many Ozark people believe that eels are inordinately fond of human flesh, and there are stories of vast numbers of eels taken by fishermen callous enough to use this sort of bait. On the lower White River, according to one account, some fishermen murdered a Negro girl and soaked thousands of dough balls in her blood; with this gruesome bait they caught a whole truckload of eels in two nights' fishing. This story was widely circulated at one time, but the peace officers who investigated the matter found no evidence of a killing, nor any trace of the truckload of eels.

There are some Ozark folk who will not touch eels at all, but most of the old-timers eat blue eels freely enough, while contending that the larger yellow species is poisonous. I have seen yel-

4 *Arkansas Gazette.* July 3, 1938.

low eels weighing five or six pounds thrown away by giggers at
Noel, Missouri, on the Cowskin River. And Mr. R. W. Church,
of Pittsburg, Kansas, tells me that people near Stuttgart,
Arkansas, think that yellow catfish are not fit to eat; he says
that the boys down there used to eat the blue catfish and throw
the "yaller bellies" to the hogs.

I know many rivermen who believe that spoonbill catfish,
which grow quite large in some of the Ozark rivers, are not
wholesome food for human beings. These fellows cut the heads
off spoonbills and sell the flesh to the tourists as ordinary catfish, but they don't eat such stuff themselves. Other fishermen
tell me that the injurious substance occurs mainly in the brain
and spinal cord; if a man *must* eat spoonbill cats, he should
split 'em open as soon as caught and remove not only the head
but the entire backbone as well. In many places one hears experienced fishermen say that a spoonbill catfish can't swim
downstream, though nobody seems to have any particular reason for this belief.

Catfish and men, it is said, are the only living creatures known
to eat pawpaws; dogs and even swine turn from them in dis-
gust. However, though it is almost proverbial that catfish are
"plumb gluttons for pawpaws," I have never seen a hillman
use them as bait. "Fish that's a-feedin' on them things," an old
man told me, "aint fit to eat nohow." It seems very odd that
these fellows eat pawpaws themselves with every sign of relish
but regard fish that have fed upon pawpaws as unwholesome.
Personally, I do not believe that catfish have any particular
fondness for pawpaws, although they doubtless eat 'em on occasion, as they will sometimes devour any sort of garbage that
falls into the water. But the catfish-pawpaw legend is heard
the length and breadth of the Ozark country, and is repeated
even by second-growth hillbillies in the cities.

Guides on the Ozark streams are always telling the tourists
that gars are deadly poison, but I have seen people eating
them on the lower White River. There is a very ancient idea

that mussels, the shells of which are collected and sold to the button factories, are poisonous. This despite the fact that shell diggers are known to eat them, when times are hard, without any fatal results. In fact, I don't mind admitting that I have eaten mussels myself. They aren't very good, but they're certainly not poisonous.

Ozark fishermen are careful never to step over a fish pole, or over a fishing line on the ground; if a man does inadvertently take such a step, it means that he will catch no more fish that day.

Country boys often leave one fish of a large catch hanging in a tree near the fishing hole. "Oh—just for the birds," a boy answered rather sheepishly when I asked him why this was done. The old-timers say that it is supposed to bring good luck next time. A woman at Calico Rock, Arkansas, told me that it was a trick learned from the Cherokees, who always left several of their best fish lying on the bank. The old Cherokees whom I interviewed, however, said they never heard of any such foolishness.

The old-timers believe that an east wind is the worst possible omen for a fisherman, but I have seen large catches of bass made in Lake Taneycomo when an east wind was blowing; I recall at least one fine jacksalmon which was taken in White River, when a regular gale was blowing from the east. There is a very general belief that all fish bite best during the dark of the moon, and also that fish exposed to moonlight are likely to spoil in a few hours. Another old story is that bass won't bite during an electrical display, but I have caught both bigmouth and black bass in a thunderstorm, with flashes of lightning illuminating the whole countryside. Many old rivermen insist that fish won't bite when the sign is in the heart or stomach, but it seems to me that there is no truth in this, either.

If dragonflies or snake feeders alight on a still-fisherman's bobber it is a sign of bad luck; but if the little black beetles called lucky-bugs gather around his cork, he may expect to catch a fine string of pan fish.

Many rivermen say that fish may be kept fresh for several days, even in the hottest weather, simply by wrapping them in green walnut leaves. Others claim that the same result is obtained by smearing the dressed fish, inside and out, with black pepper.

Any hillman will tell you that an ordinary mud turtle contains seven kinds of meat—pork, beef, mutton, venison, chicken, duck, and fish. Despite this belief, the Ozarkers as a class seldom eat turtles. The hillfolk who do eat them choose the soft shell kind, not snappers or hard-shells, although I have eaten all three and find little difference. Some of the Indians in eastern Oklahoma eat land turtles or box tortoises, and a dog which will point these creatures always brings a good price in the Osage Nation. Bird hunters will not believe this, but it is a fact that some pointers and setters will disregard quail in order to retrieve land turtles.

Miss Margaret Lillie, of Rockaway Beach, Missouri, who boasts some Cherokee blood, told me that she had eaten land turtles and that they were very good. Later on I tried one myself, as cooked by some Indians from Sallisaw, Oklahoma, and found it palatable enough. But I have never known a non-Indian hillbilly who could be induced to taste a land turtle, and the majority of them will not eat any sort of reptile.

There is an old saying that once a turtle bites a man, it never lets go until a clap of thunder is heard, but I don't think anybody really believes such an obvious falsehood. Akin to this is the idea that a snake can't possibly die until the sun goes down, no matter how badly it is injured. No snake can cross a horsehair rope, according to the old-timers, many of whom have never even seen a horsehair rope.

If a single horsehair is placed in water, in the summer time, it is believed to turn into a snake. This notion probably arose from the fact that long hairlike worms, said to mature in the intestines of grasshoppers, are sometimes seen in watering troughs and roadside pools. I found one of these creatures once, in my springhouse at Pineville, Missouri. It was about a foot long, white, and rather thicker than a horsehair. One end was tapered, the other blunt—the tapered end seemed to be the head. I kept the thing in an aquarium for several days. It was always moving, the tapered end being most active in exploring every crack and cranny as if seeking a way out. Later on some boys showed me another horsehair snake they had found in a creek. This one was about five inches long, dark brown in color, and very active. It really looked pretty much like a piece of horsehair, and the boys who found it had no doubt that it *was* a horsehair which, in the natural course of events, had "turned into a snake."

The old story of the hoop snake which puts its tail in its mouth and rolls downhill is believed by many; in most cases this creature pursues some poor hillman, misses him, and strikes the horn on its tail into a growing tree; the hoop snake's horn is deadly poison, and the tree always dies within a few days— sometimes the green leaves wither and fall within an hour. Otto Ernest Rayburn repeats the story of a woman who was attacked by a hoop snake, but the sting in the snake's tail barely touched her dress. She washed the dress next day, and the poison "turned three tubs of wash water plumb green!" [5] I have met reliable and honest farmers who say that they have *seen* hoop snakes rolling through the tall grass, and there is no doubt in my mind that they are telling what they believe to be the truth. But the scientific herpetologists are all agreed that the hoop snake is a myth.

A variety of blacksnake called the "blue racer" is popularly supposed to chase people, particularly little boys playing truant from school. Many people believe that the coachwhip snake, a big blacksnake with a red tail, has been known to catch a

[5] *Ozark Country*, p. 267.

child by the lips, take one turn round his neck, and whip him very severely; sometimes two coachwhips are said to work together, one holding the victim while the other lashes him.

Poisonous snakes, when in the water, are said to lie on the surface with the entire body afloat, while nonpoisonous serpents swim with only the head exposed; many hillmen really believe that this is a reliable way to distinguish between the venomous cottonmouth moccasin and several species of harmless water snakes. Some noodlers or rock fishermen, accustomed to catch big fish with their bare hands, say that moccasins never bite a man under water. Others believe that the snakes may bite, but are unable to inject poison into the wound while their heads are submerged.

Many persons believe that female snakes, particularly water moccasins, swallow their young at the approach of danger. One of my neighbors says that he suddenly came upon a large "bitch cottonmouth" with a number of young snakes playing about her; the moment the old moccasin saw him she opened her mouth wide, and the little ones instantly ran down her throat. A few moments later he killed the big snake, cut her open, and found fourteen little moccasins inside.

A number of sober backwoods farmers have told me seriously that before a copperhead takes a drink of water, it discharges its venom carefully out upon a flat stone; a moment later, having drunk, the creature sucks the poison into its fangs again.

There is an almost universal belief that the king snake, which has no poison fangs, can kill any copperhead or rattler. And there are people who say that the king snake is not affected by the venom of a rattlesnake, because it eats rattlesnake weed as an antidote. The story goes that every time a rattler bites the king snake, the latter hurries over to a snakeweed nearby and nibbles off a leaf or two, before returning to the fight. I have never found anybody who claims to have witnessed this performance, and the whole thing doubtless began as a tall tale, but there are people in Missouri and Arkansas today who accept it as a fact.

Many people in northwestern Taney county, Missouri, tell me that they have killed big timber rattlers with hair on 'em. "Like coarse bristles, black, about three inches long," the story runs. "Mostly there's a scatterin' of bristles just back of the snake's head, and maybe a few more shorter ones about eight or ten inches from the tip of his tail." So many people in this region tell the story that I am almost persuaded that they have seen rattlesnakes with something like bristles on them. It occurred to me that the "hairs" might be some kind of parasite, but the experts at the American Museum of Natural History tell me that nothing remotely resembling bristles has ever been found on snakes anywhere; Dr. Charles M. Bogert, of the department of herpetology, suggests that the "hairs" might be cactus spines, but this does not impress me since the only cactus in this region is the prickly pear, which has short thorns not at all like the three-inch bristles which my neighbors insist they have seen on these Taney county rattlesnakes.

All snakes are supposed to go blind and change their skins during the dog days in late summer and become more belligerent than at any other time. Uncle Israel Bonebreak, an ordinarily reliable old gentleman who lives near Pineville, Missouri, tells me that he has often seen blacksnakes, chicken snakes, milk snakes, and other harmless serpents deliberately attack human beings during the dog-day period. There is an old saying that "all snakes go blind when huckleberries are ripe," and it appears that some hillfolk accept it as a literal truth.

A great many Ozarkers fear the common blow snake or puff adder quite as much as the venomous copperhead. Visitors from the city have fallen into this error too, and even Marge Lyon says that "the spreading adder, called spread head, is very poisonous." [6] The truth is, of course, that the vicious-looking adder is completely harmless.

[6] *And Green Grass Grows All Around*, p. 294.

The innoxious little green tree snake is believed to carry a deadly poison. It is called the snake doctor, and is supposed to cure all other kinds of snakes when they are sick or injured. I once found a large timber rattler which had been badly wounded, apparently by deer or goats. An old hunter who was present said "Look out for the doctor!" and began to search the bushes nearby. Sure enough, in a few minutes he found one of these little green snakes in a blackberry bush.

The old folks say that wherever you find a scorpion—the Ozarker's name for a harmless little blue-tailed lizard—there is always a snake only a few feet away.

There are several old tales about an odd relationship between snakes and babies. According to one story, well known in many parts of the Ozark country, a small child is seen to carry his cup of bread and milk out into the shrubbery near the cabin. The mother hears the baby prattling but supposes that he is talking to himself. Finally she approaches the child and is horrified to see him playing with a large serpent—usually a rattlesnake or copperhead. The baby takes a little food but gives most of his bread and milk to the big reptile. The mother's first impulse is to kill the snake, of course, but the old-timers say that this would be a mistake. They believe that the snake's life is somehow linked with that of the child, and if the reptile is killed the baby will pine away and die a few weeks later. I have heard old men and women declare that they had such cases in their own families and knew that the baby *did* die shortly after the snake's death.

A spotted serpent called the milk snake is said to live by milking cows in the pasture. I know several persons who swear they have seen these snakes sucking milk cows, and they say that a cow which has been milked by a snake is always reluctant to allow a human being to touch her thereafter.

Some of the Holy Roller preachers are accustomed to bring poisonous snakes into the pulpit, declaring that God will protect His servants from all harm, and quoting various Biblical

references to such matters, usually the statement in Luke 10:
19, where the saints are given power to tread on serpents and
scorpions and assured that nothing shall hurt them, or the
passage about taking up serpents in Mark 16:18. I have not
seen this performance myself, but I once called on one of these
"snake-wavin' preachers" and was shown two large copperheads in a cage. The man of God refused to handle them in my
presence, although I offered to make a substantial contribution
to his church. He said that he claimed nothing for himself, but
that a temporary immunity to snake venom was sometimes given
him by God Almighty for the purpose of impressing His poor
sinful children. "I don't believe in temptin' Providence," he
added, "an' I don't never touch no sarpints only when I feel
the Power a-comin' on."

It is very generally believed that there is something about
the odor of gourds or gourd vines which repels snakes; many
people plant gourds near their cabins for this reason, although
they will seldom admit it to an outsider.

Some families have secret spells or "charms" which are supposed to protect them against snake bite, but the nature of
these has not been revealed to me. I do know, however, that
some hillfolk are very careful to avoid the use of the word
"snake." Instead of warning their children to beware of snakes
in the path, they say "look out for *our friends* down that way,"
or "there's a lot of *them old things* between here and the river."
If despite all precautions a hillman is bitten by a reptile which
he regards as poisonous, he still has recourse to some astounding remedies—but I have dealt with the treatment of snake bite
elsewhere in this book.

There are many odd notions concerning insects and arach-
nids. Big centipedes are common in the hill country, no matter
what the Chamber of Commerce people may see fit to tell the
tourists about it. Some old-timers say that a centipede tries
to count the teeth of every child who approaches him; if the
creature makes a correct count, the child will die in a few weeks.
I have seen children close their lips firmly and even cover their

mouths with their hands when a centipede appears in an Ozark cabin. Many hillfolk repeat the tale that the bite of a centipede makes the flesh fall off the bones, but I don't think there's any truth in it.

People near Natural Dam, Arkansas, told me that the Devil's horse, or praying mantis, is deadly poison, and that a boy near that place died as a result of its bite. Local physicians laughed at this story; one doctor said that he didn't know whether or not the Devil's horse was poisonous, but he knew damned well that it had never killed anybody in his neighborhood. Children in the Ozarks are often told, however, that it is bad luck to "pester" a Devil's horse, as the creature is likely to spit tobacco juice in one's eye and perhaps cause blindness.

The sting of the big Ozark hornet is a painful matter, but I never heard of hornets killing anybody. Mr. Elbert Short, however, who lives near Crane, Missouri, reports the old idea that if seven hornets sting a man at once, the poor chap dies instantly, as if he had a bullet through his heart.

Very few of the mountain people would intentionally kill a spider, since such an act is supposed to bring misfortune in its wake. It is bad luck to kill a cricket, too, though I have not heard of any definite penalty for this. My neighbors were disgusted to see me using little black crickets as fish bait. One man who looked at a fine string of perch that I had taken with crickets observed that he would not eat one of these fish or allow his children to do so. "I'd have to git mighty hungry," said he, "before I'd ever put one of them crickets onto a fish hook."

There are several peculiar superstitions relating to the larva of the ant lion, which lives in little cone-shaped pits in the dirt under rock ledges. Every boy is told that if he finds one of these nests and cries:

> Oh Johnny Doodlebug,
> Come up an' I'll give you a bushel of corn!

the insect will climb out and show itself immediately.

Mr. Lewis Kelley, of Cyclone, Missouri, tells me that practically all of the old settlers believed that spiders hatch from eggs laid by "dirt dobbers" or mud wasps. "Just open up a dirt dobber's nest," he said, "and see if you don't find it full of live spiders." The truth is, of course, that the spiders are stung by the adult wasps into a state of paralysis and placed in the mud nests to serve as food for the young dirt dobbers. The old-timers have heard of this theory, but they don't believe it.

The white foam which appears on the stems of certain weeds, produced doubtless by the activities of some small insect, is always called frog spit; this is merely an imaginative name, however, since the hillfolk don't really believe that frogs are responsible for it. Many of them are convinced, however, that horse flies somehow hatch out of frog spit. I have met old men who told me seriously that fleas are hatched from eggs, under ordinary conditions, but are sometimes produced spontaneously from dog hair.

Charles J. Finger, of Fayetteville, Arkansas, told me of his neighbors who believe that the drops of resin found on pine boards often turn into bedbugs. I have never encountered this idea but have known many hillfolk who think that bedbugs are somehow generated from bats. Some old-timers say that the daddy longlegs or harvestmen deposit their eggs on bats, and that these eggs hatch into bedbugs. "If you mash a daddy longlegs," said an old fellow in Polk county, Arkansas, "it smells just exactly like bedbugs"—this being regarded as evidence of parental relationship, apparently.

There is an old saying to the effect that dog fennel breeds chiggers and kills ticks; the hillfolk claim that chiggers swarm on the yellow flowers, and this may be true, for all I know. The old notion that fennel kills ticks seems to have no foundation in fact. The common milkweed with orange-colored blooms (*Asclepias*) is also called chigger weed and is said to be headquarters for chiggers.

The hills around Bonniebrook, the old O'Neill home near Day, Missouri, are crawling with chiggers and wood ticks all summer. There is only one place in the whole neighborhood where it is safe for campers to sit on the ground, and that is a certain hillside where pennyroyal grows. Pennyroyal is a kind of mint, and it really seems to discourage both ticks and chiggers.

Many Ozark people insist that cedar trees are poison to the tiny seed ticks which are so abundant in July and August. One often sees farmer boys take off their overalls and brush their bare legs with a cedar bough. I have tried this myself, but without any benefit whatever. And the cedar thickets or "brakes" in Taney county, Missouri, are swarming with seed ticks every summer.

There are strange theories about certain trees, and I have touched upon some of these items in connection with witchcraft elsewhere in this book. Many old people believe that there is something supernatural about the propagation of the ironwood tree, which is supposed to be planted by the Devil's agents. And there are woodsmen in Missouri who say that sassafras trees do not grow from seeds, but somehow sprout from grub worms.

One often hears that mistletoe, known as witches' broom, is used in casting magic spells and the like. Some farmers hang a bunch of mistletoe in the smokehouse, "to keep witches off'n the meat." About Christmas time the country boys make a little money by gathering mistletoe and sending it to the city markets. These fellows all say that mistletoe doesn't come from seeds but grows spontaneously out of bird manure.

The pawpaw tree is well known to be connected with witchcraft and devil worship, and even a gray-and-black butterfly (*Papilio ajax*) is looked upon as "strange" because it is so often seen fluttering about pawpaw trees. People near Goodman, Missouri, tell me that there is some direct connection between pawpaw trees and malaria, but just what this relation is I don't know. Pawpaws are becoming rare in many sections where they were formerly abundant; this is regarded by the old-timers as a bad omen, perhaps a sign that the end of the world is at hand.

Several tales about the dogwood tree are linked up with religious legends. One story, said to be very old although I never heard it until about 1935, is that the cross on which Jesus died was made of dogwood, and that He cursed the tree and doomed it to be stunted and twisted, unfit for any kind of lumber. In the center of the dogwood flower is something said to resemble a crown of thorns, while a brown mark—like the stain of a rusty nail—shows at the tip of each white sepal. A fanciful and romanticized version of this legend was written up by C. E. Barnes of Sulphur Springs, Arkansas, in the 1930's and was published by many Arkansas newspapers.[7]

In Washington county, Arkansas, a wood chopper told me that it was the willow, not the dogwood, which was cursed by Jesus. "An' since that day," said the old man, "the willer tree aint been worth a good God damn for nothin'." This man assured me that the tale of Jesus cursing the willow is in the Book— by which he meant the Bible. "I caint read myself," said he, "but it's in the Book all right, an' any o' these here spindle-assed preachers can tell you all 'bout it." A related legend of the willow tree is the "Jesus and Joses" story recorded by Professor H. M. Belden who got it in 1914 from a man at Rolla, Missouri.[8]

The wild hawthorn or redhaw (*Crataegus*) is another accursed tree, though just how this came about is unknown to me. In March, 1923, the legislature named the hawthorn bloom as the state flower of Missouri, but there are many people in the southern end of the state who avoid touching it and regard even an accidental contact with the blooming tree as a very bad omen. Both redhaw and blackhaw bushes are common in the

[7] See also a reference to the dogwood-cross story in Guy Howard's *Walkin' Preacher of the Ozarks* (New York, Harper, 1944), p. 141.

[8] *Ballads and Songs Collected by the Missouri Folk-Lore Society,* Columbia, Univ. of Missouri, 1940, p. 102.

Ozarks, and both are connected in the hillman's mind with sexual misadventures—rapes and unfortunate pregnancies and disastrous abortions and the like. Other plants which may be mentioned in this connection are the lady's-slipper (*Cypripedium*) and the stinkhorn fungus (*Phallus impudicus*).

The Oklahoma legislature, in 1937, passed a bill making the redbud Oklahoma's official state tree. This roused a great storm of criticism, because many people believe that the redbud is the unluckiest tree in the world, since Judas hanged himself on a tree of this kind. Some hillfolk who have no interest in religious matters still feel that the redbud or Judas tree is bewitched, at least in the spring, and it is well to keep away from blooming redbuds after dark. Mrs. Roberta Lawson, of Tulsa, vice-president of the General Federation of Women's Clubs, led a large number of Oklahoma clubwomen who held public meetings, telegraphed protests to Governor Marland, and so on. Some important citizens of northeastern Oklahoma were still grumbling about the matter, I am told, as recently as 1942.

Some observers have thought they found a suggestion of tree worship, or something of the sort, in the Ozarker's use of masculine pronouns as applied to trees. One of my neighbors near Pineville, Missouri, said of a certain bee tree: "*He's* holler as a gourd! I bet there's five hunderd pound o' honey in *him!*" A gentleman at Fayetteville, Arkansas, remarked that he had enjoyed the shade of a certain maple on his lawn for forty years and added: "I aim to be buried under *him* when I die." I have many other examples of this sort of thing. It does not seem particularly significant to me but has impressed several eminent scholars who have visited the hill country, and I set it down here for what it may be worth.

12. Ozark Witchcraft

The Ozark hillfolk will talk about crop failures and weather signs with any tourist who happens along, but let him mention witches and they all shut up like clams. If they say anything at all on the subject, it will be that they do not believe any such foolishness. Some of them will even deny that they ever heard of witches or witch masters.

The truth is, however, that a great many Ozarkers do believe these things. I meet people every day who are firm believers in witchcraft, and I have been personally acquainted with more than a score of so-called witches myself.

A solid citizen of Little Rock, Arkansas, contends that every good Christian must believe in witchcraft. "It's just like John Wesley said," he told me, "if you give up witches you might as well throw away your Bible!" The Bible, he went on, not only requires a belief in witches but also demands that they be persecuted. He quoted from memory at great length, but the only one of his quotations that I have been able to verify is in Exodus 22, where it says plainly "thou shalt not suffer a witch to live."

This man assured me that "witches are thicker than seed ticks" in Pulaski county, even today. "Them things are goin' on same as they always did," said he, "but it's all under cover nowadays. The young folks lives too fast an' heedless. More than half of 'em are bewitched anyhow, so they don't care what happens. It looks like the Devil's got the country by the tail, on a downhill pull!"

A witch, according to my informants, is a woman who has

had dealings with the Devil and thereby acquired some supernatural powers, and who uses these powers to bring evil upon
her neighbors. This definition excludes such estimable characters as Mrs. Josie Forbes of Taskee, Missouri, Mrs. Angie
Paxton of Green Forest, Arkansas, Miss Jean Wallace of
Roaring River, Missouri, and others of the same type. Newspaper writers call these women witches, and the tourists naturally follow suit, but no real old-time Ozarker would make such
a mistake. They may be clairvoyants, fortunetellers, seers,
mystics, purveyors of medical advice, seekers of lost property—
but they are certainly not witches.

Although I have known and interviewed twenty-four persons
who were regarded by their neighbors as witches, only three
admitted that they had sold themselves to the Devil. These three
women were quite mad, of course; the point is that their neighbors did not regard them as lunatics, but as witches. The other
twenty-one claim that their efforts are directed *against* the
forces of evil, and that their main business is the removal of
spells and curses put upon their clients by supernatural means.
These practitioners are variously known as witch masters,
white witches, witch doctors, faith doctors, goomer doctors and
conjure folks, and it is from them that I have obtained much
of my information on the subject.

Some hillfolk believe that a woman may become a witch by
some comparatively simple hocus-pocus. Professor A. W. Breedon, of Manhattan, Kansas, who was reared near Galena, Missouri, in the nineties, tells me his neighbors thought that a
woman had only to fire a silver bullet at the moon and mutter
two or three obscene old sayin's. A lady in Barry county,
Missouri, says that any woman who repeats the Lord's Prayer
backward and fires seven silver bullets at the moon is transformed into a witch instanter. But most of the genuine old-
timers are agreed that to become a witch is a rather complicated
matter.

Anybody is free to discuss the general principles of witchcraft, but the conjure words and old sayin's must be learned from a member of the opposite sex. Another thing to be remembered is that the secret doctrines must pass only between blood relatives, or between persons who have been united in sexual intercourse. Thus it is that every witch obtains her unholy wisdom either from a lover or from a male relative.

Not every woman who receives this information becomes a witch. A mother can transmit the secret work to her son, and he could pass it on to his wife, and she might tell one of her male cousins, and so on. All of these people may be regarded as "carriers," but not until someone actually uses the deadly formulae does a genuine witch appear. And thus, while a knowledge of witchcraft is admitted to exist in certain families and clans, it sometimes lies dormant for a long time.

A woman who was regarded as a witch by her neighbors died some years ago, in Greene county, Missouri. I never met the old lady but am acquainted with her daughter—a college graduate, very citified and sophisticated, who has not visited Missouri for a long time. I asked this girl if she had ever heard anything about witchcraft in the Ozarks. To my surprise she did not laugh it off. She said that she believed her own mother had possessed some measure of supernatural power, and that this power was definitely evil. She had never discussed the matter with her mother. "I always thought mamma would tell me about that some day," the daughter said, "but she never did."

Some parts of the witches' routine are well known, even to people who deny all acquaintance with such matters. The trick of reversing the Lord's Prayer is a case in point. A pious Baptist lady in McDonald county, Missouri, once denounced a schoolmarm because the children were taught to shout their multiplication tables backward as well as forward. "It's plumb risky, an' there ought to be a law ag'in it," growled the old woman. "Learn them gals to say their 'rithmetic back'ards today, an' they'll be a-sayin' *somethin' else* back'ards tomorrow!"

A virgin may possess some of the secrets of "bedevilment,"

imparted by her father or her uncle, but she cannot be a genuine witch, for good and sufficient reasons. Most of the Ozark
witches seem to be widows, or elderly spinsters who are obviously
not virgins. I knew one sprightly grass widder who was said
to "talk the Devil's language," but most people doubted this
because of her youth—she was only seventeen. A woman can
"do the Devil's work" and practice the infernal arts in a small
way without any ceremony, but to attain her full powers she
must be formally initiated into the sinister sisterhood.

When a woman decides to become a witch, according to the
fireside legends, she repairs to the family buryin' ground at
midnight, in the dark of the moon. Beginning with a verbal
renunciation of the Christian religion, she swears to give herself
body and soul to the Devil. She removes every stitch of clothing,
which she hangs on an infidel's tombstone, and delivers her body
immediately to the Devil's representative—that is, to the man
who is inducting her into the "mystery." The sexual act completed, both parties repeat certain old sayin's—terrible words
which assemble devils, and the spirits of the evil dead—and end
by reciting the Lord's Prayer backward. This ceremony is supposed to be witnessed by at least two initiates, also nude, and
must be repeated on three consecutive nights. After the first
and second vows the candidate is still free to change her mind,
but the third pledge is final. Henceforth the woman is a witch
and must serve her new master through all eternity.

The dedication of a witch is a solemn affair, not to be con-
fused with the so-called "Witches' Sabbath" which occasioned
so much talk in northwestern Arkansas, when a group of
drunken young people suddenly decided to dance naked by the
roadside. It was a mere accident that this lewd frolic was staged
at the entrance to a cemetery. The incident had no connection
with witchcraft. The term "Witches' Sabbath" was applied to
it, not by the natives, but by an imaginative newspaperman
from Illinois.

The vagaries of some nude Holy Rollers near Forsyth, Missouri, have also been connected in the public mind with the initiation of a witch. I have examined the Rutledge photographs which were given so much publicity by the late Lou Beardon and others, but have never been able to find out just what happened at the Roller camp when these pictures were made. My opinion is that the White River nudists were merely religious fanatics, together with a few thrill-seeking young men from the nearby villages. There is no evidence that they had anything to do with witchcraft.

I am told, by women who claim to have experienced both, that the witch's initiation is a much more moving spiritual crisis than that which the Christians call conversion. The primary reaction is profoundly depressing, however, because it inevitably results in the death of some person near and dear to the witch.

I once attended the funeral of a woman whose death was attributed to her daughter's participation in one of these graveyard ceremonies. The accused girl sat apart from the other members of the family and was ignored by the minister and the congregation alike. Witchcraft is very real to these people. A friend of the dead woman told me that the person who dies as a "witch's sixpence" generally goes to hell, and therefore such a crime is infinitely more horrible than an ordinary murder. It is not until after the first victim's death that the witch comes into full possession of her supernatural powers, but from that time forward she is able to do many things which are impossible to ordinary mortals.

A witch can assume the form of any bird or animal, but cats and wolves seem to be her favorite disguises. In many a backwoods village you may hear some gossip about a woman who visits her lover in the guise of a house cat. Once inside his cabin, she resumes her natural form and spends the night with him. Shortly before daybreak she becomes a cat again, returns to her home, and is transformed into a woman at her husband's bedside.

A big yellow cat once walked into a cabin where I was sitting with an aged tie hacker and his wife. The woman began to shout "Witch! Witch!" at the top of her voice. The old man sprang up, crossed the fingers of both hands, and chanted something that sounded like "Pulley-bone holy-ghost double-yoke! Pulley-bone holy-ghost double-yoke!" The cat walked in a wide circle past the hearth, stared fixedly at the old gentleman for a moment, and then strolled out across the threshold. We followed a moment later, but the animal was nowhere in sight. It may have crawled under the cabin, or under a corncrib which stood only a few yards away, but the old couple insisted that it had vanished by reason of some supernatural dispensation.

There is an old story of a drunken bravo in northwestern Arkansas who was bantered to sleep all night in a shack where witches were known to be "usin' round." He said that if they gave him a jug of whiskey he'd sleep anywhere. He lit a candle, and drank heavily, and felt very well until midnight, when suddenly there appeared an enormous cat. The creature yowled and spit at him, and the man fired his great horse-pistol—a muzzle-loading weapon loaded with buckshot. Somewhere a woman screamed, and the hillman always swore that just as the candle went out he saw a woman's bare foot, covered with blood, wriggling around on the table. Next day it was learned that a woman who lived nearby had shot her foot off accidentally and died from loss of blood. Some say that she died a-yowlin' and a-spittin' like a cat!

Another well-known tale is concerned with a witch who assumed the form of a swamp rabbit and lived on milk. A farmer saw this big rabbit sucking his cow and fired at it with a load of turkey shot; the animal was only about thirty feet off but seemed quite unharmed. The man rushed home and molded several slugs of silver, obtained by melting half dollars. Charging his shotgun with these, he fired again and killed the rabbit. A few hours later came the news that an old woman in the next holler had been shot to death; the doctor couldn't find the bullet, but everybody knew that it must have been a silver slug that killed her.

Once I was riding through the woods with two hillmen, when a timber wolf suddenly appeared in a little clearing. One of my companions fired several times with his revolver, but the wolf trotted unhurriedly away, looking back over its left shoulder. "Damn it, I don't see how I missed th' critter!" cried the pistol shooter. "You didn't miss it," the other answered quietly. Nothing more was said, but I noticed that both men rode with their fingers crossed. I crossed mine, too, not wishing to be mistaken for an ignorant "furriner."

A schoolmaster from Pea Ridge, Arkansas, used to tell the story of two young women who lived alone in a nearby farm. They owned no cattle and were never seen to do any milking but always had plenty of butter and homemade cheese. Finally a farmhand peeked in at their window and later swore that he saw these girls hang a dishcloth on the pot rack and squeeze several gallons of milk out of it. Turning about, he looked at the cows in a neighbor's pasture and saw that their udders were gradually decreasing in size.

The teacher mentioned above is an exceptionally intelligent man, not at all credulous in ordinary matters, but he seemed inclined to accept this dishrag-milking tale as true. He suggested that the phenomena which we associate with hypnosis may be identical with those formerly attributed to witchcraft. Some high-powered salesman's exploits may be of this type, he thought, and referred with feeling to a chap who sold him some worthless magazines at an exorbitant figure. "That fellow certainly got control of my mind somehow," he said ruefully. "We call it hypnotism now, but the old folks would probably say I was bewitched."

An old lady near Chadwick, Missouri, flew into a rage one Sunday morning because other members of the family insisted on going to church. Suddenly one of the horses became sick and fell right down in the harness. The women and children began to cry, and the whole expedition was thrown into confusion. Finally the menfolks managed to tail the animal up, and dragged it through a stream of running water. This broke the witch spell and cured the horse instantly, but it was too late for anybody to attend church.

I remember a poor silly old woman who tried to buy some of my neighbor's ducks. The price she offered was very low, and Aunt Rosie decided to wait for a better market. "You'll be mighty sorry," the old woman shouted. "Them ducks is all a-goin' to die Monday." My neighbor paid no heed to this prediction, but the ducks *did* die on Monday, and it was generally believed that the old witch had cast a spell on them. The possibility of poisoning, or some other material cause of death, apparently did not occur to any of the parties concerned. This unquestioning acceptance of supernatural explanations is not uncommon in the Ozark country.

Mrs. Isabel Spradley, Van Buren, Arkansas, tells me of an old woman in her neighborhood who "throwed a spell" upon a neighbor's tomato patch just by drawing a circle in the dust, marking a cross in the center of the circle, and spitting in the center of the cross. No buyer in this region, once he heard the news, would give a plugged nickel for that man's tomato crop.

Aunt Sarah Wilson, who lives on Bear Creek near Day, Missouri, was worried about one of her nephews, who had wrecked four automobiles. She believed, and told several of her friends, that some witch was throwin' spells on the boy's cars. One day she was standing in her own backyard, when something fell right beside her foot. It was a witch ball about the size of an ordinary marble, made of black horse-hair. She knew immediately that the witches were workin' on her nephew again. And sure enough, he had an accident that same afternoon.

I have been told of another Ozark witch who killed several of her enemies by means of a "hair ball"—just a little bunch of black hair mixed with beeswax and rolled into a hard pellet. The old woman tossed this thing at the persons whom she wished to eliminate, and they fell dead a few hours later. It is said that the fatal hair ball is always found somewhere in the body of a person killed in this manner. In one case, according to my informant, the little ball of combings was taken from the dead girl's mouth.

There are men and women in the Ozarks who believe that the strange feather balls known as "crowns," which sometimes form in pillows, are the work of witches and if not destroyed will inevitably cause the death of the person whose head rests upon the pillow. For a detailed account of these feather crowns see Chapter 13.

Some witches are said to kill people with graveyard dirt, which is dust scraped from a grave with the left forefinger at midnight. This is mixed with the blood of a black bird; a raven or crow is best, but a black chicken will do in a pinch. The witch ties this mixture up in a rag which has touched a corpse and buries it under the doorstep of the person who is to be liquidated. The practice of burying conjure stuff under houses and doorsteps is well known. I have heard it said of a sick woman that she "must have stepped on somethin' "—meaning that she was bewitched.

Occasionally the "bad thing" is concealed in the saddle or wagon or automobile of the person upon whom the curse is intended to fall. One often hears of such objects being sewn into clothing, especially wedding garments. The witch's desire is to put the bad-luck charm into the victim's possession without his knowledge, or in such a manner that he does not recognize it for what it is. Sometimes a pet animal or an adopted child is made to serve the witch's purpose—a sort of left-handed mascot, as it were.

A witch is delighted if she gets a chance to walk three times clockwise around a sick man, as this is supposed to kill the patient immediately. It can seldom be managed inside a house, since beds are usually placed in contact with at least one wall. So the witch comes in the dead of night and walks in a wide circle outside the cabin. Certain nondescript marks in the dirt are alleged to be witch's tracks, and some people think that by burning dry grass in these tracks they can somehow discomfit the witch and break the spell cast upon the sick person.

One old woman in my neighborhood was unable to walk without crutches, but whenever a chicken was to be killed she insisted on doing the job herself. One of the boys would catch the chicken and bring it to granny as she sat in her chair under a tree. As she wrung the chicken's neck she spoke the name of an ancient enemy of hers. I asked once what effect this would have on the woman whose name she muttered. "Well, it won't do her no good," said granny with satisfaction. Both my neighbor and the woman she hated were supposed to have dabbled in witchcraft, and each denounced the other as a witch.

Near Clinton, Missouri, only a few years ago, there were people who showed marks on their legs as evidence that a certain old woman in the neighborhood was a witch. Their story was that when they undressed to go to bed, they felt pain as if they were being beaten with switches. One girl claimed to have been whipped so severely that the blood ran down to her heels. It is not clear to me how these people knew that a particular old woman was responsible for all this, but there seemed to be no doubt in anybody's mind on that point.

A little boy near Pineville, Missouri, failed to catch any rabbits in his clumsily built traps. "Them gums is *spellt*, that's what's the matter," he told me. I thought he meant spoiled, which the local people pronounce with a long *i* sound, and asked for further information. "They aint sp'ilt" he said disgustedly, "they're *spellt!* Some old woman done it." That was the first time I ever heard *spelled* used to mean bewitched.

Here is one of the old fireside witch tales, still told at Sparta, Missouri. A young boy worked on a farm for a widow and her two daughters. They all slept in a big one-room cabin. Several times the boy woke up in the night and found all three women gone, but the door bolted inside. In the morning he awoke to find them all in their beds as usual. Finally one night he just pretended to be asleep. About midnight he saw all three women get up and place a pan of water on the hearth. They washed their faces in the water, then each one said "Out I go and touch nowhere!"—and flicked up the chimney like a swallow! When the women were gone the boy got up, washed his face in the water and cried: "Out I go and touch nowhere!" Before you could bat an eye he was up the chimney and flyin' through the air. His hat blowed off. Pretty soon he lit in a big pasture, where all kinds of people was fiddlin' and dancin' and havin' a regular picnic. Some of them gals didn't have enough clothes on to wad a shotgun! . . . the next thing he knowed he was back at the house in bed, and the women was in their beds, and the door still bolted. It wasn't no dream though, because there was soot on his nightshirt, and his hat was gone. He never did find the hat. But he quit the job before the moon changed and went to live with his kinfolks.

A woman in Springfield, Missouri, told me that her own mother was an innocent sort of witch, who never did any serious harm, but interfered with household tasks and the like. Some strangers waxed loud in praise of the daughter's light bread; this irritated the old lady, who fancied that her own bread was much better, and she threw a spell on the girl's baking. This all happened forty years ago, and the witch has been in her grave for a quarter of a century, but the spell still holds, and the daughter has never once since that fatal day succeeded in making a really good batch of light bread.

There is a common belief that if a witch stirs soft soap, it won't be any good. A farmer's wife in Christian county, Missouri, was making soap in the back yard when an alleged witch came along. Immediately the woman raked the fire out from under the kettle and invited the witch into the house. When the witch had gone, the housewife found that every bit of the soap had boiled away, although *there wasn't any fire under it.*

Mr. A. W. Breedon, of Manhattan, Kansas, told me a tale

he heard as a boy in Taney county, Missouri, in the nineties. There was a very wicked man living there—a man who opposed all religion and refused to help build the meetinghouse. His family had drifted away, and the fellow was dying all alone, cursing at every breath. Some neighbors came over to take care of him, and while they were there a bolt of lightning fell out of a clear sky and set the house on fire. Two big men tried to carry the dying infidel out but couldn't lift him off the bed. Then they tried to move the bed, but even their great strength could not budge it an inch. Soon the house became intolerably hot, and the neighbors left just before the roof fell in. A strange black dog slipped out at the same time, apparently from under the sick man's bed. When the ashes cooled, there was no sign of the infidel's body—"nary a bone!"

Mrs. C. P. Mahnkey, of Mincy, Missouri, who still lives in the neighborhood where Breedon heard this tale, tells an almost identical story, booger dog and all. And even today there are folks who say that a strange black dog is seen about that region, wherever a fatal accident, fire, cyclone, or other calamity occurs.

Some old people in the neighborhood have hinted that the infidel was really a "he witch," and that the neighbors killed him and the black dog by shooting them with silver bullets. Then they burned the house with the bodies inside, and called it a good day's work. This variant of the legend also records the detail that no bones, either human or canine, were found in the ashes of the cabin.

There are people in northeastern Arkansas who believe that the Devil appeared near the end of the eighteenth century, at a pioneer settlement called Kentertown, some say as a warning of the great earthquake that occurred there in 1812. Several versions of the tale are still in oral circulation, and they differ as to the town, the date, and the names of the witnesses. But all the stories agree that two young Arkansas boys actually met the Devil in the brush, in broad daylight, and that he first appeared as a headless man with a cloven hoof. Later on he assumed other frightful shapes, roared like a lion, belched out great quantities of smoke, and so on. Finally the Devil snatched up one of the youths, tore out most of his hair, and handled him so roughly that he was unable to walk. Upon this the other young man fell upon his knees and cried out to God, asking help in Jesus' name. Instantly the Devil vanished in a cloud of stinking smoke, and the young man carried his injured companion back to town.

Some skeptics said that the two young men had been drinking heavily and must have dreamed all this business of demons roaring and blowing smoke. But many thought that the boys really had seen the Devil, and there are people in Arkansas who believe the story to this day. The *Golden Book Magazine* for March, 1926, reprinted a pamphlet entitled *Surprising Account of the Devil's Appearing to John Chesseldon and James Arkins, at a Town near the Mississippi, on the 24th of May, 1784.* This document was written by the two men named in the title and printed in 1792, according to the *Golden Book*. Fred W. Allsopp, in his *Folklore of Romantic Arkansas*, discusses the whole matter under the caption "The Devil in Arkansas." [1]

An old man near Caverna, Missouri, told me that he once met the Devil walking along in the snow just south of the Missouri-Arkansas line. When I questioned him about the Devil's appearance he described an ordinary countryman—blue overalls, slouch hat, skinny face, long hair, shotgun on shoulder, and so on. "He just looked like any common ordinary feller," said the old man wonderingly. I pondered this for awhile. "But how did you know it was the Devil?" I asked. The old man looked fearfully around, then leaned toward me and whispered: "He didn't throw no shadder! He didn't leave no tracks!"

In various parts of Missouri and Arkansas one hears the story of a great hole in the ground, surrounded by rugged cliffs, where hunters have heard strange sounds and smelled

[1] 1931, I, 234–238.

unusual odors. Some say that the Devil lives in that hole, imprisoned under a heavy fall of rock. There are stories of old men who claim to have visited the place as children. Some of these men swear that they heard the Devil's groans and curses and smelled burning flesh and brimstone. Strange people live on the escarpments, it is said, and throw odd things into the pit at night, particularly when the moon is full. There are tales of dark-visaged "furriners" traveling at night, who make regular pilgrimages to the place from distant parts of the country.

I have made some effort to locate this legendary spot, without success. There is a deep canyon with high rugged walls near Mena, Arkansas, which is known as "Devil's Half Acre," but the story of the Devil's imprisonment is not known to the people who live there. Some old-timers connect the story with Hot Springs, Arkansas, but I have never found anybody in that vicinity able to show me the bottomless pit, where I could hear the Devil yell and smell brimstone a-burnin'.

The student of these matters must remember that the word *witch* and its derivatives are not always to be taken literally. Tangles in a horse's mane are called *witches' stirrups*, but I don't think the people who use this term really believe that witches have been riding their horses. I have heard snarls in a woman's hair called *witches' cradles*, but am not sure just what is meant by this. The great horned owl is often called a *witch chicken*, perhaps because of the belief that owls can charm a chicken off its roost. *Witch ball* is a common name for a big puffball, known also as the Devil's snuffbox; this fungus will "hold fire" for a long time, like punk, and it is said that the Indians used it to carry fire from one camp to another. Occasionally a pullet lays a very small egg, and this the housewife usually throws on the roof of the cabin, remarking humorously that it isn't big enough to cook, so she may as well "feed it to the *witches*." I know a little boy who fell down and bloodied his nose and scratched his face and tore his clothes; when he came home blubbering, his mother cried: "My God, Tommy! You're a sight to skeer the *witches!*" When everything suddenly seems to go wrong, or a series of minor accidents disorganizes her kitchen, many an exasperated housewife exclaims that "the *witches* must be a-ridin' tonight!" But this is just on old backwoods expression, and she doesn't mean it literally.

Mrs. Mabel E. Mueller, Rolla, Missouri, tells of an old man who was much alarmed when his clock suddenly began to strike at random. On one occasion it struck fifteen or twenty times before he could get it stopped. Mrs. Mueller made some humorous remark about this, but the old man was deadly serious, declaring that a witch was responsible. He carried the clock out of the house at once and sold it for a very low price. Later on a friend showed him that a part of the clock's mechanism was broken, but the old man still believed that a witch had somehow caused the trouble.

A young man in Phelps county, Missouri, had an old gasoline-power woodsaw; it was always breaking down, and he didn't know much about machinery or gasoline motors, although he regarded himself as a mechanical genius. He always spoke of the saw "taking a spell," and insisted that it was "witched" by his enemies. Once he brought the machine to a farm where he expected to saw up a big pile of wood. He had cut about one-half a rick when the saw broke down. After tinkering with it awhile he flew into a rage and told the woman who had hired him: "My saw is witched! You and your whole family are witches! To hell with you all!" And no more wood was sawed that day.

Here is another old fireside tale, current in the late eighties. I got this particular version from Clarence Sharp, who heard it near Dutch Mills, Arkansas. The story goes that a hillman was just falling asleep when a pretty girl appeared with a bridle in her hand. In a twinkling she turned the poor fellow into a pony, leaped on his back, and rode him wildly through the woods. Later on she hitched him to a tree at the mouth of a cave, and he saw a group of "furriners" carrying big sacks of money into the cavern. Finally she rode him back home, and he woke up next morning all tired out and brier-scratched. This happened night after night, and the hillman consulted a famous witch master. The witch master advised him to mark the tree to which he was tied at night, so that he could find it again in the daytime. Then, said the witch master, it would be an easy matter to waylay the witch and kill her with a silver bullet, and afterwards they could get the treasure in the cave. So the next night, being transformed into a horse, the hillman "drapped as many drappin's" as he could to mark the place and started in to chaw a big blaze on the sapling to which he was tied. "I chawed an' I chawed," he said, "an' all of a sudden come a hell of a noise an' a big flash o' light. Then I heerd a lot o' hollerin', an' it sounded like my old woman was a-doin' the hollerin'. Quick as a wink I seen I was home again, an' it seemed like"— here the hillman stole a furtive glance at his wife, who sat stolidly smoking by the fireplace—"it seemed like I'd went an' benastied the bed-blankets, an' dang near bit the old woman's leg off!"

Many people believe that a witch can ruin a man's health by placing a lock of his hair, a fingernail clipping, or even a photograph of him, under the eaves of a house where the rain from the roof will fall upon it. I have heard of a woman in Newton county, Missouri, who hung the framed pictures of her husband's parents under the eaves during a hard rain. Just for the record—both of the old persons died a few weeks later. A man in Joplin, Missouri, told me that his disease, which the doctors called neuritis, had been wished on him—wished is a common euphemism for witched. "I can lay here in bed any night when it's a-rainin'," he said, "an' just *feel* the water a-pourin' on my head an' shoulders!"

To curse any particular part of a victim's body, the witch takes the corresponding part of an animal, *names* it for him, and then buries it in the ground or suspends it in a pool of

water. There was a man near Neosho, Missouri, who said publicly that his prostatitis was "wished on him" in this manner
by a former mistress. Many people think that witches can, by
some hocus-pocus with the sex organs of a sheep, render a man
impotent or a woman sterile. A girl in McDonald county, Missouri, named sheep's testicles for a boy who had mistreated
her and put them into an anthill; this was supposed to destroy
the young man's virility but was apparently without effect, as
he was still going strong the last I heard of him.

Just across the river from Sylamore, Arkansas, I met several
persons who told me that there was a witch in the neighborhood,
adding that everyone was frightened but nobody could figure
out who the witch was. According to the story, a local man was
stricken by some mysterious disease, and a "power doctor"
decided to bleed him. When a vein in the man's arm was opened,
the blood which rushed out was jet black. The horrified healer
hurried away saying that the man was witched, and that no
earthly power could save his life. When the poor fellow died a
few days later, the relatives were all convinced that some woman
in the vicinity had sold her soul to the Devil.

A physician at Ozark, Missouri, tells me that some people in
that town became convinced that a man with an aortic aneurysm
was "goomered" by a witch who had died some time before. They
called a goomer doctor down from Springfield; he decided that
there were live lizards and frogs inside the patient—said he
could feel 'em wriggling about under the swelling in the poor
fellow's chest! The ceremony which was supposed to remove
these creatures lasted several days and nights, but the patient
died.

It is surprising how seriously many people, apparently intelligent and enlightened on other subjects, take this witchcraft
business. I have even been accused of dabbling in sorcery myself;
there is an old woman still living near Farmington, Arkansas,
who tells people that I "throwed a curse" which ruined her
whole family. A neighbor of mine, by no means an ignorant

man, seemed delighted when the doctor told him that his illness
was caused by a bad appendix, and that it could be cured by
an operation. His reaction puzzled the physician, who asked
what he was so happy about. The man answered that he had
feared the pain was "wished on him" and could not be relieved
by any natural means!

Nancy Clemens, of Springfield, Missouri, told me an old
story about a man who was shot by a witch's bullet, a ball
which leaves no mark but causes the victim to lose consciousness.
This poor chap was picking apples in a high tree at the time,
and the fall injured him so badly that he was confined to his
bed for several weeks. An outsider would have thought that the
old man just fainted and fell out of the tree, but the fellow
himself insisted that he had been shot by a witch, and his friends
and relatives agreed with him.

It is generally believed that a witch acquires extraordinary
merit by burning the body of a newborn babe. Many a granny-
woman has been suspected of selling stillborn children to the
witches. My father-in-law, a physician at Pineville, Missouri,
claims that there are no witches in the Ozarks nowadays. But
he once told me that a certain old woman was trying to obtain
the body of an infant. "I think she wants to burn it," he admitted reluctantly, "and make some kind of luck charms out
of the ashes."

It is said that a mirror framed on three sides only gives a
witch telescopic and X-ray vision, so that she can watch her
enemies no matter how far off they may be, or how well concealed. I have seen two of these mirrors, one of which was said
to have been brought from England in colonial days and used
by several generations of women who could "do things." The
present owners can't work the mirrors, I was told, because they
don't know the magic words.

There are many ways of detecting a witch, such as hiding
a Bible in her mattress, placing a broomstick in her path,
scratching a little cross under the seat of her chair, or adding

a bit of pawpaw bark to her tobacco. Any of these measures will make a witch deathly sick, while an innocent woman is not affected. Another method is to take a new awl and fix it in the seat of a chair, so that only a very little of the point sticks through. Then get the suspected woman to sit down in the chair. If she jumps and cries out, it means that she is not a witch, since a witch doesn't feel the sharp point at all.

Many people believe that witches eat very little salt. If a woman complains that food is too salty, when it does not seem so to others, she is regarded with suspicion. "The Devil hates salt" is a very old saying. Farmers have told me that bewitched cattle will not touch salt. Some hillfolk say that one can detect witchcraft by placing a little salt in the suspect's chair; if she is really a witch the salt melts like glue, and her dress sticks to the chair seat.

There is an old story that if a man kisses or embraces a witch, the silver coins in his pocket will all turn black, but I do not believe that this is taken very seriously by the real witch masters.

When a witch comes into the house, raw onions that have been cut up and peeled are supposed to sour instantly and become poisonous. I have seen a housewife, when another woman entered the room, ostentatiously remove some raw onions from the table and throw them out into the yard. In this case the housewife did not really believe that the visitor was a witch, but she wanted to *behave* as if she believed it.

The backwoods witch hunters have little confidence in the old notion that a witch must be aged, or stooped, or hatchet-faced, or hook-nosed, or swarthy according to the storybook pattern. There is no obvious physical characteristic that is relied upon to identify a witch. However, I did meet one old man, a basketmaker near Eureka Springs, Arkansas, who said that a witch always has a "shifty" eye, and "don't never look straight at nobody, unless she's got 'em cunjured."

If several persons are seated about a fire, and the sparks

which pop out seem to be directed toward one particular individual, it is said that this person is somehow connected with the powers of evil. I have often heard this notion dismissed lightly, as when a great burst of sparks flew directly at a very ugly old woman, who showed her toothless gums in a grin. "Fire follers beauty," she said. We all laughed, but some of the old-timers looked distinctly uncomfortable.

Witches can make themselves invisible, as everybody knows, but there is one method by which anybody can see them. All you have to do is throw a pinch of dust from a certain kind of puffball, known as the Devil's snuffbox, into a little whirlwind. Whirlwinds are common on the dusty roads every summer, but they are nearly always seen at a little distance. It is like the story often told children, that in order to catch wild birds, one has only to put a little salt on their tails.

A friend of mine went out to photograph an alleged witch, not far from Neosho, Missouri. The old crone posed willingly enough beside her little cabin, in the bright sunlight. When the film was developed, the building showed sharp and clear in every detail, but there was no human figure in the picture at all. "It gave me quite a turn," said the amateur photographer. "For a moment I almost believed that there *was* something supernatural about that old woman!" But I reckon the lady must have shifted the camera somehow, thus cutting the witch out of the negative.

Probably the commonest way to keep witches out of the house is to nail a horseshoe over the door; this is regarded as a sort of general prophylactic against witches, bad luck, contagious disease, and other evil influences. Many hillmen insist that it doesn't work unless the open end of the horseshoe is upward, but the reason for this has never been explained to me.

Some of the old-timers drive three nails into the outside of a door, in the form of a triangle, to keep witches away from the cabin; one man told me that the three nails represent the Father, the Son, and the Holy Ghost and were particularly efficacious in protecting an expectant mother from the powers of evil. Painting the outside of a door blue is said to be a sensible precaution also, and some people make doubly sure by driving several tiny pegs of pawpaw wood into the doorsill.

A man in Fort Smith, Arkansas, told me that his father placed the entrails of a big horned owl over the door, to keep witches away. And Otto Ernest Rayburn tells of a man on trial for hog-stealing who wore "the dried gizzard of a hoot-owl tied round his neck for good luck." [2] A hunter who lived in the woods on Spring River, near Waco, Missouri, nailed the genitals of a male fox squirrel above the door of his shanty. When I asked the purpose of this he said that it brought good luck. "It skeers the witches, too," he added, "just like deer horns."

Some of the old-timers used to make a net of horsehair—a horsehair sieve, they called it—and fasten it over a hole in the door or window. In order to reach the people in the house, it was said, a witch must go *in and out* at each of the holes in the sieve, which would slow up her activity to a very considerable extent. I have seen what was left of one of these sieves, but the woman who showed it to me explained that it had been used nearly a hundred years ago, and that she kept it only as a relic.

Some people say that, in order to protect a building against witches, one need only fasten two little hazel sticks on the wall in the form of a cross. I have never seen this in a cabin occupied by human beings but have often found such crosses nailed up in barns, where they are said to protect cattle and horses against disease.

A new house, which has not yet been occupied, is sometimes protected from evil spirits by placing an old broom across the threshold. Mrs. May Kennedy McCord, of Springfield, Missouri, says that the old folks used to set up the mop and broom so as to form a cross, in the belief that it would keep witches out of the house. Mrs. C. P. Mahnkey, of Mincy, Missouri, writes me that the woman who cleaned house for her always

2 *Ozark Country*, p. 11.

did this, when the sweeping and mopping were finished. I have seen the crossing of the mop and broom several times in my own house near Pineville, Missouri, but the woman who crossed them would not admit any connection with superstition. "It just shows I'm all done cleanin'," she said.

May Stafford Hilburn tells of an old woman who "kept the witches away by running three times around the cabin, just at dusk-dark, shaking a white rag above her head as she ran." [3]

Some hillfolk plant a cedar peg, with three short prongs, in the pathway to keep witches away from a backwoods cabin. It is said that this device is particularly favored by certain primitive Christians, who regard it as representative of the Trinity. It is very bad luck to disturb such a symbol, whether one believes in witchcraft or not. Enlightened hill people may laugh at these outworn superstitions, but they are nevertheless very careful not to step on a "witch peg."

By all odds the most striking barrier against witches is the so-called egg tree. Usually it is just a little dead bush with the branches closely trimmed, and literally covered with carefully blown egg shells. There are hundreds of egg shells on a really fine egg tree, which often requires years to perfect. It is set firmly in the ground near the cabin, a favorite place being under a big cedar in the front yard. Just how the egg tree is supposed to drive off witches I was never able to learn. Egg trees are rare nowadays, and many people have spent years in the Ozarks without seeing or even hearing of such a thing. As recently as 1921 there were two or three near Pineville, Missouri, and Southwest City, Missouri, and I saw one in 1924 not far from Sulphur Springs, Arkansas. There used to be a very fine egg tree at the old Jim Cummins place, on Bear Creek, in Taney county, Missouri. Mrs. C. P. Mahnkey tells me that she saw egg trees "now and then" when she was a child, and that the last one in her neighborhood stood in Granny Howe's yard, near Kirbyville, Missouri.

[3] *Missouri Magazine* (December, 1933), p. 10.

Many hillfolk believe that witches are discomfited by hearing the name of the Deity. A woman at Sparta, Missouri, complained that a local witch turned her into a calf and rode her all over the country. Many a morning she would awake all tired out and brier-scratched, with burs and beggars'-lice in her hair. Finally one night the witch forced her into a particularly painful brier patch, and as the thorns tore her flesh she cried out "Oh God!" Instantly the witch and the brier patch disappeared, and she found herself out in a field, sitting on a bundle of fodder.

An old woman near Conway, Arkansas, told me the following "charm," guaranteed to drive off witches, which she learned from her grandfather:

> Dullix, ix, ux,
> You caint fly over Pontio,
> Pontio is above Pilato!

A man in Hot Springs, Arkansas, claimed that he could stop any sort of supernatural evil-doing, temporarily at least, by repeating aloud:

> Old Tom Walker under your hat,
> Bound in the name of God the Father,
> God the Son, and God the Holy Spirit.

Here is a rhyme from a manuscript book which Miss Miriam Lynch, Notch, Missouri, obtained from one of her neighbors. It is supposed to be repeated by one who is about to enter a struggle or contest and fears that his adversary may be assisted by the Powers of Evil:

> God the Father is with me,
> God the Son may be with thee,
> The Holy Ghost is with us all
> But I will rise and you will fall.

In pronouncing any of these magic words against witches, it is well to clasp one's hands together, in such a manner that the thumbs cross. Some think a better move against witches is to hold the right thumb in the left hand, and the left thumb in the right hand; this can be done inconspicuously, with the hands in one's lap. Either of these positions is supposed to be more effective than the ordinary crossing of the first and second fingers of the same hand, in the "King's X" fashion affected by school children.

Another ancient method of discouraging witches is to take a buckeye and stand facing the rising sun. Then, while repeating a certain old sayin', you bore a hole in the buckeye with a sharp pointed flint-rock. The old sayin' is a secret, of course. "I wouldn't be allowed to tell," one woman said to me, "and there's some dirty words in it, anyhow."

In a really serious situation the old-time Ozarker does not rely upon his own efforts to rout a witch but obtains the services of a professional witch master. If the witch master knows the identity of the woman who is causing the trouble, he draws her picture on a board and fires a silver bullet into it. This is supposed to kill the witch, or at least to cause her great bodily and mental anguish. I interviewed one renowned witch killer who cuts a silhouette out of paper and writes the witch's name on it. Then he very slowly tears the paper doll to pieces—pulls off a hand one day, a foot the next, and so on. Finally he snips off the head, whereupon the witch is expected to die, or suffer a paralytic stroke, or become violently insane.

Some operators prefer to make a little image of mud or beeswax to represent the witch. This "poppet" is covered with cloth once worn by the guilty woman. Then the witch doctor drives nails into the poppet, or beats it with a hammer, or burns it.

Years ago in Arkansas I knew a jealous woman who tried to "witch" the girl who had stolen her man. She set a human skull on a Bible, and before it placed two dolls, representing the erring husband and his light-o'-love. The poppet dressed as a girl had four big nails driven into its back. The whole thing was a failure, apparently; I saw the girl several years later, and she seemed in good health and spirits. In 1938 Mr. D. F. Fox, a photographer of Galena, Missouri, wanted to make some pictures illustrating Ozark superstition; I fixed a skull-and-Bible altar for him, with two dolls posed exactly like those used by the jealous wife in Arkansas. The picture was later published in *Life*, June 19, 1939. William Seabrook describes Fox's photographs at some length, adding that he had helped to destroy similar hellish devices in France, in 1932. "I don't know what Messrs. Fox and Randolph think they are playing with," he writes. "They may have merely persuaded some old woman to show them how such things are set up, but the pictures intrinsically stink of murder." [4]

Mr. G. H. Pipes told me a witch story, which he had from Grandmaw Bryant of Reeds Spring, Missouri, in the early 1920's. It seems that some carpenters were building a house, and the work was going very well until a certain old woman walked slowly past. From that moment everything went wrong. The workmen couldn't hit nails but hammered their thumbs instead. They dropped their tools repeatedly, and one narrowly missed falling off the ridgepole. After two or three days of this, they called in a witch doctor. He found the old woman's trail in the dirt and drove a big nail into one of her heel prints. As soon as this was done, the carpenters went to work again, and the building was completed with no further difficulty. The old witch had a very sore foot and limped around with a bandage on her heel nearly all winter.

A witch killer near Steelville, Missouri, says that it is only necessary to draw a rude picture of the witch on the north side of a black-oak tree, then drive a nail through the heart of the picture and leave it there. All this is done secretly, in the deep woods; unless the witch can find the black oak and pull out the nail, she'll die very soon.

I once knew a man who spent half-an-hour or so every evening

---

[4] *Witchcraft, Its Power in the World Today* (New York, Harcourt, Brace, 1940), pp. 18–19.

playing with a wooden spite doll, which was dressed to resemble a local woman who could "do things." Time after time he would thrust the little image into the fireplace, until the feet touched the glowing embers, and then snatch it out again. The expression on his face was most unpleasant. I am quite indifferent to the ordinary superstitions of the hillfolk. I visit graveyards at night, shoot cats on occasion, and burn sassafras wood without a tremor. And yet, something akin to horror gripped me, as I watched the witch master's sadistic foolery. I should not care to have that man burning a poppet wrapped in *my* undershirt.

Some witch masters go into the woods and pile grass and twigs around in a big circle, perhaps fifty feet in diameter. Then they mutter their magic phrases, and one minute before midnight they set the ring of brush on fire. The idea is that this somehow forces the witch to appear within the circle, and anybody who does show up there is likely to get a silver bullet through the guts. There are several stories of travelers, usually doctors on late calls, blundering into these witch rings at midnight. Sometimes the doctor talks his way out, while in other variants of the tale the unfortunate physician is shot to death.

If it is possible to obtain any part of the witch's body—such as fingernail parings, a lock of hair, a tooth, or even a cloth with some of her blood upon it—the witch doctor has recourse to another method. Out in the woods at midnight he bores a hole in the fork of a pawpaw tree, and drives a wooden peg into the hole. Once, despite the protests of a superstitious hillman who was with me, I pulled out one of these pegs and examined it. The end was covered with beeswax, in which several long hairs were imbedded. There was a circle of what appeared to be dried blood higher up on the peg, and the auger hole contained a quantity of fine sand. A similar "pawpaw conjure" is sometimes employed by cuckold husbands, but it is primarily intended to deal with women who "talk the Devil's language."

In case the material for the pawpaw trick cannot be obtained from a witch, some hillfolk try to conjure her with any object that she has ever touched, or even a bit of wood or metal from the house in which she lives. I know a man who, as a child in McDonald county, Missouri, was sent by his parents to steal a shingle from a witch's roof. His grandmother burned the shingle and buried the ashes in the graveyard. But the little boy never understood the purpose of this business, and nobody ever explained it to him. He told me about the incident, and a few years later I met his mother, in a neighboring state, and asked her if she remembered it. "Yes," she said slowly, "I reckon Tommy got the shingle, all right. But it didn't mean nothin'. Just some of Granny Fitzhugh's foolishness. She was awful old, an' kind of weak in her mind."

The discomfort caused by the witch master's spells finally forces the witch to show her hand, and she comes to the bewitched person's home. Usually she offers some apparently innocent gift or attempts to borrow some trifle. If the witch's gift is accepted, or her request for a loan granted, the witch master's charm is broken and the witch instantly regains control of the situation. The safest plan is never to lend anything under such conditions unless the borrower speaks the words "for God's sake"—it is said that a witch cannot pronounce these words.

The witch master's immediate purpose is to check the particular "bewitchment" which is injuring his client, but his ultimate intention is to kill or permanently disable the witch. When a witch dies, every jackleg witch doctor in the country claims credit for causing her death. When old Gram French was killed by falling off a bluff, an amateur conjurer in our neighborhood stalked solemnly about with rabbit blood on his forehead for several days. "But ever'body knows," a village loafer said scornfully, "that the pore half-wit never even *seen* Gram!"

Mrs. Mabel E. Mueller, Rolla, Missouri, told me of an alleged witch in her neighborhood and repeated several stories she had heard about this woman. "A certain young man," she said, "was trying to court the old witch's pretty daughter. The old woman did not approve of the match, so she cast a spell on the boy and made him very sick. The boy's folks called the witch master, who drew a picture of the witch and pierced the head with a pegging-awl. 'I reckon that'll give the ol' devil a headache, anyhow,' he said. Next day the boy was much improved, and the old woman was in bed, with a bag of hot sand on her forehead.

"On another occasion," Mrs. Mueller added, "this same old witch put a spell on a neighbor's daughter, so that she was stricken with some kind of lumbago and couldn't walk. The witch doctor didn't tell anybody just what he did this time, but in a few days the girl was feeling much better. And for weeks after that the old witch was seen walking aimlessly about in a rocky field, so crippled that she moved very slowly and leaned upon a cane.

"These stories were told me by people who believe every word of them," said Mrs. Mueller with a smile. "There was a time when nearly all of the backwoods people believed in witchcraft and sorcery, and such beliefs are not at all uncommon today, even among the more or less enlightened younger generation."

A basketmaker at Eureka Springs, Arkansas, told me that children are best protected against witches by wearing a neck-lace of dried burdock roots, cut into small pieces and strung like beads. Some say that if a child is bewitched despite this precaution, it is only necessary to stand him on his head while you count forty-nine backwards to take the curse off. Another remedy is to strip the child and leave him naked while you boil his clothes in a kettle out of doors. Rap three times on the kettle with a stick, calling out the name of the woman whom you be-lieve to have bewitched the child. If the woman is guilty, the spell will be broken instantly.

A family named Criger, in Greene county, Missouri, had an infant bewitched; the baby cried constantly, but the doctors could find nothing wrong with it. The mother was advised to carry the child to the front door every morning, and to lick its face "in a clean sweep from the nose to the hairline." This was to continue for nine mornings, and on the ninth day the witch would appear and try to borrow something. Her request must be refused, and the refusal would break the spell forever. Sure enough, on the ninth morning an old woman appeared and wanted to borrow a cup of sugar. Mrs. Criger refused to lend any sugar, and the baby was perfectly normal thereafter. Otto Ernest Rayburn tells a very similar story,[5] but in his version the mother was told to "repeat the three highest names in the Bible" each time she licked the child's face "from nose to hairline." In Rayburn's story, too, it was a *man* who had bewitched the infant. When this man was unable to borrow anything on the ninth day the child recovered, but the woman who told the mother how to break the spell "had a nice heifer to die the following day."

The following story came to me from Phelps county, Missouri, but variants of it are heard all through the Ozark region. An infant suddenly became very ill, and the parents suspected witchcraft, so they called in the local goomer doctor. He muttered some incantations, burned a little powder in the fireplace, and boiled all the baby's clothing in a kettle outside the cabin. "Don't take no gifts from nobody," he cautioned the parents, "an' don't lend nobody nothin'." The only callers next day were two women, one of whom carried a child in her arms. Just as they were leaving a little shower came up, and the sick baby's mother handed the other woman a shawl to protect the visiting child from the rain. Later that same day the baby died. "You must have took a gift," said the witch master, "or else loaned somethin'." Forgetting the shawl, the sorrowing mother denied this but later recalled the incident and admitted her mistake. "You ought to have done like I told ye," the goomer doctor said sadly as he took his leave.

Clothing that has been bewitched is treated by burying it in the ground, "jest like if it had been stunk up by a polecat." Other hillfolk prefer to wash such clothing in milk and hang

[5] *Ozark Country*, p. 164.

it out of doors over night in freezing weather; this is supposed to take the curse off somehow, so that the garments may be worn without danger.

The rifle is still an essential part of the hillman's equipment, and in pioneer days it was even more important. There are many stories of witches who could utterly ruin a hunter by putting a spell on his rifle. One way of witching a man's weapon is to steal a bullet from his pouch and fasten it with string to a willow, so that it remains suspended in swift water. The poor fellow's rifle shakes from that time forward, just as the bullet shakes in the current, and he can never shoot accurately until the spell is removed.

Mrs. Mabel E. Mueller, of Rolla, Missouri, told me about a farmer whose wife was reputed to have supernatural powers. One day the men of the neighborhood were engaged in a shooting match, while the witch woman was working near the house. After awhile she called her husband. "John," she said, "come help me frame this here flax." John paid no attention, for he was an exceptionally good shot and didn't want to leave the shooting match. The next shot he fired went wild. His rifle was in perfect condition, but the witch had tied a little knot in the corner of her apron. After three more shots, all of which missed the target, John prepared to leave the match. "I'll have to go, boys," he said. "The old woman's done put a spell on my gun, an' she won't take it off till I 'tend to that damn' flax."

A man in Christian county, Missouri, complained that his brand-new rifle was witched. The witch doctor advised him to put it in the spring branch so that the water would run through the barrel, and not to lend anything. Pretty soon a woman who lived nearby came to borrow some medicine, but he told her no. She must have been the witch, said my informant, because she had a turrible runnin' off at the bowels, and he figgered it made the old devil sick when the spell was took off'n the gun.

There is an old story of a famous hunter whose rifle suddenly lost its accuracy. He believed that the weapon was witched by

an old woman who lived near his cabin. All smiles, the hunter
went to see this woman and borrowed a nail to fasten the heel
of his boot, which he said was loose. Returning home, he drove
the nail into the stock of his rifle; instantly the spell was broken,
and the hunter could shoot as well as ever.

It is said that a bewitched firearm can somehow be disen-
chanted with asafetida, but I have never been able to find out
anything definite about this method.

An old man at Berryville, Arkansas, claims that witch doctors
can write something on paper and place it under the metal butt
plate of a rifle; this is supposed to fix a gun so that it caint
be witched. Some gunsmiths used to *make* all their weapons
that way; it is said that many of the earlier Hawkins rifles, for
example, were warranted witch proof. A sort of built-in witch
stopper, as it were.

When the new moon comes on Friday, it is said to usher in a
favorable period for molding bullets; many old folks insist that
bullets made at this time are luckier and deadlier than those
cast at any other season. It is said also that rifle balls kept in
a human skull for awhile become more lethal than ordinary
bullets. Some old-timers believe—or at least pretend to believe
—that the man who drives a coffin nail into the butt of his gun
will never fail to kill an enemy. The coffin nail must be one
which has been used and buried in the ground, of course.

If a man threatens you with a firearm, cry out "Poxy soxy
sorrox" and the gun will miss fire; if it does go off, the bullet
won't hit you; if the bullet does hit you, it won't kill you. In
the old days, many a pioneer carried a bat's heart, dried and
powdered. Some said that it would turn bullets, others that it
would keep a wounded man from bleeding to death. A bullet
which has killed a man can be used in some kind of hocus-pocus
against witches and is carefully preserved for this purpose.

Many Ozark housewives think, when the butter doesn't come
promptly, that it must be due to witches in the churn. I have
seen these women wash a silver coin and drop it into the cream

—this is supposed to drive the witches out. Some people put a horseshoe into the churn, instead of a coin. Most of them say simply a horseshoe, but sometimes one hears that it should be a hot horseshoe. It may be that a *hot* horseshoe really would make the butter come, and not by any supernatural spells, either.

A woman near Springfield, Missouri, tells the following tale which she had from her pioneer mother. One day they churned and churned with no result, so the housewife took a hot horseshoe out of the oven, where it was kept to drive hawks away from the chickens, and dropped it into the churn. The butter came instantly, and a moment later they heard loud screams from a shanty across the road. They rushed over there and found an old woman badly burned. She said she had fallen into the fireplace, but the burn *looked* as if it had been made by a hot horseshoe.

A lady in Christian county, Missouri, was annoyed by a series of minor inconveniences, which she attributed to a neighbor who could "do things." One afternoon somebody remarked that if she shouted out the witch's name the spell would be dissipated. That very night she was sitting before the fire when she sensed the witch's approach. "I just drawed a good deep breath," she said later, "an' then I hollered 'Peggy McGee' as loud as I could! The whole thing stopped right there, an' I aint had no trouble with witches since."

Some witches seem to specialize in throwing spells on horses, cattle, and other livestock. One of my old neighbors told me that his hogs had been witched only a few years ago. When he went to feed 'em they wouldn't come to the trough at all but "jest lent back on their tails an' squole!"

When a cow gives bloody milk, it is generally due to some natural cause, but there is always the possibility of witchcraft. Put the morning's milk in a kettle, boil it over an open fire outdoors, and stir it with a forked thorny stick. If the cow *has* been witched, this procedure will send the witch into convulsions, and she will not bother your cows any more.

Old Granny Bryant, of Reeds Spring, Missouri, used to tell of a family whose cow suddenly began to give bloody milk. They talked the matter over and called in a witch doctor. "Put some of that bloody milk in a fryin' pan," said he, "an' bile it over a slow fire. While the milk's a-bilin', beat on the bottom of the pan with a hickory stick." These instructions were carried out, and people who went to the local witch's cabin said that her back and buttocks were a mass of bruises, so sore that she could not walk for several days. The spell was dissipated, and the cow gave no more bloody milk.

A lady named Barnes, at Galena, Missouri, sold her cow to a doctor. Later on she said that the physician had cheated her somehow and demanded the return of the cow, but the new owner refused to give it up. This angered Mrs. Barnes, and she "wished a sickness" on the cow, so that it took to throwing fits every day and was never of much use to the doctor or his family. "I never wished anything on anybody yet," said Mrs. Barnes in my hearing, "that it didn't happen!"

Many farmers treat witched cattle with a mixture of burnt cornbread, soot, and salt. The soot is the important ingredient, I think—the bread and salt are just added to make the stuff palatable. The water in which a blacksmith cools his irons is supposed to be good for witched cattle and is sometimes given to human beings also, particularly children. Some witch masters cure a witched horse or cow by snipping off a bit of hair from its head and burning the hair, the idea being that this will make a sore place on the witch's head and thus cause her to remove the spell.

Mrs. Mabel E. Mueller, Rolla, Missouri, told me of a neighbor whose cow was "on the lift"; the animal's eyes bulged, and it had a peculiar frightened look said to be characteristic of witched cattle. The witch master came and cut off a little curl from the cow's forelock. Next day the cow was well, and the witch came to borrow some soda, but the family refused to lend. They noticed that a lock of hair had been cut from the front of the witch's forehead. The hired man asked her about this, and the woman said she had cut it off because it "bothered" her.

Mrs. Mueller unearthed another witch tale, well known to some of the old-timers in Phelps County, Missouri. A young man wanted to marry the traditional farmer's daughter, but the match was opposed by his mother, who was able to "do things." He married the girl anyhow, and they had a baby. One day the young folks were picking blackberries, and the baby was sleeping under a tree only a few yards away. The husband heard a noise, and found that an old sow had mangled the infant so badly that it died. The boy looked at the sow and saw that it had eyes exactly like his mother's. He accused the old woman and threatened her life, but she denied everything. Their next baby was also attacked by a sow, but the father got there before it was much hurt. He looked at the sow, and the animal trotted away. The boy went home, loaded a rifle with a silver ball, and pointed it at his mother. She screamed and begged and confessed on her knees that she had killed his baby. Then in the presence of all the kinfolk she swore that she would not molest his family again, and he was persuaded by his sisters to spare her life. The old witch kept her promise, and the young couple raised their other children without any supernatural interference.

I am indebted to Mrs. Mueller also for an account of a conjure man she knew in Rolla about 1910. He was a mind reader, clairvoyant, fortuneteller, power doctor, witch master—an old fellow with strange red eyes. This man told Mrs. Mueller how he learned the art of conjuring. He said that even as a small boy he always felt that he could "do things," and one day he saw what looked like a snake or an eel at the water's edge, in a small creek. He approached, and the thing crawled out on a gravel bar. A strange animal, black all over, about a foot long, shaped exactly like a coffin, with two red eyes like balls of fire. A voice told him to kill this creature, and he smashed it with a club.

From that day forward he could conjure. There are people in Rolla today who remember the old man with the strange red eyes, like balls of fire.

I have met elderly folk near Marionville, Missouri, who remember the doings of Granny Whittaker. On one occasion she asked a neighbor's daughter to hold the Whittaker baby for a few moments, but the little girl refused to touch the infant. "It stinks," she said bluntly. "All right, young lady," cried the Whittaker woman, "you'll suffer for them remarks!" From that day forward the girl had fits, sometimes three or four fits in a single day. The poor child always cried out that she saw "old Granny Whittaker, in the shape of a turkey" just before the attacks came on. The girl's father could see nothing, but he often fired his pistol in the direction of the phantom turkey pointed out by the "fitified" girl. Once old Granny Whittaker lost a finger in some mysterious accident, and the neighbors thought that one of this man's bullets might have somehow struck her hand. The local conjurers and power doctors "sot up spells" against Granny Whittaker for years, but without any visible results. It is said that one famous witch master came all the way from Little Rock, Arkansas, to match magic with the Whittaker witch but accomplished nothing.

There is one case reported from the Cookson Hill country of Oklahoma, just across the Arkansas line, where a prominent citizen died in rather strange circumstances. Some of his backwoods relatives got the idea that a witch was the cause of this man's death and decided to avenge him in the real old-time tradition. The first step was to secure three nails from the dead man's coffin; these may be drawn before the coffin is buried in the ground, but not until after the body has been placed in the coffin. The nails must not be replaced by other nails, and the three holes in the wood should be left open. After the funeral the old-timers killed a goat, removed the heart, and thrust the three coffin nails into it. The goat's heart with the nails in it was then enclosed in a little basket-like cage of wire and suspended out of sight in the big chimney of the dead man's house. The theory is that, as the goat's heart shrivels and decays, the witch will sicken and die. If she does not sicken and die, it is regarded as evidence that she was not responsible for the man's death, after all.

The preceding paragraph seems rather fantastic, but I believe that the goat's-heart and coffin-nail business was carried out exactly as I have described it. I saw nothing of it myself, though I am intimately acquainted with some of the persons involved; I once sat within a few feet of the big fireplace above which the nailed goat's heart is suspended but did not peer up the chimney to see if the little wire cage was really there. I was told about this by two young, educated members of the family, who gave me permission to publish the story on condition that no names or identifying data were included. The man who sold the coffin refused to discuss this particular case, but admitted that "more than once" people had come to his place of business and wanted to pull nails out of coffins in which bodies were lying at the time. The nails, or screws, he thought, were to be used in "some Indian ceremony." Well, the clan in question boasts a "smidgin" of Cherokee blood—so does my own family, for that matter. But the persons concerned in this goat's-heart affair have had little contact with Indians; they know nothing of tribal religions or ceremonials, and many of them never even spoke with a fullblood in their lives.

Many of the unsolved murders, and many of the outrages attributed to masked night riders, are directly or indirectly connected with the hillman's belief in witchcraft. The Henley-Barnett feud at Marshall, Arkansas, which killed so many people that the governor sent troops to prevent further bloodshed, is said to have been fanned into flame by an old woman who could "do things." This was common talk when I interviewed members of both factions at Marshall in 1934, although vigorously denied by those in authority.

Less than a year ago I heard a man threaten an old woman's

life, because he believed that she had bewitched his son. The boy had lived quietly at home until he reached the age of seventeen, when he suddenly took to robbing tourist camps and filling-stations along the highway. "My boy was brought up honest," the old man said, "an' there aint no *natural* reason for this here trouble. He's witched, an' I know who done it!"

Most of the Ozark superstitions are harmless enough, but this belief in witchcraft frequently leads to violent crime. When primitive people imagine that their troubles are caused by supernatural "spells," and that these spells are cast upon them by their neighbors, tragedy often results. Things happen in these hills which are never mentioned in the newspapers, never reported to the sheriff at the county seat. The casual tourist sees nothing to suggest the current of savage hatred that flows beneath the genial hospitality of our Ozark villages. "Still waters run deep," as Grandmaw Tolliver used to say, "an' the Devil lays at the bottom."

13. Death and Burial

Many trivial happenings in a mountain cabin are regarded as presages of an approaching death. The falling of a window sash at night, or the spontaneous breaking of any household object when no one is touching it, is a sure sign of death in the house. When a picture falls from the wall of itself, many hillfolk believe that the person who picks it up will die within the year. Some say, however, that it is just a general sign of sickness and death for the entire household, and the individual who happens to pick up the picture is in no more danger than anybody else. But if anyone imagines that he hears the crash of glass, when no breakage actually occurs, the head of the house will meet a violent death before the year is out.

The breaking of a mirror is always a sign of seven years' bad luck, but sometimes it means a death in the family. May Stafford Hilburn tells us how the looking glass in her home was smashed and adds that "in less than seven years my father died!" [1]

Hillfolk are always upset by any unusual clicking or rumbling in a clock—they think that a relative or close friend must be dying at the moment when the sound is heard. If a clock that has not run for a long time suddenly begins to strike, there will be a death in the house within the number of days, weeks, or months indicated by the chimes, but there's a wide difference of opinion about the interpretation of this material.

Any household noise of unexplained origin, if it suggests the tearing of cloth, is a death sign. An old woman near Fort Smith, Arkansas, told me that, as a girl, she heard somebody tearing

[1] *Missouri Magazine* (October, 1933), p. 14.

cloth in the kitchen. There was nobody in the room when she looked to see, but a few days later the house was full of women tearing up sheets to lay out her sister, who died suddenly and unexpectedly. Those were the days when they buried corpses in winding sheets—long strips of cloth which were torn, not cut.

Many hillfolk claim to hear another sound called the "death bones" shortly before someone dies. An old woman once said to me: "I heerd Lucy's death bones a-rattlin' this mornin', so I reckon she'll be dead afore night." And sure enough, Lucy died that afternoon, although the local physician had expected her to live for a month or so.

If you hear raps, knocks, ticks, or bells, with no apparent cause for these noises, it is a sign that death is coming to someone near you. The famous death watch or death tick, a sharp snapping noise sometimes heard in log houses at night, is supposed to mean a death in the building within a few days. This noise is similar to the sound made by cocking a pistol and is said to be produced by a beetle with a singular gift of divination.

May Stafford Hilburn, of Jefferson City, Missouri, says that it is a very bad sign for a church bell to ring "without human hands to ring it. Calamity will certainly descend upon any community should such a supernatural event take place, for floods or fire or other dire event may be expected." [2]

A ringing in the ears—the jingle of the so-called death bells —means that somebody near you is about to die. A little tinkling sound means the death of a close friend or relative. A very loud bell, so loud it makes the hearer dizzy, foretells the death of a high official or prominent citizen, someone important to many people. The Springfield (Missouri) *News & Leader* (Dec. 10, 1933) observes that "several Springfieldians said they heard the *loud death bells* at the time of Dr. A. J. Croft's death." The name death bells is also applied to a row of little appendages found on the heart of a hog when it is butchered; Mrs. C. P. Mahnkey, of Mincy, Missouri, knows about these and says it

[2] *Missouri Magazine* (September, 1933), p. 21.

is important that they be cut off at once. Some people think that if these death bells are immediately removed, the curse is somehow lifted and the expected death may not occur.

If an Ozark girl breaks a needle while making a quilt she is depressed; some say that she will die before the quilt is finished, others think it means only that she will die before the quilt is worn out, which is much less serious, since quilts sometimes last longer than an ordinary lifetime. But it's bad luck to break a needle, anyhow. Most any mountain woman knows better than to make a dress or other garment for a person who is critically ill, as to do this means that the sick person has very little chance of recovery.

If an Ozark woman is accustomed to fasten the door every night and forgets to do so, she regards it as an evil omen and is not surprised to hear of the death of a dear friend.

The woman who washes clothes on January 1 is likely to bring about the death of a relative, according to a very common belief. "Wash on New Year's, and you'll wash away your kinfolks!" said an old woman near Carthage, Missouri. I have heard many people laugh at this idea, but I have never known a real old-timer to do any washing on New Year's Day.

It is very bad luck for an Ozarker to hang his boots against a wall, and many people regard this as a sign that he will not live to wear them out. If a woman sneezes with food in her mouth, she expects to hear of a close friend's death before another sunrise. A girl near Mena, Arkansas, once showed me that the coffee grounds in her cup formed a straight line; she said this meant there would be a funeral in the house before many months had passed. The woman who throws an egg shell into the fire on May 1 and sees a drop of blood on the shell knows that she will never live to enjoy another May Day. To sweep a floor after dark or allow a lamp to burn until the last drop of oil is consumed— these things are taboo, and many people believe that they are likely to bring death into the family circle.

When you see an oil lamp in an old-timer's cabin, very often there is a little piece of red woolen cloth, or a bit of red yarn, submerged in the oil. Some people say that this collects impurities or sediment from the kerosene and thus prevents a clogging of the wick. Others think that a lamp with a red rag in it never explodes, while oil without the rag may take fire spontaneously and burn the shanty down. But several old people in widely separated parts of the Ozarks have told me that the red wool in the oil is supposed to protect the family from death by violence or poison.

The typical hillman avoids any firewood which pops or crackles too much, in the belief that burning such wood will bring about the death of some member of his family. To burn sassafras wood is supposed to cause the death of one's mother, and although sassafras makes very fine charcoal, no decent native will burn it, or even haul it to the kiln, unless his mother is already dead. There is an old saying that the Devil sits a-straddle of the roof when sassafras pops in the fireplace; Otto Ernest Rayburn refers to this expression.[3]

It is very bad luck to burn peach trees, and dreadful results are almost certain to follow. I know a man and woman who cut down and burned some old peach trees, despite the warnings of their neighbors. Sure enough, their baby became sick a few days later. The neighbors helped them as best they could, but one and all refused to come into the house or have anything further to do with the family if any more peach trees were burned.

The Ozark children are told that if they defecate in a path or public road their sisters will die. If a mountain woman imagines that she sees the face of an absent friend in a mirror she expects to hear of this person's death, and if a young girl sees any coffin-shaped object reflected in water she is sure to die before the year is out. Most old-time hill women were taught that cloth contaminated with the menstrual discharge must be buried in the ground, never burned; to disregard this is to court death

3 *Ozark Country*, p. 157.

in some particularly terrifying form. For a menstruating woman to take a bath is almost equivalent to suicide, according to the granny-women. It is regarded as dangerous for anybody to bathe just before starting on a journey; the traveler who does so has good reason to fear death by drowning.

The farmer who carries a hoe into his house will cause the death of a near relative within the year. To carry an ax into the cabin is seldom permitted except in confinement cases, where the granny-woman puts an ax under the bed to ease the pains of childbirth.

I once traveled through rural Arkansas in a covered wagon with Mr. Lewis Kelley, of Cyclone, Missouri, an old-time mountain man. We camped by the roadside every night and slept in the wagon when the weather was bad. One morning I picked up the ax and started to put it in the wagon, but Mr. Kelley immediately stopped me, saying that it is bad luck to carry an ax in the wagon bed where men are accustomed to sleep; also, he added reasonably, it's likely to dull the blade. There is a place low down at the rear of the wagon, on the axle I think, where the ax fits perfectly, and that's where we carried it.

If a hillman steps over a spade lying on the ground he is seriously disturbed by the belief that it will shortly be used to dig his grave. The man who inadvertently kicks a rifle on the ground will die of a gunshot wound, according to the old-timers. To step over a person lying on the floor is very bad luck, and if done intentionally is almost akin to homicide. Some liberal thinkers claim that one can stop the curse by crossing his fingers and immediately stepping backwards over the sleeping individual, but there is considerable doubt about the efficacy of this.

A falling star is supposed to be somehow connected with the death of a human being; in 1917 I sat one night with a fellow soldier at Camp Pike, Arkansas, and as several stars fell the boy remarked gloomily that he reckoned "they must be a-killin' fellers right now, over thar." Some old folks claim to have seen a ball of fire travel across a field and down the chimney of a house where someone lay sick; this is a sure death sign, and the patient always dies within a few hours.

When a dog under the cabin, or on the front porch, howls four times and then stops, it is said that there will be a death in the house very soon. If a dog rolls over and over in the same direction, it is said that he is measuring the ground for his master's grave. If a cat licks the door it is a sure sign that somebody in the house will die shortly. When horses take to running about and neighing without any visible cause, or mules suddenly begin to "ride" each other near the house, it means that someone is dying not far away.

If a cow has just lost her calf, everybody expects her to bawl and pays no attention; but when a cow begins to bawl without any apparent reason and keeps it up, the hillfolk become uneasy. I have seen a group of modern, educated, bridge-playing women in Joplin, Missouri, much upset by hearing some cattle bawling. I learned later that they had been reared in the wilds near Pineville, Missouri, and that a man related to most of them was very ill at the time.

It is a bad sign for a rooster to crow in the doorway; if anybody is dangerously ill in the house it usually means death. If a rooster crows seven times in front of the door without turning around, it means that someone in the family is going to die soon, whether any of them are sick now or not.

If a hen makes any sound suggestive of crowing near the door, it is a sure sign of death, and I have been told of cases in which somebody died within ten minutes. A crowing hen will excite any group of backwoods people; I have seen a man spring up and fire his revolver wildly into a flock of chickens, killing several. Some people do not hesitate to eat a crowing hen, but this man would not allow one to be cooked in his house. "Throw it to the hogs," said he, "and if they won't eat the damn' thing, we'll sell it to the tourists!"

Whippoorwills seldom alight on buildings, but if one does come to rest on the roof of a house and gives its characteristic call from this position, there will be a death in the neighborhood within twenty-four hours. Any sort of a bird rapping on a windowpane, or trying to get into the cabin, is a very bad sign; a man from St. Paul, Arkansas, tells me that when a turtle dove flies into a house, somebody is sure to die soon.

A bat in the cabin is even worse than a songbird, but a screech owl is worst of all. One cry from this bird, even if it is only in the dog run and not in the house proper, will upset almost any backwoods family. The mother jumps instantly to throw salt on the fire, while the older children, usually crying, begin to tie knots in a string. "Owls don't often get into houses," says Mrs. May Kennedy McCord, of Springfield, Missouri, "but it's terrible when such a thing does happen." If there happens to be a sick man in the place, every effort is made to kill the owl, so that its body may be laid warm and bleeding on the patient's chest, for otherwise he will surely die. A man in Madison county, Arkansas, tells me that to throw a handful of salt or feathers on the fire will silence a screech owl outside the cabin. "Maybe it's the smell of salt a-burnin' that does the trick," he said thoughtfully.

The transplanting of cedar trees is a bad business, and the old-timers thought that the transplanter would die as soon as the cedar's shadow was big enough to cover a grave. I have heard of a case where a young fellow uprooted some little cedars that a "furriner" wanted for his lawn, dug the holes in which they were to be planted, and then hired a very old man to set them in the holes. The old codger didn't mind, knowing that he couldn't live long anyhow. One good thing is that cedars are hard to transplant successfully, and most of them die before they're big enough to shade a grave. A man told me once that the curse could be "throwed off" by putting a flat stone in the bottom of the hole where the cedar is planted, but others shook their heads at this theory. I know of some boys who hired out to transplant cedars in a nursery; these young men laughed at the old superstition, but their parents were horrified and ordered them to quit the job immediately.

Mrs. Marion B. Pickens of Jefferson City, Missouri, editor

of the *Missouri Magazine*, wrote me (Oct. 1, 1935) of her experience shortly after buying a country home on the Osage River, near Tuscumbia, Missouri. "The new place is a beautifully located farm house," she said. "We planned to move some native cedars into groupings and had great difficulty in finding someone to do the work because moving cedar trees was known to bring untoward happenings, nearly always a death to the immediate family. And these Tuscumbians cited actual cases to prove the rule. We finally found a native who was willing to risk the welfare of his family, but he had worked on the big roads out in the valley and had acquired a certain bravado or recklessness in tempting the powers that be. This is a bona fide experience."

Mrs. Frances Mathes, of Galena, Missouri, once told me that years ago she transplanted a little cedar on the Mathes farm. Her young husband just grinned when he heard of it, but her father-in-law was almost prostrated. He urged Frances to go instantly and pull the tree up. Frances refused, and always after that the old man felt that she was destined for an early death. But the cedar tree is still flourishing, big enough to cover half a dozen graves now, while Frances Mathes outlived her husband and the whole Mathes family.

The prejudice against transplanting cedars is known all through the Ozarks, and doubtless in many parts of the South. Other superstitions about trees seem to be local, or even limited to certain family groups or clans. There are people in southwest Missouri who will not under any conditions plant a willow. I once asked a hired man to "stick" some willows in a certain gravel bar, in order to turn the creek the other way and prevent it from cutting into my field. Without mentioning the matter to me, he went out and hired another man to attend to this. "It's sure death for us folks to fool with willers," he explained later, "so I just got one o' them Henson boys. The Hensons is eddicated, an' they don't believe nothin'."

When a big tree dies without any visible cause, it is a sign that some human being will die before the year is out, exactly one mile north of the tree. If nobody lives there it doesn't matter, the old folks insist that a man, woman, or child will die at the designated spot anyhow. I once tried to point out the fallacy of this theory, since one of our big walnuts had died, and there was no record of a human death to the north of us. But an old man, a deacon in the church, told me seriously that somebody had doubtless been *made away with*—by which he meant murdered—there, and the body concealed.

For a baby's cradle to rock without any visible reason is a very bad omen, and it is generally believed that the child will not live to outgrow the cradle. Many hillfolk think, however, that the cradle-rocking has a more general significance, and that the person marked for death may not be the baby at all, but one of its parents, or some other member of the household.

If a child less than a year old is permitted to see its reflection in a mirror, it will either be cross-eyed or will die before its second birthday. If a babe's fingernails are cut with a metal blade it will die within the year, or become a thief in later life. Most backwoods mothers take no chances with this dilemma; they bite the child's fingernails off.

For a baby to lose a shoe is regarded as a very serious matter, and all the people in the house drop their other affairs to hunt for it. Sometimes men are even called in from the fields to help. If the shoe is not found, it is a sure sign that somebody in the family will die.

In the Ozarks as elsewhere, of course, there are men who think they can "smell death" many days ahead. Mr. W. H. Scott, of Bennett Springs, Missouri, once wrote to the Springfield *News* (Apr. 3, 1941): "I was born with a veil over the face, May 16, 1863. If there is going to be any death in the family I know it about two weeks beforehand. Also among close and particular friends."

To see the wraith or double of a living person is a death sign. "One bitterly cold day," writes Mrs. C. P. Mahnkey, a father and his son were gathering corn. All at once the lad appeared directly in front of the wagon, busily husking out the ears. The father spoke to him, rather amazed at his working ahead of the team like that, and the boy replied from the other side of the wagon, tossing in corn as he spoke. The father wondered, but said nothing. Again, a moment later, the boy was in front. The father stopped work and turned, and there he was, busy at his rows, the other side of the wagon. Bewildered, puzzled, the father resumed his work, and suddenly the boy was at his side, snatching at the corn. But—there he was, across the wagon, in his place! In a sudden fright and unexplained agony of apprehension, the father made an excuse to stop work and go to the house, as he said it was getting colder. The boy never helped him again. In just a few days he was dead, of pneumonia.[4]

No matter what his ailment, a sick man must never be lifted from one bed to another. If it becomes necessary to move him to another room or another building, the bed and bedding must be transferred also. Some hillfolk take this matter very seriously, indeed, and put themselves to a great deal of trouble and expense because of it.

Never turn a bedfast person end to end, so that his head is where his feet have been. If you do, he'll die sure. A man who is dangerously ill must not be shaved in bed, since the old folks say that this is nearly always fatal.

To sweep under a sick person's bed, in some localities, is regarded as a bad thing, an admission by the sweeper that the patient is about to die. Mrs. May Kennedy McCord, of Springfield, Missouri, writes to the Springfield *News* (July 24, 1941): "I am so bound by these early superstitions that I can hardly get away from them, and to this day it makes me crawl all over when I am in a hospital and they sweep under my bed. The only comfort I get is that it isn't a broom—they just have dustmops. And I'm still living!"

When a sick man wants to know his true condition, he touches a bit of bread to his lips and throws it to a dog; if the dog

[4] *White River Leader*, Branson, Missouri, Jan. 4, 1934.

won't eat it, the man knows that he has a very short time to live. If cocks crow or dogs howl or foxes bark unexpectedly near a sick room, the patient may die at any moment. On this point, Mrs. May Kennedy McCord declares that "all the dogs for five miles around" howl just before an old settler breathes his last, but maybe this is taking in a little too much territory. When a sick man begins to pick at the coverlet, or to slide down toward the foot of the bed, or to emit an odor like that of crushed pumpkins, his death may be expected very soon. What is more, it is said that the last person upon whom the dying man's gaze rests will be the first among those present to follow him to the grave.

Mr. Elbert Short of Crane, Missouri, tells me that every Negro "bawls three times like a calf" just before he dies. There are no Negroes in the region about Crane, and Mr. Short has never seen a Negro die, but the old folks all repeat this bit of wisdom, so he reckons it must be true.

Those attending a dying man, particularly if he is thrashing about or struggling, are very careful to keep their fingers away from his mouth, since the bite of a dying person is said to be deadly poison. In many localities I heard the tale of the doctor who was bitten in the hand by a dying child and died two weeks later of blood poisoning.

There is a common belief that dying persons are particularly apt to take off just as the clock strikes the hour. Some say that more people die at 4 A.M. than at any other time. Mrs. Anna Bacon, of Stone county, Missouri, is an old woman who has seen many people die, and she says that "the change of the hour," meaning midnight, is the best time to go, if one has any choice in the matter.

I once sat with a man who was dying of pulmonary tuberculosis. An old woman looked at the sky and remarked that a storm was coming, adding that "as soon as it rains, he'll die." The doctor told me that rain had nothing to do with the time of the man's death and said that he would probably live for several days longer. Three hours later it rained, and thirty minutes after the rain began the poor chap was dead.

When a death finally occurs, one of the bereaved neighbors rises immediately from the bedside and stops the clock. Everybody knows that if the clock should happen to stop of itself while a corpse is lying in the house, another member of the family would die within a year, and it is considered best to take no chances. Several families near Southwest City, Missouri, are somehow persuaded that the old custom of stopping the clock is derived from the Indians. When I pointed out that the old-time Indians had no clocks, and that some local Indians have no clocks even today, these people said no more. But they still believe that the stop-the-clock business is based upon "a old Injun idy."

The next thing to be done is to cover every mirror in the house with white cloths, which are not removed until after the funeral. This is done out of consideration for those who may come in to view the body, for if one of them should glimpse his own reflection in the house of death, it is believed that he will never live to see another summer.

In some houses, immediately after a death occurs, the chairs are all turned up so that nobody can sit in them, and people who come into the presence of the dead are forced to stand. I have never been able to find out the purpose of this. One old man in Benton county, Arkansas, told me that it is a new-fangled custom, brought into the country by some "outlanders" about 1880.

When a hillman dies all his bedding and articles of clothing are immediately hung on a line out of doors. People coming far down the road see this and know that the patient is dead. In predicting a sick man's demise, I have heard people say "Poor Jim's britches will be a-hangin' out most any day now!"

The hillfolk have a veritable mania for washing dead bodies; the moment a death occurs the neighbors strip the corpse and begin to scrub it vigorously. A man may be dirty all his life, and in his last illness his body and bedding may be so foul that one can hardly stay in the cabin, but he goes to his grave clean, so far as soap and water can cleanse him. All of the work connected with a death—washing and dressing the body, and so on—is done by friends and neighbors. Not one of the near relatives of the deceased will have any part in these doings, except in case of the direst necessity.

Many hillfolk make a weak tea from the bark of the wahoo bush (*Euonymus*), widely used as a medicine for chills and fever. Mrs. May Kennedy McCord, of Springfield, Missouri, tells me that the old folks soak cloths in this wahoo tea and lay them over the face of the dead, in order to keep the face fresh so that it will look well at the funeral. Others wrap the head in a towel wet with soda water, believing that this will prevent the skin from turning dark. Mr. Hugh Wilder, a mortician of Fort Smith, Arkansas, says that country people in his territory often place a saucer of salt upon the abdomen of a corpse, "to keep the belly from bloatin'."

A county nurse in Arkansas recalled that when an old man she was attending died, she put little pieces of paper under his eyelids, so that the eyes would remain closed. But the family objected, saying: "We may be on relief, but we still got our corpse money!" They brought out two old silver dollars and laid them on the dead man's eyes. It appears that some families keep these same coins, set aside for this purpose only, for several generations. In one backwoods county a serious quarrel arose which finally ended in violence and arrest for several individuals; peace officers said that the whole thing began over the refusal of one family to lend their "corpse money" when a death occurred in their neighbor's home.

Whatever happens, the body must never be left alone for a single instant, for fear some animal should get at it; if a cat, for example, should so much as sniff at the corpse, some unspeakable calamity would overtake the whole family. The belief that cats will mutilate a dead body seems to be widely accepted in the South but appears to have little foundation in fact. It is true, however, that cats sometimes show marked symptoms of excitement in the presence of the dead, and the hillman prefers to take no chances.

Several young couples are usually called in to serve as a death watch, and at least two persons are supposed to remain beside the body, while the others may be kissing in a dark corner, or eating the elaborate lunch supplied by the sorrowing family. A jug of corn whiskey is sometimes provided for the menfolks—the Ozark women seldom drink in public—but there is very little drunkenness on these occasions. If an owl hoots or a wolf howls in the vicinity the watchers are seriously disturbed, because these sounds signify that one of the group will die before the year is out.

When a backwoodsman dies, in certain sections of the Ozarks, it sometimes happens that one of his male relatives cuts a hickory stick just the length of the corpse. I have seen a hill farmer carrying one of these sticks on the day of his brother's death, and I have seen one tied to the wagon which conveyed a corpse to the graveyard, but I have never been able to find out what became of them, or what their significance was. I first thought that the stick was simply to measure the body for a coffin, but it is something more complicated than that, and there is some sort of superstition connected with it.

If the weather and other conditions permit, a body is sometimes kept for two or three days before burial. But it is usually considered bad luck to allow a corpse to lie unburied over Sunday, and some say that it means another death in the family. When a corpse is lying in the house, members of the family and near relatives generally use the back door, although other visitors come in by the front entrance as usual.

There is often a good deal of cooking in the lean-to kitchen while a dead body lies in the cabin proper, although friends and relatives bring in quantities of food already cooked. But nearly all of the old-timers believe that it is very bad luck to

cook cabbage in a house where someone is "lyin' a corpse."
Some say this is merely because cabbage attracts flies, but I
don't think that is the real reason.

One of my neighbors, an old fellow from West Virginia, was
buried with a silver dollar in his mouth. Why this was done I
don't know. I didn't have the courage to mention it at the time,
but several years later I asked one of the younger members of
the family. "Aw, it was just some of the old folks' notions,"
he said.

A man dying in McDonald county, Missouri, said that he
wanted to be buried lying on his left side, because he had never
been able to sleep on his back. The village undertaker complained loudly about this, but the body was "laid to rest side-
ways," as one of the dead man's relatives assured me.

I know personally of an old-timer in Taney county, Missouri,
who was buried with his Winchester rifle, loaded and *cocked*,
in the coffin with him. His Colt revolver, also loaded, was in his
belt. This was according to his own directions, given to his
family during his last illness.

There are stories of several other pioneers who were buried
with loaded pistols in their belts, usually at their own request.
Many will remember that Belle Starr, notorious Missouri-born
outlaw, was buried in 1889 with a silver-mounted revolver at
her waist. I remarked to one old settler that this seemed to me
like "a heathen practice, probably got from the Indians." He
answered that he didn't think the Indians had anything to do
with it, and that it was no more "heathen" than the custom of
burying bodies with valuable rings and other jewelry, which is
common in all parts of the country.

Some hillfolk of Indian descent insist upon sprinkling a little
cornmeal over a corpse, just before the burial. This is done un-
obtrusively, without any noise or ceremony, and many whites
have attended funerals where the rite was carried out without
ever noticing it. As the mourners shuffle past the body, here
and there you see one drop a tiny pinch of meal into the coffin.

The relatives of a murdered man sometimes throw pawpaw seeds into the grave, on top of the coffin. It is said that this insures that the murderer will be punished. Other old-timers, in similar case, prefer to pull down the top of a little cedar tree and fasten it with a big stone. This somehow helps to catch the murderer. As soon as the man is punished, somebody must hurry out and move the stone; if the cedar is not released there'll be another killing in the neighborhood.

Some old people cherish a belief, said to have been borrowed from the Osages, that by burning the heart of a murdered man his relatives may make certain that the murderer will be punished for his crime. There are whispers of such things being done in the back hills even today, but the rumors cannot be verified, and it is not prudent for an amicable outsider to investigate these matters too closely.

I have heard of several families near Southwest City, Missouri, who think it is a good idea to throw chicken entrails into the grave. This is definitely an Indian idea. Christian hillfolk don't like it much, but it is still practiced. Usually the stuff is placed under the coffin, and covered with dirt so that nobody knows about it, save the bereaved family and the gravediggers.

Several methods are used in locating the bodies of persons drowned in the Ozark streams. One way is to set off charges of dynamite on the bank; this is said to bring the corpse to the surface. Some rivermen just float a loaf of light bread on the water and watch it carefully in the belief that it will stop and turn round three times at a point directly above the body. Others take a rooster in a boat and cruise about; the rooster is supposed to crow when the boat approaches the corpse. When Charles Dunlap was drowned in White River, at Elbow Shoals just below the Missouri-Arkansas line, Nov. 22, 1941, the body was not recovered for about ten days. All three of the methods noted above were suggested, and it is said that all three were tried without success.

Rube Meadows, city marshal of Branson, Missouri, claims a

peculiar ability to locate the bodies of drowned persons. He has boasted of this "sleight" since boyhood and is said to have found several corpses in White River and elsewhere. His method is comparable to water witching, but no forked stick is required. Mr. Meadows just reaches out of the boat and thrusts his bare arm into the water. There is a strange pull or attraction, he says, which indicates the location of the body. Mrs. C. P. Mahnkey, of Mincy, Missouri, first told me about this, but Mr. Meadows' claims are well known in Taney county, and many people feel that there must be something in it.

There was no embalming in the early days, and bodies must needs be buried at once. There were no automobiles or hard-surfaced roads, either, and it was impossible for relatives who lived at a distance to get together at short notice. Thus it happened that the actual "buryin' " frequently proceeded with no ceremony other than a short prayer at the grave, and the funeral was preached six months or a year later, when all the kinfolk could be present to hear the minister of their choice. These deferred funeral preachin's were held in the church house, and the mourners did not go to the graveyard at all. Such a ceremony occurred near my cabin once, when a great number of people gathered to hear a country preacher eulogize a woman who had been dead and buried for more than a year. I have heard of one case in which the funeral of a man's first wife was attended by his second spouse, who sat beside her husband and wept with him for the loss of her predecessor.

The old-timers all agree that the grave should be dug on the day of the buryin'. It is very bad luck to leave a grave open over night, as this is supposed to bring an early death to one of the dead man's relatives. A woman in Sparta, Missouri, tells how they dug a grave there for a body that was to arrive on an afternoon train; the corpse did not show up at the appointed time, so that the buryin' had to be postponed until the following day. Sure enough, as the old-timers had predicted, another member of the family died a few weeks later. This belief is taken very seriously in some places, and I have known county officials to fail of re-election because they had callously permitted a pauper to be buried in a grave dug several days previously.

It is strange that Lucile Morris, in describing the burial of Nat N. Kinney, the notorious Bald Knobber leader, near Forsyth, Missouri, Aug. 25, 1888, says positively that it was customary for the Ozarkers to leave graves open overnight. "A handful of volunteers started digging the grave," she writes. "They worked until they were well along, then stopped until the next day, for few old-time Ozarkers will complete a grave on the day it is started. That is an invitation to some catastrophe." [5] This statement seemed so much at variance with the Ozark practice that I went to Forsyth and tried to find out something definite about Kinney's burial. I located several persons who had attended the funeral, but the men who dug the grave are all gone now. Every one of the old-timers whom I interviewed assured me that if Kinney's grave actually was dug as Miss Morris says, it was a very exceptional case. Mrs. C. P. Mahnkey, whose father, A. S. Prather, was Kinney's chief lieutenant in the Bald Knobber organization, and who was herself well acquainted with the Kinney family, is very sure about this. "Lucile Morris is wrong, of course," she told me Dec. 12, 1943. "A grave is never started unless the burial is to be the same day."

It is bad taste and also very bad luck for a woman to wear a brand-new dress at a funeral, but just what would be the penalty for a violation of this rule I have never been able to find out.

Rainy weather is nothing short of calamitous on a wedding day, but at a funeral it is the best possible omen, since it means that the dead man's soul is at rest, and even a few drops of rain at this time go further to comfort the bereaved family than anything the "preacher man" can do or say. Every Ozarker knows the little verse:

[5] *Bald Knobbers,* Caldwell, Idaho (Caxton Printers, Ltd., 1939), p. 216.

Happy is the bride that the sun shines on;
Blessed are the dead that the rain falls on.

One must be careful at funerals to avoid counting the ve-
hicles, since an early death is invariably the portion of the
thoughtless individual who does so. Some say that the counter
will die in as many weeks as there are buggies or cars to be
counted. To cross a funeral procession, or to collide with a
hearse, is regarded as almost equivalent to suicide.

If a buryin' party is forced to stop on the way to the graveyard, many old-timers believe that another member of the family will be buried before the year is out. I have known interested
persons to send horsemen on ahead, to see that gates are open
and everything is in readiness. It is bad luck also if the grave
is not ready when the corpse is brought to the buryin' ground.
This sometimes happens when the gravediggers strike big rocks
or encounter some other difficulty.

Many of the old-timers think that all burials should take place
before noon; if a body is buried after 12 o'clock, another member of the family is likely to die soon. But this is no longer insisted upon, except among some very old-fashioned families.
In pioneer times the funeral lasted most of the day, with hillfolk milling around the buryin' ground for three or four hours
after the corpse was buried and the grave filled up. There was
preachin' and prayin' and singin' all day long, with time out
at noon to eat the "basket dinner" which each family brought
with them in the wagon.

On no account must the mourners leave the cemetery until
the last clod of earth is thrown into the grave—to do so evi-
dences a lack of respect for the dead and is likely to bring death
and destruction upon the family circle. Every one of the gravediggers must wait, because a man who digs a grave and does not
stay to see it filled and covered is marked for an early death.
Many hillfolk believe that deaths always come in threes, and
it may be that two more members of the group will be "called
home" within a few weeks, anyhow.

There is usually a lot of gabbling and hollering at an Ozark burial. In 1944, when Rose O'Neill was buried in the family graveyard near Day, Missouri, there was no preaching, no prayer, no religious ceremony at all. We just carried the coffin out of the house, lowered it into the grave and shoveled in the dirt, without saying a word. Some of the neighbors were horrified—it was the first non-Christian burial they had ever seen. But they all did what they could to show their respect for the dead woman, even though she *was* an unbeliever. Every man of them stood stock-still until the last shovelful of earth was thrown into the grave.

Some hillfolk become quite noisy at funerals. I have seen the immediate relatives of the deceased fling themselves on the corpse with loud yells, roll groaning and kicking on the floor, and even try to leap after the coffin when it is lowered into the grave. On the other hand, I remember one man who served his children with popcorn balls at their mother's funeral, and they all sat there eating the stuff within arm's length of the woman's body. A certain amount of noise is not regarded as bad taste at a buryin', but the old-timers do not favor long periods of mourning. Some say that protracted grieving, at least in public, is likely to interfere with the dead man's repose in the other world. "The dead caint sleep," an old woman told me, "when their kinfolks hollers too loud."

Another superstition which has to do with the welfare of the dead is the tale of the heavenly crowns, also known as feather crowns and angel wreaths. The idea is that when a very good and saintly person is dying, the feathers in the pillow form themselves into a crown, a kind of symbol of the golden crown which the dying person is soon to wear in Heaven. Variations of this tale are heard in many places, over the whole length and breadth of the Ozark country.

I have seen about twenty of these heavenly crowns. Several of them were loosely made, like inferior birds' nests. Crowns of this type may have been faked or have come together more or less accidentally. One of these loosely built crowns had a round hole in the center, something like a bird's nest with the bottom punched out. Another was in the form of a ropelike ring, smooth and firm, about five inches in diameter, more like an undersized halo than a crown.

The most finished type of feather crown, and the most impressive to my mind, is not shaped like a cap or doughnut at all, but rather like a large bun; these are very tightly woven, solid enough to be tossed about like a ball, and surprisingly heavy. They are usually about six inches in diameter and two inches thick, slightly convex on both sides. They seem to be made in a sort of spiral like a snail shell, with the feathers all pointed the same direction and no quill ends in sight. All of the crowns I have seen, whether of the rough or the finished type, seemed very clean, and I saw no grease or glue or anything of the sort to hold the feathers together. I have pulled several of the loosely built crowns to pieces but have never been allowed to dissect one of the really fine, compactly woven kind. I do not believe that crowns of this latter type were deliberately fabricated by the horny-handed folk who showed them to me.

When the bereaved family finds one of these feather crowns in the pillow of a relative who has just died, they are quite set up about it, sure that the dear departed has gone straight to Heaven and is "doin' well thar," as one old woman told me. The crown is taken out of the pillow with great care and displayed to all the neighbors; sometimes there is a mention of it in the village paper, as a sort of postscript appended to the obituary. Some families keep such a crown in a box for many years, and I have seen two crowns sealed up in a glass-topped case of polished walnut which had been made especially for them.

May Stafford Hilburn describes the "angel wreath found in the goose-feather pillow of an old saint" of her acquaintance. She makes it plain that the wreath was regarded as a good omen, "a positive proof that the sainted old man had gone straight to Heaven." [6]

There is a farmer still living near Anderson, Missouri, who

6 *Missouri Magazine* (December, 1933), p. 11.

treasures the crown left by his son. The boy spent several years in prison but finally came home to die, and the old man exhibits the crown as proof that the convict's sins were forgiven, since he not only went to Heaven but went rather ostentatiously at that. The implication is that the boy wasn't as bad as he was painted and may have been altogether innocent of the crime for which he was imprisoned.

An old friend near Aurora, Missouri, tells of a widow in that neighborhood who displayed a very fine feather crown from her husband's pillow. The deceased was not at all the sort of man who would be expected to have a crown, and this particular specimen was so large and perfect that some of the neighbors suspected that the widow had woven it herself and stuck the feathers in place with molasses.

There are stories of persons who have stolen crowns, and shifted pillows from one bed to another, and otherwise claimed crowns for persons who were by no means entitled to them. But it seems to me that such happenings are rare, since most hillfolk are too superstitious to meddle in these matters.

It is difficult for an outsider to realize how seriously this heavenly-crown business is regarded by the old-time hillfolk. Here is a letter from Mrs. W. H. Haney, Dixon, Missouri, which was published in the Springfield (Missouri) *News*, Nov. 16, 1940:

I want to tell you that I know about these feather crowns that are found in pillows of the dying. I have three now that I found in the pillow of my darling daughter's bed when she passed away over ten years ago. No human hand could place those feathers like they are. So many of the old time things are true. The Bible teaches that there are "signs" for us to go by, and I believe everything the Bible teaches.

I knew an old lady in Little Rock, Arkansas, who left instructions that she was to be buried with her husband's feather crown in her bosom; the husband had died some thirty years before, but she had kept his crown in a box at her bedside.

I once took a city feller, a dealer in antique furniture and the like, to a backwoods cabin where he saw a fine feather crown in a box. When the thing was explained to him he became much interested and insulted everybody by offering to buy it for ten dollars. The old folks became very reserved, and one of the young men advised me to "take that feller back to town. He'll be tryin' to buy the stone off'n Sally's grave next, an' Paw's a-gittin' pretty damn' mad already!"

Various theories have been advanced to explain the formation of feather crowns. Mrs. J. H. Mayes, Mountain Grove, Missouri, published a letter in the Springfield (Missouri) *News* (Jan. 15, 1942) contending that the larvae of moths live inside the quills, and "fasten the feathers together with an almost invisible thread, something like the web of a spider." She says that she has seen these larvae "emerging from the quills and dragging the feathers," and that she has found feather crowns fastened together with "almost invisible web." She adds "my pioneer mother told me that moths would get in feathers and form balls unless the feathers were periodically exposed to the sunlight." Mrs. Mayes thinks that these crowns are not found in feathers which have been scalded before storing them away.

Commenting on two feather crowns which May Kennedy Mc-Cord presented to the Missouri Historical Society, later placed on exhibition at the Jefferson Memorial, an anonymous writer in the St. Louis *Post-Dispatch* (Apr. 3, 1942) offers the following theory of their origin:

A possible explanation lies in the physiological character of feathers. From the shaft above the quill are numerous vanes composed of barbs, and on the barbs are barbules with minute hooklets on the side toward the tip of the feather. These hooklets normally are caught in indentations on the side of the barbules toward the quill. In a pillow they are likely to become loose, ready to hook any other minute thing. When two feathers come into contact, they are held together by the hooklets. Other feathers join them, and a nucleus is formed. Just as feathers can be pushed through a small hole quill first with comparative ease, but tip first with difficulty, so feathers in a clump would tend to "climb" or move along each other toward the quill point. Such movement would continue until all the quill points attained a common center and could go no farther. Since downy feathers are all curved, the tendency would be for the outward curve to fit into an inward curve, and the feather clump would assume a spherical shape.

A man in St. Louis, who used to buy and sell feathers in very large quantities, tells me that goose feathers sometimes "lump up" into firm rounded bunches, varying from the size of a biscuit to that of a washtub. These lumps have to be picked apart and broken up in order to handle the feathers. He doesn't know what causes this lumping but says that it can't be moth larvae, because feather dealers treat all their stuff with chemicals or live steam, which is certain to kill any insects that might be present.

Mrs. Eliza Polete, of Fredericktown, Missouri, reported a feather crown "in which the feathers were intertwined with a light blue silk thread." And Mrs. May Kennedy McCord, of Springfield, Missouri, mentions a crown that "appears as if it had been started around a pink thread, the like of which we do not have about the house, and never have had that I know of." Several persons have told me of crowns which contained pieces of thread from bed ticking, bits of dried chicken skin, unidentified animal matter, and long black hairs. A young widow in Greene county, Missouri, a month after her husband's death, found a crown in his pillow which contained several hairs from his head; this man's hair was dyed a peculiar color, so there was no trouble in identifying them. But how did these hairs get inside the pillow? The crowns which I have examined contained, so far as I could see with a pocket lens, nothing but feathers.

Most hillfolk seem to think that the presence of a feather crown in one's pillow means good fortune here or hereafter, but there are some who believe they are death signs, the work of the Devil. Mrs. Nelle Burger, of Springfield, Missouri, president of the Missouri State W.C.T.U., has expressed herself about this. She says that in her childhood the people regarded feather crowns as evil omens, produced by the machinations of witches, which should be instantly destroyed wherever they are found.[7] Mr. Rudolph Summers, of Crane, Missouri, recalls certain old settlers in his neighborhood who believe that feather wreaths are bad for everybody concerned and must be thrown into the fire immediately.

Mrs. Ruth Tyler, of Neosho, Missouri, is another who regards the heavenly crown as a sinister thing. Writing in *Rayburn's Ozark Guide* she tells her readers: "The feather-crown is a swirl of feathers that cling to a tiny thread or raveling. The feathers all turn in one direction, 'clockwise' to the right. It is very BAD luck to keep or give away one of these strange formations. Burn or destroy them at once." [8]

A lady whom I knew in Little Rock, Arkansas, never lets a month go by without examining every feather pillow in her house, to see if any suspicious lumps have appeared. Her husband is a politician, with many enemies, and she fears that some of them might employ witchcraft against the family. The idea is that these crowns grow slowly, over a period of several months, and that one can stop the whole business by searching the things out and burning them. But she thinks that if a feather crown ever comes to completion, the person who sleeps on that pillow will die immediately. That's why, according to her view, one never finds a perfect, finished crown excepting in the pillow of someone who has died.

Mrs. May Kennedy McCord, of Springfield, Missouri, published a letter from a woman living at Fordland, Missouri, on this subject:

According to what my husband tells me, as I have no knowledge myself, these crowns are definitely of evil. In fact very evil. As you say they are never found in a finished state only after the death of the user of the pillow and if you'll take a fool's advice you'll get rid of the specimens you have at once.

[7] Springfield (Missouri) *News*, Jan. 15, 1941.
[8] Lonsdale, Arkansas (July–August–September, 1944), p. 29.

I was taught not to believe in superstitions, and this one I never heard of until I came to Missouri. My husband's people have lived in St. Louis since the days of Laclede and Choteau, and they firmly believe in this sort of thing. But they believe that if the pillow is burned if a sick person is using it, the hex will be removed and the sick one recover. One of his nephews' wives won't have a feather pillow in the home on this account. I do not like my name in the paper but I do think people should know that these feathers are not works of art but of the Evil One, in plain English, just a way of escaping punishment for murder.—A READER.[9]

That's pretty strong language and leaves no doubt as to what the Fordland lady has in mind.

There are many miscellaneous superstitions about grave-yards, and I have listed some of these in the chapters on ghost stories and witchcraft. When a man feels a sudden chill without any obvious reason, it means that someone or something— usually a rabbit, a possum, or a goose—is walking over the spot which will ultimately be his grave.

It is very generally regarded as a bad business to move a body that has once been buried, and many hillfolk absolutely refuse to have any part in such an undertaking.

Dr. W. O. Cralle, of Springfield, Missouri, met an old woman who told him that when a nearby cemetery was moved it was found that the corpses had gone to dust, but all the hearts were just as sound as the day the bodies were buried. Another version of this tale, which I heard in Washington county, Arkansas, has it that the hearts were petrified—turned into solid reddish lime-stone. If a long-buried body is found to be well preserved, the hillfolk seem disturbed and a little frightened. They feel that it is natural for a corpse to decay and return to dust, and that a body which does *not* decay is somehow unwholesome or be-witched. Charles J. Finger, of Fayetteville, Arkansas, was struck by this idea; he suggested to me that it might be a remnant of the European belief in vampires.

An odd notion, still quoted in many parts of Arkansas, is

[9] Springfield (Missouri) *News*, Jan. 15, 1942.

that a green brier always grows where a Yankee soldier is buried, while wild roses bloom over the graves of the Confederate dead.

It is bad luck to carry anything out of a graveyard. One may move shrubs or flowering plants from one grave to another, but the person who carries a flower outside the gate will bury some member of his family within a year. May Stafford Hilburn mentions a woman who picked a bouquet from her father-in-law's grave, and sure enough her husband died the very next summer. "To this day," writes Mrs. Hilburn, "I do not take even a leaf from a cemetery!" [10] In 1936 a band of thieves carried off many tombstones from old cemeteries in southwest Missouri; it is supposed that the stones were redressed and sold elsewhere. People at Granby and Oronogo especially became very indignant about this and predicted that some supernatural calamity would overtake the criminals.

In some sections of Arkansas I have seen newly filled graves with a pick and shovel left on the mound in the shape of a cross. This was evidently the gravediggers' idea. Perhaps it is somehow related to the familiar practice of crossing the mop and broom when the house cleaning is finished, as described elsewhere in this book.

If a hillman happens to tread upon a grave, he is supposed to jump backward across it immediately, as otherwise a member of his family will die, according to the old-timers. One of my best friends, an educated Ozarker who is generally indifferent to superstition, surprised me by suddenly springing over a grave in this fashion. "It isn't a matter of what I believe," he said later, "but one must respect the prejudices of his neighbors. If I had not jumped back across that grave, it would look as if I *want* some of my relatives to die!" There are doubtless many other persons in the Ozarks who explain their observance of the old customs and taboos in similar terms.

[10] *Missouri Magazine* (October, 1933), p. 14.

14. Miscellaneous Items

The folk beliefs lumped together under this chapter's heading have little in common, beyond the fact that they do not easily fit into any of the previous chapters. How should one classify, for example, the hillman's strange notions about the physical characteristics correlated with honesty and dependability? There are still old-timers who will have no business dealings with a man whose beard is of a noticeably different color than his hair; I have talked with men and women, as recently as 1936, who refused to support a candidate for public office because his hair was gray and his mustache red.

Colonel A. S. Prather, who lived near Kirbyville, Missouri, in the eighties, always said "Never trust a man with ears too close to the top of his head." And Mrs. C. P. Mahnkey, daughter of the Colonel, told me not long ago that she thought there must be some truth in it. Mrs. Mahnkey also quoted Uncle Jim Parnell, who placed small confidence in "a feller who rattled money in his pocket whilst he was a-tradin'." A person with very small ears is generally supposed to be stingy or "close." If a man's fingers are straight and held close together in repose, so that one cannot see the light between one finger and another, it is also a sign of stinginess or at least frugality. When a man begins to speak, and then forgets what he was about to say, many hillfolk believe that the statement he intended to make was a lie.

The common expression "never trust a feller that wears a suit" does not really represent a superstitious belief, but merely the universal prejudice against men from the cities. The backwoods boys seldom wear suits. They buy expensive trousers sometimes but prefer leather jackets or windbreakers to matching coats. A woman in Branson, Missouri, once said to me: "Them Bull Creek boys is hell on big-legged pants. Don't keer much about coats, but *pants is their pride*." Many a prosperous young countryman, in possession of a farm, a car, some cattle and other livestock, has never owned a suit of clothes in his life.

It is natural perhaps, in a fox-huntin' country, that a man who doesn't make friends with dogs should be regarded as a suspicious character. Related to this, no doubt, is the old idea that a beekeeper can always be relied upon, while a fellow who doesn't get along with bees is likely to be untrustworthy in financial matters. But what can we make of the old saying that "an honest man never rides a sorrel horse"? I have heard references to this sorrel-horse business in many parts of the Ozark country, over a long term of years, but even today I'm not sure just what is meant by it.

There is a very old sayin' to the effect that a thief always looks into his cup before he drinks. This is quoted in a joking way, but I once met a deputy sheriff in Eureka Springs, Arkansas, who said that he had studied the matter for many years and was almost convinced that there was something in it. "Them old fellers that figgered out such notions," he told me, "was hunters an' Indian fighters. They had sharp eyes, an' they watched ever'thing mighty close."

In a poverty-ridden region such as the Ozarks, one would expect to find a number of superstitions relating to wealth. If a gray moth called the money miller hovers over you, or a little red money spider crawls on your clothes, you are sure to become rich some day. When a honeybee buzzes about your head, it is a sign that you will get a letter with money in it, or at least good news about financial matters. Mr. Clarence Marshbanks, of Galena, Missouri, says that the children used to cry "Money 'fore the week's out!" whenever they saw a redbird; the idea is that if you could get it all said before the bird was out of sight, there would be money coming your way by the end of the week.

A person whose initials spell a word is certain to be rich, sooner or later. A man with a wart or mole on the neck is supposed to be fortunate in money matters, according to the old rhyme:

> Mole on the neck,
> Money by the peck.

A woman with conspicuous hairs on her breasts will attain riches, if we are to believe the old-timers.

Ozark children are often told that if the lucky-bones taken from crawfish are buried in the earth, they'll turn into nickels in a fortnight. Many a credulous mountain boy has tried this, and one youngster said disgustedly: "God, what a lie old Granny Durgen told me!"

The man who has an eye tooth extracted should hasten to bury it in a cemetery, on an infidel's grave, because this is sure to bring money within six months. When you see a lot of bubbles on the surface of your coffee, try to drink them all before they disappear, for if you succeed it means that you are about to make a large sum of money.

On seeing a shooting star, always cry out "money-money-money" before it disappears, and you will inherit wealth. When you first glimpse the new moon, turn over a coin in your pocket without looking at the moon again, and you will be fortunate in money matters. It is always a good idea to be touching a silver coin whenever you see the moon, and it may be for this reason that rings hammered from silver coins are so popular in some sections. A girl who happens to see the new moon "cl'ar o' brush" hastens to kiss her hand three times and expects to find something worth a lot of money before the moon changes.

Like most primitive folk, the Ozark natives attach considerable importance to dreams, but their dream interpretations don't seem to differ greatly from those current among unlettered people in other parts of the country.

To dream of muddy water means trouble, to dream of snakes presages a battle with one's enemies, to dream of money means that the dreamer will be poorer than ever before. A dream of white horses is unlucky and may mean sickness or death in the family. A dream of death is good luck if the dream comes at night and usually signifies a wedding, but to fall asleep in the daytime and dream of death is very unfortunate. A dream of childbirth is always welcome, a sign of a happy and prosperous marriage. The man who dreams repeatedly of fishes will attain great wealth. To dream of chickens is bad luck, and the vision of a black boat means an early death. A lady at Fort Smith, Arkansas, told me that she had discarded nearly all the superstitions of her childhood, but still felt that it is bad luck to dream about cattle. To dream of a hoe or a rake signifies a happy marriage. The girl who dreams always of storms and floods will marry a rich man. It is good luck to dream of pigeons or doves, and usually means that a fortunate love affair is just around the corner.

The first dream that one has in a new house, or when sleeping under a new quilt, will nearly always come true—many mountain girls are anxious to "dream out" a new quilt or coverlet. The same may be said of a dream related before breakfast, or of one dreamed on Friday and told on Saturday:

> Friday night's dream, on Saturday told,
> Will always come true, no matter how old.

An old woman at Pineville, Missouri, told me that as a little girl she dreamed of a gigantic snake coiled around her father's log house. She says this was a sign of the Civil War which broke out a few months later, in which her father and two brothers were killed. In 1865 she dreamed that the big snake was dead, upon which she knew that the War would soon be ended.

Mrs. May Kennedy McCord, of Springfield, Missouri, says

that the best way to stop unpleasant dreams is to stuff cloth into the key hole. But I'm not sure that she means this to be taken literally.

Some people are accustomed to place a knife under the dreamer's pillow, to prevent nightmares. I once noticed a small girl, not more than ten years old, sleeping with the handle of an enormous homemade bowie knife sticking out from under her pillow. "Maizie used to wake up a-hollerin'," the mother told me, "but since I put that there knife under the piller, we aint had no more trouble." Somnambulism is related to nightmares in the hillman's mind, and there is a widespread belief that one should never awaken a sleepwalker, as this may cause instant death. The Ozarker who sees a friend walking in his sleep just strides along beside him and tries to keep him from getting into danger, but makes no effort to wake him up.

At several places in Missouri and Arkansas one hears of "electric springs." I never saw one of these, but persons in Lanagan and Anderson, Missouri, told me that if you dip your knife in the waters of a certain spring branch north of Anderson, the steel blade becomes a magnet. A boy assured me that the blade of his clasp knife retained its magnetic properties for several months, after being immersed in the "electric water" about five minutes.

Most hillfolk believe that all water which is clear and cold is good to drink—they cannot understand that such water may carry deadly organisms. Many persons contend that any spring water, no matter how contaminated, is purified by running over a hundred feet of gravel.

It is said that a man who takes three drinks in three minutes from any Ozark spring is bound to return for another drink before he dies. In one form or another, that story is heard all over the Ozark country. But whether it is really old-time stuff, or was cooked up by the Chamber of Commerce propagandists, I have been unable to find out.

There is an odd belief that stalactites or stalagmites are

somehow deadlier than other stones, and that even a slight blow from a piece of "drip rock" is generally fatal. Carl Hovey, of Springfield, Missouri, was killed years ago by bumping his head on a stalactite and is still remembered and talked about whenever this superstition is mentioned.

The "git-your-wish" class of superstitions is rather large, but I don't think it is taken very seriously by many adults nowadays. Grown people still go through the motions, but it is only the children who really believe that their wishes will come true.

When a little girl sees a redbird she "throws a kiss an' makes a wish." If she can throw *three* kisses before the bird disappears, she is certain that her wish will be granted unless she sees the same bird again, in which case all bets are off. Some say that if one spies a cardinal in a tree he should always make a wish and then throw a stone; if the bird flies upward the wish will be granted, but if it flies downward the desire will never be satisfied.

The hillman who sees a snake trail across a dusty road often spits in the track and makes a wish; such wishes are supposed to come true, particularly if nobody is within sight of the spitter at the time.

When a plowman hears the first turtle dove in the spring, he makes a wish and turns round three times on his left heel. Then he takes off his left shoe, and if he finds a hair in the shoe which is the color of his wife's or sweetheart's hair, he feels that his wish will be realized. Several sober and generally truthful farmers have told me that they have tried this and actually found the hair; one man said it was a very long hair, coiled up as if it had been placed in the shoe deliberately.

Some hillfolk "stick a wish" on a soaring buzzard high up and far away; if the bird passes out of sight without flapping its wings, they think that the wish will be granted. "When you see a little new colt," said one of my neighbors, "always spit in your hand an' make a wish; your wish is bound to come true, 'cordin' to the old folks."

Many Ozark children believe in "stamping mules," especially gray or white mules. On seeing one of these animals the child wets his thumb, presses a little saliva into the palm of the left hand, and "stamps" it with a blow of his fist. When he has stamped twenty mules he makes a wish—it's sure to be granted. In some parts of the Ozarks, where Negroes are rare but not entirely lacking, I am told that the children "stamp niggers" the same as mules. I met children near Mena, Arkansas, who were stamping white horses too, but without much enthusiasm; they said it was necessary to stamp a hundred horses before making a wish.

An old woman near Noel, Missouri, always makes a wish when she sees a spotted horse, believing that if she refrains from looking at the animal again and tells someone about the occurrence as soon as possible, her wish will come true. "But it won't work in Oklahomy," she said with a toothless grin, "there's too many paint ponies over there."

If a hillman happens to see a star before dark he shuts his eyes for a moment, spits over his left shoulder, and makes a wish. Many an Ozarker "sticks a wish" on a falling star; if he succeeds in pronouncing the words under his breath before the star is out of sight and refrains from telling anybody the nature of the wish, he believes that it will come true. When the first star of the evening appears backwoods children make a wish, then cross their fingers and chant:

> Star light, star bright,
> First star I seen tonight,
> I wish I may, I wish I might,
> Git the wish I wish tonight!

Children at Reeds Spring, Missouri, when they see a yellow boxcar standing still, stamp their feet and make a wish. If the yellow car is moving, the charm doesn't work.

Some hillfolk say that if you make a wish at the bottom of a long steep hill and don't speak or look back until you have reached the top, your wish is sure to be granted. It is well to make a wish, also, when one walks on strange ground for the first time. Some people make a wish whenever they see a woman wearing a man's hat.

In Taney county, Missouri, they say that the first time a woman sews on a button for a man, she should make a wish about that man's future, and such a wish invariably comes true.

It is bad luck to drop a comb, but when an Ozark woman does so she invariably puts her foot on it and makes a wish. When a girl's dress turns up accidentally, she knows that her lover is thinking of her and hastens to kiss the hem and make a wish, confident that it will be granted. If her shoestring comes untied she asks a friend to tie it, and while this is being done she makes a wish. When a child's tooth is extracted he doesn't throw it away but puts it under his pillow and sleeps on it, confident that this will cause his chief desire to be granted within a few days.

When a young girl in Springfield, Missouri, finds one of her eyelashes which has fallen out, she puts it on her thumb and makes a wish; then she blows the eyelash away and believes that her wish will come true.

If two Ozark children happen to pronounce the same word or phrase at the same time, they must not speak again until they have hooked their little fingers together, made wishes, and chanted the following:

First voice: "Needles,"
Second voice: "Pins,"
First voice: "Triplets,"
Second voice: "Twins."
First voice: "When a man marries,"
Second voice: "His troubles begin,"
First voice: "When a man dies,"
Second voice: "His troubles end."
First voice: "What goes up the chimney?"
Second voice: "Smoke!"

This done, the youngsters unhook their little fingers and go on about their business, each satisfied that his or her desire will be fulfilled. A girl in Stone county, Missouri, told me that all her schoolmates were familiar with this ceremony, and that many practiced it even after they were old enough to attend the village high schools.

A woman at West Plains, Missouri, places her right hand on the closed Bible, makes a wish, and opens the book at random. She does this three times, muttering the same wish under her breath. If the opened Bible shows the words "it came to pass" three times in succession, she is sure to get her wish. This woman tells me that she has been doing this for many years, and that perhaps 90 percent of her prayers have been granted. "Of course," she told me smiling, "a body shouldn't wish for somethin' that aint *reasonable*."

Another semi-serious ceremony occurs when the first louse is found on a boy baby's head. This is quite an occasion in some families, and the other children all gather round while the mother kills the louse by "popping" it on the family Bible. While doing this she intones a wish about the children's future profession and salutes him as lawyer, doctor, merchant, farmer, preacher or what-not. This ritual is not exactly a joke—children are not allowed to laugh at anything in which the Bible is concerned—but I do not think many adults really believe that the child's future is determined by "louse poppin'."

One sometimes hears cryptic references to one hillman "drivin' a stake" or "plantin' a bush" in another's dooryard. My first impression was that these phrases referred to what the hillfolk call "family matters," but I learned later that sometimes they are to be taken quite literally. A lawyer in McDonald county, Missouri, told me that our local rich man, in a towering rage, had exhibited a "green stake" which an enemy had driven into his front lawn at midnight. He wanted the lawyer to see that the stake driver was arrested and flung into jail. "He thought the fellow had made a *wish* on the stake, or something," the attorney chuckled. "A kind of spooky business. No sense to it at all. I just threw the stake in the fire, an' advised my client to go back home an' forget it."

In the *Taney County Republican*, a weekly newspaper published at Forsyth, Missouri, Feb. 20, 1941, appeared the following bit of gossip: "Rita Reynolds and Arnold Davis are planning on planting a tree in Alvin Huff's yard." The neighbors told me that Rita had been "goin' with" Alvin, but the two had quarreled, and now she was "goin' with" Arnold Davis instead. Some members of the Huff family were said to be considerably displeased about this item in the *Republican*. But nobody seemed willing to tell me just what was meant by it.

Some hillfolk believe that if the cicadas or "locusts" have a black *W* on their wings it is a sure sign of war. Mrs. May Kennedy McCord insists that there is something in this notion and recalls that she saw the fatal *W* on locusts' wings the year of the Spanish-American War.[1]

An old man near Bentonville, Arkansas, told me that it was no trouble to predict the result of any national election. If the Democrats are going to win, every garden is full of dog fennel; if a Republican victory is in the cards, dog fennel will be scarce, and plantain will choke every fence corner in Arkansas—which God forbid! Asked about the best method of doping out the Democratic primaries, the old chap just grinned and shook his head.

During the presidential campaign of 1928, many Ozarkers saw a strange light in the sky, doubtless the aurora borealis. Some people in Christian county, Missouri, were very much frightened; they thought the end of the world was at hand, so they held a big prayer-meeting. Clay Fulks, a professor at Commonwealth College, near Mena, Arkansas, told me that his neighbors believed that the light was a sign from God Almighty, warning the people not to vote for Al Smith.

In the early days of the New Deal, many Holy Roller preach-

[1] Springfield (Missouri) *News & Leader*, Jan. 4, 1933.

ers wandered through the backwoods of Missouri and Arkansas denouncing the "Blue Eagle" of the NRA, claiming that it was the evil sign described in the Apocalypse. The Joplin (Missouri) *Globe* (Aug. 29, 1933) discussed this matter seriously at some length, estimating that "between 20 and 25 percent of the population of the foothill region" identified the NRA symbol with the seven-headed beast of doom mentioned by St. John. In 1942 I heard one of these fellows in the courtyard at Galena, Missouri, preaching against the government sugar rationing; he placed great emphasis upon the "mark" or "stamp" which he said was predicted in the Bible. "Right over thar at Troy Stone's store," he cried, "you caint even git a little poke o' sugar without that stamp!"

Many Ozarkers feel that there is some religious or political significance connected with any unusual mark on an egg shell, and such marks are carefully studied. Old-timers in southern Missouri and northern Arkansas still talk of the "hen-egg revivals" which swept over this region in pioneer days. The story goes that some old woman found an egg with the words "Judgment is at Hand" plainly marked on the shell. Ministers of various sects came long distances to examine this egg and preached about it. The general impression prevailed that it was a "token" or omen and meant that the end of the world was soon to come. People became very religious for awhile, but after a year or so had passed and nothing happened, the excitement gradually died down, and the "hen-egg revival" was regarded as a sort of joke.

As recently as 1935 a similar excitement arose in the village of Couch, Missouri, when Mrs. Henry Bennett found an egg imprinted with the phrase "Here my Word 35." Viewing this as a religious portent, Mrs. Bennett told her neighbors about it. "A wave of excited piety overtook Couch," reports *Time*, Feb. 4, 1935. "To Mrs. Bennett's home went visitor after visitor, to emit fervent prayers. When, in a fit of devout jitters, a female preacher dropped the egg and broke it, Mrs. Bennett succeeded in gluing enough pieces on another egg so that the words were still visible." Mrs. Bennett said that she did not know what the egg meant, but "it was sent to us for some good reason, and there is no need for the children of God to be afraid."

A woman once showed me a strange scar, something like a Chinese ideograph, on an egg shell. Later she told me privately that her husband, who was a Pentecostal preacher, had fallen into a trance at sight of the "inscription" and translated it. The message stated, he said, that Jesus Christ was going to visit the United States, run for President on the Democratic ticket, and "stump the whole State of Arkansas!"

Well, so much for superstition in the Ozark country. When I began to collect material for this book, more than twenty-five years ago, it seemed to me that these old folk beliefs were disappearing very rapidly and would soon be rejected and forgotten. I intimated as much in my first paper on the subject, published in 1927.[2] We all talked at length about scientific progress, and enlightenment, and the obvious effect of popular education. But now, I am not so sure. I am not so sure about anything, nowadays.

[2] *Journal of American Folklore,* Vol. 40 (1927), pp. 78–93.

Bibliography

Not many studies of Ozark superstition have been published. The titles listed below make up the entire literature of the subject, so far as I know.

There are several important manuscript collections. Dr. Benjamin A. Cartwright, of Norman, Oklahoma, has more than 30,000 superstitions typed on cards, and some of these items were collected in Barry and McDonald counties, Missouri, where he lived for many years. Mrs. Mabel E. Mueller, of Rolla, Missouri, showed me a large file of ghost stories and witch tales, mostly from Phelps county, Missouri. Mrs. Isabel France, of Mountainburg, Arkansas, recorded a lot of folk remedies in the backwoods of northwest Arkansas. Mr. Otto Ernest Rayburn, of Eureka Springs, Arkansas, has much unpublished material, and so has Mrs. May Kennedy McCord, of Springfield, Missouri. A considerable amount of miscellaneous information about folklore was assembled by the Federal Writers' Project in the 1930's; this material has since been delivered to the Library of Congress, where it is being worked over by Dr. B. A. Botkin, formerly a professor at the University of Oklahoma, editor of *A Treasury of American Folklore* (New York, 1944; 932 pp.).

Allsopp, Fred W. Folklore of Romantic Arkansas. New York, Grolier Society, 1931. 2 vols., 333, 371 pp.

> Only one short chapter entitled "Some Early Superstitions" (II, 121–128) is ostensibly devoted to this subject, but both volumes contain much interesting information. Badly indexed, no documentation. Allsopp was managing editor of the *Arkansas Gazette* in Little Rock for many years.

Arkansas, a Guide to the State. New York, Hastings House, 1941. 447 pp.

> Compiled by the Federal Writers' Project, sponsored and copyrighted by the Secretary of State at Little Rock, Arkansas. The word "superstition" does not appear in the index, but there is a brief section (pp. 97–102) entitled "Folklore and Folkways" which contains a few items.

Barker, Catherine S. Yesterday Today; Life in the Ozarks. Caldwell, Idaho, Caxton Printers, Ltd., 1941. 263 pp.

> Chapter XV, pp. 241–253, is entitled "Superstition" and contains a list of Ozark folk beliefs. Mrs. Barker lived at Batesville, Arkansas, for eleven years, and was a case worker for the Federal Emergency Relief Administration; she collected the material for this book in the country near Batesville.

Bauersfeld, "Mirandy." Breezes from Persimmon Holler. Hollywood, California, Printed by the Oxford Press, 1943. 207 pp.

Behymer, F. A. "The Legend Lady of the Ozarks," St. Louis *Post-Dispatch*, St. Louis, Missouri, July 7, 1943, p. 3-C.

Brief article about Mrs. Mabel E. Mueller, of Rolla, Missouri, and her studies of witchcraft and other Ozark superstition.

Broadfoot, Lennis L. Pioneers of the Ozarks. Caldwell, Idaho, Caxton Printers, Ltd., 1944. 195 pp.

Charcoal portraits of elderly Ozarkers, with names and addresses attached. There is a page of printed matter opposite each drawing, usually a direct quotation from the subject. Note references to superstition, pp. 28, 30, 40, 100, 142, and 146. Broadfoot is a self-taught artist, a native of Shannon county, Missouri.

Clemens, Nancy. Girl Scouts in the Ozarks. New York, Alfred A. Knopf, 1936. 233 pp.

—— "Grandma's Charm String," *Mothers' Home Life,* Winona, Minnesota (November, 1936), pp. 3, 11.

—— "Heavenly Crown," *University Review,* University of Kansas City, Kansas City, Missouri (Summer, 1937), pp. 263–266.

—— "Mountain Sibyl," *University Review,* University of Kansas City, Kansas City, Missouri (Winter, 1937), pp. 105–107. Reprinted in Lowry C. Wimberly's *Mid Country,* University of Nebraska Press, Lincoln, Neb., 1945, pp. 403–406.

—— "Taking My Medicine," *Atlantic Monthly* (February, 1938), pp. 265–266.

A native of Cedar County, Missouri, Miss Clemens does features for the Kansas City *Star* and the St. Louis *Post-Dispatch* and has written several books and numerous magazine articles. What she says about superstition is trustworthy, because this material has come to her from kinfolk and intimates. She lives in Springfield, Missouri.

Cralle, Walter O. "Social Change and Isolation in the Ozark Mountain Region of Missouri," *American Journal of Sociology,* Vol. 41, No. 4 (January, 1936), pp. 435–446.

This is an abstract of a Ph.D thesis, presented at the University of Minnesota in 1934. Cralle refers briefly to "the geographic configuration of myth, superstition, magical practices, and a wealth of folklore which still abounds in the more isolated sections" but does not treat this material in detail. Almost the only groups available for study are those in schoolrooms, he says, "and here superstition, as well as dialect, finds itself in strained and hostile environment. It seems to the writer that superstition is more widespread and tenacious than dialect because less often exposed to criticism and ridicule." Dr. Cralle teaches sociology at the Southwest Missouri Teachers College, Springfield, Missouri, and has considerable firsthand knowledge of the hillbilly population.

Davis, Clyde Brion. The Arkansas. New York, Farrar and Rinehart, 1940. 340 pp.

One short section (pp. 216–221) is devoted to folk beliefs. "Many of the superstitions prevalent in the Ozarks have some universality," writes Davis. "Others are, I believe, peculiar to that region."

DeHaven, Pearl. "Add Folklore," *Country Gentleman* (May, 1944), p. 2.

A brief letter to supplement "Folklore on the Farm" by Moran and Gale Tudury, in the March, 1944, issue of *Country Gentleman*. The Tudury article dealt with rural America in general, but Mrs. DeHaven adds a number of Ozark items. She lives in Greene County, Missouri.

Finger, Charles J. Ozark Fantasia. Fayetteville, Arkansas, Golden Horseman Press, 1927. 342 pp.

The sketch entitled "As to the Well Walter Dug," pp. 125–130, deals with water witches.

France, Isabel. "The Hills of Home," a weekly column in the *Southwest Times-Record,* daily newspaper published at Fort Smith, Arkansas, April, 1936—.

Mrs. France now lives near Mountainburg, Arkansas, but was formerly a resident of Van Buren and taught several country schools in that vicinity, where she will be remembered as Isabel Spradley. She refers to superstitions only incidentally, but what she has to say is always worth attention. Mrs. France knows vastly more about Ozark folklore than most people who have written on the subject.

Hilburn, May Stafford. "Traditional Beliefs of the Hill People, *Missouri Magazine,* Jefferson City, Missouri (September, 1933), pp. 20–21.

—— "Rites and Sayings of Pioneer Folk," *Missouri Magazine,* Jefferson City, Missouri (October, 1933), pp. 14–15.

—— "Culled from My Memory Box," *Missouri Magazine,* Jefferson City, Missouri (December, 1933), pp. 10–11.

Mrs. Hilburn is a native Ozarker, who makes her home at Jefferson City, Missouri. She is inclined to be sentimental and poetic in her writing, but these three papers contain a great deal of valuable material, much of it derived from the author's childhood experience.

Hogue, Wayman. "Don't Pity the Mountaineer," New York *Herald-Tribune,* Feb. 22, 1931, pp. 13–15.

This article is reprinted in my *Ozark Anthology* (Caldwell, Idaho, Caxton Printers, Ltd., 1940), pp. 241–256. It contains some good witchcraft references.

—— Back Yonder, an Ozark Chronicle. New York, Minton, Balch & Co., 1932. 303 pp.

One of the finest nonfiction books ever written about the Ozark country. Hogue is a native of Van Buren County, Arkansas. He knows the truth about this region, and sets it down without any sentimental twaddle. Chapter XX, pp. 270–285, is entitled "Folklore and Superstition," but other valuable items are scattered throughout the book.

Lain, Myrtle. "A Dummy Supper in the Ozarks," *Arcadian Magazine,* Eminence, Missouri (August, 1931), pp. 9–10.

Miss Lain's material came from Old Linn Creek, Missouri.

Lyon, Marguerite. And Green Grass Grows All Around. New York, Indianapolis, Bobbs-Merrill, 1942. 307 pp.

Chapter 23, pp. 200–210, "The Seer of the Ozarks," is apparently an account of the author's interview with Josie Forbes, the "Witch of Taskee."

—— Fresh from the Hills. New York, Bobbs-Merrill Co., 1945. 283 pp.

This author, who writes for the Chicago *Tribune,* spent some time in the hills near Mountain View, Missouri, and now lives at Eureka Springs, Arkansas. The section entitled "Don't Believe It," pp. 120–130, is devoted to Ozark superstitions and folk remedies.

McCord, May Kennedy. "Hillbilly Heartbeats," weekly column in the Springfield (Missouri) *Leader-News,* 1932–1938; appeared thrice weekly in the Springfield (Missouri) *News,* 1938–1942.

This column was made up almost entirely of old songs, pioneer reminiscences, folk remedies, ghost stories, and the like, sent in by Mrs. McCord's fans in southern Missouri and northern Arkansas, and the files afford a vast reservoir of interesting material. Mrs. McCord was reared at Galena, in Stone county, Missouri, and both her family and that of her husband are well known in this vicinity, while she has "kinfolks an' connection" all over the Ozark country. She lectured on Ozark folklore in many places, played her guitar, and sang old songs at all the folk festivals and similar gatherings. Since 1942 Mrs. McCord has engaged in radio work and is heard on KWK in St. Louis and KWTO in Springfield, Missouri.

Mahnkey, Mary Elizabeth. "In the Hills," Springfield (Missouri) *News,* and the Springfield (Missouri) *Leader & Press,* 1932—.

Brief articles scattered at frequent but irregular intervals through the files of the two newspapers noted above. Many of these sketches contain important references to superstition.

—— "When Roseville Was Young," *White River Leader,* Branson, Missouri, July 27, 1933—March 22, 1934.

A leisurely series of reminiscences in a little weekly paper. Mrs. Mahnkey was born at Harrison, Arkansas, but grew up in Taney county, Missouri, near Kirbyville—which is the Roseville of her story. It is a true chronicle, from the early 1880's down to the middle 1930's. A valuable source of information about folklore and old customs.

Martin, Roxie. "May Day Superstitions," *Arcadian Magazine,* Eminence, Missouri (May, 1932), pp. 14–15.

It appears that Mrs. Martin once lived at Lanagan or Anderson, in McDonald county, Missouri, and gathered much of her material in that vicinity.

Missouri, a Guide to the "Show Me" State. New York, Duell, Sloan & Pearce, 1941. 625 pp.

Compiled by the Writers' Project in Missouri, sponsored and copyrighted by the Missouri State Highway Department. Old-time superstitions are mentioned on pp. 63, 136–139, and 534.

Moore, Tom. Mysterious Tales and Legends of the Ozarks. Philadelphia, Dorrance & Co., 1938. 148 pp.

There are seven ghost stories in this book, all set in southwest Missouri. The names of the central characters are thinly disguised, and in many cases the place names are not disguised at all. The author is a prominent attorney in Christian county, Missouri.

Mueller, Mabel E. "Sparks from the Spindle," weekly column in the Rolla *New Era* and the Rolla *Herald,* Rolla, Missouri, 1938–1940.

Some of the same material appeared in a monthly called *What Not,* published at Rolla by Eleanor Tolman in 1942; also in *Hillbilly News,* printed at Winslow, Arkansas, by Gene Barnes in 1943–1944. Mrs. Mueller is especially interested in tales of ghosts and witches.

Oklahoma, a Guide to the Sooner State. Norman, Oklahoma, University of Oklahoma Press, 1941. 442 pp.

Compiled by the Writers' Program of the WPA, sponsored by the University of Oklahoma. "It is in the hills of eastern Oklahoma that the beliefs and customs of another century are best preserved," we are told. A few superstitions are listed on pp. 119–120, but most of them have Indian or Negro references.

Randolph, Vance. "Folk-Beliefs in the Ozark Mountains," *Journal of American Folklore,* Vol. 40 (1927), pp. 78–94.

—— The Ozarks, an American Survival of Primitive Society. New York, Vanguard Press, 1931. 310 pp.

Chapter V, pp. 87–137, is devoted to "Signs and Superstitions."

—— "Witches and Witch-Masters," *Folk-Say,* University of Oklahoma Press, Norman, Oklahoma, 1931, pp. 86–93.

Reprinted in B. A. Botkin's *Treasury of American Folklore* (New York, Crown Publishers, 1944), pp. 692–696.

—— Ozark Mountain Folks. New York, Vanguard Press, 1932. 279 pp.

Chapter II, pp. 30–41, is a revised version of the "Witches and Witch-Masters" paper from the 1931 *Folk-Say*.

—— "Ozark Superstitions," *Journal of American Folklore*, Vol. 46 (1933), pp. 1–21.

—— "The Witch on Bradshaw Mountain," *University Review*, University of Kansas City, Kansas City, Missouri, June, 1936, pp. 203–206.

This is an account of Angie Paxton, Green Forest, Arkansas, with a drawing of Mrs. Paxton by Thomas Hart Benton.

—— "Ozark Superstitions," *Life*, June 19, 1939, pp. 82–83.

With six photos by D. F. Fox, of Galena, Missouri.

—— "Ozark Superstitions," *Click*, December, 1939, pp. 20–21.

With nine photos by D. F. Fox, of Galena, Missouri.

—— Ozark Ghost Stories. Girard, Kansas, Haldeman-Julius Publications, 1944. 24 pp.

—— Tall Tales from the Ozarks. Girard, Kansas, Haldeman-Julius Publications, 1944. 31 pp.

The section entitled "The Taskee Witch" (pp. 20–22) is an account of Mrs. Josie Forbes of Taskee, Missouri.

Ray, Celia. Many short articles and paragraphs in the Springfield (Missouri) *News & Leader;* also in the Springfield (Missouri) *Leader & Press,* 1927–1932.

Celia Ray is not particularly interested in folklore, but she sometimes used references to Ozark superstition in her regional gossip columns. Under her real name, Lucile Morris, she wrote *Bald Knobbers* (Caldwell, Idaho, Caxton Printers, Ltd., 1939; 253 pp.) which is still the best book available on the Ozark night riders.

Rayburn, Otto Ernest. Numerous short articles and paragraphs, usually captioned "Ozark Folklore," in *Ozark Life* (Kingston, Arkansas, 1925–1930), *Tulsa Tribune* (Tulsa, Oklahoma, 1930–1931), *Arkansas Gazette* (Little Rock, Arkansas, 1930–1931), *Arcadian Magazine* (Eminence, Missouri, 1931–1932), *Arcadian Life* (Caddo Gap, Arkansas, 1933–1942), and *Ozark Guide* (Eureka Springs, Arkansas, 1943—).

Rayburn is a schoolmaster from Iowa who wandered into the Ozark country shortly after World War I and has been here ever since. His writings deal with folksong, dialect, pioneer dances, play parties, old customs, ghost stories, and backwoods history of a sort not often found in textbooks. Rayburn has done a great deal to arouse popular interest in folk material, and the files of the little magazines *Ozark Life, Arcadian Magazine, Arcadian Life,* and *Ozark Guide*—all of which he edited and published himself—are full of fascinating stuff.

—— Rayburn's Roadside Chats. Beebe, Arkansas, Underhill Press, 1939. 48 pp.

—— Ozark Country. New York, Duell, Sloan & Pearce, 1941. 352 pp.

This is the fourth volume of the "American Folkways" series edited by Erskine Caldwell. It is Rayburn's best work—a summary of all his writings about the Ozarks. There are many references to Ozark superstitions, especially pp. 6–11, 139–147, 156–167, 249–260.

Russell, V. C. "Old Superstitions of the Ozark Mountains," St. Louis *Post-Dispatch,* rotogravure section, St. Louis, Missouri, Oct. 31, 1937, p. 2.

Seven posed photographs, illustrating superstitious practices in Taney county, Missouri. Each picture is accompanied by a brief explanation.

Seabrook, William. "Beheaded Women Sacrificed to Witchcraft?" *American Weekly,* New York, July 2, 1944, p. 15.

A fantastic story about the murder of two women near the Lake of the Ozarks, in Missouri, where the headless bodies were found in April, 1944. For a typical Ozark reaction to Seabrook's theory of this crime, see an editorial in the Springfield (Missouri) *News & Leader,* July 30, 1944, p. 6.

Shiras, Tom. "Weather Signs in the Ozarks," *Arkansas Gazette,* Little Rock, Arkansas, Feb. 20, 1944, pp. 5–6.

Reprinted in Rayburn's *Ozark Guide,* Lonsdale, Arkansas, Vol. II, No. 3 (October–December, 1944), pp. 51–54. Tom Shiras is a newspaperman who has lived in Mountain Home, Baxter county, Arkansas, for many years. He contends that some activities of birds, reptiles, and so on are conditioned by atmospheric pressure and thus serve as natural barometers.

Simpich, Frederick M. "Missouri, Mother of the West," *National Geographic Magazine,* Vol. XLIII, No. 4 (April, 1923), pp. 421–460.

One short section (pp. 425–428) is devoted to "Missouri Signs and Superstitions." Even this brief reference to the subject aroused the ire of many Missourians. See the comment on Simpich's article in the *Missouri Historical Review,* XVII, 419–434.

Smith, Walter R. "You Can't Tell About the Weather," *Folk-Say,* University of Oklahoma Press, Norman, Oklahoma, 1930, pp. 173–185.

Starr, Fred. "Hillside Adventures," a weekly column in the *Northwest Arkansas Times,* Fayetteville, Arkansas, May 6, 1937—.

The record is a bit muddled by the fact that Starr's column was formerly called "Plain Tales from the Hills" and later "Plain Tales from the Ozarks"; also that the newspaper was formerly known as the Fayetteville *Daily Democrat.* Under whatever name, the references to folk belief in Starr's copy are always worth reading.

—— From an Ozark Hillside. Siloam Springs, Arkansas, Bar D Press, 1938. 90 pp.

A selection of Starr's newspaper columns, with a preface by Lessie Stringfellow Read. The book contains one section entitled "Hill Beliefs" (pp. 29–34), which is concerned with Ozark superstition in general, and another (pp. 73–75) dealing briefly with herb remedies. See also the items on pp. 22, 23–24, 42, and 72.

—— Pebbles from the Ozarks. Siloam Springs, Arkansas, Bar D Press, 1942. 55 pp.

More extracts from Starr's newspaper column. Note especially the references to superstitions, pp. 15, 25, 37, 50–53. Starr is a schoolteacher by profession, writes about the Ozarks in his spare time, and lives on a farm near Greenland, Arkansas.

"Superstition and Folklore," *Clinton Eye Centennial Edition,* Clinton, Missouri, Sept. 7, 1936, pp. 3–4.

A list of several hundred Ozark superstitions, without comment.

"Superstition Still Rules in Remote Parts of the Ozarks," Kansas City *Times,* Kansas City, Missouri, April 15, 1938, p. 6.

A report of "Folklore and Folkways of the Ozark Region," an "address by Vance Randolph of Pineville, Mo., delivered at the annual dinner of the Missouri State Historical Society, Columbia, Missouri, April 14, 1938."

Taylor, Jay L. B. "Luminous Spectre Hunted to Its Lair," *Missouri Magazine,* Jefferson City, Missouri, October, 1934, pp. 11–12.

A surveyor in Joplin, Missouri, Mr. Taylor thinks that the ghost which so many people have seen at the Devil's Promenade is produced by the lights of cars on a distant highway.

Thanet, Octave. "Folklore in Arkansas," *Journal of American Folklore,* V (April–June, 1892), 121–125.

Octave Thanet was a popular novelist, whose real name was Alice French; she spent her winters at Clover Bend, on Black River, in Lawrence county, Arkansas, for some thirty years previous to World War I. The whites at Clover Bend, she says, were just as superstitious as the Negroes, but they took little stock in the black conjurers and conjure doctors. "Charms of all kinds are favored both by whites and blacks," she writes, "but I observe

that the white charms and the black charms are usually quite different."
Miss French knew one Negro conjurer, "a pious man and a deacon in the
church," who was supposed to have killed ten persons by his magic.

Thomas, John L. "History of Victoria," *Missouri Historical Review,*
Columbia, Missouri, II, 1907–1908, 17–22.

The story of Prudence Bevis, also known as "Queen Bevers," an alleged
witch who terrorized people in Jefferson county, Missouri, between 1826
and 1854. Compare the note in the WPA guidebook *Missouri, a Guide to the
"Show Me" State* (New York, Duell, Sloan & Pearce, 1941), p. 534.

Webb, W. L. "Burning Witches in Missouri," Kansas City *Post,* Kansas City, Missouri, Jan. 16, 1916, p. 12A.

Webb says that the Shawnee Indians in southeast Missouri burned witches
at the stake but offers no evidence that white Missourians ever did so. He
tells several good stories of witches and witch masters in Jackson county,
Missouri, and leaves no doubt that many of the pioneers were firm believers
in witchcraft.

Wilson, Charles Morrow. "Folk-Beliefs in the Ozark Hills," *Folk-
Say,* University of Oklahoma Press, Norman, Oklahoma, 1930,
pp. 157–172.

Material from "isolated communities in the Arkansas hill counties of Newton, Franklin, Madison, Benton, Carroll, Jackson and Washington, and in
Stone and Taney counties of Missouri."

—— Backwoods America. Chapel Hill, N.C., University of North
Carolina Press, 1934. 209 pp.

Chapter VI, "Folk Beliefs," pp. 47–60, contains much good material on
Ozark superstitions, most of it from Newton and Washington counties,
Arkansas. Wilson is a native of Arkansas and spent his youth in Fayette-
ville and its environs.

Wolverton, F. E. "The Woman of Taskee," in *Eve's Stepchildren,*
edited by Lealon N. Jones. Caldwell, Idaho, Caxton Printers,
Ltd., 1942, pp. 265–271.

Wolverton is a state supervisor of public schools, who lives in Cape Girardeau, Missouri. This piece is an account of his interview with Josie Forbes,
of Wayne county, Missouri, known as "the Witch of Taskee."

Index

A CATALOG OF SELECTED
DOVER BOOKS
IN ALL FIELDS OF INTEREST

A CATALOG OF SELECTED DOVER
BOOKS IN ALL FIELDS OF INTEREST

CONCERNING THE SPIRITUAL IN ART, Wassily Kandinsky. Pioneering work by father of abstract art. Thoughts on color theory, nature of art. Analysis of earlier masters. 12 illustrations. 80pp. of text. 5⅜ x 8½. 0-486-23411-8

CELTIC ART: The Methods of Construction, George Bain. Simple geometric techniques for making Celtic interlacements, spirals, Kells-type initials, animals, humans, etc. Over 500 illustrations. 160pp. 9 x 12. (Available in U.S. only.) 0-486-22923-8

AN ATLAS OF ANATOMY FOR ARTISTS, Fritz Schider. Most thorough reference work on art anatomy in the world. Hundreds of illustrations, including selections from works by Vesalius, Leonardo, Goya, Ingres, Michelangelo, others. 593 illustrations. 192pp. 7⅛ x 10¼. 0-486-20241-0

CELTIC HAND STROKE-BY-STROKE (Irish Half-Uncial from "The Book of Kells"): An Arthur Baker Calligraphy Manual, Arthur Baker. Complete guide to creating each letter of the alphabet in distinctive Celtic manner. Covers hand position, strokes, pens, inks, paper, more. Illustrated. 48pp. 8¼ x 11. 0-486-24336-2

EASY ORIGAMI, John Montroll. Charming collection of 32 projects (hat, cup, pelican, piano, swan, many more) specially designed for the novice origami hobbyist. Clearly illustrated easy-to-follow instructions insure that even beginning papercrafters will achieve successful results. 48pp. 8¼ x 11. 0-486-27298-2

BLOOMINGDALE'S ILLUSTRATED 1886 CATALOG: Fashions, Dry Goods and Housewares, Bloomingdale Brothers. Famed merchants' extremely rare catalog depicting about 1,700 products: clothing, housewares, firearms, dry goods, jewelry, more. Invaluable for dating, identifying vintage items. Also, copyright-free graphics for artists, designers. Co-published with Henry Ford Museum & Greenfield Village. 160pp. 8¼ x 11. 0-486-25780-0

THE ART OF WORLDLY WISDOM, Baltasar Gracian. "Think with the few and speak with the many," "Friends are a second existence," and "Be able to forget" are among this 1637 volume's 300 pithy maxims. A perfect source of mental and spiritual refreshment, it can be opened at random and appreciated either in brief or at length. 128pp. 5⅜ x 8½. 0-486-44034-6

JOHNSON'S DICTIONARY: A Modern Selection, Samuel Johnson (E. L. McAdam and George Milne, eds.). This modern version reduces the original 1755 edition's 2,300 pages of definitions and literary examples to a more manageable length, retaining the verbal pleasure and historical curiosity of the original. 480pp. 5⁵⁄₁₆ x 8¼. 0-486-44089-3

ADVENTURES OF HUCKLEBERRY FINN, Mark Twain, Illustrated by E. W. Kemble. A work of eternal richness and complexity, a source of ongoing critical debate, and a literary landmark, Twain's 1885 masterpiece about a barefoot boy's journey of self-discovery has enthralled readers around the world. This handsome clothbound reproduction of the first edition features all 174 of the original black-and-white illustrations. 368pp. 5⅜ x 8½. 0-486-44322-1

STICKLEY CRAFTSMAN FURNITURE CATALOGS, Gustav Stickley and L. & J. G. Stickley. Beautiful, functional furniture in two authentic catalogs from 1910. 594 illustrations, including 277 photos, show settles, rockers, armchairs, reclining chairs, bookcases, desks, tables. 183pp. 6½ x 9¼. 0-486-23838-5

AMERICAN LOCOMOTIVES IN HISTORIC PHOTOGRAPHS: 1858 to 1949, Ron Ziel (ed.). A rare collection of 126 meticulously detailed official photographs, called "builder portraits," of American locomotives that majestically chronicle the rise of steam locomotive power in America. Introduction. Detailed captions. xi+ 129pp. 9 x 12. 0-486-27393-8

AMERICA'S LIGHTHOUSES: An Illustrated History, Francis Ross Holland, Jr. Delightfully written, profusely illustrated fact-filled survey of over 200 American lighthouses since 1716. History, anecdotes, technological advances, more. 240pp. 8 x 10¾.
0-486-25576-X

TOWARDS A NEW ARCHITECTURE, Le Corbusier. Pioneering manifesto by founder of "International School." Technical and aesthetic theories, views of industry, economics, relation of form to function, "mass-production split" and much more. Profusely illustrated. 320pp. 6⅛ x 9¼. (Available in U.S. only.) 0-486-25023-7

HOW THE OTHER HALF LIVES, Jacob Riis. Famous journalistic record, exposing poverty and degradation of New York slums around 1900, by major social reformer. 100 striking and influential photographs. 233pp. 10 x 7⅞. 0-486-22012-5

FRUIT KEY AND TWIG KEY TO TREES AND SHRUBS, William M. Harlow. One of the handiest and most widely used identification aids. Fruit key covers 120 deciduous and evergreen species; twig key 160 deciduous species. Easily used. Over 300 photographs. 126pp. 5⅜ x 8½. 0-486-20511-8

COMMON BIRD SONGS, Dr. Donald J. Borror. Songs of 60 most common U.S. birds: robins, sparrows, cardinals, bluejays, finches, more—arranged in order of increasing complexity. Up to 9 variations of songs of each species.
Cassette and manual 0-486-99911-4

ORCHIDS AS HOUSE PLANTS, Rebecca Tyson Northen. Grow cattleyas and many other kinds of orchids—in a window, in a case, or under artificial light. 63 illustrations. 148pp. 5⅜ x 8½. 0-486-23261-1

MONSTER MAZES, Dave Phillips. Masterful mazes at four levels of difficulty. Avoid deadly perils and evil creatures to find magical treasures. Solutions for all 32 exciting illustrated puzzles. 48pp. 8¼ x 11. 0-486-26005-4

MOZART'S DON GIOVANNI (DOVER OPERA LIBRETTO SERIES), Wolfgang Amadeus Mozart. Introduced and translated by Ellen H. Bleiler. Standard Italian libretto, with complete English translation. Convenient and thoroughly portable—an ideal companion for reading along with a recording or the performance itself. Introduction. List of characters. Plot summary. 121pp. 5¼ x 8½. 0-486-24944-1

FRANK LLOYD WRIGHT'S DANA HOUSE, Donald Hoffmann. Pictorial essay of residential masterpiece with over 160 interior and exterior photos, plans, elevations, sketches and studies. 128pp. 9¼ x 10¾. 0-486-29120-0

THE CLARINET AND CLARINET PLAYING, David Pino. Lively, comprehensive work features suggestions about technique, musicianship, and musical interpretation, as well as guidelines for teaching, making your own reeds, and preparing for public performance. Includes an intriguing look at clarinet history. "A godsend," *The Clarinet,* Journal of the International Clarinet Society. Appendixes. 7 illus. 320pp. 5⅜ x 8½. 0-486-40270-3

HOLLYWOOD GLAMOR PORTRAITS, John Kobal (ed.). 145 photos from 1926-49. Harlow, Gable, Bogart, Bacall; 94 stars in all. Full background on photographers, technical aspects. 160pp. 8⅜ x 11¼. 0-486-23352-9

THE RAVEN AND OTHER FAVORITE POEMS, Edgar Allan Poe. Over 40 of the author's most memorable poems: "The Bells," "Ulalume," "Israfel," "To Helen," "The Conqueror Worm," "Eldorado," "Annabel Lee," many more. Alphabetic lists of titles and first lines. 64pp. 5³⁄₁₆ x 8¼. 0-486-26685-0

PERSONAL MEMOIRS OF U. S. GRANT, Ulysses Simpson Grant. Intelligent, deeply moving firsthand account of Civil War campaigns, considered by many the finest military memoirs ever written. Includes letters, historic photographs, maps and more. 528pp. 6⅛ x 9¼. 0-486-28587-1

ANCIENT EGYPTIAN MATERIALS AND INDUSTRIES, A. Lucas and J. Harris. Fascinating, comprehensive, thoroughly documented text describes this ancient civilization's vast resources and the processes that incorporated them in daily life, including the use of animal products, building materials, cosmetics, perfumes and incense, fibers, glazed ware, glass and its manufacture, materials used in the mummification process, and much more. 544pp. 6⅛ x 9¼. (Available in U.S. only.) 0-486-40446-3

RUSSIAN STORIES/RUSSKIE RASSKAZY: A Dual-Language Book, edited by Gleb Struve. Twelve tales by such masters as Chekhov, Tolstoy, Dostoevsky, Pushkin, others. Excellent word-for-word English translations on facing pages, plus teaching and study aids, Russian/English vocabulary, biographical/critical introductions, more. 416pp. 5⅜ x 8½. 0-486-26244-8

PHILADELPHIA THEN AND NOW: 60 Sites Photographed in the Past and Present, Kenneth Finkel and Susan Oyama. Rare photographs of City Hall, Logan Square, Independence Hall, Betsy Ross House, other landmarks juxtaposed with contemporary views. Captures changing face of historic city. Introduction. Captions. 128pp. 8¼ x 11. 0-486-25790-8

NORTH AMERICAN INDIAN LIFE: Customs and Traditions of 23 Tribes, Elsie Clews Parsons (ed.). 27 fictionalized essays by noted anthropologists examine religion, customs, government, additional facets of life among the Winnebago, Crow, Zuni, Eskimo, other tribes. 480pp. 6⅛ x 9¼. 0-486-27377-6

TECHNICAL MANUAL AND DICTIONARY OF CLASSICAL BALLET, Gail Grant. Defines, explains, comments on steps, movements, poses and concepts. 15-page pictorial section. Basic book for student, viewer. 127pp. 5⅜ x 8½. 0-486-21843-0

THE MALE AND FEMALE FIGURE IN MOTION: 60 Classic Photographic Sequences, Eadweard Muybridge. 60 true-action photographs of men and women walking, running, climbing, bending, turning, etc., reproduced from rare 19th-century masterpiece. vi + 121pp. 9 x 12. 0-486-24745-7

CATALOG OF DOVER BOOKS

ANIMALS: 1,419 Copyright-Free Illustrations of Mammals, Birds, Fish, Insects, etc., Jim Harter (ed.). Clear wood engravings present, in extremely lifelike poses, over 1,000 species of animals. One of the most extensive pictorial sourcebooks of its kind. Captions. Index. 284pp. 9 x 12. 0-486-23766-4

1001 QUESTIONS ANSWERED ABOUT THE SEASHORE, N. J. Berrill and Jacquelyn Berrill. Queries answered about dolphins, sea snails, sponges, starfish, fishes, shore birds, many others. Covers appearance, breeding, growth, feeding, much more. 305pp. 5¼ x 8¼. 0-486-23366-9

ATTRACTING BIRDS TO YOUR YARD, William J. Weber. Easy-to-follow guide offers advice on how to attract the greatest diversity of birds: birdhouses, feeders, water and waterers, much more. 96pp. 5³⁄₁₆ x 8¼. 0-486-28927-3

MEDICINAL AND OTHER USES OF NORTH AMERICAN PLANTS: A Historical Survey with Special Reference to the Eastern Indian Tribes, Charlotte Erichsen-Brown. Chronological historical citations document 500 years of usage of plants, trees, shrubs native to eastern Canada, northeastern U.S. Also complete identifying information. 343 illustrations. 544pp. 6½ x 9¼. 0-486-25951-X

STORYBOOK MAZES, Dave Phillips. 23 stories and mazes on two-page spreads: Wizard of Oz, Treasure Island, Robin Hood, etc. Solutions. 64pp. 8¼ x 11.
0-486-23628-5

AMERICAN NEGRO SONGS: 230 Folk Songs and Spirituals, Religious and Secular, John W. Work. This authoritative study traces the African influences of songs sung and played by black Americans at work, in church, and as entertainment. The author discusses the lyric significance of such songs as "Swing Low, Sweet Chariot," "John Henry," and others and offers the words and music for 230 songs. Bibliography. Index of Song Titles. 272pp. 6½ x 9¼. 0-486-40271-1

MOVIE-STAR PORTRAITS OF THE FORTIES, John Kobal (ed.). 163 glamor, studio photos of 106 stars of the 1940s: Rita Hayworth, Ava Gardner, Marlon Brando, Clark Gable, many more. 176pp. 8⅜ x 11¼. 0-486-23546-7

YEKL and THE IMPORTED BRIDEGROOM AND OTHER STORIES OF YIDDISH NEW YORK, Abraham Cahan. Film Hester Street based on Yekl (1896). Novel, other stories among first about Jewish immigrants on N.Y.'s East Side. 240pp. 5⅜ x 8½. 0-486-22427-9

SELECTED POEMS, Walt Whitman. Generous sampling from Leaves of Grass. Twenty-four poems include "I Hear America Singing," "Song of the Open Road," "I Sing the Body Electric," "When Lilacs Last in the Dooryard Bloom'd," "O Captain! My Captain!"–all reprinted from an authoritative edition. Lists of titles and first lines. 128pp. 5³⁄₁₆ x 8¼. 0-486-26878-0

SONGS OF EXPERIENCE: Facsimile Reproduction with 26 Plates in Full Color, William Blake. 26 full-color plates from a rare 1826 edition. Includes "The Tyger," "London," "Holy Thursday," and other poems. Printed text of poems. 48pp. 5¼ x 7.
0-486-24636-1

THE BEST TALES OF HOFFMANN, E. T. A. Hoffmann. 10 of Hoffmann's most important stories: "Nutcracker and the King of Mice," "The Golden Flowerpot," etc. 458pp. 5⅜ x 8½. 0-486-21793-0

THE BOOK OF TEA, Kakuzo Okakura. Minor classic of the Orient: entertaining, charming explanation, interpretation of traditional Japanese culture in terms of tea ceremony. 94pp. 5⅜ x 8½. 0-486-20070-1

FRENCH STORIES/CONTES FRANÇAIS: A Dual-Language Book, Wallace Fowlie. Ten stories by French masters, Voltaire to Camus: "Micromegas" by Voltaire; "The Atheist's Mass" by Balzac; "Minuet" by de Maupassant; "The Guest" by Camus, six more. Excellent English translations on facing pages. Also French-English vocabulary list, exercises, more. 352pp. 5⅜ x 8½. 0-486-26443-2

CHICAGO AT THE TURN OF THE CENTURY IN PHOTOGRAPHS: 122 Historic Views from the Collections of the Chicago Historical Society, Larry A. Viskochil. Rare large-format prints offer detailed views of City Hall, State Street, the Loop, Hull House, Union Station, many other landmarks, circa 1904-1913. Introduction. Captions. Maps. 144pp. 9⅜ x 12¼. 0-486-24656-6

OLD BROOKLYN IN EARLY PHOTOGRAPHS, 1865-1929, William Lee Younger. Luna Park, Gravesend race track, construction of Grand Army Plaza, moving of Hotel Brighton, etc. 157 previously unpublished photographs. 165pp. 8⅞ x 11¾. 0-486-23587-4

THE MYTHS OF THE NORTH AMERICAN INDIANS, Lewis Spence. Rich anthology of the myths and legends of the Algonquins, Iroquois, Pawnees and Sioux, prefaced by an extensive historical and ethnological commentary. 36 illustrations. 480pp. 5⅜ x 8½. 0-486-25967-6

AN ENCYCLOPEDIA OF BATTLES: Accounts of Over 1,560 Battles from 1479 B.C. to the Present, David Eggenberger. Essential details of every major battle in recorded history from the first battle of Megiddo in 1479 B.C. to Grenada in 1984. List of Battle Maps. New Appendix covering the years 1967-1984. Index. 99 illustrations. 544pp. 6½ x 9¼. 0-486-24913-1

SAILING ALONE AROUND THE WORLD, Captain Joshua Slocum. First man to sail around the world, alone, in small boat. One of great feats of seamanship told in delightful manner. 67 illustrations. 294pp. 5⅜ x 8½. 0-486-20326-3

ANARCHISM AND OTHER ESSAYS, Emma Goldman. Powerful, penetrating, prophetic essays on direct action, role of minorities, prison reform, puritan hypocrisy, violence, etc. 271pp. 5⅜ x 8½. 0-486-22484-8

MYTHS OF THE HINDUS AND BUDDHISTS, Ananda K. Coomaraswamy and Sister Nivedita. Great stories of the epics; deeds of Krishna, Shiva, taken from puranas, Vedas, folk tales; etc. 32 illustrations. 400pp. 5⅜ x 8½. 0-486-21759-0

MY BONDAGE AND MY FREEDOM, Frederick Douglass. Born a slave, Douglass became outspoken force in antislavery movement. The best of Douglass' autobiographies. Graphic description of slave life. 464pp. 5⅜ x 8½. 0-486-22457-0

FOLLOWING THE EQUATOR: A Journey Around the World, Mark Twain. Fascinating humorous account of 1897 voyage to Hawaii, Australia, India, New Zealand, etc. Ironic, bemused reports on peoples, customs, climate, flora and fauna, politics, much more. 197 illustrations. 720pp. 5⅜ x 8½. 0-486-26113-1

THE PEOPLE CALLED SHAKERS, Edward D. Andrews. Definitive study of Shakers: origins, beliefs, practices, dances, social organization, furniture and crafts, etc. 33 illustrations. 351pp. 5⅜ x 8½. 0-486-21081-2

THE MYTHS OF GREECE AND ROME, H. A. Guerber. A classic of mythology, generously illustrated, long prized for its simple, graphic, accurate retelling of the principal myths of Greece and Rome, and for its commentary on their origins and significance. With 64 illustrations by Michelangelo, Raphael, Titian, Rubens, Canova, Bernini and others. 480pp. 5⅜ x 8½. 0-486-27584-1

PSYCHOLOGY OF MUSIC, Carl E. Seashore. Classic work discusses music as a medium from psychological viewpoint. Clear treatment of physical acoustics, auditory apparatus, sound perception, development of musical skills, nature of musical feeling, host of other topics. 88 figures. 408pp. 5⅜ x 8½.　　0-486-21851-1

LIFE IN ANCIENT EGYPT, Adolf Erman. Fullest, most thorough, detailed older account with much not in more recent books, domestic life, religion, magic, medicine, commerce, much more. Many illustrations reproduce tomb paintings, carvings, hieroglyphs, etc. 597pp. 5⅜ x 8½.　　0-486-22632-8

SUNDIALS, Their Theory and Construction, Albert Waugh. Far and away the best, most thorough coverage of ideas, mathematics concerned, types, construction, adjusting anywhere. Simple, nontechnical treatment allows even children to build several of these dials. Over 100 illustrations. 230pp. 5⅜ x 8½.　　0-486-22947-5

THEORETICAL HYDRODYNAMICS, L. M. Milne-Thomson. Classic exposition of the mathematical theory of fluid motion, applicable to both hydrodynamics and aerodynamics. Over 600 exercises. 768pp. 6⅛ x 9¼.　　0-486-68970-0

OLD-TIME VIGNETTES IN FULL COLOR, Carol Belanger Grafton (ed.). Over 390 charming, often sentimental illustrations, selected from archives of Victorian graphics—pretty women posing, children playing, food, flowers, kittens and puppies, smiling cherubs, birds and butterflies, much more. All copyright-free. 48pp. 9¼ x 12¼.
0-486-27269-9

PERSPECTIVE FOR ARTISTS, Rex Vicat Cole. Depth, perspective of sky and sea, shadows, much more, not usually covered. 391 diagrams, 81 reproductions of drawings and paintings. 279pp. 5⅜ x 8½.　　0-486-22487-2

DRAWING THE LIVING FIGURE, Joseph Sheppard. Innovative approach to artistic anatomy focuses on specifics of surface anatomy, rather than muscles and bones. Over 170 drawings of live models in front, back and side views, and in widely varying poses. Accompanying diagrams. 177 illustrations. Introduction. Index. 144pp. 8⅜ x11¼.　　0-486-26723-7

GOTHIC AND OLD ENGLISH ALPHABETS: 100 Complete Fonts, Dan X. Solo. Add power, elegance to posters, signs, other graphics with 100 stunning copyright-free alphabets: Blackstone, Dolbey, Germania, 97 more—including many lower-case, numerals, punctuation marks. 104pp. 8⅛ x 11.　　0-486-24695-7

THE BOOK OF WOOD CARVING, Charles Marshall Sayers. Finest book for beginners discusses fundamentals and offers 34 designs. "Absolutely first rate . . . well thought out and well executed."—E. J. Tangerman. 118pp. 7¾ x 10⅝.　0-486-23654-4

ILLUSTRATED CATALOG OF CIVIL WAR MILITARY GOODS: Union Army Weapons, Insignia, Uniform Accessories, and Other Equipment, Schuyler, Hartley, and Graham. Rare, profusely illustrated 1846 catalog includes Union Army uniform and dress regulations, arms and ammunition, coats, insignia, flags, swords, rifles, etc. 226 illustrations. 160pp. 9 x 12.　　0-486-24939-5

WOMEN'S FASHIONS OF THE EARLY 1900s: An Unabridged Republication of "New York Fashions, 1909," National Cloak & Suit Co. Rare catalog of mail-order fashions documents women's and children's clothing styles shortly after the turn of the century. Captions offer full descriptions, prices. Invaluable resource for fashion, costume historians. Approximately 725 illustrations. 128pp. 8⅜ x 11¼.
0-486-27276-1

HOW TO DO BEADWORK, Mary White. Fundamental book on craft from simple projects to five-bead chains and woven works. 106 illustrations. 142pp. 5⅜ x 8. 0-486-20697-1

THE 1912 AND 1915 GUSTAV STICKLEY FURNITURE CATALOGS, Gustav Stickley. With over 200 detailed illustrations and descriptions, these two catalogs are essential reading and reference materials and identification guides for Stickley furniture. Captions cite materials, dimensions and prices. 112pp. 6½ x 9¼. 0-486-26676-1

EARLY AMERICAN LOCOMOTIVES, John H. White, Jr. Finest locomotive engravings from early 19th century: historical (1804–74), main-line (after 1870), special, foreign, etc. 147 plates. 142pp. 11⅜ x 8¼. 0-486-22772-3

LITTLE BOOK OF EARLY AMERICAN CRAFTS AND TRADES, Peter Stockham (ed.). 1807 children's book explains crafts and trades: baker, hatter, cooper, potter, and many others. 23 copperplate illustrations. 140pp. 4⅝ x 6. 0-486-23336-7

VICTORIAN FASHIONS AND COSTUMES FROM HARPER'S BAZAR, 1867–1898, Stella Blum (ed.). Day costumes, evening wear, sports clothes, shoes, hats, other accessories in over 1,000 detailed engravings. 320pp. 9⅜ x 12¼. 0-486-22990-4

THE LONG ISLAND RAIL ROAD IN EARLY PHOTOGRAPHS, Ron Ziel. Over 220 rare photos, informative text document origin (1844) and development of rail service on Long Island. Vintage views of early trains, locomotives, stations, passengers, crews, much more. Captions. 8⅞ x 11¾. 0-486-26301-0

VOYAGE OF THE LIBERDADE, Joshua Slocum. Great 19th-century mariner's thrilling, first-hand account of the wreck of his ship off South America, the 35-foot boat he built from the wreckage, and its remarkable voyage home. 128pp. 5⅜ x 8½. 0-486-40022-0

TEN BOOKS ON ARCHITECTURE, Vitruvius. The most important book ever written on architecture. Early Roman aesthetics, technology, classical orders, site selection, all other aspects. Morgan translation. 331pp. 5⅜ x 8½. 0-486-20645-9

THE HUMAN FIGURE IN MOTION, Eadweard Muybridge. More than 4,500 stopped-action photos, in action series, showing undraped men, women, children jumping, lying down, throwing, sitting, wrestling, carrying, etc. 390pp. 7⅞ x 10⅝. 0-486-20204-6 Clothbd.

TREES OF THE EASTERN AND CENTRAL UNITED STATES AND CANADA, William M. Harlow. Best one-volume guide to 140 trees. Full descriptions, woodlore, range, etc. Over 600 illustrations. Handy size. 288pp. 4½ x 6⅜. 0-486-20395-6

GROWING AND USING HERBS AND SPICES, Milo Miloradovich. Versatile handbook provides all the information needed for cultivation and use of all the herbs and spices available in North America. 4 illustrations. Index. Glossary. 236pp. 5⅜ x 8½. 0-486-25058-X

BIG BOOK OF MAZES AND LABYRINTHS, Walter Shepherd. 50 mazes and labyrinths in all–classical, solid, ripple, and more–in one great volume. Perfect inexpensive puzzler for clever youngsters. Full solutions. 112pp. 8⅛ x 11. 0-486-22951-3

PIANO TUNING, J. Cree Fischer. Clearest, best book for beginner, amateur. Simple repairs, raising dropped notes, tuning by easy method of flattened fifths. No previous skills needed. 4 illustrations. 201pp. 5⅜ x 8½. 0-486-23267-0

HINTS TO SINGERS, Lillian Nordica. Selecting the right teacher, developing confidence, overcoming stage fright, and many other important skills receive thoughtful discussion in this indispensible guide, written by a world-famous diva of four decades' experience. 96pp. 5⅜ x 8½. 0-486-40094-8

THE COMPLETE NONSENSE OF EDWARD LEAR, Edward Lear. All nonsense limericks, zany alphabets, Owl and Pussycat, songs, nonsense botany, etc., illustrated by Lear. Total of 320pp. 5⅜ x 8½. (Available in U.S. only.) 0-486-20167-8

VICTORIAN PARLOUR POETRY: An Annotated Anthology, Michael R. Turner. 117 gems by Longfellow, Tennyson, Browning, many lesser-known poets. "The Village Blacksmith," "Curfew Must Not Ring Tonight," "Only a Baby Small," dozens more, often difficult to find elsewhere. Index of poets, titles, first lines. xxiii + 325pp. 5⅝ x 8¼. 0-486-27044-0

DUBLINERS, James Joyce. Fifteen stories offer vivid, tightly focused observations of the lives of Dublin's poorer classes. At least one, "The Dead," is considered a masterpiece. Reprinted complete and unabridged from standard edition. 160pp. 5$\frac{3}{16}$ x 8¼. 0-486-26870-5

GREAT WEIRD TALES: 14 Stories by Lovecraft, Blackwood, Machen and Others, S. T. Joshi (ed.). 14 spellbinding tales, including "The Sin Eater," by Fiona McLeod, "The Eye Above the Mantel," by Frank Belknap Long, as well as renowned works by R. H. Barlow, Lord Dunsany, Arthur Machen, W. C. Morrow and eight other masters of the genre. 256pp. 5⅜ x 8½. (Available in U.S. only.) 0-486-40436-6

THE BOOK OF THE SACRED MAGIC OF ABRAMELIN THE MAGE, translated by S. MacGregor Mathers. Medieval manuscript of ceremonial magic. Basic document in Aleister Crowley, Golden Dawn groups. 268pp. 5⅜ x 8½. 0-486-23211-5

THE BATTLES THAT CHANGED HISTORY, Fletcher Pratt. Eminent historian profiles 16 crucial conflicts, ancient to modern, that changed the course of civilization. 352pp. 5⅜ x 8½. 0-486-41129-X

NEW RUSSIAN-ENGLISH AND ENGLISH-RUSSIAN DICTIONARY, M. A. O'Brien. This is a remarkably handy Russian dictionary, containing a surprising amount of information, including over 70,000 entries. 366pp. 4½ x 6⅛. 0-486-20208-9

NEW YORK IN THE FORTIES, Andreas Feininger. 162 brilliant photographs by the well-known photographer, formerly with *Life* magazine. Commuters, shoppers, Times Square at night, much else from city at its peak. Captions by John von Hartz. 181pp. 9¼ x 10¾. 0-486-23585-8

INDIAN SIGN LANGUAGE, William Tomkins. Over 525 signs developed by Sioux and other tribes. Written instructions and diagrams. Also 290 pictographs. 111pp. 6⅛ x 9¼. 0-486-22029-X

ANATOMY: A Complete Guide for Artists, Joseph Sheppard. A master of figure drawing shows artists how to render human anatomy convincingly. Over 460 illustrations. 224pp. 8⅜ x 11¼. 0-486-27279-6

MEDIEVAL CALLIGRAPHY: Its History and Technique, Marc Drogin. Spirited history, comprehensive instruction manual covers 13 styles (ca. 4th century through 15th). Excellent photographs; directions for duplicating medieval techniques with modern tools. 224pp. 8⅜ x 11¼. 0-486-26142-5

DRIED FLOWERS: How to Prepare Them, Sarah Whitlock and Martha Rankin. Complete instructions on how to use silica gel, meal and borax, perlite aggregate, sand and borax, glycerine and water to create attractive permanent flower arrangements. 12 illustrations. 32pp. 5⅜ x 8½. 0-486-21802-3

EASY-TO-MAKE BIRD FEEDERS FOR WOODWORKERS, Scott D. Campbell. Detailed, simple-to-use guide for designing, constructing, caring for and using feeders. Text, illustrations for 12 classic and contemporary designs. 96pp. 5⅜ x 8½. 0-486-25847-5

THE COMPLETE BOOK OF BIRDHOUSE CONSTRUCTION FOR WOOD-WORKERS, Scott D. Campbell. Detailed instructions, illustrations, tables. Also data on bird habitat and instinct patterns. Bibliography. 3 tables. 63 illustrations in 15 figures. 48pp. 5¼ x 8½. 0-486-24407-5

SCOTTISH WONDER TALES FROM MYTH AND LEGEND, Donald A. Mackenzie. 16 lively tales tell of giants rumbling down mountainsides, of a magic wand that turns stone pillars into warriors, of gods and goddesses, evil hags, powerful forces and more. 240pp. 5⅜ x 8½. 0-486-29677-6

THE HISTORY OF UNDERCLOTHES, C. Willett Cunnington and Phyllis Cunnington. Fascinating, well-documented survey covering six centuries of English undergarments, enhanced with over 100 illustrations: 12th-century laced-up bodice, footed long drawers (1795), 19th-century bustles, 19th-century corsets for men, Victorian "bust improvers," much more. 272pp. 5⅜ x 8¼. 0-486-27124-2

ARTS AND CRAFTS FURNITURE: The Complete Brooks Catalog of 1912, Brooks Manufacturing Co. Photos and detailed descriptions of more than 150 now very collectible furniture designs from the Arts and Crafts movement depict davenports, settees, buffets, desks, tables, chairs, bedsteads, dressers and more, all built of solid, quarter-sawed oak. Invaluable for students and enthusiasts of antiques, Americana and the decorative arts. 80pp. 6½ x 9¼. 0-486-27471-3

WILBUR AND ORVILLE: A Biography of the Wright Brothers, Fred Howard. Definitive, crisply written study tells the full story of the brothers' lives and work. A vividly written biography, unparalleled in scope and color, that also captures the spirit of an extraordinary era. 560pp. 6⅛ x 9¼. 0-486-40297-5

THE ARTS OF THE SAILOR: Knotting, Splicing and Ropework, Hervey Garrett Smith. Indispensable shipboard reference covers tools, basic knots and useful hitches; handsewing and canvas work, more. Over 100 illustrations. Delightful reading for sea lovers. 256pp. 5⅜ x 8½. 0-486-26440-8

FRANK LLOYD WRIGHT'S FALLINGWATER: The House and Its History, Second, Revised Edition, Donald Hoffmann. A total revision—both in text and illustrations—of the standard document on Fallingwater, the boldest, most personal architectural statement of Wright's mature years, updated with valuable new material from the recently opened Frank Lloyd Wright Archives. "Fascinating"—*The New York Times.* 116 illustrations. 128pp. 9¼ x 10¾. 0-486-27430-6

PHOTOGRAPHIC SKETCHBOOK OF THE CIVIL WAR, Alexander Gardner. 100 photos taken on field during the Civil War. Famous shots of Manassas Harper's Ferry, Lincoln, Richmond, slave pens, etc. 244pp. 10⅝ x 8¼. 0-486-22731-6

FIVE ACRES AND INDEPENDENCE, Maurice G. Kains. Great back-to-the-land classic explains basics of self-sufficient farming. The one book to get. 95 illustrations. 397pp. 5⅜ x 8½. 0-486-20974-1

A MODERN HERBAL, Margaret Grieve. Much the fullest, most exact, most useful compilation of herbal material. Gigantic alphabetical encyclopedia, from aconite to zedoary, gives botanical information, medical properties, folklore, economic uses, much else. Indispensable to serious reader. 161 illustrations. 888pp. 6½ x 9¼. 2-vol. set. (Available in U.S. only.)   Vol. I: 0-486-22798-7   Vol. II: 0-486-22799-5

HIDDEN TREASURE MAZE BOOK, Dave Phillips. Solve 34 challenging mazes accompanied by heroic tales of adventure. Evil dragons, people-eating plants, blood-thirsty giants, many more dangerous adversaries lurk at every twist and turn. 34 mazes, stories, solutions. 48pp. 8¼ x 11.   0-486-24566-7

LETTERS OF W. A. MOZART, Wolfgang A. Mozart. Remarkable letters show bawdy wit, humor, imagination, musical insights, contemporary musical world; includes some letters from Leopold Mozart. 276pp. 5⅜ x 8½.   0-486-22859-2

BASIC PRINCIPLES OF CLASSICAL BALLET, Agrippina Vaganova. Great Russian theoretician, teacher explains methods for teaching classical ballet. 118 illustrations. 175pp. 5⅜ x 8½.   0-486-22036-2

THE JUMPING FROG, Mark Twain. Revenge edition. The original story of The Celebrated Jumping Frog of Calaveras County, a hapless French translation, and Twain's hilarious "retranslation" from the French. 12 illustrations. 66pp. 5⅜ x 8½.
                                                            0-486-22686-7

BEST REMEMBERED POEMS, Martin Gardner (ed.). The 126 poems in this superb collection of 19th- and 20th-century British and American verse range from Shelley's "To a Skylark" to the impassioned "Renascence" of Edna St. Vincent Millay and to Edward Lear's whimsical "The Owl and the Pussycat." 224pp. 5⅜ x 8½.
                                                            0-486-27165-X

COMPLETE SONNETS, William Shakespeare. Over 150 exquisite poems deal with love, friendship, the tyranny of time, beauty's evanescence, death and other themes in language of remarkable power, precision and beauty. Glossary of archaic terms. 80pp. 5³⁄₁₆ x 8¼.   0-486-26686-9

HISTORIC HOMES OF THE AMERICAN PRESIDENTS, Second, Revised Edition, Irvin Haas. A traveler's guide to American Presidential homes, most open to the public, depicting and describing homes occupied by every American President from George Washington to George Bush. With visiting hours, admission charges, travel routes. 175 photographs. Index. 160pp. 8¼ x 11.   0-486-26751-2

THE WIT AND HUMOR OF OSCAR WILDE, Alvin Redman (ed.). More than 1,000 ripostes, paradoxes, wisecracks: Work is the curse of the drinking classes; I can resist everything except temptation; etc. 258pp. 5⅜ x 8½.   0-486-20602-5

SHAKESPEARE LEXICON AND QUOTATION DICTIONARY, Alexander Schmidt. Full definitions, locations, shades of meaning in every word in plays and poems. More than 50,000 exact quotations. 1,485pp. 6½ x 9¼. 2-vol. set.
                       Vol. 1: 0-486-22726-X   Vol. 2: 0-486-22727-8

SELECTED POEMS, Emily Dickinson. Over 100 best-known, best-loved poems by one of America's foremost poets, reprinted from authoritative early editions. No comparable edition at this price. Index of first lines. 64pp. 5³⁄₁₆ x 8¼. 0-486-26466-1

THE INSIDIOUS DR. FU-MANCHU, Sax Rohmer. The first of the popular mystery series introduces a pair of English detectives to their archnemesis, the diabolical Dr. Fu-Manchu. Flavorful atmosphere, fast-paced action, and colorful characters enliven this classic of the genre. 208pp. 5³⁄₁₆ x 8¼.   0-486-29898-1

THE MALLEUS MALEFICARUM OF KRAMER AND SPRENGER, translated by Montague Summers. Full text of most important witchhunter's "bible," used by both Catholics and Protestants. 278pp. 6⅛ x 10. 0-486-22802-9

SPANISH STORIES/CUENTOS ESPAÑOLES: A Dual-Language Book, Angel Flores (ed.). Unique format offers 13 great stories in Spanish by Cervantes, Borges, others. Faithful English translations on facing pages. 352pp. 5⅜ x 8½.
0-486-25399-6

GARDEN CITY, LONG ISLAND, IN EARLY PHOTOGRAPHS, 1869–1919, Mildred H. Smith. Handsome treasury of 118 vintage pictures, accompanied by carefully researched captions, document the Garden City Hotel fire (1899), the Vanderbilt Cup Race (1908), the first airmail flight departing from the Nassau Boulevard Aerodrome (1911), and much more. 96pp. 8⅞ x 11¾. 0-486-40669-5

OLD QUEENS, N.Y., IN EARLY PHOTOGRAPHS, Vincent F. Seyfried and William Asadorian. Over 160 rare photographs of Maspeth, Jamaica, Jackson Heights, and other areas. Vintage views of DeWitt Clinton mansion, 1939 World's Fair and more. Captions. 192pp. 8⅞ x 11. 0-486-26358-4

CAPTURED BY THE INDIANS: 15 Firsthand Accounts, 1750-1870, Frederick Drimmer. Astounding true historical accounts of grisly torture, bloody conflicts, relentless pursuits, miraculous escapes and more, by people who lived to tell the tale. 384pp. 5⅜ x 8½. 0-486-24901-8

THE WORLD'S GREAT SPEECHES (Fourth Enlarged Edition), Lewis Copeland, Lawrence W. Lamm, and Stephen J. McKenna. Nearly 300 speeches provide public speakers with a wealth of updated quotes and inspiration–from Pericles' funeral oration and William Jennings Bryan's "Cross of Gold Speech" to Malcolm X's powerful words on the Black Revolution and Earl of Spenser's tribute to his sister, Diana, Princess of Wales. 944pp. 5⅜ x 8⅜. 0-486-40903-1

THE BOOK OF THE SWORD, Sir Richard F. Burton. Great Victorian scholar/adventurer's eloquent, erudite history of the "queen of weapons"–from prehistory to early Roman Empire. Evolution and development of early swords, variations (sabre, broadsword, cutlass, scimitar, etc.), much more. 336pp. 6⅛ x 9¼.
0-486-25434-8

AUTOBIOGRAPHY: The Story of My Experiments with Truth, Mohandas K. Gandhi. Boyhood, legal studies, purification, the growth of the Satyagraha (nonviolent protest) movement. Critical, inspiring work of the man responsible for the freedom of India. 480pp. 5⅜ x 8½. (Available in U.S. only.) 0-486-24593-4

CELTIC MYTHS AND LEGENDS, T. W. Rolleston. Masterful retelling of Irish and Welsh stories and tales. Cuchulain, King Arthur, Deirdre, the Grail, many more. First paperback edition. 58 full-page illustrations. 512pp. 5⅜ x 8½. 0-486-26507-2

THE PRINCIPLES OF PSYCHOLOGY, William James. Famous long course complete, unabridged. Stream of thought, time perception, memory, experimental methods; great work decades ahead of its time. 94 figures. 1,391pp. 5⅜ x 8½. 2-vol. set.
Vol. I: 0-486-20381-6   Vol. II: 0-486-20382-4

THE WORLD AS WILL AND REPRESENTATION, Arthur Schopenhauer. Definitive English translation of Schopenhauer's life work, correcting more than 1,000 errors, omissions in earlier translations. Translated by E. F. J. Payne. Total of 1,269pp. 5⅜ x 8½. 2-vol. set.   Vol. 1: 0-486-21761-2   Vol. 2: 0-486-21762-0

MAGIC AND MYSTERY IN TIBET, Madame Alexandra David-Neel. Experiences among lamas, magicians, sages, sorcerers, Bonpa wizards. A true psychic discovery. 32 illustrations. 321pp. 5⅜ x 8½. (Available in U.S. only.) 0-486-22682-4

THE EGYPTIAN BOOK OF THE DEAD, E. A. Wallis Budge. Complete reproduction of Ani's papyrus, finest ever found. Full hieroglyphic text, interlinear transliteration, word-for-word translation, smooth translation. 533pp. 6½ x 9¼. 0-486-21866-X

HISTORIC COSTUME IN PICTURES, Braun & Schneider. Over 1,450 costumed figures in clearly detailed engravings–from dawn of civilization to end of 19th century. Captions. Many folk costumes. 256pp. 8⅜ x 11¾. 0-486-23150-X

MATHEMATICS FOR THE NONMATHEMATICIAN, Morris Kline. Detailed, college-level treatment of mathematics in cultural and historical context, with numerous exercises. Recommended Reading Lists. Tables. Numerous figures. 641pp. 5⅜ x 8½. 0-486-24823-2

PROBABILISTIC METHODS IN THE THEORY OF STRUCTURES, Isaac Elishakoff. Well-written introduction covers the elements of the theory of probability from two or more random variables, the reliability of such multivariable structures, the theory of random function, Monte Carlo methods of treating problems incapable of exact solution, and more. Examples. 502pp. 5⅜ x 8½. 0-486-40691-1

THE RIME OF THE ANCIENT MARINER, Gustave Doré, S. T. Coleridge. Doré's finest work; 34 plates capture moods, subtleties of poem. Flawless full-size reproductions printed on facing pages with authoritative text of poem. "Beautiful. Simply beautiful."–*Publisher's Weekly.* 77pp. 9¼ x 12. 0-486-22305-1

SCULPTURE: Principles and Practice, Louis Slobodkin. Step-by-step approach to clay, plaster, metals, stone; classical and modern. 253 drawings, photos. 255pp. 8⅛ x 11. 0-486-22960-2

THE INFLUENCE OF SEA POWER UPON HISTORY, 1660–1783, A. T. Mahan. Influential classic of naval history and tactics still used as text in war colleges. First paperback edition. 4 maps. 24 battle plans. 640pp. 5⅜ x 8½. 0-486-25509-3

THE STORY OF THE TITANIC AS TOLD BY ITS SURVIVORS, Jack Winocour (ed.). What it was really like. Panic, despair, shocking inefficiency, and a little heroism. More thrilling than any fictional account. 26 illustrations. 320pp. 5⅜ x 8½. 0-486-20610-6

ONE TWO THREE . . . INFINITY: Facts and Speculations of Science, George Gamow. Great physicist's fascinating, readable overview of contemporary science: number theory, relativity, fourth dimension, entropy, genes, atomic structure, much more. 128 illustrations. Index. 352pp. 5⅜ x 8½. 0-486-25664-2

DALÍ ON MODERN ART: The Cuckolds of Antiquated Modern Art, Salvador Dalí. Influential painter skewers modern art and its practitioners. Outrageous evaluations of Picasso, Cézanne, Turner, more. 15 renderings of paintings discussed. 44 calligraphic decorations by Dalí. 96pp. 5⅜ x 8½. (Available in U.S. only.) 0-486-29220-7

ANTIQUE PLAYING CARDS: A Pictorial History, Henry René D'Allemagne. Over 900 elaborate, decorative images from rare playing cards (14th–20th centuries): Bacchus, death, dancing dogs, hunting scenes, royal coats of arms, players cheating, much more. 96pp. 9¼ x 12¼. 0-486-29265-7

MAKING FURNITURE MASTERPIECES: 30 Projects with Measured Drawings, Franklin H. Gottshall. Step-by-step instructions, illustrations for constructing handsome, useful pieces, among them a Sheraton desk, Chippendale chair, Spanish desk, Queen Anne table and a William and Mary dressing mirror. 224pp. 8⅛ x 11¼.
0-486-29338-6

NORTH AMERICAN INDIAN DESIGNS FOR ARTISTS AND CRAFTSPEOPLE, Eva Wilson. Over 360 authentic copyright-free designs adapted from Navajo blankets, Hopi pottery, Sioux buffalo hides, more. Geometrics, symbolic figures, plant and animal motifs, etc. 128pp. 8⅜ x 11. (Not for sale in the United Kingdom.) 0-486-25341-4

THE FOSSIL BOOK: A Record of Prehistoric Life, Patricia V. Rich et al. Profusely illustrated definitive guide covers everything from single-celled organisms and dinosaurs to birds and mammals and the interplay between climate and man. Over 1,500 illustrations. 760pp. 7½ x 10⅛. 0-486-29371-8

VICTORIAN ARCHITECTURAL DETAILS: Designs for Over 700 Stairs, Mantels, Doors, Windows, Cornices, Porches, and Other Decorative Elements, A. J. Bicknell & Company. Everything from dormer windows and piazzas to balconies and gable ornaments. Also includes elevations and floor plans for handsome, private residences and commercial structures. 80pp. 9⅜ x 12¼. 0-486-44015-X

WESTERN ISLAMIC ARCHITECTURE: A Concise Introduction, John D. Hoag. Profusely illustrated critical appraisal compares and contrasts Islamic mosques and palaces–from Spain and Egypt to other areas in the Middle East. 139 illustrations. 128pp. 6 x 9. 0-486-43760-4

CHINESE ARCHITECTURE: A Pictorial History, Liang Ssu-ch'eng. More than 240 rare photographs and drawings depict temples, pagodas, tombs, bridges, and imperial palaces comprising much of China's architectural heritage. 152 halftones, 94 diagrams. 232pp. 10¾ x 9⅞. 0-486-43999-2

THE RENAISSANCE: Studies in Art and Poetry, Walter Pater. One of the most talked-about books of the 19th century, *The Renaissance* combines scholarship and philosophy in an innovative work of cultural criticism that examines the achievements of Botticelli, Leonardo, Michelangelo, and other artists. "The holy writ of beauty."–Oscar Wilde. 160pp. 5⅜ x 8½. 0-486-44025-7

A TREATISE ON PAINTING, Leonardo da Vinci. The great Renaissance artist's practical advice on drawing and painting techniques covers anatomy, perspective, composition, light and shadow, and color. A classic of art instruction, it features 48 drawings by Nicholas Poussin and Leon Battista Alberti. 192pp. 5⅜ x 8½.
0-486-44155-5

THE MIND OF LEONARDO DA VINCI, Edward McCurdy. More than just a biography, this classic study by a distinguished historian draws upon Leonardo's extensive writings to offer numerous demonstrations of the Renaissance master's achievements, not only in sculpture and painting, but also in music, engineering, and even experimental aviation. 384pp. 5⅜ x 8½. 0-486-44142-3

WASHINGTON IRVING'S RIP VAN WINKLE, Illustrated by Arthur Rackham. Lovely prints that established artist as a leading illustrator of the time and forever etched into the popular imagination a classic of Catskill lore. 51 full-color plates. 80pp. 8⅜ x 11. 0-486-44242-X

HENSCHE ON PAINTING, John W. Robichaux. Basic painting philosophy and methodology of a great teacher, as expounded in his famous classes and workshops on Cape Cod. 7 illustrations in color on covers. 80pp. 5⅜ x 8½. 0-486-43728-0

LIGHT AND SHADE: A Classic Approach to Three-Dimensional Drawing, Mrs. Mary P. Merrifield. Handy reference clearly demonstrates principles of light and shade by revealing effects of common daylight, sunshine, and candle or artificial light on geometrical solids. 13 plates. 64pp. 5⅜ x 8½. 0-486-44143-1

ASTROLOGY AND ASTRONOMY: A Pictorial Archive of Signs and Symbols, Ernst and Johanna Lehner. Treasure trove of stories, lore, and myth, accompanied by more than 300 rare illustrations of planets, the Milky Way, signs of the zodiac, comets, meteors, and other astronomical phenomena. 192pp. 8⅜ x 11. 0-486-43981-X

JEWELRY MAKING: Techniques for Metal, Tim McCreight. Easy-to-follow instructions and carefully executed illustrations describe tools and techniques, use of gems and enamels, wire inlay, casting, and other topics. 72 line illustrations and diagrams. 176pp. 8¼ x 10⅞. 0-486-44043-5

MAKING BIRDHOUSES: Easy and Advanced Projects, Gladstone Califf. Easy-to-follow instructions include diagrams for everything from a one-room house for bluebirds to a forty-two-room structure for purple martins. 56 plates; 4 figures. 80pp. 8¾ x 6⅜. 0-486-44183-0

LITTLE BOOK OF LOG CABINS: How to Build and Furnish Them, William S. Wicks. Handy how-to manual, with instructions and illustrations for building cabins in the Adirondack style, fireplaces, stairways, furniture, beamed ceilings, and more. 102 line drawings. 96pp. 8¾ x 6⅜. 0-486-44259-4

THE SEASONS OF AMERICA PAST, Eric Sloane. From "sugaring time" and strawberry picking to Indian summer and fall harvest, a whole year's activities described in charming prose and enhanced with 79 of the author's own illustrations. 160pp. 8¼ x 11. 0-486-44220-9

THE METROPOLIS OF TOMORROW, Hugh Ferriss. Generous, prophetic vision of the metropolis of the future, as perceived in 1929. Powerful illustrations of towering structures, wide avenues, and rooftop parks–all features in many of today's modern cities. 59 illustrations. 144pp. 8¼ x 11. 0-486-43727-2

THE PATH TO ROME, Hilaire Belloc. This 1902 memoir abounds in lively vignettes from a vanished time, recounting a pilgrimage on foot across the Alps and Apennines in order to "see all Europe which the Christian Faith has saved." 77 of the author's original line drawings complement his sparkling prose. 272pp. 5⅜ x 8½. 0-486-44001-X

THE HISTORY OF RASSELAS: Prince of Abissinia, Samuel Johnson. Distinguished English writer attacks eighteenth-century optimism and man's unrealistic estimates of what life has to offer. 112pp. 5⅜ x 8½. 0-486-44094-X

A VOYAGE TO ARCTURUS, David Lindsay. A brilliant flight of pure fancy, where wild creatures crowd the fantastic landscape and demented torturers dominate victims with their bizarre mental powers. 272pp. 5⅜ x 8½. 0-486-44198-9

Paperbound unless otherwise indicated. Available at your book dealer, online at **www.doverpublications.com**, or by writing to Dept. GI, Dover Publications, Inc., 31 East 2nd Street, Mineola, NY 11501. For current price information or for free catalogs (please indicate field of interest), write to Dover Publications or log on to **www.doverpublications.com** and see every Dover book in print. Dover publishes more than 500 books each year on science, elementary and advanced mathematics, biology, music, art, literary history, social sciences, and other areas.